A SHORT HISTORY OF
MUSIC IN AMERICA

A SHORT HISTORY OF

MUSIC IN AMERICA

BY

JOHN TASKER HOWARD

AND

GEORGE KENT BELLOWS

THOMAS Y. CROWELL COMPANY, NEW YORK

TO
Ruth and Lydia

———

L.A.P.C.E.T

Preface

It has become increasingly obvious for some time that a brief history of American music is needed for use both as a textbook and a conventional guide for those who are interested in becoming better acquainted with the nation's incredible musical growth.

It has taken America three and a half centuries to become the world leader in music that she is today, yet our Western art music, developing rapidly after the birth of opera in Florence in 1600, is scarcely much older. Few realize how much has been accomplished since the first colonists came to our shores, and how dramatic and colorful has been the emergence of American music.

This is a history of that development from the first native Indian music, down to the present day. To keep the picture of America's musical evolution moving, many details have of course had to be omitted. To remain within the province of a short history, only the most significant musicians and outstanding events could be chronicled.

America's musicians have been a part of their times, and in many cases, helped to create them. An attempt has also been made to correlate our music with the history of a growing country, and the development of the related arts. For the student and layman having little or no musical background, there has been a consistent tie-in with the traditional movements and currents in European music.

Along with the American composers (whether native-born or citizens by adoption), must be considered the many important men whose residence in this country has greatly influenced both our music and our composers. Because of wars, revolutions, and persecution, many now have no country except America, and so they and their works are referred to wherever they have influenced the contemporary American scene.

A bibliography of American music, even in condensed form, is a lengthy affair, for the literature of our native music and composers has grown to vast proportions. Rather than include in this short volume a list of references that would of necessity be woefully incomplete, the reader is referred to the extensive bibliography of John Tasker Howard's *Our American Music*. Newer and more important books that have more recently been published, have, of course, been added.

There have been powerful implications in this chronological unfolding of American music that few have taken the trouble to trace from beginning to end. As America came of age musically, and became a world center of music, her position was due to the sum total of many persons and countless events, many of which were unique among the nations of the world. Thus, every phase of her phenomenal growth and ultimate maturing gives a clue to the destiny of her art. For this reason, the authors hope that the reader will be as fascinated and as deeply impressed as they have been.

Montclair, New Jersey   JOHN TASKER HOWARD
Glyndon, Maryland   GEORGE KENT BELLOWS

Contents

Illustrations

(Following page 234)

Introduction

If only a Bach or a Mozart had been born on this side of the Atlantic in colonial times, how tidy and orthodox our American musical lineage might have been made to appear. No matter what our music became, we would always have been able to explain it, or rationalize it, in reference to *him*, the father of American music and the source of it all. Just one universally acknowledged musical genius would have taken care of everything for all time.

Unfortunately, musical genius is something America did not, could not, produce and cultivate in its formative years. Latent talent was probably here, but the leisure, wealth, and cultural application required to nurture and employ it were in notably short supply on this continent until well into the nineteenth century. Therefore, we now look for our musical ancestors among myriad non-geniuses whose widely varied musical tastes and practices went into the making of an incredibly complex American musical ethos.

Over the years, this ever-churning, ever-changing ethos has produced from time to time a Stephen Foster, a John Philip Sousa, a Charles Ives, a George Gershwin, an Aaron Copland, a Duke Ellington, or a John Cage. Any parentage capable of producing such differently gifted offspring should automatically inspire pride. In this case, however, that pride tends to be dulled by the fear that, musically speaking, we may somehow still be illegitimate.

We are obviously lacking in old masters to claim as direct musical forebears, but we certainly do not want for industrious purveyors of music on our national family tree. Some of them were rich, some were poor; some were free, some slave; some were gifted, some were not. What most of them had in common, especially in the earliest days, was a lack of musical sophistication and virtuoso skills.

In the 1770s, for example, Europe was heading into one of the most dazzling musical epochs of all time. Bach and Handel had already died, and Beethoven was still a child, but Haydn, in his forties, was composing voluminously at Esterhazy, and Mozart, at twenty, was well into his spectacular career.

Here in the American colonies, by contrast, William Billings was impressing New England with his crude "fuging tunes." They were naïve, even incorrect by strict theoretical rules, but they were sincere and seem to have been the most authentic American musical statements of the time. Billings earned most of his living as a tanner, but he managed to publish six collections of his compositions, teach, conduct, argue with his critics, and become somewhat famous. If he had been handsome, glamorous, and erudite, he might have been a Leonard Bernstein of his time and place.

Billings was not the only American musician of his day. Francis Hopkinson, a well-to-do Philadelphia aristocrat and dilettante who signed the Declaration of Independence, referred to himself in a letter to George Washington as "the first Native of the United States who has produced a Musical Composition." He may have been just that. The matter is of little more than factual interest, however, for Hopkinson's songs are at best reminders of period charm. No genius he, nor hundreds of others encountered in a survey of music in America.

Let us forget about genius, then, and simply enjoy ourselves as we look through the mementos of our musical past. They and the personalities associated with them are almost unfailingly intriguing and are sometimes startling.

A glance at the Contents page of this book suggests in an instant the astonishing variety of experiences that went into the making of our musical background. One reason these experiences are so often colorful is that they follow the growth of the nation in all its corners, crises, and cultures. At every point and on every occasion there was always someone singing, playing in a band, improvising jazz for dancing, or composing a piece suited to some special purpose.

The subjects mentioned on this Contents page are surprising now and then and raise unexpected questions in your mind. Did James Lyon capture Nova Scotia? If so, why? What did he do with it? What was the "Foreign Invasion of 1848" and did it start a war? How did the financial crash in 1929 affect music in America? As you go through the book you discover what Tom Thumb and Jenny Lind had in common, the significance of minstrel shows, and you are set to thinking about the effects of Marconi's invention of wireless telegraphy on the course of music, American and otherwise.

In the end, you find that the history of music in America has been writing itself in a thoroughly original way ever since it began, and that every musical sound made here has contributed to it in some way.

A century ago, Walt Whitman wrote "I hear America singing, the varied carols I hear." In our own time, Virgil Thomson has suggested why those "carols" were varied and why Whitman's observation is still 100 per cent applicable today.

"The United States," Thomson has written, "is the one country in all the world that produces all kinds of music that there are. Only here do composers write in every possible style and does the public have access to every style."

This, I think, tells us why the title of this book refers to "Music in America" rather than "American Music." It implies, too, that our musical life is probably richer now than it would have been if we had had to follow in the footsteps of genius musical ancestors.

In any case, it seems to me that we have long since created our own musical legitimacy and that whatever we may have lacked in orthodoxy of means, we have more than made up for in variety, energy, and excitement.

New York, N. Y.   ALLEN HUGHES

A SHORT HISTORY OF
MUSIC IN AMERICA

CHAPTER I

Before the Settlers

For many years after Columbus discovered America, it was thought that the American Indians were composed of various races; but it is now known that the "red race," from the Arctic Circle to the tip of South America, emanated from the same stock. The Indians had been on the American continent for so many centuries that their beginnings were lost in the dim past. Their culture, for the greatest part, was one of the most primitive in the world; and their inventions, tools, and methods were of the crudest sort.

The Indians in the eastern part of the continent, with whom the first settlers came in contact, were hunters and fishermen who also lived off wild plant life, with agriculture of secondary importance. Though the Indians on the plains west of Mississippi wore elaborate headdresses of feathers, the pictures of Columbus and John Smith meeting with Indians so bedecked showed nothing more than the artists' disregard for the correct styles of Indian dress in the East. Like the very name "Indian," the feathers came to be a symbol of all Indians.

General Characteristics

Music for the Indians, as for all primitive peoples, was not only functional, but the very breath of life, and they cherished their tribal songs and dance music. Many of the Indians' songs were thought by them to have supernatural powers, and were a medium of communication between the individual and his god. The Indians

1

were a deeply animistic race. They had a simple faith in the ultimate victory of right and justice, their heroes were honored and
worshiped, and many individuals were said to have visions and converse with their gods. For these, there existed a sacred, unwritten
body of beliefs (they would be called a folklore today). Ceremo-
nials were common, with rituals composed of songs and dances, with
offerings of tobacco and incense to the deities. Even the most casual
social gatherings were prescribed, often incredibly tedious, and the
early foreign traders and explorers soon had to learn to be patient
as well as tolerant.

The sun god and the maize god were two of the many worshiped,
and even though many Indians were later converted to Christianity,
they never gave up their old animistic faith. This was to have a
potent influence on the early colonists.

Today we realize that America had within her borders one of the
most interesting of all primitive races. In the musical scales and
patterns of the Indians, resemblances may be found to the primitive
musics of China and Russia. Intervals found in the songs were not
those of our modern tempered scale, but were more suggestive of
pure intervals. The basic scale was the pentatonic or five-tone scale,
found in one form or another among all primitive peoples. The
irregular intonation of the Indian, as he slurred from tone to tone,
had something in common with the intervals of Oriental music,
many of which are smaller than the half-steps of Western music.
An interesting similarity may be seen in a gambling song of the
Rogue River Indians of Oregon and the Russian folk theme Tchaikovsky used in the Finale of his Fifth Symphony.

Songs

It is agreed by those who have made an exhaustive study of Indian music that rhythm was more important than melody. The
intervals used were generally simple, the rhythms complicated.
About half the songs were in the major mode and half in the minor.
It must not be forgotten that the Indian had not the European
musician's conceptions of scales and modes, tonality, or harmony.
He achieved his results without awareness of their technical structure. His songs, sung either solo or in unison by a group, followed
the pattern of all primitive music in that they showed a movement
from one extreme to another, from wild excitement to quiet repose.

Melodies began typically on a high note, and sank to a final low note.

From the collector's point of view Indian songs fall into three classes: (1) the old songs that are still sung by the old singers; (2) the ancient ceremonial and medicine songs, which originally belonged to men long since dead, but which can still be sung with reasonable accuracy by the younger Indians who heard them; and (3) the comparatively modern songs, composed on the reservations. These last, of course, represent a transitional culture, and show influences of the white man.

When one realizes that the United States Office of Indian Affairs now deals with fifty basic linguistic stocks, which are further divided into separate tribes of which there are some 342—each a separate and distinctive group with different customs and ways of life—it is possible to comprehend the vastness of the body of Indian music, which is just becoming known today. Just as European music is the sum total of the many countries that have contributed to it, so Indian music includes all types of music from the three-hundred-odd tribes.

Many tribes had lullabies and children's songs, while others had relatively few, as in the agricultural sections, where the women did the farming and the children were left to lie quietly in their hammocks. The Chippewa, Yuma, Makah, Mandan, Ute, and Hopi tribes had children's songs for the purpose of teaching the young to do essential tasks through games. Except with the Makahs, love songs were comparatively rare, as marriages were usually arranged by the parents, and the songs in this case were associated with disappointment in love. The various tribal musics were easily differentiated by those who sang them. Thus, the singing of the bison hunters of the West would be found to be quite different from the singing of the salmon hunters in the Northwest.

Instruments

The instruments in use when Columbus reached the New World were basically of two types—wind and percussion. Melodic instruments included whistles or flageolets, made from the wing bone of some large bird, pierced with three holes, and capable of producing five shrill tones. These were used by magicians and doctors for treating the sick. The wooden flute, about eighteen inches in length and one and a half inches in diameter, was blown from the end, pierced with six holes, and sounded a complete octave, with corresponding overtones. As the instruments were not always accurately made, there were sometimes irregularities of intonation.

The drums were of greater importance, and varied in size from the tambourine to a large bass drum. They were made of hides stretched over a frame, tied with thongs, brightly painted with tribal symbols, and warmed by a fire to tighten the heads before they were played. One interesting drum was shaped like a keg, and partially filled with water. Its pitch could be changed by wetting the skin head covering it, or by scraping it with the hand when it was dry. This instrument might be said to have anticipated the modern timpani. Rattles were also customary, made from gourds and often thought to be sacred, so that they were used mostly on religious occasions.

Performance

The Indian admired a singing voice with a noticeable vibrato, and a proficient singer strove for a clear falsetto tone. Love songs, however, invariably were sung with a decided nasal twang. Common to the Indians was the ability to sing in one rhythm and beat a drum in another, a feat that would tax many a well-trained professional musician of today. At the great tribal ceremonies or festivals there would be polychoral effects, as several groups would sing their songs at the same time. Indian melodies, as far as any formal structure was concerned, were based largely on the repetition of one or two motives or phrases, without development, and continued indefinitely. This, too, was common to the Orient, and today it finds a counterpart in art music, as for example in the incessant repetitions Ravel used in his *Bolero*.

In singing, the Indian often interrupted long sustained tones by fluttering his hand before his lips, the sharp cries suggestive of animal calls. Songs were invariably associated with some tribal custom, and were used only for the performance of that custom, such as the popular harvest or planting songs. Other songs were the property of the individual, songs which were believed to have been received in a dream or vision, and could only be sung by their owners. It was sometimes possible to purchase songs from the owner, especially if they were supposed to have some magic power for healing the sick. There were songs for friends, enemies, gods, animals, forests, lakes, and even clothing, and they were always sung to gain some end—to treat the sick, or to win success in hunting or in battle.

The rhythms of Indian music were often irregular, with the rhythmic units varying from two to five beats and occurring in one melody. This discovery was of particular interest to students, for it was thought for many years that such irregularity occurred only in certain European folk music, such as that of the Russians.

PERPETUATION OF INDIAN MUSIC

When George Catlin (1796-1872) published the report of his "eight years travel [1832-1839] amongst the wildest tribes of Indians in North America," he included a description of Indian music and dances. Henry Rowe Schoolcraft (1793-1864), in 1851, gave an account of the rites and symbolic notation of the songs of the Walbeno, and showed how these people used mnemonic symbols to refresh their memories for traditional songs. But it was not until 1880 that a serious attempt was made by musicians to make an exact record of Indian songs. It was then that Theodore Baker, an American student at the Leipzig University, chose the music of the North American Indians as the subject for his doctor's thesis. He returned to America in the summer of 1880 and lived among the Indians on the Seneca Reservation and at the Training School for Indian Youth at Carlisle, Pennsylvania, where he collected and wrote down many songs, studying and analyzing them. He discussed them under the following headings: Scales, Melodic Progressions, Rhythm, Recitative, Notation, and Instruments.

Baker's thesis, written in German, was well received in 1882, and he was graduated with the highest honors. For many years he was the editor and translator for G. Schirmer, Inc., in New York, yet he never found time to translate his own great contribution to American music, and the thesis is now out of print.

Many scholars have since followed the pioneer work of Dr. Baker, the group including Alice C. Fletcher, Frederick R. Burton, Benjamin Ives Gilman, Natalie Curtis (Mrs. Paul Burlin), Frances Densmore, Helen H. Roberts, and Willard Rhodes. Many of these investigators have used the phonograph to record the songs, and the recordings have been deposited in museums where students may hear them. In 1911 the United States government undertook the great task of perpetuating Indian music. Trained investigators were appointed to gather the songs and dances of the many tribes, which were recorded and placed in the Smithsonian Institution in Washington. Today, the main source is to be found in the Library of Congress. Many authentic recordings have also been issued by Folkways Records and Service Corporation in New York.

MODERN USE OF INDIAN THEMES

Quite a number of composers have sought to capture the music of the Indians in their compositions. One of the earliest attempts may be found in the score of James Hewitt's ballad-opera *Tammany* (1794), of which we shall hear more in chapter 5. This is a song called *Alknomook*, "the death song of the Cherokee Indians." It was published and became popular in England as well as in America. However, in its printed arrangement, it became wholly conventional and sounded very little like the singing of actual Indians.

Except for the lonely figure of "Father Heinrich" (Anton Philipp Heinrich, 1781-1861), whom we shall meet in the years before the Civil War, it was not until near the end of the nineteenth century that composers began to be aware of the possibilities of native music.

It was owing to Antonin Dvořák's residence in America from 1892 to 1895 that what might be termed a small national movement got under way. He advised his students to consider both Indian and Negro themes for their compositions, and various American composers attempted to use Indian song material. Edward MacDowell also used a few themes (taken from Baker's thesis) in his second *Indian Suite*, but he stated that he did not pretend to compose authentic Indian music by so doing.

In the course of the years, a number of highly effective compositions have resulted from experiments with Indian material. The most significant composers were Arthur Farwell, Henry B. F. Gilbert, Charles Wakefield Cadman, Charles Sanford Skilton, Arthur Nevin, and Charles T. Griffes (all of whom will be discussed in subsequent chapters), but for the most part they are isolated examples. There has been no fundamental merging of Indian idioms with a musical heritage that is essentially European.

Today we know that this national movement was but a passing phase, important at that time because it was one of the earliest manifestations that serious composers were seeking something which they felt was truly American. Today the musician is interested in Indian music primarily for its own sake and as an example of primitive music that was created within the borders of our own country. Nationalism of the type that was urged in the early years of the twentieth century gradually became unimportant, and since the 1920s interest on the part of composers has lagged and shows no signs of being revived.

CHAPTER II

Music in the Colonies

THE SPANIARDS IN MEXICO

When the Gregorian plain song of the Christian Church was at its height, there took place two of the most important events in the entire history of Western music. One was the birth of polyphony (or plural melody); the other—not obviously connected with music— was the discovery and exploration of North America. From the former was to come the great structure that is the art music of the present day; from the latter was to develop the great nation that is now the United States of America, a nation that was to be a world center of music by the midpoint of the twentieth century.

The Norsemen could not know, as they reached Greenland in the tenth century, that this new country was as vast and rich as it later proved to be, any more than could the early European musicians realize, as they combined their melodies in their scattered and often isolated monasteries, that the seeds they cultivated so carefully would one day blossom into an abundant harvest.

The Spaniards who captured Mexico City in 1521 lost no time in transforming their new country according to their own ideas. Their zeal in the spread of Christianity, with force if necessary, soon led them to replace with their own the elaborate Aztec traditions, in which music had played a great part, especially in regard to worship. Within three years of the fall of Mexico City to the Spanish invaders, Pedro de Gante, a Franciscan missionary, had founded a school of music in Texcoco.

A printing press was set up in 1539, and in less than twenty years the first book with music was printed in America—an Ordinary of the Mass, in 1556. Eleven other liturgical books came from the press in rapid succession, a truly remarkable feat, when in the home country of Spain, in the same half-century, there appeared only fourteen liturgical books with music. The Spanish influence on music, architecture, and way of living was to color the life of Mexico and the Southwest for many years to come. Earlier buildings were soon replaced with Spanish-type structures, and the great Cathedral in Mexico City, started in 1573, recalls the luxuriant Spanish baroque style. In the years that followed, as the missionaries traveled farther and farther from their center, building missions and preaching to the people, this influence was extended through Texas, New Mexico, Arizona, and along the California coast.

Probably the first European music that was heard upon either coast of North America, north of the Spanish settlements, was that of the French Huguenots, who not only settled in Acadia and Canada, but along the eastern seaboard as far south as Florida in the 1560s. Their greatest concentration would soon create the state of South Carolina.

A few years later, the English songs of Drake's seamen might have been heard along the California coast, during their stay of several weeks in June, 1579, at what is now known as Drake's Bay.

THE FIRST ENGLISH SETTLEMENTS

When John Smith and his company of gentlemen and merchants established the first permanent English settlement at Jamestown, Virginia, in 1607, it is certain that they kept up their spirits by the singing of catches around their campfires, and psalms in their houses of worship. Only the diaries and similar records of those early years give us any clues as to their life in the new country, and because music was obviously so much a part of daily life, no one took the trouble to mention it.

The England from whose shores these men had sailed had enjoyed a rich musical life in the previous century, one which had given new impulses to European music. It was music worthy of the age in which Shakespeare wrote and over which Queen Elizabeth reigned. As the curtain went up on the seventeenth century, it heralded an era pregnant with promise for the future. Little could the heartsick band of Pilgrims, separating from the Church of Eng-

land and fleeing the terrible persecution of their native land, have
known that this move of theirs would change the history of the
world.

THE PURITANS AND SEPARATISTS IN ENGLAND

In England, Queen Elizabeth disliked the Puritans for their bare
and simple worship and also because she felt the teachings of John
Knox opposed her royal power. The Puritans, steadfast in their belief that the English Reformation had not gone far enough in its
separation from the Roman Catholic Church, had suffered untold
tortures, even death. Some of them had been dubbed Separatists
because they wished independence for their church, refusing to bow
to either king or bishop, wanting only to manage their own affairs.
In the early years of the seventeenth century these Separatists
had already established Independent (Congregational) churches at
Scrooby (near York), as well as at Gainsborough.

James I, ascending the throne, yearned toward absolute sover-
eignty and richly hated the Separatists who defied his wishes. He
swore that they should conform or be run out of the country, and
at last both Puritans and Separatists had no alternative but to leave.
In the same year that Captain Smith landed in America, they sought
refuge across the Channel in Holland. With grim fortitude and
cheerful courage, the Puritans tried to make a new home among the
hospitable Dutch, but within a dozen years it became quite clear
that they and their ideals would soon be absorbed by another nationality. One of their greatest ambitions was to spread the gospel
of Christ to the furthermost corners of the earth, and it was only
natural that at last their eyes turned toward that land of promise—
America. There, at no matter what cost, they would found a Puritan
state.

THE SEPARATISTS OR PILGRIMS LAND IN 1620

It was in 1620, after feasting and the singing of psalms, that an
advance group of the English Separatists who had been living in
Holland left Delfthaven in the ship *Speedwell*, bound for Southampton, where they were to be joined by their friends from London,
sailing in the *Mayflower*. We learn of their love for music, especially
the joy of singing, from the vivid account of Edward Winslow. In

his book, *Hypocrisie Unmasked* (1646), he describes the ceremony which took place on the eve of their departure:

> ... they, I say, that stayed at Leyden feasted us that were to go, at our pastor's house . . . . ; where we refreshed ourselves, after tears, with singing of psalms, making joyful melody in our hearts, as well as with the voice, there being many of our congregation very expert in music; and indeed it was the sweetest melody that ever mine ears heard.

At Southampton, serious leaks were discovered in the *Speedwell*, and it was the *Mayflower* alone that sailed from Plymouth with a hundred and one persons aboard. Fervently religious, with high ideals and an iron strength of character, these brave souls were to leave an indelible impression on the new land to which they came.

Their Psalm Book

The music which these Separatists (whom we now call Pilgrims) took with them was contained in a book of average size, Henry Ainsworth's *Book of Psalmes,* which had been prepared for the little congregation in Holland in 1612, the year after the appearance of the King James Version of the Bible. Ainsworth's 342-page book contained thirty-nine psalm-tunes, about half being taken from English psalm books (many of them of French origin), the rest being the longer and finer French and Dutch tunes in a considerable variety of meters. Musically it was better than any other available English psalm book.

In Longfellow's poem, *The Courtship of Miles Standish,* he refers to the Ainsworth Psalter as he describes Priscilla singing the 100th Psalm:

> Open wide in her lap lay the well-worn psalm-book of
>   Ainsworth,
> Printed in Amsterdam, the words and music together,
> Rough-hewn, angular notes, like stones in the wall of a
>   churchyard,
> Darkened and overhung by the running vine of the verses.

The Ainsworth Psalter is a book whose musical importance is now coming to be realized. The tunes, some with sources so obviously from the people, have a refreshing freedom and vitality.

Origins of the Psalms

Because of the importance of psalm singing in the early colonies, and the many books which were used, it would be well to recall just how very ancient was the practice of this kind of singing. The music of the early Christian Church, up to the end of the fifth century, had its roots in the music of the Jewish Synagogue, where not only psalms were chanted, but hymns were sung. As the first generations of those converted to the Christian faith still thought of themselves as a part of the various Jewish religious communities, it was natural that the music preserved all of the traditions of Jewish cantillation.

Many of the psalms were taken from the *Book of Psalms*, those magnificent songs of David which have been one of the most influential sources of text throughout the history of music. In their original form they were not pure poetry, but were songs written in the style of poetic prose, and when sung, were often accompanied by instruments similar to the harp.

The early hymns had texts which paraphrased those in the Bible, and by the third century this very fact caused them to become unpopular, and only Biblical texts were allowed. We shall meet this same situation centuries later, as the English Puritans scorned any music whose texts were not directly from the Scriptures.

Sources of Puritan Music

All of the music of the Reformation had naturally centered around the ideas of Martin Luther (1483-1546), who had urged congregational singing when he broke away from the Roman Catholic Church. Luther favored texts that were simple and in the vernacular, and tunes that were easy to sing. Many Catholic hymns had been translated into German, and numerous secular folk songs were provided with new, and sacred, texts. These simple hymns or chorales were usually sung in unison, and became the communal song of the Protestant Church. They perfectly expressed the spirit of the German Reformation, and were soon to be transplanted to America by the Pietist groups.

But Luther's music was not acceptable to every country, and England was one of them. The Puritans, following the teachings of John Calvin (1509-1564), thought it proper to sing only words taken from the Scriptures, and would have no part of the texts of the German Reformation writers.

THE PURITANS MIGRATE IN 1630

The group of non-Separatist Puritans that had remained in England, emigrating ten years after the Separatist Pilgrims, in 1630, brought with them a different psalm-book, one which had been produced by the English exiles in Geneva, the "Protestant Rome." These Puritans, starting a great exodus that was to continue for many years, came to America as members of the Church of England, with no desire to break away from the mother Church. They wished merely a purified worship, which, with the rise of the Stuart despotism in England, they knew they could not have there. Conditions had become intolerable, and, like the Separatist Pilgrims before them, they set their sails westward, toward the land which they planned to dedicate to God and a democratic self-government.

The Puritan music book had tunes which were drawn from the French psalter and was commonly called *Sternhold and Hopkins.* Their English edition had been printed in 1562 by John Day. By that time the English churches had somewhat altered the older way of singing the psalms by casting them into popular ballad meters, hoping in this way to appeal to the masses. In Day's edition the music of the psalms was printed with the words, a single melody line, which was to be sung in unison, a note to each syllable.

To modern ears many of these early psalms may seem dry and stilted, sometimes crude, but for the Puritans they had a simple dignity and solemnity. One of their tunes is still in constant use— *Old Hundredth,* or, in our time, the *Doxology.* Its original name came from the fact that it was used in the singing of the 100th Psalm. Its melody is attributed to Louis Bourgeois, the music editor of John Calvin's Genevan psalters. At first it had been set by Beze in 1551 to the 134th Psalm, and in adopting it, the English Puritans had used it instead for the 100th Psalm in Day's edition of *Sternhold and Hopkins.* The familiar verses start:

> All people that on earth do dwell,
> Sing to the Lord with cheereful voyce
> Him serve with feare, His praise forth tel,
> Come ye before Him and rejoyce.

The Puritans sang it with quick notes that expressed the joyousness of the words, and it was thought to be a "lively and jocund tune."

Once landed in America, the Puritan fathers had little time or inclination to do more than clear the land, build homes, and organize their religious and social life. Because they were so far from England, they soon adopted the Congregational or Independent form of church government which the Pilgrims had already set up. The Independents (Congregationalists) were often called Brownists, after their founder, Robert Browne, who was known as a "singular good lutenist" and taught his children to play.

It is a tribute to the keen intelligence of this band of people that within six years of their arrival in a vast and almost unbroken country, America's first college—Harvard—was founded, in 1636. In creating their college, the Puritans felt it the best way to train future leaders, and from the beginning we find that music was a part of daily life. Drums and trumpets were used to summon the people to church (where the music of the service was always decorously conducted), until the time came when bells were available. These instruments were also used to sound an alarm in case of Indian attacks, or other emergencies. Before long Jew's-harps were imported in quantities for barter with the Indians, who delighted in the sounds they made.

From the painstaking research of recent years and from the discovery of documents hitherto unknown, ideas about the Puritans and their life, and most especially about their music, have radically changed. For generations Americans have been taught that the Puritans hated music and tolerated it only in their Sunday services. In this supposedly enlightened day it may come as a shock to some to discover how very wrong many of the early writers have been.

The Puritans possessed all the best qualities for the founding of a cultured civilization. In the holds of the *Mayflower* there were undoubtedly scores of excellent books besides those on music. William Brewster, one of the first arrivals, is said to have owned some three hundred volumes on widely diversified subjects. Many of the first colonists had been well-educated in England and therefore it is not surprising to find an early flowering of poetry in the Puritan community. America's first known poet was a woman, Anne Bradstreet (1612-1672), who had arrived with her father Thomas Dudley, a Puritan in every sense of the word. Already married to Simon Bradstreet when she arrived in 1630, Mrs. Bradstreet wrote and dedicated her verses to God, expressing in them the Puritan sense of His presence. Her frequent allusions to music give brief glimpses of contemporary life and the pleasure afforded by both sacred as well as secular music.

THE BAY PSALM BOOK

It did not take long for the New England ministers—forceful, well-educated men—to realize that the older translations of the psalms in their *Sternhold and Hopkins* music book were both inaccurate and faulty. They knew their Hebrew, and while they had no objection to metrical verse, they soon agreed that the texts should be closer to the original meaning. A committee was formed to prepare a new set of translations, led by Richard Mather, Thomas Welde, and John Eliot, all of whom had studied in England. Their translation, soon to become known as the *Bay Psalm Book* (its actual title was *The Whole Booke of Psalmes Faithfully Translated into English Metre*), was printed by the little press of Stephen Day at Cambridge, in 1640. Day's press was the gift of Puritan friends in Holland, and had been sent from England in 1638. Aside from a small pamphlet and a broadside (1639), the *Bay Psalm Book* was the first item to be printed in the English-speaking colonies, almost a century after the first books printed in the Spanish colony in Mexico City.

The early editions of the *Bay Psalm Book* contained no music, probably for lack of anyone capable of engraving the plates. Forty-eight melodies were suggested for the singing of the psalms, and an "Admonition" about the tunes to which they might be sung read (in part) as follows:

> The verses of these psalmes may be reduced to six kindes, (metres), the first whereof may be sung in very neere fourty common tunes; as they are collected out of our chief musicians by Tho. Ravenscroft.

This psalter of Ravenscroft had appeared in 1621 in London, and contained four-part settings of some of England's finest composers: Thomas Morley, Thomas Tallis, Giles Farnaby, John Dowland, John Farmer, as well as Ravenscroft. It is important to remember that although the editors were unable to print music in the *Bay*

Psalm Book, they obviously knew and recommended to its users the best collection of tunes which the time afforded.

Only eleven copies of the original edition of the *Bay Psalm Book* are known to survive, and only three of them are in perfect condition. In 1651, a revised edition appeared (the third), containing considerable improvements in versification, and its use soon spread throughout New England.

GENERAL PICTURE OF PURITAN MUSICAL LIFE

In coming to their new home, the Puritans had had to forsake two very important musical influences—the court and the cathedral. But it is to be expected that once they were settled, secular music became as much a part of their lives as it had been in England. In the same way their writings reflected the fine heritage of Elizabethan prose and poetry, as well as the influences of the Reformation and Renaissance. The writing was either descriptive or argumentative, and for nearly a century it varied from narratives to such complex books as Cotton Mather's monumental history of New England, the *Magnalia Christi Americana* (1702). There was, however, a simple dignity in the chronicles of adventure, and a fundamental strength in the fiery sermons which expressed the Puritan conception of life. Together with the poetry, always the handmaiden of religion, these early expressions of the arts were functional, and mirrored the sternness of the times, yet there is a sweetness and a joy of living which cannot be denied, and therefore they will ever remain a storehouse of seventeenth-century life in America.

Not much of the Puritan poetry was good, and there is no better example of its pedestrian quality than that which is contained in the *Bay Psalm Book*, and which Richard Mather instinctively sensed when he wrote in the preface: "If therefore the verses are not alwayes so smooth and elegant as some may desire or expect; let them consider that Gods Altar needs not our pollishings . . . for wee . . . have attended Conscience rather then Elegance, fidelity rather then poetry . . ."

Despite the popularity of their new psalm-book, not all of the Puritans approved of singing in the church, and some were set and fanatical in their views. They insisted that the Christian should hear melodies within himself, and some went so far as to stuff cotton in their ears, that they might not hear. This sort of thing no doubt led many to believe that all Puritans shared the views of this minority group, and went so far as to make laws against music, a legend which has persisted to our own day. There is proof enough now that there were never any laws passed against music or the playing of certain instruments. Singing was enjoyed, and in 1647, John Cotton, the revered leader of the Puritan congregation in Boston, reminded his flock that the singing of the psalms was a Gospel ordinance, while he backed the objection of some who protested the use of instruments in public worship. This objection to instruments was a purely religious one, some feeling them too reminiscent of "church ceremonies" and "popery." Cotton expressly said, however, that the use of instruments in the home, to accompany psalms, might be allowed.

Secular music there was, for as the older men died, many specifically mentioned in their wills the instruments they owned. Nathaniell Rogers, in 1664, left a "treble viall" (viol), and the Reverend Edmund Browne, in 1678, listed a "bass Vyol," books of music, and left behind the reputation of having been a good musician.

Youth, too, made its music, for around 1650, when Harvard College was still in its infancy, Tutor Wigglesworth recorded the admonitions he gave a young student whom he caught idling ". . . in the forenoon with ill company playing musick, though I had solemnly warned him but yesterday of letting his spirit go after pleasures." Thus spoke age to youth, lest he forget the seriousness of life. Some ten years later, another Harvard student, freshman Josiah Flynt, wrote his uncle in London for a fiddle. His uncle's reply was again an admonition: "Musick I had almost forgot. I suspect you seek it both to soon and to much. This be assured of that if you be not excellent at it Its worth nothing at all. . . . were it for your sisters, for whom it is more proper and they also have more leisure to look after it: For them I say I had provided the instruments desired." The day was yet to come when a young man in America might earn his living as a fiddler.

From such scattered bits of information as these it has been possible to piece together the fact that secular music was made and cherished in the colonies as it had been in the homes of Elizabethan England. It would not be many years before this amateur activity would lead to Boston's first public concert of which there is a record.

Life, therefore, was not as dull as we have been led to believe, for the American Calvinists, like those in Europe, countenanced the games and simple amusements of everyday life as long as they were temperately indulged in. Songs with indecent words, wanton dancing, gambling, and disorder would not be tolerated, and Sabbath observance was rigidly enforced, with the music of the Sunday services kept firmly in hand at all times. But even dancing was not wholly condemned.

Four years after the Pilgrims landed at Plymouth, one Thomas Morton arrived (1624) and outraged the citizens by his celebration of May Day at Merry Mount, his settlement at Mount Wollaston (used by Howard Hanson as the locale for his opera *Merry Mount* [1934]), which turned out to be the wildest of orgies. As the song which was sung was "Drink and be merry, merry, merry boys," and as the admiring Indians were drawn into the revelry (probably much the worse for a bit of fire-water), there were doubtless sound reasons for the objections. But the crux of the situation was the discovery that Morton was selling guns and ammunition to the Indians, a grim threat to the safety and welfare of the young colony, and it does not take much imagination to see why Morton was asked to leave the settlement.

As the years passed and the colonists' generations succeeded one another, it became increasingly obvious that there was a perceptible decline in the quality of singing in the Sunday services. The lack of music in the first editions of the *Bay Psalm Book,* and the inability of the younger members of the congregation to read the music in the older English books, became a serious problem.

MANNER OF SINGING THE PSALMS

The singing in the Sunday services was led by a precentor, generally one of the elders of the church, who set the tunes, and "lined out" the psalms, as had been the custom in the Old Country. The precentor would sing the psalm line by line, pausing each time for the congregation to repeat the line he had just sung. Naturally this procedure disrupted the sense of the text, and destroyed musical continuity. If the precentor had an ear for music and a good sense of pitch, the singing might be acceptable. Otherwise the tunes were either pitched too high or too low, and were frequently altered or embellished by the gentleman in charge. These whims of the leader greatly confused the congregation and so corrupted the melodies that the results were anything but musical. Soon no two congregations sang the same tune alike, and as the century drew to a close the cultivation of music became more and more neglected.

Many early writers on American music considered the lining-out of the psalms deplorable and held the custom up to ridicule. But the custom, with its roots in England, persisted and the people refused to change their way of singing without a fight. We shall meet something closely related to this Puritan lining-out in the congregational singing of the southern Negroes in the nineteenth century.

EARLY MUSIC IN THE OTHER COLONIES

The times were troubled, and this did not help the cause of music. The spirit of unrest hung heavily over the colonies from Maine to Florida. There was increasing resentment over the Quakers, from Massachusetts to Virginia. Quaker missionaries had come to America as early as 1656, settling anywhere they could along the coast. But they would not conform to the religious practices of others, and violently attacked all who differed from them. It was they, and not the Puritans, who detested music. George Fox, the founder of the Sect, wrote in his Journal (1649): "I was moved to cry out against all kinds of music." It was only their interest and activity in the field of education, as well as their philanthropies, which offset their dislike of music. For all of this, the Quakers, of course, were unmercifully treated for a number of years. In 1661 four of them were hanged for heresy on the Boston Common.

Attitudes changed considerably in the next few years and in spite of the Quakers' views on music the leader of their Society opened the way for several of the most ardent music-loving groups that settled in America. When this leader, William Penn, proclaimed his "glorious new world" in 1682 and founded Philadelphia, the "City of Brotherly Love," he offered what at last was to be religious freedom for all sects and denominations, and in quick succession many groups settled all through Pennsylvania. The Swedish emigrants had already preceded Penn, and a year later

(1683), the Mennonites became the first large group to follow him, settling in Germantown, near Philadelphia.

In 1694 an important group of German Pietists settled on the Wissahickon River, about eight miles from Quaker Philadelphia. They were mystics who believed that the end of the world was near, and they renounced marriage as sinful. Their leader was Johannes Kelpius, an educated and cultured man and a lover of music. These people brought with them not only a rich heritage of both sacred and secular music, but the ability to put it into practice as soon as they were settled. Their instruments made a choice group for a young nation and were as representative as those to be found in many small German towns. These folk were the first to transplant a Germanic culture to the new country.

In New England, the era of witchcraft trials had ended in a sharp public reaction against such excesses, but somewhere along the way music had been almost forgotten. This development undoubtedly helped the progressive ministers to become more and more aware of its value, and to realize how much meaning it gave to life. Because music was in such a deplorable state, they set about taking steps to correct it.

THE FIRST MUSIC BOOK

In 1698 a new edition of the *Bay Psalm Book* was issued, and this time music was added. It is possible that future research may unearth an earlier edition with music, but at any rate this ninth edition had thirteen tunes inserted in the back of the book, doubtless those in frequent use at the time—*Oxford, Lichfield, Low-Dutch, York, Windsor, Cambridge Short Tune, St. David's, Martyrs, Hackney, 119th Psalm Tune, 100th Psalm Tune, 115th Psalm Tune,* and *148th Psalm Tune.* Most of them were in common meter, and the music was printed from crudely engraved wooden blocks, in diamond-shaped notes. It was the first music book published in the English-speaking colonies, and the second on the North American continent. The preachers felt that new interest would be created when the people could be taught to read notes, and the music would thereby improve. This new *Bay Psalm Book* was to go through twenty-seven editions in all—the last, the second edition of Thomas Prince's revision in 1773—and even appeared in England, requiring some eighteen or more editions there. In 1947 a copy of the first (1640) edition was sold at auction for $151,000. No other book has ever brought such a price, not even the rarest Gutenberg Bible.

The ministers, rightly priding themselves on their perception, could hardly have anticipated the bitter controversy which ensued between those who thought the old way of singing from memory was good enough, and those who were eager to learn the new way of singing from notes, which came to be called "regular singing." The die-hards considered the note names blasphemous and popish, merely a scheme to get money for singing teachers. They insisted it was sure to cause disturbances in the church and would grieve good men, making them disorderly.

It is significant that these violent controversies on the part of the clergy were characteristic of the many attempts in the history of music to preserve a medium that was becoming old-fashioned. We can see today that there was a strong undercurrent which stemmed from the people who fiercely resented any kind of regimentation or standardization in the way they sang. But the crusade on the part of the ministers for better singing soon bore fruit, and early in the eighteenth century instruction books began to appear, and itinerant singing teachers began to hold singing schools in the various settlements. At the same time the people grimly held to the way of singing they loved, and in the not-too-distant future they would take things into their own hands and create in their revival services and camp meetings the great body of song, that, although ignored for years by historians and musicians alike, has finally come to be recognized as one of America's most singular manifestations of musical activity along the frontier.

AMERICA: A VAST MELTING-POT

By 1700 the colonies were already a vast melting-pot, a fact that has always been peculiar to America. In California and the Southwest were the Spanish; New Orleans was a mixture of Spanish and French; to the Carolinas had come the French Huguenots after the Revocation of the Edict of Nantes (1685), to be joined by the French refugees from Acadia later in 1755; while the Swedes and Finns were entrenched on the lower Delaware. The German groups of Pennsylvania, the Dutch in New York, and the French around Quebec were all mixed with the English, who seemed to be everywhere. The first slave ships, brought by the Dutch to Virginia as early as 1619, had thrust the African Negro into the midst of colonial life; his primitive music would have a profound influence on later generations of American musicians. Before all of these people and their influences, there had, of course, been the Indians. In each permanent colony were to be found the traditions of an older way of life, but almost at once they were slowly but surely absorbed into the new life, and there began to emerge a new individual—the American.

THE PIETISTS IN PENNSYLVANIA

It is astonishing how fast music took root and flourished in Pennsylvania. The Wissahickon Hermits (as the Pietists were soon called) had already achieved a reputation for their music, and in 1700, when the Old Swedes' Church (Gloria Dei) in Philadelphia was dedicated, the nearby hermits were asked to act as choristers and also to furnish instrumental music. With the original group had come a German Lutheran pastor, Justus Falckner, whose interest in music had caused him to ask for help from Germany, particularly for an organ. He wrote that he felt music would not only greatly "attract and civilize the wild Indian, but do much good in spreading the Gospel truths among the sects" (the younger Quakers), whose fathers, he knew, had abolished all music.

In 1703, when Falckner was ordained a minister—the first German to be ordained in the new country—an organ was used in the service. Whether one had been sent him or whether it belonged to the hermits is not known, but in addition to the organ (played by Jonas Auren), music was furnished by a choir and a group of instrumentalists, including viols, oboes, trombones, and kettledrums.

Within the year the hermits had a new member, Dr. Christopher Witt, an English physician, who built an organ for private use, the first to be constructed in this country. Besides leading his group, Johannes Kelpius composed nineteen hymns which appeared in the Kelpius hymnal. The book contained seventeen other hymns, probably by Heinrich Bernhard Köster and Johann Gottfried Seelig (also members of the group). It was completed in 1705, and is still extant. There is no evidence that Kelpius wrote the hymn tunes, most of which are of German origin. He was probably the first musician to come to the Pennsylvania colony.

MUSIC IN THE SOUTH

Maryland, Virginia, and the Carolinas had a different way of life from the northern colonies, and it is natural that their music reflected that existence. Many of the settlers, like Cecilius Calvert, who founded Maryland (1634), or the Carolina Huguenots, were members of noble families, and were used to a leisurely and easy life. With the land divided into large plantations and manors, recreating English country life as nearly as possible, the daily tempo of living was gay and alive. It may be assumed that the first music was that of the small virginal and spinet, brought over on the ships that crowded the tidewater wharves. There must also have been the singing of madrigals after the bountiful meals, as had been the custom in Elizabethan England.

Although the cities, such as Annapolis and Williamsburg, were built in the style of English cities, they were already assuming certain architectural qualities that were entirely American. Yet the life was a reflection of London society, and probably because it merely continued the customs of the home country, formal records of music were practically nonexistent. Charleston, South Carolina, one of the brightest of the southern cities and already noted for her beautiful landscaped gardens, alludes to some sort of operatic entertainment as early as 1702.

Williamsburg (where the Episcopal Church had created its first college, William and Mary, in 1693), must have seemed altogether cosmopolitan and worldly in comparison with Quaker Philadelphia or Puritan Boston. The first real playhouse known to have existed in America may have flourished earlier than the records of 1722 indicate, but from that year on it was to have regular seasons by the best players in the country. The Episcopalians always championed the lighter entertainments, and enjoyed their dancing and music.

THE FIRST ORGAN IN NEW ENGLAND

In New England the Congregational Church had gained further momentum and founded its second school, Yale College, at New Haven, Connecticut, in 1701—the third college in the colonies. All of the major colleges in colonial America were founded by religious groups.

Boston citizens were acquiring wealth and position, and those who loved music were importing instruments from England. Thomas Brattle was among the first to send for an organ for his home, the earliest known to be brought into New England. The Reverend Joseph Green noted in his *Diary* on May 29, 1711: "I was at Mr. Thomas Brattle's; heard ye organ and saw strange things in a microscope."

When Brattle died in 1713, he willed this organ to the Brattle Square Church, of which he had been a leading member. He foresaw a possible rejection of the organ on the part of the church authorities (and they did reject it on two different occasions), so he stipulated that it then be given to King's Chapel. A year later the organ was accepted by King's Chapel, and a further request of Brattle's was carried out, namely, that the chapel would "procure a sober person that can play skilfully thereon with a loud noise." Edward Enstone was brought over from London expressly to play the new organ, which was sold a few years later to Newburyport (1756) and then to St. John's Church in Portsmouth, New Hampshire (1836), where it still exists today in a usable condition.

Boston's social life was beginning to relax its austerity, for the dancing schools, which had been so bitterly opposed in the last years of the seventeenth century, were allowed to be held and were well attended. Music in the home must have been in a healthy state when various shops advertised all types of instruments for sale. Edward Enstone, to cite one example, arriving to play the organ in King's Chapel, lost no time in setting up business on the side, and in the *Boston News Letter* of April 16-23, 1716, ran the following advertisement:

This is to give notice that there is lately sent over from London, a choice Collection of Musickal Instruments, consisting of Flageolets, Flutes, Haut-Boys, Bass-Viols, Violins, Bows, Strings, Reads for Haut-Boys, Books of Instructions for all these Instruments, Books of ruled Paper. To be Sold at the Dancing School of Mr. Enstone in Sudbury Street near the Orange Tree, Boston
NOTE. Any person may have all Instruments of Musick mended, or Virginalls and Spinnets Strung and Tuned at a reasonable Rate, and likewise may be taught to Play on any

of these Instruments above mention'd; dancing taught by a true and easier method than has been heretofore.

TYPICAL INSTRUMENTS OF THE DAY

The imposing array of instruments Enstone offered for sale, many of which were like those of the Pietists outside Philadelphia, clearly indicates just how active the musical amateur was becoming. These were the same instruments that could be heard in the courts and churches of Europe, and for which men like Bach and Handel were writing. It may be helpful briefly to describe them.

The most aristocratic stringed instruments of the day were the viols, which had descended from the fifteenth-century troubadour fiddles. Their tone was soft and discreet, perfectly suited to the intimacy of a small room and the musical amateur. The seventeenth century had been the classical period for the viols. They were ordinarily of four sizes: the treble, approximating the violin in range; the alto, comparable to the modern viola; the tenor, pitched somewhat like the modern violin but an octave lower; and the bass, the equivalent of our modern violoncello. The "chests of viols" so frequently referred to in English music, were sets of instruments—for example, two trebles, two tenors, and two basses—made by English craftsmen and fitted into a "chest"—apparently a shallow vertical cabinet.

But a new instrument was encroaching on the territory of the old viols—the violin. The older viols lacked the brilliance and versatility of the violin, and with the magnificent violins (and other stringed instruments) made in Cremona by the Amati family and Stradivarius, the obsolescence of the viols was soon to come. The violin was much better suited to the larger concert halls and cathedrals as well as to the demands of the increasing body of professional musicians.

The oboes (hautboys) of the eighteenth century had a much more strident and piercing tone than our modern instruments, and were descendants of the aulos of the Greeks and the early European shawms. Flutes, among the most ancient of all instruments, and widely used, existed in the early days in Mexico and South America, where they were frequently made of clay. In the seventeenth century the cross-blown flute was mainly a military instrument (the fife), and so closely connected with the music of Germany that for years it was called the German flute. For artistic playing the end-blown flute or recorder was preferred. Bach and Handel and others used the word *flauto* when they meant the recorder, the flute being called *flauto traverso* (cross-flute). The flageolet, mentioned in so many of the early advertisements in the colonies, was not greatly different from the recorder; that is, it had a whistle mouthpiece and was end-blown.

The viols had roughly the same relation to the violin as the harpsichord had to the piano, and the recorder to the flute. In each instance the newer instrument (violin, piano, flute) was given a bigger, more brilliant tone, a wider compass, and increased technical possibilities that led it gradually to displace its less assertive ancestor.

Trombones had been popular throughout the sixteenth century in the court bands of princes as well as in churches. Their sliding mechanism made them suitable for the performance of art music when the horns and trumpets were still in primitive form, and limited to sounding military signals.

NEW IMPULSES IN CHURCH MUSIC

Side by side with this growth of secular musical activity, church music was broadening its horizons as new books were issued abroad and quickly found their way to the colonies. Tate and Brady's *New Version* (1696) of the metrical psalms had not quite superseded the early book of *Sternhold and Hopkins*—hereafter known as the *Old Version*. However, new life began to be felt, like a breath of fresh air, as an important book by Isaac Watts (English minister and physician, 1674-1748) appeared, *Hymns and Spiritual Songs* (1707). Watts had strong objections to the style of the older psalms, and the literary quality of his new psalms and hymns was far superior to that of the earlier verses, much more pleasing to ears that had become accustomed to the style of Addison and Pope. Watts was becoming known in America as a theologian and a religious writer. He frequently corresponded with Cotton Mather, who approved of Watts' verses for private devotional reading.

In 1719 Watts published *The Psalms of David Imitated*, of which the American edition was printed in 1729 by Benjamin Franklin in

Philadelphia. It must not be thought that Watts did away altogether with the older psalms. He merely chose those which he felt most fitting for religious services and wrote paraphrases on them. Eventually Watts was to dominate the hymnody in most of the Protestant churches in the colonies.

EARLY POETS

At the height of this new impetus in church music, New England saw the emergence of the first major poets since the early verses of Anne Bradstreet. Michael Wigglesworth (1631-1705) and Edward Taylor (ca. 1645-1729), whose works were not discovered until 1937 in the Yale Library. Wigglesworth's verses were a "popular summary in doggerel verse of Calvinistic belief" but were widely read. Rough jingles had always been a part of the sermons and chronicles over a period of years, showing that with the Puritan writers poetry was closely allied to prose. When Wigglesworth's *Day of Doom* came out in a sixth edition (1715) its popularity was instantaneous, and within the year there were over eighteen hundred copies. Soon after, there was one for every thirty-five persons in New England. Such enormous popularity was not to be encountered again until *Uncle Tom's Cabin* was published nearly a century and a half later. Taylor, on the other hand, living in Boston and Westfield, was less touched by gloom than any of the other writers, and his poems are charming jewels of verse.

EARLY INSTRUCTION BOOKS: TUFTS AND WALTER

It was the young church ministers who fought for "regular singing"—singing from notes—fiercely overriding the objections of those who persistently advocated singing the old psalms from memory, and were thus perpetuators of an oral tradition. Much to the chagrin of the reformers, the young people, as well as the oldsters, resisted any change. Out of this bitter conflict of principles was to emerge a new music of the people.

When the first of many instruction books appeared, published by one of the reforming ministers—the Reverend John Tufts of Newburyport, Massachusetts (1689-1750)—and announced for sale in the *Boston News Letter* of January 2-9, 1721, it was to be followed by countless others. Tufts called his book *AN INTRODUCTION To the Singing OF Psalm-Tunes, In a plain & easy method with A COLLECTION of Tunes In Three Parts,* and he provided a musical notation that he thought might be simpler to read than the older sort. Letters were used on the staff instead of notes, and the time was marked by placing one or more dots on the right of each letter. Actually this made things even more complicated and difficult and the book was not destined to be a lasting success, although at the time it had a wide circulation. By 1744 it had gone through eleven editions. Tufts included thirty-seven tunes, in arrangements copied from publications of John Playford (such as his *Whole Book of Psalms,* published in England in 1677), and very likely some from Thomas Walter's book, mentioned below. They were arranged for three-part singing—cantus, medius, and bass, and the volume will always be of interest, despite its limitations, because it was the first instruction book compiled in the colonies. Tufts was a pioneer in this movement for the improvement of church music, in the hope that the congregations might be made more literate. It might be said that Tufts began music education in America; he remains the most outstanding figure in music teaching until the pioneering work of Lowell Mason in the nineteenth century. The 1721 edition of Tufts' book (any earlier editions have never been authenticated) was followed by an important fifth edition in 1726, which is considered the definitive one, for all later editions were never materially changed.

In 1721 there also appeared the famous book of the Reverend Thomas Walter (1696-1725) of Roxbury—*The Grounds and Rules of Musick Explained; Or An Introduction to the Art of Singing by Note.* Walter was another of the reforming ministers and, like that of Tufts, his book contained a set of "Rules for Tuning ye Voice." These scale exercises, in musical notation, were yet another important step forward. Walter gives an admirable description of the state of music at that time when he writes:

> Tunes are now miserably tortured, and twisted, and quavered, in some Churches, into an horrid Medley of confused and discordant Noises; much time is taken up in shaking out these Turns and Quavers, and besides no two men in the Congregation quavering alike, or together, which sounds in the

Ears of a Good Judge like five hundred different Tunes roared out at the Same Time.

The "shaking out" he refers to was the movement of a whole tone above or below, on one syllable, as on the word "praise." "The Grace of Transition" meant to slur or break the note; and to "sweeten the roughness of a leap" was to slide from one note to the other. One can imagine the confusion when an entire congregation did these things, each in terms of his own individual interpretation.

But underneath this description of singing are far deeper implications. This kind of congregational freedom (each singing his own variation, highly embellished, no two "quavering alike") had been going on for years, handed down from one generation to another. In it were all the elements of true folk song, an oral tradition the people liked and were determined to hold onto.

The idea of "singing by note" gradually caught on—in the larger towns first—and singing societies were eventually established throughout New England. These societies were of a higher standard than the singing school. A few of them still exist today. At the same time in a large number of the churches the first seats in the gallery were reserved for the best singers, who were to lead in the singing of the psalms. From this custom was to develop the church choir.

THE FIRST CONCERT IN BOSTON

In 1731, Boston's population had become cosmopolitan, the development hastened by her position as a seaport. Numerous musical instruments were being imported, and the amateur musicians of the city were more numerous and proficient. Entries in diaries have been invaluable in giving an idea of contemporary life. One of the most revealing diaries was that of Judge Samuel Sewall (1652-1730), a graduate of Harvard College, a minister, and one of the first justices of Boston. (He had taken a notable part in the Salem witchcraft trials.) Judge Sewall enjoyed good food and wine, and had a special fondness for music, whether in the home or at the public concerts he attended while on a visit to London. The following entries in the Judge's diary clearly reveal just how widespread was the practice of making and listening to secular music. December 1, 1699: "Was at Mr. Hiller's to enquire for my wife's virginals" (the

popular keyboard instrument of the day) which were obviously being repaired; "May 23, 1717. To Salem, Meadford, Lodge at Cousin
Porter's: See and Hear the Dulcimer"; or with reference to a Harvard classmate: "We were Fellows together at College and have
sung many a tune in Consort." (By *consort* was meant a group of
singers or players, likewise a small group of instruments, as well as
the concerted music.)

With the regular arrival of visitors from Europe, as well as of new
instruments, it is not surprising to read an advertisement in the
Boston Weekly News Letter, December 16-23, 1731. It ran as follows:

> On Thursday the 30th of this instant December, there will be
> performed a *Concert of Music* on sundry Instruments at Mr.
> Pelham's great Room, being the House of the late Doctor
> Noyes near the Sun Tavern.
> Tickets to be delivered at the place of performance at *Five*
> *shillings* each. The Concert to begin exactly at Six o'clock, and
> no Tickets will be delivered after Five the day of performance.
> N. B. There will be no admittance after Six.

Considering the fact that in Europe public-paid concerts were
just coming into vogue, Boston's first concert is all the more remarkable, and its significance has only recently been appreciated.
Similar concerts were to follow in Charleston, New York, and Philadelphia.

Mr. Pelham, in whose "great Room" the concert was held, was an
engraver who had come to America in 1726. A versatile man, he
had to make a living on the side, as did all the musicians in the
colonies in those days. Pelham was an excellent maker of mezzo-
tints, a painter of sorts, and an instructor of writing, reading, and
arithmetic in a boarding school.

THE EPHRATA CLOISTER

Germans poured into the colonies, at first through New York, but
the news of Penn's hospitality soon reached Europe, and for the
next thirty years, beginning in 1727, about two thousand of the emigrants from the Palatinate arrived in Pennsylvania each year. Many
were too poor to pay for their passage, and so became "redemp-

tioners," selling their services in the new country for a period of years, that somehow they might get to America. They were thrifty and hard-working farmers, and soon made good citizens. Gradually their houses were scattered through the rich valleys of eastern Pennsylvania, patterned for the most part after the primitive rural farm buildings of their native Germany.

One of the Germans, a man who was banished from his native land, and who sought refuge in America, was Johann Conrad Beissel. He was responsible for one of the most interesting settlements in the early colonies, one which provided a colorful chapter in America's music. Beissel was born in 1690, the son of a baker, and when forced to leave Germany, he reached America via the port of Boston in 1720. He traveled south and settled at Germantown, Pennsylvania, where he lived on and off for several years. He was a difficult, quarrelsome man, and he never stayed long in any one place.

Beissel finally joined a sect of the Seventh Day Baptists (Dunkers), whose members, known as the Solitary Brethren, took Saturday as the Lord's Day. A dominant and compelling personality, Beissel soon gathered together enough people who believed in him and were willing to follow his teachings, and in 1732, he founded the beautiful Ephrata Cloister, in Lancaster County. Beissel was ever the moving spirit in the life of the Cloister, designing a special garb for the members and insisting on a rigid diet. It was a bare, hard life, likely a subconscious revenge for his own pitiful younger days when he had been mistreated by his drunken father.

From the beginning the group concerned itself with music, and a visitor in 1735 reported that "many of the younger sisters are just now constantly employed in copying musical note books for themselves and their brethren." Beissel taught practically every subject, and as a result of the fine penmanship he insisted upon, there have come down to us some of the most beautiful illuminated manuscripts of colonial America.

Using religion as a pretext to dominate (although it must be said everything was motivated by a desire to be sincere), Beissel would tolerate no interference, and when men like Conrad Weiser and the Eckerlin brothers joined the Cloister and might have proved to be of the greatest help, they did not remain long. Beissel obviously enjoyed the sound of his own voice, for it is said that his sermons often lasted for over two hours, well into the night. The excellent study of the Cloister by Dr. Hans T. David (*Ephrata and Bethlehem in Pennsylvania: a Comparison*) has unearthed many interesting details. In the matter of music alone, one may see to what lengths Beissel's conceit carried him. His pretensions were nothing more than an attempt to cover up his own lack of knowledge on the subject. His education in Germany, where he had been for a while a mere baker's assistant, had been so scant that he was practically self-taught. He had played the violin, but his knowledge and understanding of harmony was literally nonexistent. But when the sisters complained of their vocal instructor, Beissel discharged him and took over the classes himself. He soon found that he had a way with his choir, and as he followed his own dictates, he made great use of the falsetto, claiming he had captured the music of the heavenly hosts. Visitors were constantly amazed by the sounds they heard, so different were they from any type of contemporary singing. Beissel wrote hundreds of hymns for his choir, providing the melodies for the verses that came from Europe, and for all his own. Many of them were published by Benjamin Franklin and Christopher Saur, and later by the Ephrata community itself, whose press was the first in Pennsylvania outside Philadelphia.

Taking up composition around 1743, and because he knew only the merest fundamentals, Beissel made himself a set of rules, with charts of the harmonies, writing for a number of voices, from four to eight. The rhythms of his settings followed the structure of the text in an unusual fashion, but the hymns were sung in chordal harmony with no imitation or counterpoint. One of the most interesting and beautiful of the many Ephrata collections is the *Turtel-Taube* manuscript, compiled in 1746 and now in the Library of Congress. Its full title is: *Das Gesang der einsamen und verlassenen Turtel-Taube Nemlich der Christlichen Kirche (The Song of the Solitary and Deserted Turtle-Dove, namely, the Christian Church).* It was also printed as a book in 1747, with texts only, Beissel describing in the Foreword his ideas on harmony.

In all, Beissel composed thousands of pieces, setting whole chapters of the Old Testament, and making two settings of *The Song of Solomon.* However, as Hans David has said: "it must have appeared like food without seasoning, for it was harmony without dissonance," and so Ephrata's contribution is far more important historically than it is musically.

Charleston, South Carolina—gay city of the South—recorded its first public concert the same year in which Beissel founded his Ephrata Cloister. *The South Carolina Gazette* for April 8/15, 1732, announced a "Consort of Musick at the Council Chamber, for the Benefit of Mr. Salter."

Three years later Charleston—far less aware of sin than either the Puritans or Quakers—had its first theatrical season, from January to March. For the fourth performance, *The South Carolina Gazette* of February 8, 1735, advertised:

> On Tuesday the 18th inst. will be presented at the Courtroom the opera of "Flora, or Hob in the Well," with the Dance of the two Pierrots, and a new Pantomime entertainment, called the Adventures of Harlequin Scaramouch . . .

This was the first recorded performance of opera in America. (*Flora,* a ballad opera, had been performed in London earlier and published there in 1729.)

The performance in Charleston inaugurated three regular theatrical seasons, which became quite a social event. Ballad opera was to become the favorite form of musical entertainment until after the Revolution. It was the rage in England, where in 1728 London had witnessed the première of *The Beggar's Opera,* by John Gay, with music arranged by John Pepusch. This, one of the finest ballad operas, and the most successful, was soon to become known in all the important colonial cities. These productions, comic in nature, contained spoken dialogue, and the musical numbers were principally folk songs, or well-known tunes of contemporary composers, fitted out with new verses.

With the first public concerts in America came the visiting celebrity from Europe, who appeared in all the leading cities. Among the first was Charles Theodore Pachelbell (1690-1750), son of the great German organist and composer, Johann Pachelbell, who had been an intimate friend of the Bach family and had taught Johann Sebastian Bach's eldest brother (Johann Christoph). Young Pachelbell appeared first in Boston about 1730, went on to Newport, Rhode Island (where he was organist at Trinity Church), and eventually to New York, where he performed in that city's first recorded concert in 1736. He finally moved on to Charleston, South Carolina, where until his death he was active in the city's musical life.

The focus of musical interest now moves back to Pennsylvania, where the last major settlement was made, that of Bethlehem.

THE MORAVIANS AT BETHLEHEM

By far one of the most important emigrations to America, from the standpoint of music, was that of the German religious group, the Moravians. They came as missionaries, in the name of religion, and although music was their very life, it was always to remain secondary to the propagation of their beliefs. A small group of these Moravian missionaries had come to Georgia in 1735, sailing from England on the same ship with John and Charles Wesley (who had been at Oxford and active in a new group of religious enthusiasts called "Methodists"). Both Wesleys were to remember the beautiful Moravian hymns they heard sung during the voyage. The hymns not only made a deep impression, but were also to have far-reaching effects, of which we shall soon speak. The Georgia colony of the Moravians was a failure, and it would not be until six years later that a permanent home in America would be established. In Europe the Moravians had been known as Unitas Fratrum, a devoutly religious congregation, the followers of John Hus and the first independent reformed church. The Moravians, as they decided to call themselves, symbolized the original spirit of the traditions of the Reformation. The Protestant Church, which had been considerably weakened, had received a new impetus in the eighteenth century under Count Zinzendorf, and was known as the Renewed Church. Zinzendorf's greatest ambition was to have a unified Protestant Church, and with this in mind he came to America. He sought out Beissel at Ephrata, begging his help in the carrying out of his great plan, but Beissel was too well entrenched in his own particular kingdom to follow any group in which he might have to take second place. Beissel's refusal was a blow, but Zinzendorf took his followers on some sixty miles, where, on Christmas Eve, 1741, he named their new home Bethlehem.

Both Bethlehem and Ephrata were about the same distance from Philadelphia, and had similar traditions, but as far as their purpose in life was concerned they might have been worlds apart. Ephrata was a retreat, the realm of a fantastic personality. Bethlehem, on the other hand, was an active settlement, practicing the principles of democracy. Like the Pietists, we have seen that the Moravians believed in the singing of hymns. Both groups likewise realized the immense value of instrumental music. In this respect they were different from other Protestant congregations in America at that time.

Many of today's musical pilgrims who journey to Bethlehem for the now-famous Bach Festival, held each May, have secured lodgings in the quaint old houses which still line the city's streets, whose residents still carry on the tradition of singing in the Festival chorus, just as their fathers and grandfathers had done. From its founding—as it is today—Bethlehem was a center of music. Its musicians were the teachers, the artisans, the preachers of the town, working by day at their tasks or trades, and making music in their free time. Early manuscripts frequently contained figured basses for the organ, so that the hymns might be sung by voices with instrumental combinations.

The first hymn collections contained hymns from the older church books compiled by Johann Daniel Grimm, and a selection published by Christian Gregor. These two men, with other Moravian composers, wrote many anthems and arias for voices, with organ accompaniment and strings obbligato, and before long, with combinations of wind instruments.

The first Singstunde (singing class) was formed in 1742, and in 1744 the Collegium Musicum (a small body of vocalists and instrumentalists) was founded. There were many performances of concerted music from the 1760s on and all were impressive to Bethlehem's visitors. Franklin wrote his wife in 1756 about the excellent music in the Moravian Church, and George Washington, in the midst of the Revolution, passed a night in Bethlehem and found great pleasure in a concert of chamber music.

Handel's *Messiah* had been written and performed (first in Dublin and then in London) when the Bethlehem colony was only a year old (1742). Some twenty-eight years later, parts of the score were written out for performances in Bethlehem. By 1780, an extensive repertoire of orchestral music—mostly symphonies—had been gathered for the concerts. The music was the best of its day, such as one might hear in the capitals of Europe, and included works of Johann Christian Bach, Carl Friedrich Abel, Haydn, and Mozart. Today, it amazes us to learn how rapidly some of this music crossed the Atlantic. In the archives of Bethlehem's museum are manuscript copies of six trios and three symphonies of Mozart, dated 1785, when the composer was only twenty-nine. Some of Haydn's quartets and early symphonies are claimed to have been first played in America at Bethlehem, and his *The Creation* had its first American performance there in 1811.

The earliest surviving music of the Moravian composers is that of Jeremiah Dencke, who arrived from Europe in 1761. He wrote for the Christmas services of 1767 and 1768. The most important, as well as the most prolific composer to settle in Bethlehem, was John Frederick Peter (1746-1813). He arrived in America in 1769 and reached Bethlehem in 1770, where he soon became the church organist and directed its music. His sacred music shows him to have been a talented composer, one devoted to his art. It was he who brought from Germany, where he had studied, his own copies of the best contemporary music such as those already mentioned. His only secular works were six string quintets, written in Salem (now Winston-Salem), North Carolina, one of the most important southern settlements of the Moravians. The quintets are dated 1789, and there is a strong Haydn influence in their style. They have recently been published for the New York Public Library by Peters and recorded by New Records.

Another tradition (which still may be heard at the spring Bach Festivals) was the playing of chorales by a trombone choir from the church tower, their rich tones echoing among the hills. This was a custom on occasions of joy as well as of sorrow.

When it is recalled that it was religion, and not music, which brought the Moravians to America, it is easy to see why they exerted so little influence, musically speaking, outside their immediate circle. Bethlehem was like a deep spring, refreshing all who sought it out. At that time it was not a part of the swifter currents which were already flowing into the larger body of American music.

AMERICAN HYMNODY

In the late eighteenth century a new spirit pervaded the church music of the colonies, and congregational singing received great stimulation from the dynamic religious leader from England, George Whitefield (1714-1770). In spite of the many new books issued, and the instruction in reading from notes, the fact was all too clear that the music of the old psalms was too formal and monotonous. The language of the Psalter was that of another day, and the worshiper could not be blamed for wanting to sing words that expressed his religious feelings in terms of his everyday speech. The composed hymn text began to make its appearance, and was at once widely adopted by Protestant congregations, especially the rural people who had all the while fought against "regular singing." Whitefield was a great believer in singing, and his enthusiasm was contagious. Before long, especially in the churches where he preached while on tour (1739-41) the people began to neglect the psalms, and used only the hymns of Watts, of whom Whitefield greatly approved.

It was Jonathan Edwards who had initiated the "Great Awakening" on the eastern coast, where revivals like the one at Northhampton, Massachusetts, in 1734 had created a sensation, and whose great success had undoubtedly come from the many newly composed hymns. When John Wesley (1703-1791) stirred Savannah, Georgia, and the surrounding countryside with his powerful sermons (1735-38), he, too, introduced the singing of hymns. Thanks to his contacts with the Moravian missionaries who were his shipmates on the voyage to America, John Wesley had become greatly aware of the value of singing, and his first hymnbook, published in 1737 in "Charles-Town," South Carolina, soon became almost as popular as Watts' books. It was called *A Collection of Psalms and Hymns*, and contained metrical psalms, translated from the Greek and German, some forty-two lyrics of George Herbert, hymns by Watts, and original hymns by other Wesleys. (John's brother Charles had stayed only a short while in America, so that none of his hymns were in this collection.) This book, with its mingling of sources, is the first of the modern type. The Methodist movements, both in England and America, made great use of the singing of hymns, and the many subsequent publications of the Wesleys kept them well supplied. Charles Wesley, alone, was eventually to write over six thousand hymn texts, a staggering accomplishment, and it is no wonder that his generation witnessed the great flowering of English and American hymnody. For the most part, the hymns of the Wesleys had a high poetical standard, for John Wesley had strongly protested the "scandalous doggerel" of *Sternhold and Hopkins.*

The New Hymn

The term *hymn* was soon restricted to the newly written ones, as distinguished from the older scriptural psalms and canticles. It would not be long before the newer hymns would get out of hand, as the emotions of the congregations in the revivals and camp meetings became completely unrestrained, and the people themselves would create a whole new body of song. Once again there would come a great conflict of wills, like the one which had had such dramatic consequences in New England a half-century before.

In 1767, another valuable hymnbook was issued from Newburyport—an American reprint of the third (1764) London edition of William Tans'ur's *Royal Melody Compleat* (first edition London, 1764). This was to become an authority for many of the early composers, particularly William Billings, who used it as a model for his own composing.

Josiah Flagg's *A Collection of the Best Psalm Tunes,* published in Boston in 1764, is of more than passing interest because it was engraved by one of America's first, and greatest, patriots—Paul Revere.

WILLIAM TUCKEY IN NEW YORK

One of the last important musicians to reach the colonies before the Revolution was William Tuckey (1708-1781), who docked in New York in 1753. He had been Vicar Choral of the British Cathedral in England, and was to have a profound influence on the city's music. Tuckey quickly established himself as an organist, choirmaster, concert artist, and composer. He organized and directed the first American performance of Handel's *Messiah* in 1770, two years before it was heard in Germany. Tuckey led an orchestra and chorus in the Overture and sixteen numbers from the oratorio. To earn a living, Tuckey became clerk at Trinity Church, and soon convinced the vestry that music should be taught to the pupils of the church's charity school. In this way he was able to develop a choir to sing in the church, and the Trinity Choir eventually became famous for its concerts, its fame extending even outside New York. Tuckey hoped and planned to develop choral singing in his newly adopted country, but he was not to be successful in realizing his dream. He anticipated the later work of Lowell Mason, but unfortunately for Tuckey, the time was not ripe in America.

SECULAR MUSIC

In the course of the century, in the years before the Revolution, the cultural leadership of the colonies was centered in Philadelphia, at that time the largest city in the country, and the second largest in the British Empire, second only to London. There was an obvious change to be seen and felt, and by 1750, with the slow but steady recession of the frontier and with increased religious freedom, life seemed full of hope and promise. There was much travel back and forth, and America's slowly expanding cultural life was greatly helped by the many newspapers, libraries, and floods of books from Europe.

The magic of the theater gave added zest to life in Philadelphia as the Kean-Murray company, among America's first acting troupes, began to give performances in 1749. Philadelphians had already enjoyed "an agreeable comedy or tragedy" which Franklin's *Pennsylvania Gazette* advertised in 1742 as acted "by changeable figures two feet high" every evening "at the Sign of the Coach-and-Horses, against the State House in Chesnut-Street," and a performance of live actors of Addison's *Cato*, in 1749. By 1754, Lewis Hallam's American Company (known later as the Old American Company), which had played in New York and the southern cities, gave Philadelphia a season which ran from April to June. Ballad operas and musical plays also became popular among the less strict members of Philadelphia society. The Southwark Theatre was opened by David Douglass in 1766.

Music in the private homes of the well-to-do became the vogue in Philadelphia, a musical activity which no other city was enjoying to the same extent, except perhaps Bethlehem and Charleston. Evenings of chamber music were frequent and regular, with the Colonial Governor John Penn as one of the leaders. Stringed instruments were combined with winds—flutes, a French horn or two, and so on. The music was the best European music of the day—Handel, Pergolesi, Scarlatti, Corelli, Vivaldi, Arne, and Purcell, to name but a few of the composers.

Professional musicians continued to arrive from England. One such was John Beals, "musick master from London," who taught in Philadelphia from 1749 to 1758. Two others, destined to play major roles in the city's musical life, were the Scottish musician, James Bremner, who arrived in 1763, and Andrew Adgate, who reached Philadelphia in 1784.

Bremner immediately opened a music school, where he taught "young ladies" the harpsichord and guitar, and "young gentlemen" the violin, flute, harpsichord, or guitar. He was also the organist of Christ Church and an active composer whose manuscripts are still extant. Among his pupils was a young man whom fate had chosen to play several leading roles. He was Francis Hopkinson, a great patriot, a signer of the Declaration of Independence, and America's first native composer.

Philadelphia's first public concert, January 20, 1757, had been given under the direction of a Mr. John Palma, and a second concert on March 25 had been distinguished by the presence of George Washington, who had bought fifty-two shillings, sixpence worth of tickets eight days in advance. Washington's military career had just opened with his promotion to the rank of a lieutenant colonel. This had been a reward for the valuable information he had brought back to the British as to the strength of the French fortifications along the Ohio.

Things were not too different in New York, although it was still a relatively small city. It was not too conscious of wrongdoing, and there were many diversions to be had. The Kean-Murray company opened a season of theater, the repertory consisting of seven works, including *The Beggar's Opera*. That same year, 1750, there was a regular theater on Nassau Street, despite opposition on the part of some of the inhabitants. But because theatrical performances were not wholly acceptable, many of the small companies gave concerts of music to augment their income.

Some were given for charity, as those of March 18, 1756, and January 14, 1760, when New York heard its first subscription concert, with William C. Hulett, actor, dancing and music master, as one of the two musicians in charge. Hulett had arrived in America in 1752 as a violinist in Hallam's·American Company, and he appears to have managed concerts for several years. New York's first outdoor concerts began under Hulett in June, 1765, and were held in the Ranelagh Gardens. All of the cities of any size in those early years had their own particular replica of the celebrated Vauxhall Gardens in London. Charleston's Vauxhall concerts began in 1767, and the *South Carolina Gazette* of June 1-15, reminded its readers that "Tea and coffee is not included in the price of the ticket."

The first musical society to be formed in the colonies was Charleston's St. Cecilia Society (originally spelled St. Cœcilia), founded in 1762. Designed to support concerts of vocal and instrumental music, it remained in existence until the twentieth century.

IN RETROSPECT

In tracing America's music so far, we have discovered along with the psalm-singing of the Puritans, a healthy admiration for and practice of making secular music. As the eighteenth century began, our music was largely vocal, whether sung in the New England meetinghouses in the numerous singing schools which began to spring up, among the isolated Pietist groups in Pennsylvania, or on the large southern plantations. In fact, vocal music would predominate in the nation for years to come, almost up to the twentieth century. While the so-called fine arts were slow in getting started, we may assume that, along with the earliest poetry and writing, there must have been many men who made up tunes as settings for the poems and paraphrases written in these years, long before any collections were issued. The sudden rash of native talent in the second half of the eighteenth century, producing many songs that are still sung today, would indicate the possibility of an early flowering of serious composition.

There are many threads, seemingly isolated, to be found in these early years, which will soon be woven into the larger fabric of America's music. One such was the bitter conflict between the old established manner of singing from memory and the newer singing from notes. The forces that were already shaping the course of our music were evident in various parts of the colonies, although the initial stimulus came from New England. As singing schools were established, new songbooks issued, and emotions were released in a near frenzy of religious excitement, these currents eddied and swirled into a mountainous tide which swept through the length and breadth of the land, and would remain a vital force for years to come, especially in the South and the trans-Alleghany region that was then called West.

The singing schools in the cities would soon grow into large choirs and singing societies which would eventually perform and keep alive the best European music. In the rural South and West, the great gathering together of people to share the joys of singing, was the means of keeping alive many of the old psalms and hymns, and very shortly, these same people would create the great body of American song—the spirituals—in their camp meetings and revivals.

CHAPTER III

First Native Composers

FRANCIS HOPKINSON

His Versatility

We might search a long time and never find another figure who so perfectly suited and embodied all of the elements of Philadelphia's era of culture as did Francis Hopkinson (1737-1791), a man who was one of the great figures of his time, and who practiced the arts in the finest sense of the word. He is given the credit of being America's first native composer, but politically he was a still stronger personality. His uncompromising, satirical pamphleteering on the part of the Revolutionary forces was of great help in molding public opinion, and during the war he assumed many governmental responsibilities. He was a signer of the Declaration of Independence and a close friend of Franklin, Washington, and Jefferson.

There was in Philadelphia a dilettante circle of amateurs, musicians, poets, and theatrical people, who enjoyed music-making. They were highly intelligent men, some of whom were well educated, and they had a keen interest in all that was going on in this teeming city in the middle of the colonies. Music gave Francis Hopkinson the greatest possible pleasure; it was a luxury which he could enjoy in private, but his interest in the other arts was just as keen. He had a flair for painting, he was something of an inventor, and he wrote easily. A member of a well-to-do family, Hopkinson had been sent to college, and he was one of the first class graduated from the College of Philadelphia (later the University of Pennsylvania), which the Episcopal Church had created in 1755.

(Opening a year after the founding of Columbia College in New York in 1754, this was the third college in the colonies to be sponsored by the Episcopalians.)

John Adams thought Hopkinson an oddity, ". . . one of your pretty, little, curious, ingenious men. His head is not bigger than a large apple. . . . I have not met with anything in natural history more amusing and entertaining than his personal appearance; yet he is genteel and well-bred, and is very social." None of the early statesmen could realize that soon there would emerge in America a professional class whose main occupation would be the practice of the arts. No wonder Hopkinson's love of all things beautiful made him seem a bit odd to his contemporaries in public life. He would have been perfectly at home in one of the musical and artistic salons in Paris or Vienna, whereas in the colonies, though he was given the utmost respect, he was not altogether understood.

Hopkinson at his harpsichord soon became a dominant figure in the musical life of Philadelphia, and his own compositions, which he started to write while still a student at school, were to be found on concert programs through the years. He wrote songs for his college, and even after graduation he accompanied from the harpsichord the choruses and instrumental music for subsequent exercises.

His First Songs

It is believed that his musical education was gained principally from James Bremner, whose death in 1780 Hopkinson commemorated by composing a memorial *Ode*. But it is his group of four secular songs, the manuscripts of which are in the Library of Congress, that make Hopkinson one of the outstanding musicians of early America. Strangely enough, these were composed as a private venture, but they are practically all the record we have of pre-Revolution secular song. The first is dated 1759—making him the earliest American composer on record to date. The very titles suggest the sensitive nature of the man: *My Days Have Been So Wondrous Free; The Garland; Oh! Come to Mason Borough's Grove;* and *With Pleasures Have I Past My Days*. Hopkinson wrote them in the current style of the eighteenth century, that is, in two parts (treble and bass). It was the custom for the person accompanying at the harpsichord to elaborate the indicated harmonies.

The Temple of Minerva

Many of Hopkinson's musical works have never been found, and they are only known to us through the words, also by Hopkinson, which were printed in current magazines. If the music of one of these works were in existence today it would be the score of the first American opera. The libretto was published, a few weeks after the first performance, in the New York *Royal Gazette*, of 1781, and was called, not an opera, but an "oratorial entertainment," which he composed to celebrate America's alliance with France during the Revolutionary War. Titled *The Temple of Minerva*, it included an overture, arias, ensembles, and choruses. A contemporary news account dates its performance as December 11, 1781, "by a company of gentlemen and ladies in the hotel of the minister of France in the presence of his Excellency General Washington and his Lady."

Songs Dedicated to Washington

Hopkinson's *Seven Songs for the Harpsichord or Forte Piano* are his own particular glory, for they are pioneers in the field, the first known published collection of secular American songs. Advertised in the newspapers of 1788 as "composed in an easy, familiar style . . . the first work of this kind attempted in the United States." their style and content were influenced quite naturally by the best contemporary English song writers, and they show a faint foreshadowing of authentic art-song technique. There were really eight songs in the volume and a note explained that the eighth was added after the title page announcing seven had been engraved. They are of more than passing interest, historically, because of their dedication to George Washington, soon to be President of the United States. Hopkinson, sending a copy of the book to Washington, wrote in the printed dedication as follows:

> With respect to the little Work, which I now have the honour to present to your notice, I can only say that it is such as a Lover, not a Master, of the Arts can furnish. I am neither a profess'd Poet, nor a profess'd Musician; and yet venture to appear in those characters united; for which, I confess, the censure of Temerity may justly be brought against me. . . .
>
> However small the Reputation may be that I shall derive from this Work, I cannot, I believe, be refused the Credit of

being the first Native of the United States who has produced a Musical Composition. If this attempt should not be too severely treated, others may be encouraged to venture on a path, yet untrodden in America, and the Arts in succession will take root and flourish amongst us.

Washington replied with his usual good grace, and in accepting the dedication, he made a statement which contradicts the popular belief that he played the flute, or any other musical instrument. He wrote that he unfortunately could do nothing to promote his friend's songs, for "I can neither sing one of the songs, nor raise a single note on any instrument to convince the unbelieving. . . . But I have, however, one argument which will prevail with persons of true taste (at least in America)—I can tell them that *it is the production of Mr. Hopkinson.*"

Hopkinson also sent a copy to Thomas Jefferson (an accomplished violinist) who was then in Paris. He remarked in his letter that the last song—*The trav'ler benighted and lost, O'er the mountains pursues his lone way*—"if played very slow, and sung with Expression," was "forcibly pathetic—at least in my Fancy." Its pathos was corroborated by Jefferson in acknowledging receipt of the songs:

I will not tell you how much they have pleased us, nor how well the last of them merits praise for it's pathos, but relate a fact only, which is that while my elder daughter was playing it on the harpsichord, I happened to look toward the fire & saw the younger one all in tears. I asked her if she was sick? She said "no; but the tune was so mournful."

While in Europe, Jefferson had attempted to interest foreign manufacturers in Hopkinson's improved method of quilling the harpsichord.

Music for the Church

In the 1759 manuscript which contained Hopkinson's four secular songs were two religious compositions: a setting of *The Twenty-Third Psalm* and *An Anthem from the 114th Psalm.* These are evidences of his interest in music for the church. When James Bremner, his teacher, temporarily relinquished the post of organist at Christ Church, Hopkinson filled the vacancy. He taught singing to the children of the church and he was the editor of *A Collection of*

Psalm Tunes, with a few Anthems and Hymns, Some of them Entirely New, for the Use of the United Churches of Christ Church and St. Peter's Church in Philadelphia (1763). This book was widely used in other Episcopal churches, particularly in New York. What has not been generally known is that Hopkinson, who had been chosen by the Consistory of the Reformed Protestant Dutch Church in New York to edit, in 1767, the English translation of the Dutch psalm book, was again called upon in 1774 when a new psalm book was published. The first book had contained only the single-line Genevan tunes and is frequently spoken of as the first book of music in the colonies to be printed from type. The second book, printed in 1774, contained a harmonization in four parts of the psalm-tunes, derived from the older version by Claude Goudimel. Titled: *A COLLECTION of the Psalms and Hymn Tunes, Used by the Reformed Protestant Dutch Church of the City of New-York, agreeable to their Psalm Book, published in English. In Four Parts, Viz. Tenor, Bass, Treble, and Counter. New-York: Printed by Hodge and Shober. M.DCC.LXXIV,* it has become known only in recent years, and it clearly shows what an important figure Hopkinson was in both the religious music of his day as well as the secular.

His Importance Historically

Hopkinson's music must be judged historically, rather than critically. His works are possessed of a freshness and ingenuous point of view that lends them considerable charm. They were like countless other pieces of the eighteenth century, and did not have enough originality to exert any influence in themselves. It is rather as an indication of the existing vogue in the colonies that they are interesting, and to the historian, important. It is as a musical amateur that we cherish the figure of Francis Hopkinson, for he is the first of many whom we shall meet in succeeding generations.

Hopkinson's life in Philadelphia clearly demonstrates the liberality of those days in the colonies, a true picture of life in the largest American city of that time. Many of those years were filled with pain, the pangs accompanying the birth of a new nation. It matters not that the music was not the greatest, nor the performances as fine as those that might be heard in Europe. What is far more important is the fact that America was slowly but surely coming into her own. The seed must sprout before the plant can grow.

JAMES LYON

A contemporary of Hopkinson's in Philadelphia was a young, modest Presbyterian minister named James Lyon (1735-1794). He was a mild-mannered man, perhaps absent-minded, whose life was a direct antithesis of that which Hopkinson led. Born in Newark ("East New Jersey") on July 1, Lyon was educated at the College of New Jersey, which was in his home town. In 1756 the college, which was to become Princeton University (it had been founded in 1747 by the Presbyterian Church) was moved to its present site at Princeton. Lyon was graduated in 1759 and received his M.A. in 1762.

Commencement Odes

Like Hopkinson, Lyon composed music for the commencement exercises, his *Ode* being sung in 1759, the year he received his Bachelor of Arts degree. Going to Philadelphia in 1760, an anthem of his was featured at a graduation concert given by the College of Pennsylvania, sharing the program with an *Ode* by Hopkinson. The *Pennsylvania Gazette* (1761) stated:

> On Saturday last the public COMMENCEMENT was held in the College of this City, before a vast Concourse of People of all Ranks. Besides the usual Exercises . . . there was performed in the Forenoon an elegant *Anthem* composed by James LYON, A.M. of New Jersey College, and in the Afternoon an *Ode,* sacred to the Memory of our late gracious Sovereign George II, written and set to Music in a very grand and masterly Taste by Francis Hopkinson, Esq. A.M. of the College of this City.

Urania

While living in Philadelphia and working toward his degree, Lyon gathered material for a collection of music which was published in 1761 as:

> *Urania, or a Choice Collection of Psalm-Tunes, Anthems and Hymns from the most approved Authors, with some Entirely*

New; in Two, Three, and Four Parts; the whole Peculiarly adapted to the Use of Churches and Private Families; to which are Prefixed the Plainest and most Necessary Rules of Psalmody.

Urania was an important work in its time, and obviously became popular, for there are supposed to have been five later editions (although none have been definitely located), and it was dedicated to "the Clergy of every Denomination in America." Included in the collection were six original compositions by Lyon: settings of the 8th, 23rd, 95th, and 104th Psalms; *Two Celebrated Verses by Sternhold and Hopkins;* and *An Anthem taken from the 150th Psalm.* Among the other psalm-tunes, hymns, and anthems was probably the first American printing of *America* (or the English *God Save the King*). Lyon called it *Whitefield's Tune,* and it was set to the words, "Come thou Almighty King."

Lyon followed the popular custom in the psalm and singing books of his time of offering a few "directions for singing." They were elementary but nevertheless practical and no doubt necessary. They read:

1. In learning the 8 Notes, get the assistance of some Person well acquainted with the Tones and Semitones.
2. Choose that Part which you can sing with the greatest ease, and make yourself Master of that first.
3. Sound all high Notes as soft as possible, but low ones hard and full.
4. Pitch your Tune so that the highest and lowest Notes may be sounded distinctly.

Plan for Capturing Nova Scotia

But like the not-too-distant Moravians, Lyon dedicated himself to God and the Church, and with him music was subordinated to his spiritual work. He soon left Philadelphia for Nova Scotia, where he worked among the isolated people in a frontier church. He became so familiar with the country that when the Revolution broke out he wrote George Washington, seeking permission to lead an expedition to conquer the province and outlining his plan of attack. The offer had to be refused because the colonies could not spare the men, but a later Canadian historian wrote that Lyon's plan was so practical that it was fortunate for the British it was never carried out.

Life as Minister and Composer

Because of his pitifully small salary, Lyon was soon forced to give up his Canadian church. In 1771 he accepted a call to Maine, where he lived at Machias (with a few brief interruptions) until his death, December 25, 1794.

That he returned to New Jersey at least once is indicated by the diary of a Southerner named Fithian, who spent his vacations in Cohansie, New Jersey. Fithian's diary affords a meager portrait of the minister-composer. Under date of April 22, 1774:

> Rode to the Stage early for the Papers thence I went Mr. Hunters where I met with that great master of music, Mr. *Lyon* —He sung at my request, & sung with his usual softness & accuracy—He is about publishing a new Book of Tunes which are to be cheiffly of his own Composition.

Throughout his ministry Lyon apparently kept up his composing, even though his later work, mentioned by Fithian, was evidently never published. He must have been a beloved figure, for he was never the fanatical type, so predominant in the colonies in those days. Lyon believed that usefulness was of more importance than display in religion, and his influence was ever practical and wholesome, as was his music.

While there is little of value for us today in Lyon's music, it certainly was far in advance of its few predecessors, and superior to some that came later. More important in his own time was the fact that he was highly regarded by his contemporaries, who not only praised his music but performed it.

WILLIAM BILLINGS

William Billings (1746-1800) was as much a force in America's democratic upheaval as were the instigators of the Boston Tea Party. Like many of his generation he was swept off his feet by music and devoted all his energies to its promotion. He was a man who, despite physical handicaps, attracted and won the friendship of the great men of his day, among them Samuel Adams, the leading figure of the new democracy in Boston, where Billings was born on October 7.

Tanner-Musician

Billings was an uneducated artisan, a tanner by trade, and an unattractive figure of a man: blind in one eye, with a withered arm and legs of uneven length. He was self-taught as far as music was concerned, learning most of what he knew from the American reprint of Tans'ur's *Royal Melody Compleat, or New Harmony of Sion* (London, 1755), whose third edition (1764, London) was published in America by William M'Alpine in 1767 in Newburyport. Billings never ceased to be impatient with rules, insisting they hampered his compositions.

Throughout his life, because of his appearance, Billings was the butt of jokes by the boys in the street. His large family kept him impoverished, but he was always well thought of in musical circles and in later years had frequent financial aid from musical benefits.

"The New-England Psalm-Singer" and Its Fuging Tunes

In 1770, the year in which Beethoven was born and when Bach had been dead for twenty years, Billings declared his musical independence by producing a volume which he called *The New-England Psalm-Singer*. It contained a miscellaneous assortment of church music, all composed by himself, the first sacred music collection entirely composed by an American. Billings stated that his own "fuging pieces" in the book were "more than twenty times as powerful as the old slow tunes." These fuging pieces (to keep the original spelling) are interesting examples of the influence exerted in America by composers like Handel, whose music was now being heard in the more important centers.

The fuging tunes were not the creation of Billings, for they were to be found in the earlier English music, whose precursor, found in the older psalm tunes, had been known as "rapports." Billings was so successful in using them, however, that many persons have thought of the fuging tunes as his own. Popular with the American composers of this period, the fuging tunes had been familiar in the American colonies since the 1760s (Lyon had published the first English fuging psalm-tunes in 1761, in his *Urania*). They developed amazingly in most of the New England states in the 1780s, and reached their peak of popularity in the last decade of the century. The important writers included Daniel Read, Jacob French, Supply Belcher, and Daniel Belknap, who undoubtedly had considerable influence on the work of Billings. These fuging tunes were most successful in the rural sections of the country, but were never as popular around Boston or in the other cities.

In the beginning a fuging or imitative section might be added to the psalm-tune, depending on the desire of those singing it. As developed in America, the fuging tune typically began with a section that was homophonic in style, and most often ended on the tonic. Making a new start, the individual voices entered imitatively, one after the other, in whatever order the composer desired. This section, which was known as the "fuge," was actually nothing more than free imitation and was usually repeated, making the piece a compact two-part form with the second part repeated (ABB). It was into this already familiar form that Billings poured his enthusiasm and musical ideas, and *The New-England Psalm-Singer* not only had wide acceptance, but his later books were also warmly received. Billings' innovations, while championed by some, were bitterly fought by others, but the strife only proves how vital they must have been.

For years Billings carried on a public conversation about his music and what he believed, through the naïve prefaces he wrote for his published collections. There were six of them, and they are milestones in the story of America's early music. In order of publication they are:

The New-England Psalm-Singer, 1770
The Singing Master's Assistant, 1778
Music in Miniature, 1779
The Psalm-Singer's Amusement, 1781
The Suffolk Harmony, 1786
The Continental Harmony, 1794

His Enthusiasm for Music

Billings' enthusiasm for music knew no bounds. He often chalked music exercises on the hides hanging in his shop, and even on the very walls. Surely his was the most vivid musical imagination to manifest itself in the early colonies and his ideas were revolutionary for his day. His tunes, texts, harmony, and even his rules of composition fitted into the time of conflict in which he lived and wrote. In the preface of *The New-England Psalm-Singer* he stated:

> Perhaps it may be expected by some, that I should say something concerning Rules for Composition; to these I answer that *Nature is the best Dictator,* for all the hard dry studied Rules that ever was prescribed, will not enable any Person to form an Air any more than the bare Knowledge of the four and twenty Letters, and strict Grammatical Rules will qualify a Scholar for composing a Piece of Poetry . . .

He added that if he were to follow slavishly the rules against consecutive octaves and fifths, he would "certainly spoil the Air, and Cross the Strain, that fancy dictated . . ."

The collection contained both psalm and hymn-tunes, harmonized for four-part singing, as well as a number of anthems and the fuging pieces. Billings was enchanted with his fuging pieces, and painted a vivid description of them in his introduction to the book:

> Each part striving for mastery and victory. The audience entertained and delighted, their minds surprisingly agitated and extremely fluctuated, sometimes declaring for one part and sometimes for another. Now the solemn bass demands their attention; next the manly tenor; now the lofty counter; now the volatile treble. Now here, now there, now here again! O ecstatic! Rush on, you sons of harmony!

Eight years later, in *The Singing Master's Assistant,* Billings told of the boyish delight he had taken in his first book:

> . . . Oh! how did my foolish heart throb and beat with tumultuous joy! With what impatience did I wait on the Book-Binder, while stitching the sheets and putting on the covers, with what extacy did I snatch the yet unfinished Book out of his hands and pressing to my bosom with rapturous delight . . . go forth my little Book . . . and immortalize the name of your Author; may your sale be rapid and may you speedily run through ten thousand Editions, may you be a welcome guest in all companies and what will add tenfold to thy dignity, may you find your way into the Libraries of the Learned.

But by that time he had turned against his "Reuben," (as he had called his first book), saying it was as "unsuitable as water, it did not excell." In the preface to *The Singing Master's Assistant,* he confessed that: "After impartial examination," he found that many pieces in the first book "were never worth my printing, or your inspection; . . ." Therefore, he stated, "in order to make you ample amends for my former intrusion, I have selected and corrected some of the Tunes which were most approved of in that book and have added several new peices [sic] which I think to be very good ones; . . ."

His Answer to Critics

Billings might see faults in his first "child," but he was ready to go into battle should anyone else venture a criticism. Some thought his arrangements of tunes too simple—that the constant succession of thirds and sixths was too cloying and should be varied by an occasional dissonant interval. Highly annoyed, Billings included in his second book a piece of his own called *Jargon*, which he made intentionally dissonant, and in which the words began: "Let horrid Jargon split the Air, And rive the Nerves asunder." A "manifesto" accompanying the composition read:

> Let it be performed in the following manner, viz. Let an Ass bray the Bass, let the fileing of a saw carry the Tenor, let a hog who is extream weak squeal the Counter, and let a cart-wheel, which is heavy loaded, and that has been long without grease, squeek the Treble; and if the Concert should appear to be too feeble you may add the cracking of a crow, the howling of a dog, the squalling of a hungry cat, and what would grace the Concert yet more, would be the rubbing of a wet finger upon a window glass . . .

Billings' critics had an answer. They hung two cats by their tails to the sign BILLINGS MUSIC which swung outside his door!

"Chester" in the Revolutionary War

As his reputation spread through the new nation, Billings' compositions were to be found on the programs of concerts in other cities, as well as Boston. One of the favorites with the public was the anthem *The Rose of Sharon*, but the most popular tune was *Chester*. By the time the Revolutionary War had been waged for two years, *Chester*, which had appeared in *The Singing Master's Assistant*, was a hit with the Continental troops (almost as popular as *Yankee Doodle*), and had the following words written by the composer himself:

> Let tyrants shake their iron rod,
> And Slav'ry clank her galling chains,
> We'll fear them not, we trust in God,
> New England's God forever reigns.

For its second appearance in printed form Billings added four additional verses expressing scorn for the British generals and their men. One of the verses proudly claimed:

> The Foe comes on with haughty Stride
> Our troops advance with martial noise,
> Their Vet'rans flee before our Youth,
> And Gen'rals yield to beardless boys.

When Boston was occupied by British troops Billings paraphrased the 137th Psalm:

> By the rivers of Watertown, we sat down;
> Yea we wept as we remembered Boston.

A courageous and ingenious composer, Billings also wrote most of the verses for his published works, both secular and religious. He proved himself something of a predecessor of W. S. Gilbert in the opening lines of a choral piece called *Modern Music:*

> We are met for a concert of modern invention
> To tickle the ear is our present intention.

The frontispiece of his last book, *The Continental Harmony,* carried a clever design of his own, showing a tune, accompanied by the words, engraved in a succession of enlarging circles, which was meant to prove that "every tune is a Compleat circle; & that what may be deficient in the first barr is supplied in the last," and that praise should "eternally go round." The upper corners showed cupids holding a floating banner above the circles, and in the lower corners were musical instruments and music books. With his natural instinct for pedagogy, one that was increasingly apparent in the colonies among other musicians, Billings gave instructions in the rudiments of music in the form of a dialogue between *Scholar* and *Master.*

Billings' rousing enthusiasm filled the land, and his influence crept into more than one phase of New England's musical life. Through his efforts the cello added richness to church music and held the pitch as the precentors lined out the hymns.

Itinerant Singing Master

As a popular itinerant singing master, Billings trained group after group in Boston and its environs. He was the leading spirit in the second revival of singing in New England, standing midway between the first revival of the 1720s, and Lowell Mason's efforts in the next century. The singing class he formed at Stoughton, Massachusetts, became, in 1786, the Stoughton Musical Society, and continued in active existence until it became the oldest singing society in America. The society was soon to prove to be much more stable as an organization than the first singing classes, or "schools" as they were called.

His Significance

Billings' compositions have been called "clumsy and crude" through the years, but time has shown they were exultant, full of praise and happiness, with rhythms that were contagious. Not only were they a novelty in their day, but much of their popularity was due to the fact that they were easy to memorize. A deeper significance, however, was that they came at a time when the unison singing of the older psalms was going out of fashion. This music had been in the hands of the clergy, but the newer music was for, and of, the people. The struggle between those who admired it and those who reviled it seems almost ridiculous to recall, but it produced at that time an exhilaration that was most beneficial. One man's initiative and independence stirred up a tempest in a teapot, and the attacks of the ministers merely show how daring this new sacred music was. It matched the religious freedom that was slowly permeating the country, just as it also revealed how broad the musical life of the time was becoming.

In his style Billings was a musical "primitive" far ahead of his time. His music was vital and rugged, and even though it was based on previous models it was sparked with a certain originality. All that he wrote was inspired by his natural genius, and it was he who fanned into life New England's smoldering musical interest. After the Revolution it would blaze with a passionate intensity.

IMPORTANCE OF OUR FIRST COMPOSERS

It was men like the aristocratic amateur, Francis Hopkinson, and the mild-mannered James Lyon (who might be said to personify the rising middle class), who, through their love of music and the practice of it both at home and in public, set an example that was soon recognized by the general public. The vitality and freedom of William Billings' fuging tunes were like a breath of fresh air, and became an important part of the transitional period as the music in the churches changed from the old metrical psalms to the emotional freedom of the newer composed hymns. Hopkinson was the first of many American amateur composers; Billings was the embodiment of the ingenuity, the freedom, and the daring, that is, and always has been, the spirit of America. He was the sturdiest and most revolutionary of our first native composers, more of whom we shall meet in the next chapter.

CHAPTER IV

The Years of the Revolution

GENERAL PICTURE OF THE COLONIES

It would seem that the year 1750 might be a good one to pause and take stock of the American colonies, when they were, so to speak, on the eve of the Revolutionary War. In less than a century and a half, the group of colonies, made up of nearly every nationality, had grown rapidly and had matured with amazing swiftness. As the Revolution seemed a certainty, America had already declared her independence of both England and the Continent through her arts and crafts, her architecture, and to a great extent, her way of life. Her silverware was as fine as any from England; her furniture, sturdy and simple, already showed a distinctive American design; and by mid-century the colonies' standard of living was above that of any like area in the world.

As tension mounted in the colonies in the years before the final break with England, musical activity was greatly restricted. Many of the musical amateurs were too busy writing pamphlets and broadsides to indulge in music, and even the theater began to suffer. The season of 1773-74 was the last before the War, for in October, 1774, the newly formed Continental Congress, realizing that a struggle with England was not only impending, but inevitable, found it advisable to pass a resolution which every one respectfully observed. All types of extravagant and reckless expenditure of money were discouraged, and soon plays and entertainments of all kinds came almost to a full stop. It seemed that the only type of music people had time for was the singing of war songs.

MUSIC OF THE REVOLUTION

Influences of Popular Song

Out of the many skirmishes and battles of the colonies—even as far back as the French and Indian War—came many songs. Older tales were made into ballads, telling their stories or praising their heroes to a people who never tired of hearing them. These verses spoke a common language which at once appealed to the illiterate as well as the educated. They became an easy and spirited way to communicate, whether taking sides in an argument, launching a satire, or expressing grief at the passing of some prominent and loved figure. Broadsides of these verses were published in increasing abundance on every known subject, and soon many flowed into song. This was particularly true during the days of the Revolution, for only in this way could the thoughts and emotions of the people be truly expressed. Thus it has come about that from the earliest days America has had a vigorous body of military songs. At first many of them were parodies, set to familiar tunes, often those belonging to the enemy. Countless ballads were written when General Burgoyne was defeated, when English tea was boycotted. Fighting at home, whether in towns or countryside, gave an urgency, an intensity to these songs that is still discernible. Billings' *Chester* (of which we spoke in the last chapter) had a conviction and sturdiness that must have grown out of the composer's experiences during the siege of Boston. But it also had a dignity that made it as suitable for church and public gatherings as for the battlefield.

Andrew Law (whom we will meet further on in this chapter) composed his song *The American Hero* to the tune *Bunker Hill*. It was heard on all sides and its style was typical of the songs of the day.

"Yankee Doodle"

The song that became the rallying cry of the Revolution was *Yankee Doodle*. It crystallized a figure that had been slowly emerging in the years before the war—the "Yankee," symbol of the new America. Shrewd, dry of speech, lovable, he was at the same time fiercely independent, bowing his head to no one. The British had first used "Yankee" as a term of derision. The "Doodle" might have been a corruption of "do little," meaning a simpleton, but whatever its derivation, its use by the enemy was unmistakable. British troops, scornful of the unmilitary appearance of the untrained colonials, sang *Yankee Doodle* upon every occasion, even standing before the churches and bellowing at the top of their voices.

The Yankees soon turned the tables. When the British troops marched out of Boston on an April night in 1775, bound for Lexington to capture John Hancock and Samuel Adams, they kept step to the strains of *Yankee Doodle*. At Concord the British were routed with *Yankee Doodle*, as well as Yankee fire, and forever after it was to be an American song.

In succeeding years the merry tune, so suggestive of folk dancing and festivities, perfectly fitted the jauntiness of the young nation. The words clearly indicate its origins in popular gatherings.

> Yankee Doodle keep it up.
> Yankee Doodle dandy;
> Mind the music and the step,
> And with the girls be handy.

The endless verses that were later sung to the tune (so obviously one that had been evolved on the fife or flute) attest the song's great popularity. Searches as to its origin always come back to America. It might well have come from the very section of the country where it was sung back to the British. Its first known printing was in Scotland (*c.* 1775-76) by James Aird (a Glasgow music dealer), in his *Selection of Scotch, English, Irish and Foreign Airs, for the fife, violin, or German Flute*, Volume I, which included "Virginian airs," a "Negro Jig," and the like. The inclusion of several Virginia airs and a "Negro Jig" in this collection suggests that *Yankee Doodle* also may have come from America. The first known printing of the tune in America was as one of the themes of Benjamin Carr's *Federal Overture*, published in 1794.

Tradition has the last ironical words, for on the day of Cornwallis' surrender at Yorktown (1781), the British band is said to have played *The World Turned Upside Down*. The Americans would not be outdone—they naturally replied with *Yankee Doodle:*

> It suits for peace, it suits for fun;
> And just as well for fighting!

Hardly had the guns of the Revolution grown silent when foreign travelers began to swarm to America, to see the new nation in its first flush of victory. Here was the hope of the world, a people who had not feared to fight to the death for a principle, and who had at last thrown off the bonds of the tyrant. To their surprise, the visitors heard music on all sides, as the marching fife and drum corps, in celebration of a great victory, were stirring a joyful people with their tunes. America was singing and dancing as she had never done before.

MUSIC AT THE CLOSE OF THE REVOLUTION

The fife well fitted the mood of the day, as it kept feet moving and people singing to its gay and lilting tunes. Its sound could be heard as Washington entered the cities, where cheering crowds were celebrating their first taste of peace. The fife became the instrument of the humble virtuoso, to be heard for many generations as he played his tunes in the taverns or at fairs. It was music of the people, often improvised, but reflecting in those happy days the affection and warmth of a grateful and adoring nation. In a few years most of the tunes would be forgotten, save *Yankee Doodle* and an early march in honor of Washington, soon to become the accompaniment of *Hail Columbia*.

With the close of the Revolution life took on new meaning and the theaters began to flourish again, as though the people would like to forget the horrors of war. Most often the productions were in the form of pageantry, and they became so popular that new theaters had to be built. In the year of the first balloon ascent (1793), Philadelphia had a new Chestnut Street Theatre, built for Thomas Wignell, and modeled after the Royal Theatre at Bath. Wignell began seasons of opera, too, and took the productions to Baltimore and Washington.

With this new flurry of entertainment, outdoor concerts again became fashionable, and were often set amid arbors, summerhouses, and near mineral springs, where one might bathe and have a drink, and later watch the display of fireworks.

This musical growth was aided by the new respect America had gained among nations. No one better demonstrated this than Benjamin West, colonial-born artist, who had gone to London in 1763 at the command of George III, to exhibit his work and to become the most influential figure and artistic personality of the closing century. European artists began to come to America and undertook commissions from the prominent men in the government. Franklin, as ambassador to the Court of France, admired the work of Houdon, who sculptured a bust of him. Franklin urged Houdon to visit the new country, and in 1785 the sculptor came to America, going to Mount Vernon where Washington also commissioned a bust. Later the Italian, Ceracchi, executed busts of Washington, Hamilton, and Jay.

Musically, these years after the war, when the new republic was struggling for its continued existence, were notable for two things: the immigration in the 1790s of certain gifted English musicians (this will be discussed in the following chapter) and the establishment of publishing firms in Philadelphia, which, in issuing only musical works, would be of the greatest service in the development of America's music.

The early statesmen, in spite of all they had done and seen, could not yet comprehend an era of the arts. John Adams remarked: "I wish I had leisure and tranquility to amuse myself with those elements and ingenious arts of painting, sculpture, and music." He added, however, that he thought them luxuries, for he did not believe that a democracy would provide patrons for them. After the Revolution Franklin wrote the young Maryland artist Charles Willson Peale: " 'Tis said the Arts delight to travel Westward, and there is no doubt of their flourishing on our side of the Atlantic," yet even George Washington, the new President, thought that "only arts of a *practical* nature would for a time be esteemed."

Perhaps they were all too close to the war, with its inevitable sequel of poverty and heartache, and perhaps they also remembered that the arts had flourished in Europe because of the patronage of a rich and cultivated nobility, and so should be avoided by a young and rising democracy.

FIRST FLOURISHING OF THE ARTS

As we look back, it seems almost incredible that the arts took root so rapidly, and at the very moment when the nation's fathers were urging caution. Of all places least likely to give them birth (if we are to believe many of the later historians), it was in New England, supposedly stern and cold. Yet Anne Bradstreet's early poems had been but an expression of Puritan minds, as had the verses of Wigglesworth and Taylor later in the century. Once again, after the Revolution, it was in the land of the Puritans where there was a first manifestation of the arts. And in New York, in 1787, America's first professional comedy was performed, Royall Tyler's *The Contrast*. From the stronghold of the rigorous Quakers came, a few years later, our first major novelist, Charles Brockden Brown, who published six novels in Philadelphia from 1798 to 1801. As in writing and poetry, the most vigorous growth of painting came from the towns of the Puritans and the countryside of the Quakers.

For nearly two centuries America's folk arts had not only existed, they had been growing and developing into a sturdy native expression. No matter how much the European cultures had been transplanted to the new country, they had from the beginning been shaped and colored by the needs of the colonists in ways that were at once peculiar to America. Today we know how great has been their influence on generations of American taste through the countless colonial reproductions, which never have lost their popularity. Now they were ready to blossom into the fine arts; acquiring a heritage of local expression, they were now ready to speak a world language.

THEATRICAL ACTIVITY

As the traveling theatrical companies moved West, the frontier receded with each year. Pittsburgh became important as a frontier town and had a lively theatrical life. As in so many isolated cities, its citizens welcomed the actors, not only for their performances but for their sprightly additions to the social life of the town and for the news they might bring of the goings-on in the East. Like the medieval troubadours of France, the players moved from town to town, carrying the gossip and news of the day, as well as entertaining. Far from being ostracized, they made a definite place for themselves in the various local communities, and as many of them had inclusive talents, there was not much that they could not do. Their skiffs might be seen floating down the rivers, sometimes through thick and unbroken forests. There were flatboats on the

Ohio, and soon the smaller towns, like Lexington and Louisville, Kentucky, had their share of theatrical entertainment.

New Orleans, whose whole history might be told in terms of opera, saw its first performance in a tent, later in the open air, and finally in a makeshift theater. Here the planters from Mississippi and the traders from the Ohio River came and congregated.

In Boston there was less and less enforcement of the anti-theater law of 1750. Although repeated attempts to repeal the law had failed, actors got around it by giving occasional performances of plays, which they called "readings" or "moral lectures." One such, given by a Mr. and Mrs. Smith in Concert Hall, was announced as a "dialogue on the horrid crime of murder, from Shakespeare's Macbeth." Defiance of the law grew more open, and the "New Exhibition Room" offered a reading of "THE GALLERY OF PORTRAITS, OR THE WORLD AS IT GOES," by Mr. Harper, and also "songs, feats of tumbling and ballet pantomiming." This theatrical speakeasy was never actually stopped, although Governor Hancock, out of respect for the law, started legal action. In 1793, the anti-theater law was talked to death in the Legislature; and, while it was never taken off the books, public sentiment began so to favor the theater that the law gradually faded into the background and was soon forgotten. The new Federal Street Theatre was built, designed by Bulfinch, and later came the Haymarket. Before long the many foreign musicians would gather in these houses, and their music would have the greatest possible influence on Boston's musical life.

New York, throughout the War, had seen little theater or heard much music. Most of the activities were carried on by the British officers, who, with their Tory friends, tried desperately to alleviate their boredom and amuse themselves. As soon as hostilities were declared at an end, musical life once again started.

As the structure of the new government seemed on the verge of falling apart in those uncertain years, one had only to look at the amazing growth of life in every part of the land to know that it would succeed.

SHAPE NOTES

In New England, the postwar years were to see a significant new answer to the perpetually vexing problem of reading musical notation. The musical independence and revolutionary thinking of Billings had split the churches. Two groups existed: those who had caught the spirit of his lively fuging tunes, and those who opposed them as trivial and undignified. John Hubbard, a Dartmouth professor, delivered "An Essay on Music" on September 9, 1807, which expressed the sentiment of many of the ministers who opposed the new songs. "Devotion ever assumes a dignity," he wrote. "It cannot delight in the tinkling bustle of unmeaning sounds. The air of a catch, a glee, a dance, a march, or a common ballad is very improper for the worship of the most High."

When the fuging tunes were at the height of their popularity, and every effort was being made to raise the level of musical literacy in the churches and singing societies, there appeared the American invention of "shape notes." Music-reading being taught primarily by solmization—that is, the assigning of a distinctive syllable to each note of the scale—it was thought that a visual distinction in the notes themselves, as they appeared in their usual places on the staff, would make learning even easier.

The solmization that the early colonists had practiced was the old one of Elizabethan England, requiring only four syllables, three of them repeated, to sing the ordinary ascending major scale, thus: *fa, sol, la, fa, sol, la, mi.* (The corresponding minor scale: *la, mi, fa, sol, la, fa, sol.*) The sequence of syllables suggested the familiar name, "fasola" system.

Only four different shapes, it will be apparent, were required to make the notes of the solmization scale correspond to the four fasola syllables still widely sung at the end of the eighteenth century. As the seven-syllable system we are familiar with today (*do, re, mi, fa, sol, la, si* [or *ti*]) came into general use—its partisans considered it a manifest improvement over the older system, whose duplicated syllables were said to confuse the learner—three new shapes were added to the earlier four, making a series of seven, each one visually different from the next. Singers who adhered to older solmization (and the many songbooks that were published in the fasola notation) were known as "four-noters"; those progressives who learned the seven-syllable system were called "seven-noters." There was considerable rivalry, of a hairsplitting sort, between the two groups, and it continues even today among the country singers of the South, where songbooks continue to be published in both the fasola and doremi notations. However, the point to bear in mind is that the music *itself* was the same, whether printed in four shapes or seven. The same large body of American song appeared in both notations as the years went on; the shape notes were simply the means by which the music was taught and learned.

Little and Smith

The public first learned of shape notes in 1802, when the New York *Chronicle Express* of November 25 announced: *THE EASY INSTRUCTOR;* or A New Method of Teaching Sacred Harmony by William Little & William Smith. . . . An earlier reference to *The Easy Instructor* and shape notes had occurred in 1798, when the title page (now in the Library of Congress) was entered for copyright in the Southern District of Pennsylvania on August 15. For some unknown reason it would be four years from this date before the first edition appeared in 1802, the scene meanwhile shifting from Philadelphia to New York.

Little and Smith placed their four shapes (a triangle representing *fa;* round, *sol;* square, *la;* diamond, *mi*) on the staff lines or spaces, printing them in outline form for whole notes and half notes, solid for smaller values, and giving them stems in the normal manner. The other aspects of the notation were entirely orthodox. *The Easy Instructor* soon became the cornerstone of the system, widely used and often copied. From the beginning the shape notes were popular with the country people, the simple folk who liked to sing for the sheer pleasure it gave them. In the cities, where "reformers" would soon raise their voices against the homespun music of Little and Smith, Billings, and their peers, the leaders would have no part of the shape-note notation. They were much too aware of the music of Haydn and Handel and the musical traditions of Europe, and as many of these reformers were to become the first to teach music in the public schools, shape notes were never to find their way into the classrooms.

Andrew Law

One of Billings' colleagues who took to the new florid style of the fuging tunes (although he was to oppose them in later years) was Andrew Law of Connecticut (1748-1821), who published such music in his many tune books. He was the grandson of Governor Law of Connecticut, and had a master's degree from Brown University. An ordained minister, he was also a musician of discriminating taste, and he composed hymn tunes that were stately and dignified. It was he, copying the Europeans, who introduced the practice of giving the melody in a four-part arrangement to the soprano. Before Law, the melody was assigned to the tenor.

In the fourth edition of his *The Art of Singing,* printed in Cambridge, Massachusetts, in 1803, Law announced that his book was "printed upon a new plan." This edition (as well as his later publications) used the same four shapes that were to be found in *The Easy Instructor,* though Law's *fa* was a square, his *la* a triangle. His contribution was to do away with the staff entirely, the shape notes being printed simply higher or lower to suggest their differences in pitch. Law never claimed to have invented his shape notes, but did stress the fact that he had done away with all staff lines.

Law's various collections of music included:

A *Select Number of Plain Tunes* (Boston, 1767)
Select Harmony (Cheshire, Conn., 1778)
The Art of Singing in Three Parts (New Haven, Conn., 1780):
    I. The Musical Primer
    II. The Christian Harmony
    III. The Musical Magazine
The Rudiments of Music (Cheshire, Conn., 1785)
Harmonic Companion (1807)

The most popular hymn tune Law composed was *Archdale.* He was one of the first American writers on music. His series of *Essays on Music* announced his intention of publishing reviews of new music.

The many later books in shape notes attest the system's great popularity. William Little sold or signed over his copyright to three printers in Albany, New York, where *The Easy Instructor* came into its own, and from 1805 until 1831, a flood of editions came from their presses. As has been said, the system is still used and taught in the South among those who keep alive the old ways of choral singing. Undoubtedly the most important book in the spreading of the shape notes to the South was John Wyeth's *Repository of Sacred Music, Part Second* (issued in Harrisburg, Pennsylvania, in 1813 and again in 1820). The Valley of Virginia became the home of singing schools that used the shape notes, and it was here that the first southern hymnals were published.

THE GREAT REVIVAL

The appearance of the shape notes coincided with the emotional impact of the Great Revival, which began in Kentucky around 1800, and whose fires were to burn brightly in every hamlet and town in the South and the old West. The emotions that were set free found expression in song—the spiritual—and were originally the response to the traveling Methodist preachers, with Bishop Asbury as their leader. All Protestant sects were aroused, and with music at its head, the Great Revival swept a wide path through the country. At first there were only pamphlets and books containing the words of the hymns, but soon books appeared that offered the music as well —the majority printed in shape notes—and hundreds learned to follow.

The songs that became popular during the Great Revival numbered many revival spiritual songs, the texts of which often came from such literary sources as Isaac Watts. This fact for a long time misled students of America's music into thinking that the music of the songs was not deserving of interest. The truth of the matter is the melodies put to religious use by the untutored singers of the Great Revival were often ancient folk tunes of striking beauty. *Wondrous Love* and *I am a poor wayfaring stranger,* spirituals that have gained a larger audience in recent years, are examples of the approximately 550 songs that make up the body of American religious folk song.

LESSER NATIVE COMPOSERS

America's earliest native musicians were mostly self-taught, and could not (nor did they try to) compete with the foreign professional musicians who had most of the paid positions in the churches and theaters. But they had the ability to compose or arrange hymn tunes, which were often exceptionally fine, and in this way they greatly contributed to the musical needs of a rapidly growing nation. In their own way, and at just the right time, they appealed to the musical tastes of the average man, the artisans, merchants, and farmers who, as an important middle class, were shaping the future of the country. These men who could compose a good hymn were to be found in every community. Hymn books were published in increasing quantities, and the many tunes and settings circulated rapidly among the people. Our earliest composers showed a self-reliance which has always been a part of America's heritage, and because music was so essential to their enjoyment of life, we discover in the latter years of the eighteenth century an amazing number of these musical pioneers. Some of them may be of interest as much for their trades and occupations as for their music. Among this group were two who wrote fuging pieces—the comb maker Daniel Read (1757-1836) and the lawyer Jacob Kimball (1761-1826). The latter was the son of a blacksmith father who had been chosen "to set ye psalms," but (in true American fashion) Jacob, Junior, was sent to Harvard. Timothy Swan (1758-1842), a hatter, wrote hymns and fuging tunes that survived him by many years, some of them still in use today in the South, along with numbers by Read, Kimball, and Billings.

Oliver Holden (1765-1844), a contemporary of Billings, was as opposed to the fuging tunes as Andrew Law had been. A carpenter by trade, Holden composed and taught a singing school in his free time. In true American fashion he climbed the ladder of success, going into real estate and becoming a member of the Massachusetts House of Representatives. His music was frequently used on occasions honoring the memory of Washington, and he is best known today for his hymn *Coronation* ("All hail the power of Jesus' name"), published in his collection *The Union Harmony* in 1793.

Holden, with the assistance of Samuel Holyoke (1762-1820), a native New Englander, collaborated with their teacher, Hans Gram (a foreigner, who had arrived in Boston before 1790) in making a collection which they called *The Massachusetts Compiler*. It was published in 1795, the most progressive work on psalmody to appear before 1800. Its harmonization of tunes was unusually good, and the book not only contained psalms, hymns, and anthems, but a treatise on sacred vocal music, and a musical dictionary.

Gram, becoming organist of the Brattle Street Church (which nearly a century before had refused Brattle's organ), is remembered for the first orchestral score published in the United States: *The Death Song of an Indian Chief*. It was printed on a flyleaf of the *Massachusetts Magazine* for March, 1791, and was scored for voice, strings, two clarinets, and two horns.

BENJAMIN FRANKLIN'S INTEREST IN MUSIC

The history of these years during and after the Revolution would not be complete without some mention of the musical interests of Benjamin Franklin. He was the embodiment of all the characteristic qualities which we have come to consider as truly American. Versatile, competent, shrewd, practical, resourceful, always at ease, whether with king or common man, he was at once a statesman, scientist, and inventor—a man who sought to improve and advance the society in which he lived. He could, with equal ease, edit and print a paper, produce a newer and better stove, help in the drafting of the Declaration of Independence and later the Constitution, play the guitar, and improve the currently popular musical instrument known as the glassychord or musical glasses.

This instrument, which was eventually to be called the glass harmonica, or simple harmonica, was first heard by Franklin while on a visit to London, when E. H. Delaval performed for an audience of which Franklin was a member. "Being charmed by the sweetness of its tones," he wrote in one of his letters, "and the music he produced from it, I wished only to see the glasses disposed in a more convenient form, and brought together in a narrower compass, so as to admit of a greater number of tones, and all within reach of hand to a person sitting before the instrument. . . ."

Musical glasses had been known in Persia and Arabia for centuries, and consisted of a series of glasses filled with various amounts of water, so as to produce various pitches. The sound was obtained by lightly rubbing the rims of the glasses with a wet finger.

Franklin did not fill his glasses with water, but used instead a series of graduated, tuned glass bowls mounted on a spindle that was revolved by means of a foot pedal. He wrote that they were "played upon by sitting before the middle of the set of glasses as before the keys of a harpsichord, turning them with the foot, and wetting them now and then with a sponge and clean water."

The sound of the harmonica enchanted the listeners of two continents, and Mozart and Beethoven were but two of the many composers who wrote for the new instrument.

From his years of traveling, both in America and in Europe, Franklin had many musical contacts, which he mentioned frequently in his letters. It is from these that we discover what a sound and sensible critic he was, and how catholic were his tastes. He could enjoy the simple music in a Moravian church, or the complex choruses of Handel's oratorios in London. He also recognized the intrinsic qualities that were to be found in the folk music of America, which the people loved and sang, and he urged that this music be kept for the pleasures of the common man, who, most of the time, did not enjoy the modern inventions of the great musicians. It was at times like these that Franklin showed his awareness and understanding of the relationship of music to man, and because of this, it can be rightfully said that he was the first important critic of music to appear on the American scene.

CHAPTER V

The Turn of the Century, to the 1830s

ARRIVAL OF THE FOREIGN MUSICIANS

With the French Revolution at its height in Europe, and general unrest everywhere, immigrants and foreign musicians continued to pour into America's ports. The European aristocracy, no longer the patrons of music they had been in the old days, left the musicians with no choice but to try their luck in the New World. Many, of course, had a genuine interest in America, and were more than glad of the opportunity to settle there. Of all who came, it was the English musicians who had a wider influence on America at this time, rather the French. They threw themselves wholeheartedly into the life of the new country, joining the many theatrical orchestras or helping to produce ballad operas and entertainments, as well as becoming organists, leaders of church music, and teachers.

It was not that these men—Reinagle, Taylor, Carr, or Hewitt—were actually distinguished, but rather it was their adventurous spirit, their versatility, and their love of the theater, that made them the right men for that particular moment. Their work was also greatly shaped by popular demand, and their music served its purpose. Public taste had not had time to be formed, and consequently the music of this period after the Revolution was of a practical nature. Marches, fife tunes, airs to set the mood of a play or to show the exaltation of a deep religious experience—this was the chief music as the century drew to its close.

Offsetting this bright, almost carefree period, the heads of the government did their best to be practical and cautious. They had been in the midst of the grimness of war, and they still labored to launch the new ship of state properly, and on a good, straight course. One can fully understand Franklin's words as he warned the people to do first things first. "All things have their reason," he said, "and with young countries, as with young men, you must curb their fancy to strengthen their judgment. . . . To America, one schoolmaster is worth a dozen poets, and the invention of a machine or the improvement of an implement is of more importance than a masterpiece of Raphael. . . . Nothing is good or beautiful but in the measure that it is useful: yet all things have a utility under particular circumstances. Thus poetry, painting, music are all necessary and proper gratifications of a refined state of society but objectionable at an earlier period, since their cultivation would make a taste for their enjoyment precede its means."

Alexander Reinagle

Alexander Reinagle, friend of Carl Philipp Emanuel Bach and other outstanding musicians of his day, was one of the most active of the English composers who came to America after the war. Born in 1756 (not long after Mozart) in Portsmouth of Austrian parents, Reinagle's early musical education was received in Scotland, where he studied with Raynor Taylor, who followed him to America in 1792, and of whom we shall hear more later. Reinagle was an excellent pianist and skillful on the violin. In London he came under the influence of Johann Christian Bach, at the time the dominant figure of London's musical life, now that Handel was dead. After traveling extensively on the Continent (where he met Carl Philipp Emanuel Bach in Hamburg), Reinagle landed in New York in 1786, where he announced that "Mr. Reinagle, member of the Society of Musicians in London, gives lessons on the piano forte, harpsichord, or violin." But the New Yorkers did not offer the encouragement and patronage he needed, and he soon departed for Philadelphia, where he was to find surroundings more similar to the life he had known in London. At thirty Reinagle was a handsome man with a compelling personality, one who had all the attributes of a gentleman, even though the professional musician of that day had not attained such a status. Philadelphia had not heard such fine piano playing as that of Reinagle, and from the beginning he exerted an influence that made for high standards in the city's musical life. General Washington is known to have attended several of Reinagle's concerts, and chose him to teach his adopted daughter (really his wife's granddaughter), Nelly Custis. Her harpsichord still may be seen in the music room at Mount Vernon, Virginia, a mute reminder of the many pleasant evenings of music that the Washingtons must have enjoyed.

Reinagle joined the orchestra of one of the leading theatrical troupes, and assisted in the subscription concerts in both New York and Philadelphia. It is rather startling to discover the apparent ease with which these early musicians commuted between the two cities, in the days when travel was neither easy nor fast. As Reinagle became increasingly interested in the theater, he formed a partnership with Thomas Wignell, the brilliant English actor and singer, and with him built the famous Chestnut Street Theatre in Philadelphia. The opening was delayed a year, due to the yellow fever epidemic which raged during the winter of 1793 and caused the postponement of any but necessary gatherings. Despite the three concerts given in February, 1793, to appease the stockholders, it was not until February 17, 1794, that the new playhouse commenced its career as a theater with a performance of Samuel Arnold's *The Castle of Andalusia.*

Reinagle was a prolific composer, and much of his music is still in existence in early prints or in manuscript. It was widely played during the composer's lifetime, but was then completely neglected until this century, when it was rediscovered and some of it republished in modern editions. He composed in the style of the German composers he knew, like Carl Philipp Emanuel Bach, and also Haydn. Four piano sonatas, composed about 1800, have been in the manuscript collection of the Music Division of the Library of Congress for many years. They are perfect examples of the sonata form as C. P. E. Bach developed it and Haydn perfected it, and they show some individuality and excellent taste. All of the sonatas, save the first, are in the fast-slow-fast three-movement form that Philipp Emanuel Bach favored. The one in E major is available in a modern edition and it has been recorded. A *Federal March* by Reinagle was composed for and played at the mammoth celebration and parade that was held in Philadelphia on July 4, 1788, to celebrate the signing of the Constitution by ten of the states.

One of Reinagle's many songs became widely used as a patriotic number, *America, Commerce and Freedom,* supposedly sung in the ballet pantomime of *The Sailor's Landlady*. Like many musicians of the day, Reinagle arranged and adapted the music and songs used in the ballad operas at the theaters. Practically none of his efforts in this field is in existence today. He later moved to Baltimore, where he remained active until his death in 1809.

Benjamin Carr

The Carrs will always be remembered as one of America's most important and influential musical families, largely because they were among our earliest music publishers, without whose help the music of the young nation could not possibly have reached the people as rapidly as it did.

The senior Carr, Joseph, was the head of a publishing house in London, and it was his eldest son Benjamin (1768-1831) who first arrived in New York in 1793 (later going on to Philadelphia), where he was joined within the year by his father and brother Thomas. Benjamin, who had been born in London, had all the advantages of his father's position in England, where he studied with the foremost musicians of the day. When he reached Philadelphia, he established himself on High Street, under the firm name of B. Carr and Company.

Joseph Carr did not linger long in the Quaker City, but moved on to Baltimore, where with Thomas he opened a "Musical Repository," and advertised as follows:

J. Carr, Music Importer, lately from London, Respectfully informs the public that he has opened a Store entirely in the Musical line, and has for sale, Finger and barrel organs, double and single key'd harpsichords; piano fortes and common guitars.

The "repository" proved a prosperous business, and was to win national distinction in 1814, when it published the first edition of *The Star Spangled Banner*.

Benjamin Carr's Philadelphia music store was the second such established in that city (it had been preceded only a few months before by the firm of Moller and Capron). The business grew so rapidly and so well that a year later Carr opened a branch in New York. He was an excellent musician and appeared as a singer, pianist, organist, choral conductor, and composer. His theatrical works had a great vogue, and his music for William Dunlap's *The*

Archers; or, the Mountaineers of Switzerland was produced in New York in 1796, and might be considered the first American ballad opera. His use of the *William Tell* legend antedated Rossini's opera on the same subject by thirty-three years. Two numbers from the score have been preserved: a graceful song, *Why, Huntress, Why,* published by Carr as No. 39 in his *Musical Journal,* and a Rondo from the Overture, which appeared as No. 7 in Joseph Carr's *Musical Miscellany* in 1813.

Carr was among the musicians who founded the Musical Fund Society of Philadelphia in 1820. The organization was formed to give concerts for the benefit of needy musicians, and it still exists today, having had a long and honored history.

A prolific song writer, Carr did his finest work after the turn of the century. His *Hymn to the Virgin—Ave Maria* (1810), is quite remarkable for the time, and might well be said to be the beginning of true art song in America.

Another successful ballad opera, given within a few months of Carr's *The Archers,* was Victor Pelissier's *Edwin and Angelina,* first heard in December, 1796, its libretto adapted from Oliver Goldsmith.

James Hewitt

James Hewitt, whose life span was exactly that of Beethoven's (1770-1827), came to New York in 1792, and was to that city what Carr was to Philadelphia. He had led the court orchestra of George III and had been fortunate enough to play under Haydn, whom the impresario Salomon had brought to London in 1791. Hewitt had been a publisher in England, and five years after his arrival in America he bought Carr's New York store. One of Hewitt's sons continued to run the store well into the new century.

Arriving from England, Hewitt announced a concert in company with four musicians who had come with him—"professors of music from the Operahouse, Hanoversquare, and Professional Concerts under the direction of Haydn, Pleyel, etc., London." One of the works on the program was a composition by Hewitt, an *Overture in 9 movements, expressive of a battle.* This was no doubt a programmatic piece in the style of Kotzwara's *Battle of Prague,* a piece which had been published in London a few years earlier and had become tremendously popular. Various notations in the score indicated the episodes the music was intended to describe: cannon, the attack, cries of the wounded, victory, and so forth.

Although Hewitt's battle score is not in existence, it must have been similar to one he published in 1797 and dedicated to George Washington. Written as a sonata for the piano, it was called *The Battle of Trenton*, and its numerous episodes described the battle and ultimate victory. *Yankee Doodle* appears on one of its pages. These program pieces were widely admired, and had honorable ancestors in the Biblical Sonatas (1700) of Johann Kuhnau, J. S. Bach's predecessor at Leipzig. They were to have such descendants in the Victorian era as *The Storm*, a trivial work that became the rage of parlor and drawing room throughout the land.

Hewitt became the organist of New York's Trinity Church, led outdoor concerts, and was the director of all the military bands in the city from 1805 to 1809. Like his contemporaries he wrote for the theater, and one of his original scores was *Tammany*, produced in 1794. It was given under the auspices of the Tammany Society (the ancestor of the present Tammany Hall), with its libretto naturally about Indians. Unfortunately nothing of the score survives, but its première was an exciting event. At that time New York was a stronghold of the anti-Federalist Party, whose members urged America to support the French Revolution, while the Federalists wished their country to remain neutral. The Tammany Society was anti-Federalist, so it is not surprising to read of the hisses and boos which offset the cheers at the première, depending on which side could make the greater noise. Hewitt's songs were among his finest compositions. *In a Far Distant Clime* is simple and charming, almost Mozartean in style, and *In Vain the Tears*, written before 1810, shows remarkable harmonic variety for that day.

In 1812 Hewitt moved from New York to Boston, where he directed the music at the Federal Street Theatre and was organist of Trinity Church. In 1818 he was back in New York and for a time led the orchestra at the Park Theatre there. He died in Boston in 1827 at the home of his second son, James L. Hewitt. This son became a music dealer and publisher, in both Boston and New York. Others of the family were prominent in American music life throughout the nineteenth century. The eldest son, John Hill Hewitt, was a song composer and literary figure whom we shall meet in later pages. The third and fourth sons, Horatio Nelson Hewitt

and Hobart Doane Hewitt, were musicians, as were the two daughters. The elder, Sophia, was organist of the Boston Handel and
Haydn Society from 1820 to 1829. Through her marriage to Louis
Ostinelli, a violinist, she became the mother of Eliza Ostinelli, who
became by marriage Eliza Biscaccianti. After studying in Naples
this granddaughter of James Hewitt became a leading prima donna
in Europe and America. The younger of James Hewitt's daughters,
Eliza, was a music teacher.

Raynor Taylor

For this period of great theatrical activity Raynor Taylor (1747-
1825) produced what were called "olios and entertainments" (in the
style of Charles Dibdin of London) in which he introduced various
original songs, comic sketches, and burlesques of Italian opera.
Taylor had taught Reinagle in Scotland, and later, in London, had
become the music director of the Sadler's Wells Theatre. He came
to Baltimore in 1792 and in October was appointed organist of St.
Anne's Church in Annapolis. He then moved on to Philadelphia,
becoming organist at St. Peter's Church, where he soon became
known for his masterly improvisations, as well as for his extravaganzas in the theaters. With Benjamin Carr, he was one of the
founders of the Musical Fund Society, of which we have already
spoken.

The Van Hagens

Charleston, South Carolina, had the Dutch Peter Albrecht Van
Hagen and his wife, who taught and gave concerts both before and
after the Revolution. When Van Hagen made his New York debut
in 1789, he introduced his eight-year-old son. Peter, Junior, having
been born in America, was probably the first professional child
prodigy to appear on the stage in the new nation, as both singer
and pianist. The family later moved to Boston, where they established a music store and publishing firm.

William Selby

One of the earliest arrivals of the many musicians from England
was a man who was primarily responsible for the rapid progress of
music in Boston during the last quarter of the eighteenth century—
William Selby (1738-1798). He was an organist and composer from

London who came to Boston about 1771, well in advance of many of his contemporaries. Selby first appeared at one of Josiah Flagg's concerts and soon after was appointed organist of King's Chapel. Although he was at first concerned principally with instrumental music and played his own "Concerto on the Organ" and harpsichord concerto in Boston concerts, his interests shifted to choral music. Through his efforts in organizing choral concerts he is considered an indirect founder of the Boston Handel and Haydn Society, even though it was established seventeen years after his death.

During the difficult years of the Revolution Selby found it necessary to turn to other activities for a livelihood, and in his shop near Broomfield's Lane he advertised himself in the *Continental Journal* of January 13, 1780, as selling "Port, Teneriffe, Malaga Wines, Tea, Brown and Loaf sugar, logwood, English soap, etc."

Selby was to Boston what William Tuckey had been to New York, but coming almost two decades later, and at a time when interest in better singing was increasing, he was able to accomplish far more than Tuckey could. He tried to start a monthly magazine, which unfortunately seems never to have been issued. It was to have been called *The New Minstrel* and each issue was to have contained "at least one composition for the harpsichord, piano forte or spinnett, one for the guittar, and one for the German flute, also of one song in French, and two songs in the English language." Selby solicited subscriptions for this project in 1782 and it may have been that conditions following the war were one of the reasons for his lack of success, for in his advertisement in the *Boston Evening Post* of February 2 he asked:

> And shall those arts which make her [this young country] happy, be less courted than those arts which have made her great? Why may she not be "In song unequall'd as unmatch'd in war?"

Here was a challenge for the young nation, which, having already won its War of Independence, was now ready to scale the heights in music.

Gottlieb Graupner

Boston had a music store that matched Carr's in Philadelphia and Hewitt's in New York. The man who issued music from this store was perhaps to be the greatest influence of his day. He was not only in large part responsible for Boston's vastly superior music, but earned the title of "father of American orchestral music." He was the German-born but English-trained Johann Christian Gottlieb Graupner (1767-1836), who sailed to America around 1795. Graupner was an experienced musician and an excellent oboist. He had been a member of a Hanoverian regimental band when a youth of twenty, and later he played under Haydn in London during the 1791-92 season. He and his wife, who was in the theater, gave many vocal concerts. There is a legend that Graupner planted the seed of Negro minstrelsy by singing a Negro song in blackface, and it is definitely recorded that Mrs. Graupner sang a ballad entitled *I Sold a Guiltless Negro Boy* at a concert in December of 1799.

Graupner had a vital interest in choral music and became one of the founders of Boston's Handel and Haydn Society. It was in March of 1815 that he and two others signed an invitation to a meeting to consider "the expediency of forming a society for cultivating and improving a correct taste in the performance of sacred music, and also to introduce into more general practice the works of Handel, Haydn and other eminent composers." From this meeting was to come one of the great oratorio societies of the United States.

Inspired by his performances under Haydn, Graupner had made a beginning in Boston by gathering together a small group to meet socially on Saturday evenings to play Haydn symphonies and similar compositions. These meetings soon grew into public concerts and the professionals who started them were joined by the amateurs of the city. The little orchestra was called the Philharmonic Society (1809) and continued in existence until 1824. No one would have been prouder than Graupner himself could he have foreseen the magnificent orchestra—the Boston Symphony—which was to emerge before the close of the century to make Boston's name synonymous with the finest music in the world.

It was these professional musicians who brought to their new home the finest music of their day, and with their ability to view the American scene with complete objectivity, they saw the possibilities of musical growth in the years ahead. They were like a strong tonic to the young republic not yet recovered from the ravages of war, for each worked with all his might and against all odds to help

America start toward the heights which she would reach in another century and a half.

"HAIL COLUMBIA"

Out of an extraordinary period of theatrical activity came one of the most popular of the country's anthems, *Hail Columbia,* which for years was to rival *The Star Spangled Banner* in the affections of the people. It originated at one of the many theatrical entertainments in 1798. These years had indeed been difficult, as there existed between the United States and France a state of undeclared war. France, just barely over her own Revolution of 1789, was at war with Prussia, and the sentiment of the anti-Federalist Party in America was for the support of France. The anti-Federalists could not forget the great help France had given the colonies during the American Revolution. President Washington, however, had kept the country neutral, but when John Adams, a strong Federalist, was inaugurated President in 1797 matters reached a crisis. The French government was most arrogant and had so grossly insulted the American ministers and violated American rights that by 1798 the country was on the brink of war.

In the spring of 1798 a young actor by the name of Gilbert Fox was about to give a special performance at the Chestnut Street Theatre. Philadelphia was then the capital of the United States and Fox, whose advance sale was not going at all well, knew he must have something unusual to attract attention and sell tickets. He called on Joseph Hopkinson (1770-1842), son of Francis, and asked him to write words to an instrumental piece that was at the height of its popularity, *The President's March.* Hopkinson not only obliged with the verses of *Hail Columbia* but avoided taking sides in the current controversy over France. Instead he emphasized American patriotism. Fox printed the refrain in his advertisement in the newspapers and Philadelphians flocked to hear the "new Federal song," as it was called, insuring its immediate success.

The music has been established as that of Philip Phile, and was originally one of the many popular marches honoring Washington. Phile was another of the immigrants who had made their way to America. He was active in both New York and Philadelphia as a member of theater orchestras.

THE EXPANDING NATION

The early years of the nineteenth century presaged a still greater era in American music, as well as a new period in the nation's political and economic life. In 1800 Thomas Jefferson was elected the third President of the United States, only a few months after the death of George Washington. This marked the defeat of the Federalist party and it brought with it many administrative changes. In that year Napoleon's ambitions were threatening all of Europe as well as the security of the United States, and it was only because he had too many problems at hand that Napoleon made a treaty with the United States, just before John Adams left office, early in 1801. With the purchase of Louisiana in 1803, all of the land west of the Mississippi, as far as the Rocky Mountains, became part of the United States. Everywhere there was bustling activity, in which music played a noticeable part. Traveling musicians gave concerts, and music teachers, dancing masters, and theatrical companies ventured farther into the new lands.

In New Orleans opera had begun to flourish while Washington was still President. An audience of five thousand was entertained by *Le Spectacle de la Rue St. Pierre,* and in 1791, Louis Tabary, a manager, brought over a company of comedians from Europe. In 1799, refugees from the San Domingo insurrection (in which the plantation slaves rose up against the whites) gave performances in the city. Le Theatre St. Pierre opened in 1808, and by 1810 New Orleans had three theaters, and was the first American city to have a permanent opera.

The extensive building after the Revolution began to affect the arts and crafts. The great Georgian mansions in the South had been influenced by the beautiful creations of the Englishman Christopher Wren. After the war the houses of the wealthy New Englanders followed a newer trend, that of the federal style, so brilliantly developed by a group of architects of whom Charles Bulfinch (1763-1844), of Boston, was the leader. Here the skillful woodcarvers were doing exquisite work in their decorations of the moldings, mantelpieces, and furniture. New churches had adopted the Georgian designs of James Gibbs (1682-1754), and in the South, Virginia's state capitol at Richmond was patterned after a Roman temple and the Library of the University of Virginia, built in Charlottesville in

1817, was designed after the Pantheon in Rome. The last two buildings reflected the influence of Thomas Jefferson, who anticipated in architecture the eclecticism of later years, an eclecticism which implied freedom to choose among the styles of the past that which seemed the most appropriate. Philadelphia's artistic life had a new impetus when Charles Willson Peale and William Rush founded the Pennsylvania Academy of the Fine Arts in 1805.

Between the cities anonymous journeymen traveled the dusty roads, carving useful objects wherever they stopped. When they visited the coastal cities they devoted their talents to carving imaginative figureheads for ships. Thus decorated, the clipper ships sailed from American harbors, unlocking the door to the China trade and bringing back teas, silks, pepper, camphor, and spices to the new nation. This in turn created a great desire for all things Chinese among the wealthy Americans, and soon lacquered chairs and screens, Oriental carvings, and exotic bric-a-brac brightened the houses of the merchants and skippers. No less a person than Thomas Chippendale came under the Chinese influence, and his furniture designs of this period were to produce a style which has come to be known as Chinese Chippendale. From the more sophisticated coastal towns to the crude and primitive life on the frontier were to come the finest manifestations of the folk arts, all of which exhibited a genuine quality that was truly American.

WAR OF 1812: "THE STAR SPANGLED BANNER"

The dark clouds that had gathered over the young republic broke in the deluge of the War of 1812. This second conflict with Great Britain was started as a war for "free trade and seamen's rights," and out of its horror and destruction was to come America's immortal song—*The Star Spangled Banner*.

The year was 1814, following the burning of the Capitol, the Library of Congress, and the White House by the British. Not too far from Baltimore a physician of Upper Marlborough, Maryland— a Dr. Beanes—had been taken prisoner by the British, and was held by the fleet which was anchored off the city. Francis Scott Key, a young lawyer, sought the release of his friend, Dr. Beanes, going to the British admiral under a flag of truce. Although accorded the most courteous treatment, Key was kept a virtual prisoner, for he was not allowed to return to Baltimore on that fateful night of September 13. It was feared that he might have seen the formation of British ships, and would tell of the plans to attack Fort McHenry, Baltimore's chief defense.

Key watched the bombardment all night long, thinking each time the firing stopped that the fort had surrendered. As dawn slowly broke, Key could make out the outline of the fort, and behold— the Stars and Stripes was still flying! The moment was so thrilling that Key was inspired to capture it in verse. Taking an envelope from his pocket he hastily sketched a few lines which he expanded, while in a boat taking him back to Baltimore later in the day, into the verses of *The Star Spangled Banner*, adapting them to a popular tune of the day, *To Anacreon in Heav'n*. This had been an English drinking song, whose earliest known edition was arranged by John Stafford Smith for the Anacreontic Society of London about 1775, as their constitutional song. Its many adaptations and parodies had become familiar to Americans, the most famous of the political songs being *Adams and Liberty* (1798). By the time the War of 1812 came, it was possibly the most popular patriotic air.

When Key reached Baltimore, he wrote out a fresh copy of his verses in his hotel room, and the next morning took it to his friend, Judge Nicholson. The judge liked the poem and it was sent at once to a printer with directions that copies be made in handbill form. On September 20, 1814, the *Baltimore Patriot* printed the words, as did the *Baltimore American* the next day. The imprint on the original broadside of Key's verses reads: "Printed and Sold at Carr's Music Store. . . ." Publishers in other cities soon followed with their own editions.

For many years the original manuscript (the completed draft) of *The Star Spangled Banner* was in the Walters Art Gallery in Baltimore, but in 1953 it was bought and given to the Maryland Historical Society by Mrs. Thomas Jenkins (whose husband was a descendant of Key). It is now housed in the fine old mansion of Enoch Pratt on West Monument Street, Baltimore, as part of the Society's permanent collection. The song was not officially made the nation's anthem until 1931, when the Seventy-first Congress passed "Public No. 823." The bill was signed on March 3 by Herbert Hoover.

AMERICA'S INTELLECTUAL AWAKENING

After the War of 1812, America found herself in the midst of an intellectual movement which was concurrent with that of the so-called Romantic movement in Europe. When Washington Irving sailed for Europe in 1815 (where he was to stay for seventeen years), literary leadership had centered in New York, where it would remain until some two decades later when Boston would take over. The literary giants of the day were Irving, James Fenimore Cooper, and William Cullen Bryant. Irving, rightly called the "father of American letters" was greatly admired for his fine style by the English romantic writers, such men as Byron, Scott, and Coleridge. Cooper, the greatest of the frontier writers, combined with the new spirit of democracy his own loyalty to the common man, and warned America that she had nearly forgotten her hard-earned lesson of freedom. Cooper's tale of the Revolution *The Spy* (1821), and *The Leatherstocking Tales* (1823-1841), won him admirers in every land, as they were translated and circulated. No less a musician than Franz Schubert, incidentally, became one of his most avid readers.

The time was not yet ripe for America's art music, which for many years would lag behind the other arts. But the excellent works of this first literary group were to inspire later musicians, who based operas, choral works, and descriptive orchestral pieces on the creations of men like Irving and Cooper.

NEW YORK'S FIRST GRAND OPERA

In 1823, New York saw Bishop's ballad opera *Clari, the Maid of Milan,* just after London had witnessed performances in May. The author of the libretto was John Howard Payne (1791-1852), noted American actor and dramatist, who was then living in Paris. His *Home, Sweet Home* was sung for the first time in the production.

November 29, 1825, was a far more important date in New York's music annals, for it was on that evening that the city had its first performance of Italian grand opera in its original form and language. The opera was Rossini's *The Barber of Seville,* which had been given in English translation and greatly modified form at the Park Theatre some six years earlier. The troupe that came in 1825 was brought from Italy by Manuel García and was a full company of experienced singers which included García's wife and daughter, the latter soon to be known as a famous singer, her name changed by marriage to Maria Malibran. Some of García's singers had been in the Rome première of *The Barber* and the choice of this delectable score with which to please New York was a fortunate one. In *The Barber*, Rossini had summed up all the traditions of eighteenth-century opera buffa at its most triumphant period. For the New York première the orchestra included the best musicians the city could produce, and the next day the *New York Evening Post* described the audience as "so fashionable, so numerous, and so elegantly dressed. . . ." The auditors were "surprised, delighted, and enchanted by the performance." It was indeed a gala occasion and among the important personages to be seen were Joseph Bonaparte, Fitz-Greene Halleck, James Fenimore Cooper, and Lorenzo Da Ponte. Da Ponte, Mozart's famous librettist who had written the texts for three of Mozart's most successful operas (*The Marriage of Figaro, Così fan Tutte,* and *Don Giovanni*), had arrived in New York in 1805. It is believed that the wine merchant, Dominick Lynch, had much to do with the proposed opera season and the arrangements for García's appearance. The first season lasted almost a year, and started a Rossini vogue in New York. Soon his *Semiramide, Il Turco in Italia (The Turk in Italy),* and *La Cenerentola (Cinderella)* were heard, as well as two operas of García's with libretti by Da Ponte, and Mozart's *Don Giovanni.*

Two years later (1827) a French Opera Company from New Orleans played at the Park Theatre, and during the same season the Bowery Theatre presented the first French ballet on an American stage. The Richmond Hill Theatre opened in 1832 and presented a succession of opera companies. In 1833 the Italian Opera House opened (the first built in New York and later called the National Theatre), and Niblo's Gardens was yet another popular rendezvous, where every important artist was heard during the next fifty years. Palmo's Opera House in Chambers Street, between Broadway and Centre Street, was built in 1844; the Astor Place Opera House opened in 1847; and in 1854, the famous Academy of Music on Fourteenth Street became the principal opera house until the Metropolitan was built some thirty years later.

Despite the fact that many of the theatrical performances were of a light nature, with frivolous and inconsequential music, these early opera performances are again indicative of the influence of the immigrant professional musician and his desire to give only the best music. As America's lyric theater continued to grow, some of the world's greatest operas were given in the larger cities, such as Weber's *Der Freischütz*, sung in New York in the English version on March 2, 1825, while Philadelphia had the American première of his *Oberon* in 1827 (two years after it was composed for London), as well as Mozart's *Magic Flute* in 1832. Beethoven's *Fidelio* was heard in 1839 in New York, in an English translation.

CONCERTS AND SONG WRITERS

With such a cosmopolitan population as New York was now attracting, concert life was bound to have its frivolous side. One might read in the New York *Herald* of January 7, 1839, that:

"A musical party will meet this evening, at 8 o'clock, at Davies' Hot Pie House, No. 14 John Street. A professor will preside at the Piano Forte. Admission 12½ cents." Or another would boast, as did Signor de Begnis, buffo singer from the Italian Opera House in London, that at his forthcoming recital he would sing "six hundred words and three hundred bars of music in the short space of three minutes."

With America's advancement of science there came a flood of songs recording the development of the nation. Ballads were composed to celebrate many of the important events, such as the completion of the Erie Canal in 1825; New York State's first train; the United States' first horse-drawn streetcars in New York City in 1831; as well as the Abolition movement against slavery. Statesmen, political figures, movements, became the subjects of songs. Fashions in dress were ridiculed and the fads and foibles of the day satirized. The American Society for the Promotion of Temperance, founded in Boston in 1826, was extolled on one side, derided on the other. Many of the songs were sugar-sweet with sentiment, and they covered all emotions from love to sorrow and self-pity.

One of the pleasant customs was to write "answer songs" to popular ballads. Sometimes they were written by other composers but often the writers supplied the "answers" to songs of their own. When *Rise Gentle Moon* became popular it was answered by *The*

Moon Is Up, "a Serenade in answer to *Rise Gentle Moon.*" Similarly *Oh, no, we never mention her* was answered by *She never blam'd him, never.* Publishers would announce new songs with all of the exaggerations accorded today's super-colossal films from Hollywood.

Charles Edward Horn

Not all of the musicians and singers of this period, however, were on the light side. One of the better of them was Charles Edward Horn (1786-1849), who, with his talented wife, was offering New Yorkers six *soirées musicales* in 1839, on the Thursday of each alternate week during February, March, and April. Horn was born in England and achieved considerable reputation there as a singer, pianist, composer, and conductor. He had composed and produced twenty-two English operas in London, acted as musical director at the Olympia, and was highly popular as an opera singer. He was forty-seven when he came to America (1833) and for a time produced English operas at New York's Park Theatre. Horn became one of the founders of the Philharmonic Society and sang at its first concert in 1842.

In the hundreds of recitals or ballad concerts that Horn and his wife gave, there was a variety of works by such composers as Purcell, Rossini, and Beethoven, but there was also a generous sprinkling of his own compositions. The song by which he is best known today is *Cherry Ripe,* and there is also his familiar setting of Shakespeare's *I know a bank whereon the wild thyme grows.* A number of his songs were grouped together in a cycle called *National Melodies of America,* which used poems of George P. Morris. The melodies Horn used in these songs were of supposedly native origin; for example, the *Northern Refrain,* based on a "carol of the sweeps of the city of New York," and the *Southern Refrain,* a Negro air. The ballad singer became extremely popular, and two other Englishmen enjoyed considerable vogue—Joseph Philip Knight, ever the favorite of basses for his *Rocked in the Cradle of the Deep* (1839); and Henry Russell, who set George P. Morris' *Woodman, Spare that Tree* (1837).

Henry Russell

Perhaps the most popular of all the ballad singers of this period was Henry Russell (1812-1900), who gave concerts in America from

1833 (when he arrived in Canada) until 1841. As a singer Russell had a keen sense of drama and of platform effectiveness. A master of hokum, he could draw cheers from his audience at will. Known best today as the composer of *Woodman, Spare that Tree,* he had just sung the song for an audience on one occasion when an old man arose and asked in a shaking voice if the tree had actually been spared. "It was, sir," Russell replied. "Thank God! Thank God! I breathe again!" sighed the old man as he sank back into his seat.

Russell was well educated musically, studying in Italy with Rossini and getting to know Donizetti and Bellini, and later on in Paris the celebrated Meyerbeer. Coming to America to seek his fortune, he became organist of the First Presbyterian Church in Rochester, New York. It was here that he started to compose the many songs which he sang throughout the country. Some of his others were: *The Old Arm Chair, The Old Bell, A Life on the Ocean Wave,* and *The Old Sexton.* Although a favorite with the public, Russell had his critics, for there were some who did not fall victim to his theatrical charms. Russell continued his activities until his death at the age of eighty-eight. In 1889 his *A Life on the Ocean Wave* was made the official march of the British Royal Marines, and his song *Cheer Boys, Cheer* has for years been the only air played by a British regimental fife and drum corps when a regiment goes abroad. Russell's sons likewise achieved fame. One, Henry Russell, became an opera impresario and was at one time manager of the Boston Opera Company (1909-14). The other took the name of Landon Ronald and was a well-known English composer, accompanist and conductor.

John Hill Hewitt

A very important musician who helped shape this era of light song was the eldest son of James Hewitt—John Hill Hewitt (1801-1890), who was given the title of the "father of the American ballad." He might be called the composer of the first all-American hit song—*The Minstrel's Return from the War,* composed in 1825. Born in New York, Hewitt moved to Boston with his parents in 1812. Because his father objected to his having a career of music, young John ran away, and enjoyed a life of adventure which was to make him a wanderer, off and on, for a large part of his life. In

1818 he went to West Point, but left at the end of his third year. Then he went South, having joined a theatrical company which his father had organized, only to have the venture end in failure when the company was burned out in a fire in Augusta, Georgia. He stayed in Augusta for a short while, and then went to Columbia, South Carolina, where he taught music, composed, and commenced the study of law. It was about this time (1825) that he composed his first song, *The Minstrel's Return from the War*. On the original manuscript, now in the Library of Congress, Hewitt's brother, James L., wrote a penciled note. He was at the time carrying on the father's publishing business and in the note he stated that when he published the song he thought so little of it that he did not bother to take out a copyright. As a result, dozens of others published their editions when the song became popular, and the Hewitts lost at least ten thousand dollars by not having the exclusive right to it.

John Hill returned to the North because of his father's death in 1827, but he soon departed for the South again, planning to visit in Baltimore. He liked that city so well that he spent most of the rest of his life there. He immediately became active in newspaper work, music, and matters theatrical, achieving some contemporary fame as both composer and poet. He became editor of the *Saturday Visitor*, and when that paper sponsored a literary contest, he entered a poem under a nom de plume. He called it *The Song of the Wind*, and it was awarded the prize over Edgar Allan Poe's *The Coliseum*. In his memoirs; *Shadows on the Wall*, Hewitt tells the story of the contest:

> The proprietors of the journal . . . offered two premiums; one of $100 for the best story, another of $50 for the best poem. . . . The committee on the awards . . . decided that Poe's weird tale entitled "A Manuscript Found in a Bottle" should receive first premium. . . . The judges were brought to a stand, but, after some debate, agreed that the latter [Hewitt] should receive the second prize, as the author of the former had already received the first. This decision did not please Poe, hence the "little unpleasantness" between us.

Hewitt is the perfect example of the newspaper and literary man of his day. He missed very little in his travels all over the country. He saw Fulton's first steamboat on the Hudson (1807); he was a passenger on the first train to be pushed out of Baltimore by a locomotive in 1829 (the Baltimore and Ohio Railroad's *Tom Thumb,* the creation of Peter Cooper, ironmaster of Baltimore); and he was present when the first dispatch was sent over Morse's telegraph between Baltimore and Washington in 1844. At the beginning of the Civil War, Hewitt offered his services to the Confederacy. He was sixty and not acceptable for active military service, but because of his West Point training, Jefferson Davis appointed him to the thankless task of drill master of raw recruits.

Hewitt's music has not lived as have some of the songs of Russell and Knight. His best-known song today is the Civil War song *All quiet along the Potomac tonight,* which, although it was written as a Confederate song, was popular in both the South and North. He wrote hundreds of songs, achieving his greatest success in narrative ballads. Hewitt's oratorio *Jephtha* was successfully given in New York at the Broadway Tabernacle, as well as in Washington, Georgetown, Norfolk, and Baltimore.

These sentimental songs of men like Hewitt, Russell, and the rest cannot be ignored, for they were a part of America's maturing. They greatly appealed to the masses, and were to have a counterpart in every succeeding generation. They were a part of the nineteenth century's period of exhibitionism, when both singers and instrumentalists (as we will discover in succeeding chapters) stopped at nothing to insure personal success and popularity. Contrived and artificial as many of these songs were, they had few of the emotional and timeless elements of the true folk song, which was already treasured within the borders of the nation. It would be many years before America could see beyond this sentimental and superficial coating and recognize the artistic values of her finest heritage—her folk songs.

CHAPTER VI

Continuing Growth in the Nineteenth Century, to 1860

THE FIRST EDUCATOR: LOWELL MASON

One of the greatest of all American musical figures to make his appearance in the new century was Lowell Mason (1792-1872), a keenly intelligent man who was remarkably gifted as a composer of hymn tunes, many of them among the finest of the early writers. Mason will always be remembered, too, as the founder of the public-school music system. The material for music in the schools had long been available in New England, with the century of the singing schools and musical societies. These elements needed but the perception of a man like Mason to see the great potentialities for the future of American music, for he was a man who not only had the vision of a great ideal, but who also had the patience and fortitude to carry it through against great odds.

Mason's ancestors went all the way back to the early days of Puritan migration to America, to Thomas Mason who settled in the town of Medfield, Massachusetts, in 1653. Lowell was the son of Colonel Johnson Mason and Catherine Hartshorn, and was born in Medfield on January 8, 1792. His parents wisely encouraged the boy's growing fondness for music (he played both the organ and piano, as well as several instruments, including flute and clarinet), but, in keeping with the spirit of the day, they did not wish him to become a professional musician. When Lowell was twenty, he left for Savannah, Georgia, to take a position which had been offered him as a clerk in a bank.

Mason continued his study of music in Savannah after his banking hours, finding in F. L. Abel (typical of the many Germans who came to our shores in succeeding years) a capable teacher, and soon he became choirmaster and organist in the Independent Presbyterian Church. Mason was an apt student and he soon began to compose hymns and tunes, as well as anthems, which were good enough to be published in later years when Mason had an established reputation as a musician. It was during this period of study with Abel that Mason collected and edited a book of psalm and hymn tunes based on William Gardiner's *Sacred Melodies*. This work of Gardiner's was in six volumes, an English compilation, whose tunes for the religious verses were drawn from the instrumental works of Mozart, Haydn, and other similar composers, with the hope that such outstanding music would greatly improve the standard of English church music still under the domination of the clumsy verses to be found in the books of Sternhold and Hopkins, as well as Tate and Brady. Mason soon had an adequate collection prepared and decided to have it published. No printer in Savannah could handle the job, so Mason attempted to find a publisher in Boston or Philadelphia. Even though he asked no royalties, he had no success and was about to lay his book aside when he met a fine Boston musician—George K. Jackson—who was at that time the organist of the Handel and Haydn Society. Jackson at once saw the merits of the book and recommended its publication to the Society. *The Boston Handel and Haydn Society Collection of Church Music* (as it was newly named) went to press late in 1821 and was copyrighted on March 5, 1822. Mason's name did not appear as editor, for, as he explained later, he was a bank officer of standing in Savannah and he had no desire to become known as a musician and (at that time) not the slightest intention of attempting a career of music. The book had an immediate popularity, going through twenty-two editions from 1822 to 1858, selling more than 50,000 copies, and earning thousands of dollars which were divided between Mason and the Society. The book exerted a strong influence on the church music of America at that time.

When Mason had arranged the details of publication, he returned to Savannah, where he stayed five more years. He had married Abigail Gregory in 1817, and now had the responsibility of a growing family. But at last the call of music became too great, and in

July, 1827, he accepted an offer in Boston—at two thousand dollars a year—to lead the music in three churches. Had he done nothing else, his own hymn tunes, still cherished in the conservative hymn-books of the nation, might have kept his name alive, for they have brought comfort to countless thousands. The most familiar are: "Nearer my God to Thee" (*Bethany*), "My Faith looks up to Thee" (*Olivet*), and "From Greenland's icy mountains" (*Missionary Hymn*), and, of course, they are still sung.

Fate had further plans for Mason. At heart he was not only a reformer, but a true educator, and for him life began at forty. His years of teaching and directing (he had been honored with the presidency of the Handel and Haydn Society in 1827) began to make him increasingly aware that music's greatest value would come only if children could come in touch with it in the formative years of their lives, that is, in the schoolroom. Mason withdrew as president of the Handel and Haydn Society in 1832 so that he might have more time to teach vocal music to children and also to try out the Pestalozzian methods of teaching which the Reverend William C. Woodbridge—author of school geographies—had brought back from Europe. Mason had been quick to sense that what was being accomplished with other subjects might be successfully applied to the teaching of music, and he had begun trying out his ideas with the classes of vocal music which he held in the Bowdoin Street Church. The several hundred children who came to these classes were taught free of charge if they promised to attend for a year. At the same time the public school was coming to be recognized as a fundamental American institution, and Mason began to preach the right of every child to receive elementary instruction in music. The school boards did not welcome these revolutionary ideas and Mason knew that he would have to prove his theories, so he arranged a series of public concerts during the season of 1832-33 as a demonstration of his principles. So great was their success that on January 8, 1833, Mason and "an association of gentlemen" founded The Boston Academy of Music, which would be a work-shop for his ideas. Like all of Mason's earlier classes, the children would be taught free of charge if they were "over seven years of age, and engage[d] to continue in the school one year." The work grew so rapidly that George J. Webb (at that time organist of St. Paul's Church) was appointed associate professor and the end of the first season saw an incredible enrollment of five hundred students.

Mason had the ability to gather disciples and to impart his enthusiasm to others, and his Academy was a success from the beginning. The various boards of education grew more and more impressed as the children who had music became better students. By 1837, the idea was introduced into the schools, but the board neglected to appropriate any money to pay the teachers. Mason did not let this trouble him; he went on teaching, not only without pay, but also buying materials and music out of his own pocket.

After the first year's demonstration (1837-38), particularly the public concert by the scholars from South Boston's Hawes School in August, 1838, Mason was put in charge of the vocal music in Boston's public schools, and by action of the Boston School Committee on August 28, 1838, he was made the world's first superintendent of public school music. The report of the Board of Education in making this great step contained words of great moment, just as applicable today as they were over a century ago. From the middle of the 1836 memorial sent to the school committee, "praying that instruction in vocal Music be introduced into the Public schools of this City," came the following words:

> Now, the defect of our present system, admirable as that system is, is this, that it aims to develop the intellectual part of man's nature solely when for all the true purposes of life, it is of more importance, a hundredfold, to feel rightly than to think profoundly. Besides, human life must and ought to have its amusements. Through vocal music you set in motion a mighty power which silently, but surely, in the end, will humanize, refine and elevate a whole community.

This, then, was the spirit of New England, land of the Puritans, speaking. This was the final glory after two centuries of singing; the philosophy which had the wisdom to see man's need for music with its great humanizing qualities. The dream of Lowell Mason would attain its greatest fulfillment in the twentieth century, and set America finally apart from the world's other nations in this field of public service.

Mason's project continued to grow, and true educator that he was, he knew to keep going forward he must train teachers who could carry on through the years. He met the new challenge with his "musical conventions," where teachers might have an intensive two-week training period. Twelve came the first year, 1834; four years later there were brought together "ninety-six gentlemen and forty-two ladies" from all over New England and the states of New York, Ohio, Kentucky, as well as the District of Columbia; and by 1850 fifteen hundred registered. Mason also went to other cities, as far west as Rochester, New York, and Cleveland, Ohio, and down to Harrisburg, Pennsylvania. By this time he had made Boston self-sufficient, and with his work there at an end he went to Europe for fifteen months, lecturing in England on his new methods of music teaching.

Back in America in 1853, Mason made New York City the head-quarters for his business activities, and in the following summer, with George F. Root, Mason established another school of teacher-training—the New York Musical Normal Institute. The meetings and classes ran for three months, and Thomas Hastings and William B. Bradbury were members of the faculty. Mason bought a home on the side of the Orange Mountains in New Jersey, and he continued his activities until his death at the age of eighty, August 11, 1872. His sons carried on the musical traditions of the family, publishing music in New York, and later manufacturing the Mason & Hamlin pianos. The youngest son, William, became a prominent pianist and teacher, and Mason's grandson, Daniel Gregory Mason, became one of America's best-known symphonic composers in the early twentieth century.

Lowell Mason had opposition in his lifetime, and even after his work had borne fruit in Boston the intelligentsia of the day said that he and his fellow writers of hymn tunes were degrading and cheapening music. For a while the native American composers, those pioneers of whom we have already spoken, were forced to take a back seat, while the newer hymns, often merely an adaptation of melodies from the instrumental pieces of Haydn, Mozart, Weber, Rossini, and other eminent composers, began the uphold-ing of the European tradition which was to dominate most of the music of the nineteenth century. But Mason was the first to preach music for the masses, and he was responsible for the higher stand-ards of choral singing in America. He bridged the work of the old-fashioned traveling singing-teacher and the modern music school.

He was one of the most powerful and original personalities of the nineteenth century, and he did more, perhaps, than any other one man in his time to further the cause of American music.

"AMERICA"

It was through Mason's search for suitable songs for children of school age that *America*, or "My country 'tis of thee, sweet land of liberty," was written. Apparently the composer of the original tune, *God save the King* (or as sung today, *God save the Queen*), will never be known. No one has done more research on the history of the British National Anthem than the eminent scholar Percy A. Scholes, and he clears away, at long last, any idea that Henry Carey (*c.* 1690-1743) might have composed the words and music of *God save the King*. The earliest recorded accounts of the singing of the "Anthem" may be found in two London newspapers—the *Daily Advertiser* of September 30, 1745, and the *General Evening Post* of September 28-October 1, 1745—who reported to their readers:

> On Saturday Night last the Audience at the Theatre Royal in Drury Lane were agreeably surpriz'd by the Gentlemen belonging to that house performing the Anthem of *God save our noble King*.

The song had been arranged by the Drury Lane Theatre's musical director, Thomas Augustine Arne, one of England's most important eighteenth-century composers, whose autograph manuscript may still be seen today in the British Museum. The song had appeared in print the year before (the first known appearance) in the collection of songs *Thesaurus Musicus* (1744). The boldness of the air and the passionate quality of the words perfectly suited the mood of the Londoners, and other theaters were quick to take up the song. Thus it was that Charles Burney (that inimitable historian of the period), himself a pupil of Dr. Arne, made an arrangement for Covent Garden, while six weeks later, the Drury Lane audience heard:

A SONG MADE FOR THE GENTLEMEN VOLUNTEERS
OF THE CITY OF LONDON

Set to Music by Mr. Handel.

Dr. Scholes points out that the tune is obviously in the style of the popular galliard, a gay and rollicking dance in triple time, which had been a favorite since the sixteenth century, but the composer "has never been discovered, and . . . never will be." It might be a combination of folk song and an old carol, as well as a tune which was attributed to John Bull. It is a traditional song, into which various phrases have drifted from time to time, until the final song emerges, from whence, no one knows. The tune came to the colonies soon after it became popular in London, and it was well known at the time of Lyon's *Urania*, for he included it as *Whitefield's Tune*, set to the words "Come thou Almighty King," and thus gave it its first known printing in America. After the Declaration of Independence, many sets of words were sung to the tune, such as "God Save America," "God Save the Thirteen States," and upon Washington's election, "God Save the President" and "God Save Great Washington."

The familiar words "My country 'tis of thee" were written in 1831 by a young student, Samuel Francis Smith (who later became a minister), at the request of Lowell Mason. Smith later admitted (in a letter of June 5, 1887) that he had not composed his words with reference to any particular or special occasion, but Mason liked the verses and had the song sung at a celebration on July 4, 1831, by a group of school children. That Smith had found the tune in a collection of German and Danish songs attests to the wide popularity of the song, and his words, now familiar to every school child, are considered one of the most beautiful patriotic hymns ever written.

NEW ERA FOR THE MUSIC TRADES

New developments in music ushered in a new era for the music trades, as the publication of tune books, hymnals, chorus and anthem books reached an all-time high. As the cities in the North began to grow and great wealth was amassed from the extensive shipping and trade, especially with the Orient, the nation's population (thanks to the thousands of immigrants who continued to pour into the country) grew with phenomenal rapidity. It was at this time that the music industry, as such, began to emerge as a big business. The manufacture of pianos became important as William Knabe and Charles M. Stieff carried on the old-world traditions in

Baltimore. At the same time Boston had the piano firm of Jonas Chickering (1823), and New York that of the Steinway family (1853). The Steinway firm had the distinction of completing the evolution of the piano that had started with those produced in 1711 by Christofori in Italy. A. Babcock of Boston had introduced full cast-iron frames in 1825, and in 1830 cross-stringing made its appearance. This arrangement of the strings was not generally adopted until the Steinway pianos used the newer arrangement of the higher strings placed in the form of a fan, spreading over the largest part of the soundboard with the bass strings crossing them at a higher level. By mid-century, the manufacture of pianos was nearly a three million dollar business, along with which went the manufacture of band instruments, made by American craftsmen. At the same time many of the composers who were writing church music and songs for Sunday Schools were making large sums of money, which, as we look back today, is another indication of the burgeoning of American prosperity.

NEW HYMNS

Three men helped Mason establish his educational system in New York, but they are today remembered best for the hymn tunes they wrote. Thomas Hastings (1784-1872), who composed over a thousand hymn tunes, is best known for the tune *Toplady (Rock of Ages, cleft for me)*. Hastings had published his *Utica Collection* in 1816, and in 1822 the first edition of his *Dissertation on Musical Taste*. In 1823 he went to Utica, New York—at that time an unusually musical community—where he became editor for *The Western Recorder*, a religious paper. He returned to New York City in 1832, where he remained active as choirmaster in various churches until his death in 1872. George James Webb (1803-1887) arrived in Boston from England in 1830, and was appointed organist of St. Paul's Church. He was appointed associate professor in Mason's Academy the first season and went on to New York with Mason, gave normal courses for teachers at Binghamton, New York, and left his best-known hymn tune, *Webb (Stand up, stand up for Jesus)* for us to remember him by. Mason's youngest pupil and disciple, William Batchelder Bradbury (1816-1868), came from York, Maine. He had a deep understanding of children, and he left them a priceless legacy of Sunday School hymns: *Aughton (He leadeth me);* *Woodworth (Just as I am, without one plea); Bradbury (Savior, like a shepherd lead me);* and *Consolation, Walford, Sweet Hour (Sweet hour of prayer).*

THE FIRST PERMANENT ORCHESTRA:
THE PHILHARMONIC SOCIETY OF NEW YORK

New York, artistically stimulated by assuming the cultural leadership of American cities through the writers, actors, and musicians who filled her places of entertainment, was the home of many excellent societies. Up to 1842, the most important of these was the Sacred Music Society, which presented Handel's *Messiah* in 1831, and the American première of Mendelssohn's *St. Paul* in 1838 (when the work was only two years old). An orchestra of twenty-seven accompanied this chorus, which consisted of some sixty members. Unfortunately, New York's critics did not write too kindly of the Mendelssohn oratorio, passing the overture off as "good," and the now-famous aria "But the Lord is mindful of His own" as "untunable, a very poor air." The Society's career reached its climax in 1839 with a "Great Union Performance" in the Broadway Tabernacle, when choirs from surrounding towns—a thousand singers in all—gave a gala concert.

The leader of the Society at this time was Ureli Corelli Hill (1802-1875), a native of Connecticut, who had studied in Germany with Ludwig Spohr. Hill returned to America and settled in New York, where, if he was not a great musician, he was at least energetic and enthusiastic about the city's musical life, and exerted a lasting influence. One of his musical ventures, which was to be of far greater moment than he could have dreamed, was a "Musical Solemnity," which was given in 1839 in memory of Daniel Schlesinger—a German pianist who had been living in New York. The concert, which was mostly orchestral, was so well received that Hill and some of his colleagues felt the time might be ripe for the establishment of a permanent orchestra. With Hill as the leading spirit, a new organization called the Philharmonic Society of New York, gave its first concert on December 7, 1842, at the Apollo Rooms, on Broadway. These rooms had for some time been a popular resort for genteel entertainments, dances, and parties. There were no chairs, so the audience sat on hard benches and in uncomfortable pews. Not only was the concert a success, it was the actual beginning of the present New York Philharmonic-Symphony, the third oldest permanent orchestra in the world. Only the Leipzig Gewandhaus Orchestra (1781), and the Societé des Concerts du Conservatoire in Paris (1792), are older. Until the next century the orchestra was a cooperative venture on the part of the musicians. Whatever money was left after expenses of hall rental, program printing, and other such items were paid, the players divided equally, with deductions for missed rehearsals. With a membership of about sixty-three, the first season of three concerts netted each player twenty-five dollars apiece.

The inaugural program—which was repeated when the orchestra's centennial was celebrated—included Beethoven's Fifth Symphony and Weber's Overture to *Oberon,* mixed with an assortment of vocal, chamber, and orchestral pieces. In the second season the new orchestra gave four concerts, and seventeen years later the number was increased to five.

THE SINGING FAMILIES

The New England singing families who toured the country from 1840 to 1860 were a typical American institution but their roots were deep in Europe. In the 1820s and 1830s small ensembles of folk singers from the Bavarian, Austrian, and Swiss Alps roamed the continent of Europe, yodeling and fiddling their music in the beer gardens and concert halls. The Rainer Family were one of the earliest vocal groups, having great success on their first tour in 1824, and becoming the rage of London during the 1827-28 season. In 1839 some of their relatives came to America, where they toured for four years. They made their headquarters in Boston for the season of 1840-41 and were highly praised by Lowell Mason, who held them up as models during the years that he and his disciples were trying to awaken Mr. Average American to the pleasures of choral singing.

Among the most famous of the American singing families were the Hutchinson and Baker families of New Hampshire and the Cheney Family of Vermont. Each troupe usually consisted of four singers, including one or two women, and they sang wherever they could get an audience—in concert halls, churches, and even in barns. The music they sang was not great, for it was designed to appeal to the masses. It was not folk music (as we know it today), but rather "ballads" of every description—sentimental, dramatic, comic, and realistic—and the singers wrote their own verses and sometimes their tunes.

In Europe medieval ballads were originally dancing songs, but as early as the thirteenth century they lost their dance connotation, and became stylized forms of solo song. In England there was still a further development, and by the sixteenth century, the "ballad" came to mean a simple story told in verses. Characteristically it had many verses, either with or without a refrain, and was simple and unaffected. In nineteenth-century America, the ballad became a popular song which usually combined narrative and romantic elements, often mixed with the morbidly gruesome. In the twentieth century the term "ballad" is applied to almost any type of sentimental song, particularly those of Tin-Pan Alley, many of which are meretricious, while others, especially those of Broadway's musicals and Hollywood's better movies, are of the finest contemporary writing of the type.

The Hutchinson family—one of the best known and most popular of these groups—had a farm in Milford, New Hampshire. They started their concertizing about 1842, and they used their singing to further the social causes they devoutly believed in—abolitionism, temperance, revivalism, and so on. The songs, as entertainment, gained them audiences, but the message was the important thing. Longfellow, William Lloyd Garrison, and Frederick Douglass admired the Hutchinsons for their championship of the Negro. One of their best-known songs of this type was called *Get Off the Track*. The programs of the Hutchinsons seem allied to the radio shows of the present century, for they used a theme song, *The Old Granite State*, to open and close all their concerts.

A modern counterpart of these family groups is seen in the Trapp Family Singers, who have spread their native Austrian folk songs and carols, as well as the fine religious and secular music of the best German composers, throughout America.

THE MINSTREL SHOWS

In the realm of the theater there was yet another manifestation of this era of singing, one which has been called America's most individual contribution to the theater—that of Negro minstrelsy. This impersonation of Negroes in action and song by white men was thoroughly American in its origin and development, and, making its appearance around 1820, lasted well into the twentieth century. It came at a time when the theaters were still offering a variety of mixed entertainment in one evening—short dramas, farces, dances, and songs. Black-face acts came to be included, and from them various types of Negro impersonations developed. One type might be in ragged clothes, typifying the Southern plantation worker, while the other—the dandy—portrayed the Northern Negro, who, with his ridiculous effects, seemed to be trying to imitate the white man.

The man who first popularized the type, and now known as "the father of American minstrelsy," was Thomas Dartmouth ("Daddy" or "Jim Crow") Rice (1808-1860), who started the idea more or less spontaneously by borrowing an old Negro's clothes and imitating his singing of *Jim Crow*. The favorite impersonation of the Northern Negro was that of the "Broadway swell," who swaggered about the stage in his modish coat, or "long-tail blue," wearing a silk hat, flourishing a walking cane, all the while boasting of his conquests among the ladies, and his song was one of the earliest and most popular of all the minstrel songs—*Long Tail Blue*.

The banjo became one of the favorite instruments of the minstrel shows. The earlier Negroes had played a type of gourd banjo, which was known variously as a "bonja," "banga," or "bamjar." The banjo as we know it today was said to have been created by Joel Walker Sweeney (1813-1860) in 1830 by cutting an old cheesebox in two, covering the half with skin and stringing it with five strings. Many believe this story to be a myth, but nevertheless the black-face solo banjoist became popular and the music that he played, often syncopated, was to have its share in the evolution of that larger body of secular Negro music: ragtime. Along with the popularity of the solo banjo performer came the solo "Negro" dancer. The early jigs and clogs that were danced by the black-face impersonators to currently popular songs were a mixture of Irish and Scotch dances that had been popular with the Western boatmen and backwoods-men, and now were done with all the gestures and quips of the Negro. Equally popular were the traditional fiddle "breakdowns," one of the favorites being *Zip Coon,* a minstrel song which later became popular as the fiddle tune *Turkey in the Straw.* These dances were characterized by comic jumps, and a heel-and-toe tech-nique which anticipated modern tap dancing, and by the end of the century the virtuoso footwork of such dancers as William Henry Lane (billed as Master Juba) set a standard for artistic brilliance. The climax of the minstrel performance was the "walk-around," consisting of two sections of about equal length. The first section consisted of a song in which solo passages alternate with recurrent choral ejaculations. The second section, with its competitive danc-ing in the maze of a circle, was patterned after the dancing of the Negroes in the compounds of the great Southern plantations.

From the early 1840s on, small groups of "Negro" performers ap-peared in increasing numbers on the stage and in the circus ring, in all kinds of combinations. Comic scenes or skits called "Negro extravaganzas" were often included, as well as "Negro" plays which were longer and had larger casts. These became featured as "Ethi-opian Operas" and were the successors of the English ballad operas and the forerunners of the later musical comedies.

In 1843, the first minstrel band—an early "jazz" band—made its appearance, and with it came the first full-fledged minstrel show. A troupe called the Virginia Minstrels was the first to become suc-cessful. Daniel Decatur Emmett ("Old Dan Emmit" of *Dixie* fame) was the leader of the band, playing the fiddle, with Billy Whitlock playing the banjo, Frank Brower the bones, and Dick Pelham the tambourine. Bones, a plantation instrument, were clackers of bone struck together, somewhat in the manner of castanets. These men performed in a semicircle, with the bone and tambourine players at either end. Their programs consisted of songs, banjo solos, comic stump speeches, jokes, and breezy repartee. As the shows grew more stereotyped and had more performers, the man in the middle was generally in white-face and was called the interlocutor. The first full-length show of the Virginia Minstrels was given on March 7, 1843, at the Masonic Temple in Boston. Other companies soon appeared, the bands grew to about a dozen players, and modern instruments were added.

E. P. Christy, who was born in Philadelphia in 1815, became for a time the unchallenged leader of his profession, and his group—the Christy Minstrels—after appearing in 1846 in New York at Palmo's Opera House, opened the following year in Mechanics' Hall (on Broadway), where they played almost continuously for ten years. Christy's and other important minstrel troupes had a great vogue in Europe in the middle and latter part of the nineteenth century. The name Christy became so generic (for after copying the original pattern as set by the Virginia Minstrels, it was Christy that gave the minstrel show its stereotyped form) that the English called all Ethiopian performers "Christys" or "Christy Minstrels." Many English cockneys tried to imitate American minstrel performers by blacking their faces and presenting minstrel acts in Paris cafés and elsewhere in Europe.

The music of the minstrels was taken from anything that might serve their purpose. They borrowed as freely from folk music as from Italian opera, fitting to the tunes their own dialect words. But more important still was the creation of their own music, which, in a few years, proved to be more indigenously American than the works of more learned composers. The early songs of the 1820s and 1830s show the style of eighteenth-century opera buffa, while others, like *Zip Coon,* cannot hide their Irish origin. As the years passed, however, they all blended into something that bore the flavor of the American scene—nonchalant humor, brevity, sturdiness, and the inflection of Negro dialect or everyday slang. How much the Southern slaves contributed to this style is difficult to ascertain. Perhaps the greatest influence was that of rhythm rather than melody. Banjo jigs, and variants of songs, full of tricky syncopations, were all a part of Negro minstrelsy.

What was important, as these troupes played on small country stages, dimly lit by guttering candles, or in the flickering gaslight of the large cities, was the bold comic quality of nonsense, which had not developed elsewhere in American humor, and which was to prove more times than can be counted one of America's saving graces. Before they passed entirely out of the picture, the minstrel-show tunes were to lead into one of the most important types of American music—ragtime.

Daniel Decatur Emmett

The outstanding composer of the texts and tunes of the first minstrel shows was Daniel Decatur Emmett (1815-1904), famous today for his *Dixie*. The son of early Virginia pioneers, he was born and grew up in Mount Vernon, Ohio, where he worked as a newspaper printer. When he was seventeen he joined the army as a fifer, where he had his only musical training: learning to read music, and to play the drum under John J. Clark. He first appeared in public in 1841 as a black-face singer and banjoist in a circus ring. He eventually arrived in New York and was seen in a variety of shows and circuses before he became the leader of the Virginia Minstrels. By 1858 he was a member of Bryant's Minstrels, Christy's principal rival, and it was for this troupe that he wrote *Dixie* in 1859. The story of that song is told in the chapter on Civil War songs. Emmett wrote hundreds of songs, many of which became the popular songs of the day, such as *De Boatman's Dance; I'm Gwine Ober de Mountains; Jordan is a Hard Road to Trabbel; Old Dan Tucker;* and *Johnny Roach.*

STEPHEN FOSTER

"Dear friends and gentle hearts"—the words were scribbled on a slip of paper, and were found in the pockets of a man who had just died. The "gentle heart" of Stephen Collins Foster (1826-1864), America's first poet of song, had ceased to beat, and his sensitive soul had returned to his Maker. The few pennies found along with the scrap of paper merely highlighted the terrible tragedy of Foster's last years; years of poverty and suffering, of seeking forgetfulness in drink; years which were like a steady and inexorable decrescendo from the climax of the early golden days down to the last despairing silence.

His Gift of Melody

Foster's gift of melody was akin to that of Schubert. He accomplished with his scanty musical training what many of our well-trained musicians failed to do. Unconsciously, and without any attempt at nationalism, Foster wrote into his simple and poignant songs the flavor and characteristic traits peculiar to America. He captured for all time this period of secular song, and his genius still shines like a star in the firmament.

Early Influences

Foster was born in Lawrenceville, Pennsylvania, near Pittsburgh, on July 4, the day the United States was exactly fifty years old. On the same day, two great American patriots died—John Adams and Thomas Jefferson—yet who could foretell that the name of Foster would some day stand beside theirs in America's Hall of Fame? Stephen showed an early interest in music. His family had no objection to music, but they felt it was no way of earning a living, and the increasingly popular minstrel shows were definitely not for a conservative, simple people. Living so far inland, Foster had not the foreign influences he would have had in the East. As he grew older he knew best the songs of these current minstrel shows, and the tunes he heard whistled and sung along the wharves of the Ohio River. He also became familiar with the sentimental songs of the singing families, and the hymns and spirituals from the camp meetings.

His First Songs

Foster may have had a little music study with a Pittsburgh musician and music dealer, Henry Kleber, but it was for such a short while that his writing was almost entirely instinctive. So it was that he dreamed through his youthful days, scribbling down his tunes, until, when he was seventeen, he had a song accepted and published—*Open Thy Lattice, Love*, set to George P. Morris' poem. When he was twenty Stephen moved to Cincinnati, to work as a bookkeeper for his brother, Dunning, but he still worked over his beloved songs. It was in the Ohio city that he met a publisher friend of the family, W. C. Peters, and he virtually made him a gift of some new songs: *Old Uncle Ned, Oh! Susanna*, and two others, which were published as *Songs of the Sable Harmonists*. The first two songs became immediate hits, and Foster obviously gained enough fame from them (it is said his publisher made over ten thousand dollars from the songs) to encourage him to give up bookkeeping and make a business of writing songs. His reputation soon grew to the extent that publishers sought him out, and he chose two firms to issue his music on a royalty basis: Firth, Pond and Company, New York; and F. D. Benteen of Baltimore. By 1849 Foster was a full-time composer, writing both the words and music of his songs.

From 1850 to 1860 were Foster's golden years, when page after page of manuscript was filled, waiting to be released into magical sound. Most of his best songs date from this decade, which ended with *Old Black Joe*, published in 1860. Gradually Stephen's inspiration seemed to wane, and the later songs lacked the spark and vitality of the earlier ones. Here, too, began the real tragedy, for it was too late for Foster to learn to write with the mind as well as the heart, and there were no outside inspirations that could challenge and stimulate him and cause him to grow and deepen as a composer. Soon the "evil propensities" that his father had feared became realities, and Stephen had nothing with which to fight them.

Foster's marriage was not always happy, although he worshiped his wife and daughter. Jane Denny McDowell, whose father was a Pittsburgh physician, had been an amateur singer and a member of the Stephen Foster Quartet that gathered to sing at the Foster home and for which Stephen wrote many of his early songs. He and Jane were married in 1850, the year of his first successes. At times he was unable to support her, and there were apparently two separations.

"Old Folks at Home"

In the meantime Foster tunes and melodies were heard everywhere. A writer in the *Albany State Register* (1852), less than a year after the immortal *Old Folks at Home* was published, gave an account of the incredible popularity of the song:

> *Old Folks at Home* the *last* negro melody, is on everybody's tongue, and consequently in everybody's mouth. Pianos and organs groan with it, night and day; sentimental young ladies sing it; sentimental young gentlemen warble it in midnight serenades; volatile young "bucks" hum it in the midst of their business and their pleasures; boatmen roar it out stentorially at all times; all the bands play it; amateur flute players agonize over it at every spare moment; the street organs grind it out at every hour; the "singing stars" carol it on the theatrical boards, and at concerts; the chamber maid sweeps and dusts to the measured cadence of *Old Folks at Home;* the butcher's boy

treats you to a strain or two of it as he hands in the steaks for dinner; the milk-man mixes it up strangely with the harsh ding-dong accompaniment of his tireless bell; there is not a "live darkey", young or old, but can whistle, sing, dance and play it, and throw in "Ben Bolt" by way of good seasoning; indeed at every hour, at every turn, we are forcibly impressed with the interesting fact, that—

> "Way down upon de Swanee ribber
>   Far, far away,
>   Dere's whar my heart is turnin ebber
>   Dere's whar de old folk stay."

Relations with Minstrel Performers

Such popularity strikingly shows the influence of the theater entertainments of those days. The minstrel shows had used so many of Foster's songs that the Christy troupe finally asked for the privilege of being the first to sing them. For ten dollars a song, Foster permitted E. P. Christy that right, and on several occasions, for an extra five dollars, Foster permitted Christy's name to appear as composer, instead of his own. This very thing had happened with *Old Folks at Home*, for the simple truth was that Foster was at first not very proud of writing Negro dialect songs. The song's later success caused Foster to ask permission for his own name to appear, but Christy refused. It is known now that Foster never saw the Suwanee River. He and his brother found the name on a map and it sounded better than the "Pedee" he had used in his first draft of the song.

Last Years

As Foster's musical star began to set, his income grew less, and there was never enough money for his needs. While he was not actually exploited by his publishers (he got the usual two or three cents a copy on all music sold), he borrowed more and more ahead, and soon was constantly overdrawn. In 1860, with new contracts, he moved with his wife and daughter to New York, hoping for better days. But the new songs did not sell, and many were returned by the publishers, whereupon Foster had to sell them outright for small amounts to other publishers who wanted his name in their catalogues. He began to have recurrent spells of "fever and ague" (which may have been malaria or tuberculosis), and his drinking increased. When there was no money on which to live, Jane left him to take a job as a telegrapher in Greensburg, Pennsylvania. In January, 1864, weak and ill in a cheap lodging house on the Bowery, Foster fell in a faint across his washbasin, breaking it as he lost consciousness, the broken pieces gashing his throat. He was taken to Bellevue Hospital, but he never recovered, and died there on January 13, a spent and beaten man.

The tattered slip of paper reading "Dear friends and gentle hearts," might well have been the beginning of his last will and testament, the legacy of golden song he left to the people of America. He had reformed the minstrel song of his day, salvaging it from the crude and vulgar ditties which reeked of the alleys and barrooms, and in so doing, he caught the humor and spirit of the America of his day.

His Two Hundred Songs

Foster composed over two hundred songs, and a few instrumental pieces. The songs fall into several types. Among the so-called "Ethiopian" songs are the nonsense type—*Oh! Susanna, Camptown Races, Ring de Banjo;* and the homesick plantation songs *Old Folks at Home, My Old Kentucky Home, Old Black Joe, Massa's in de Cold Ground.* The best of the sentimental ballads, in the style of the English lyric ballads that had been so popular in America, are *Jeanie With the Light Brown Hair* and *Come Where my Love Lies Dreaming.* His Civil War and other topical songs, comic songs of the English music-hall type, and Sunday School hymns were the least interesting musically, nor did they last. But what matter? There were more than enough songs that would live on.

Posthumous Tributes

In 1940, Foster became the first musician to be elected to the Hall of Fame at New York University. By act of Congress in 1951, January 13 was made an annual Stephen Foster Day, and, most impressive of all, on the campus of the University of Pittsburgh there is the Stephen Foster Memorial, which houses the collection of Fosteriana assembled by Josiah K. Lilly of Indianapolis.

THE NEW ENGLAND RENAISSANCE

In the years before the Civil War, America witnessed at long last, after two centuries, the final flowering of the Puritan intellectual tradition. All fields were affected—history, philosophy, poetry, fiction, and to a lesser degree, music. No period in America's history has been more brilliant, nor has surpassed those glorious years of Cambridge and Concord. It was America's first "Golden Age," and into it went many currents. There was greater freedom in religion, and America, now less under the domination of European culture, was awakening.

It would not be until the end of the century that Boston would become the leader of the nation's musical life, and music still lagged behind the literary and cultural development that had its climax around the middle of the century. We shall see in the succeeding sketches of individual composers that many were to use the novels of Hawthorne, the poetry of Whittier and Longfellow, and the dreams and thoughts of Thoreau as inspiration for operas, cantatas, and orchestral pieces, but none of them grasped the essence of this golden era as did Charles Ives, coming nearly fifty years later. Ives had a spiritual affinity, a freedom of thought and creation, that was the embodiment of New England's renaissance, and when we meet him further on, we will discover that he achieved in his music what the earlier group had achieved in their writing and philosophies.

THE EXPANDING WEST

The West was at the same time coming to life. Long trails were pushing toward the Pacific. The "Great Emigration" to Oregon had started in 1843; California was finally wrested from Mexico in 1846; in 1847 the Mormons settled in the valley of the great Salt Lake. When gold was discovered in California at Sutter's Mill on January 24, 1848, men began to swarm there from the four corners of the earth.

From 1848 on, there was another flood of foreign musicians making their way to America. Europe had been torn with wars and revolutions, and many of the lesser musicians came to America, a younger and freer country, where already there were relatives and friends.

As important as the great New England writers were the outstanding political figures of the day—Calhoun, Clay, and Webster—playing their last roles in the debates of 1850, as to whether the Southern states should secede, or whether there should be a compromise between the North and the South. We shall meet Daniel Webster in the Stephen Vincent Benét story that Douglas Moore made into an opera—*The Devil and Daniel Webster*—which was first performed in 1939. He is also one of many important figures in the opera that Virgil Thomson wrote to Gertrude Stein's libretto, *The Mother of Us All,* in 1947.

As America's population began to move into the new West, the inland towns and cities began to grow. The cultural life of these growing centers was greatly enhanced by the advent of immigrant musicians, predominantly German. It was these journeymen musicians who traveled the highways (as the older artisans had done a century before), playing in orchestras, conducting choral societies, and giving lessons, who were so important for the middle West. St. Louis may thank them for giving her a music store, that of Charles Balmer and C. Henry Weber, which was to become one of the largest in the West, as music publishing flourished mightily in the years before the Civil War.

Fort Dearborn, Illinois, became the incorporated village of Chicago in 1833, with six hundred residents, and within a year had established the Old Settlers' Harmonic Society. Chicago's first glimpse of opera was brought by boat, over the lake from the city of Milwaukee. This small touring company gave Bellini's *La Somnambula* on July 9, 1850, and within the decade Chicagoans saw such novelties as Verdi's newest operas: *Rigoletto, La Traviata,* and *Il Trovatore;* Bellini's *Norma;* and Mozart's *Don Giovanni.* Milwaukee had the Moravian musician Hans Balatka to direct its newly formed Musikverein, and when the annual Northwest Saengerfest was held in Chicago in 1857, he conducted that also. Minneapolis, a mere town at that time, had a singing school in the village of St. Anthony, and when the city was opened for settlement in 1855, most of the people who came there were Germans and Scandinavians. There were visits of the Hutchinson Family Singers in those years, as well as Emmett's minstrel troupe.

San Francisco had its musicians soon after the discovery of gold at Sutter's Mill in 1848. In 1850 came Henri Herz, a Viennese pianist, to give a concert. Opera was the first love of the new city of the West, and in 1852 San Francisco had its first opera season. Although the population of some twenty-five thousand was principally male, the Pellegrini opera troupe sang *La Somnambula, Norma, Ernani* and *La Favorita* for them. By 1854, incredible as it may seem, there were eleven different series of opera in the city.

GEORGE PEABODY CREATES THE FIRST FOUNDATION
TO ENCOURAGE THE ARTS

In Baltimore a most important event took place in 1857, when George Peabody, wealthy merchant and philanthropist, established a foundation for the advancement of the arts. He wished to establish an institute that would consist of a library, a school of lectures, an art gallery, and an academy of music. Peabody's gift was one of the first important bequests that were to inspire the donations of Enoch Pratt (whose home now houses the original revised draft of *The Star Spangled Banner*) and Johns Hopkins, whose medical school became one of the greatest in the world. These were but the first of a long series of such gifts from wealthy art patrons all over the country. The Peabody Institute building was started in 1860, on the site of the marble yard where had been fashioned the blocks that went into Baltimore's famous monument to George Washington, which the school was to face. Unfortunately, the Civil War delayed the completion of the building and the school's opening until 1868.

PHILADELPHIA'S ACADEMY OF MUSIC

The same year of Peabody's bequest, Philadelphia celebrated a gala event, when the building of the present Academy of Music was opened with a gala ball, January 26, 1857. Opera was very popular in the city, and audiences had witnessed the American première of Mozart's *Magic Flute* in 1832, given by the Musical Fund Society's opera group. With the new Academy of Music, there were a series of brilliant opera seasons (beginning with a performance of Verdi's *Il Trovatore* on February 25, 1857). The orchestra's concertmaster for the German operas was young Theodore

Thomas, who from that time on was to divide his time between the Quaker City and New York.

The years before the country was to be plunged into the horrors of civil war seemed happy ones indeed, and they were given a gaiety and color by the small orchestras and bands that came over from Europe, as had the yodelers and singers of a few years before. One such group was the Steyermark Orchestra of eighteen players, under the leadership of Francis Riha. Their music was light—operatic airs, marches, and galops—and they did not survive for long. When they disbanded Riha stayed in America, and became a member of the famous Mendelssohn Quintette Club in Boston.

In 1848 a small orchestra of about twenty-five players came to America from Germany and toured the country for half a dozen years. They called themselves the Germania Orchestra, but they were familiarly known as the Germanians. It was a unique group, for it was the only orchestra which had daily rehearsals (unheard of in this country at that time) and its programs included the finest music—as the overtures to Wagner's *Tannhäuser* and Mendelssohn's *A Midsummer Night's Dream*—which it performed with a finesse and polish new to American audiences. When the Germanians finally disbanded, their flute player, Carl Zerrahn, went on to Boston, where he made his home and became one of the greatest influences for fine music in the city. He led one of the orchestras there, which was known as the Philharmonic, from 1855 to 1863, and after that conducted the concerts of the Harvard Musical Association, which had been formed in 1837. This last group had been started to raise the standards of music at the University through concerts, and to prepare the way for a professorship of music there, as well as to collect scores for a music library. In this respect the Society was a direct predecessor of the Boston Symphony Orchestra, which would be founded in 1881. Some idea of Zerrahn's activities may be imagined when it is realized that he also conducted the Handel and Haydn Society for over forty years, as well as the Worcester (Massachusetts) Festival for more than thirty years. Boston, already basking in the glory of her great poets and writers, was slowly assuming the cultural leadership which not too many years before had centered in New York, and the city was to reign supreme in the realm of American music for many years to come.

One of the most important of all the musical cities at this time was Cincinnati, Ohio, where there had been a Haydn Society as early as 1819. Excellent bands and singing schools had existed there at the turn of the century, and it was one of the first cities outside of New England to have music in the public schools. Concerts had been given by German musicians all through the Ohio Valley, and on down through the smaller Southern cities as far as New Orleans.

THE TRAVELING VIRTUOSI

An interesting phenomenon of these years may be found in the almost incessant travels of the visiting virtuosi, and the worship of stars that beset America early in the 1800s. Life in the smaller cities had little artistic variety, and so the coming of the musical or literary celebrity, much publicized in the newspapers of the day, made of each visit a social event of major importance. Charles Dickens was only twenty-nine when he paid his first visit to America in the 1840s, and he received an adulation which in his own country would have been given only to royalty.

Ole Bull

One of the greatest favorites with American audiences of the day was a Norwegian violinist Ole Bull (1810-1880). He came to America in 1843, and although he may have resorted to tricks to impress his audiences he was a fine musician and an excellent violinist. In his five visits he became a legendary figure, and soon became so popular that he was frequently caricatured in the minstrel shows as Ole Bull and Ole Dan Tucker. His first tour lasted for two years, and from his two hundred concerts in the Eastern cities and states —including even Havana—he made about $100,000. One of his favorite tricks was to play on all four strings at the same time, and he never divulged his secret. Whether he accomplished this with a loosely strung bow, or a flat bridge, or merely through colossal strength will ever remain a mystery.

Ole Bull returned in 1852. This time he stayed for five years, and toured through the Middle West, and on to California, still in its first flush of excitement over the finding of gold. In the party was a child prodigy by the name of Adelina Patti.

Of the many ideas which Ole Bull hoped to carry out in the new country, one was for a Norwegian colony in Pennsylvania, but he merely became the victim of two sharpers who all but ruined him. In 1855 he attempted to manage an opera company in New York at the newly opened Academy of Music, and even went so far as to offer a prize of one thousand dollars for an American opera by an American composer on an American subject, but the company failed before the contest could be carried through.

Jenny Lind

It is doubtful if any event in the history of American music created the furor of Jenny Lind's debut in New York in 1850. The Swedish Nightingale, as she was called, was already a great favorite in London, a plain little lady with an angelic voice. Deeply religious by nature, she eventually abandoned opera and stage life because she felt it was too immoral. She was a consummate artist, beloved of musicians and the masses alike. Lind was a favorite of Mendelssohn, whose music she sang, and Clara Schumann called her "a pure, true artist soul!"

Phineas Taylor (P. T.) Barnum, the man who created our American circus and who still might tell modern press agents a thing or two, and who had made a fortune in managing Tom Thumb and other freaks, decided to broaden his activities and become a musical impresario. He conceived the idea of bringing Jenny Lind to America, first to make money, as he knew he would, but also to show that he could offer something that was not pure humbug. To convince the diva Lind that he meant business (for she mistrusted him), Barnum had to guarantee her a thousand dollars each for one hundred and fifty concerts, pay all of her expenses, and deposit $187,500 in cash with his London bankers as security for the fulfillment of the contract.

In New York tickets to Lind's debut concert were auctioned off for charity and some brought several hundred dollars apiece. The affair was held at Castle Garden on September 11, 1850, and its program was typical of the day. Singers rarely gave a recital, but appeared two or three times and the remainder of the evening was devoted to assisting artists and orchestral music. Jenny Lind made

over $100,000 during her two years in America, touring in the East
and West, conquering wherever she went.

Other great singers of the day included Maria Malibran, daughter
of the Manuel García who gave New York its first Italian opera, and
Henriette Sontag, who had sung in the first performance of Beethoven's Ninth Symphony, had made a great success in opera, and
was a sensation in concert before going on to sing in opera in Mexico
City.

Louis Moreau Gottschalk

The pianists of the day included Henri Herz (who had appeared
in California), and was typical of the salon-type performer so popular in Paris, as well as Sigismund Thalberg, whose stunts at the
keyboard were much more appreciated then his fine musicianship.
The king of them all, however, was an American, Louis Moreau
Gottschalk, who was born in the teeming and brilliantly colorful
city of New Orleans on May 8, 1829. His father, Edward Gottschalk,
was an Englishman who had studied medicine in Leipzig, and had
arrived in New Orleans when he was about twenty-five, where he
met and married the charming and beautiful Aimée Marie de
Bruslé, a Creole whose European parentage had been a mixture of
French and Spanish nobility. Because of his precocious talent, little
Moreau was given music lessons when he was three years old.
When he was six, he was able to substitute for the organist of one
of the churches, and at eight he gave a public concert for the benefit
of one of the violinists from the French opera in New Orleans. He
was thirteen when he was sent to Paris, where he studied with
Charles Hallé, Camille-Marie Stamaty, and Maledan, and eventually became a pupil of Hector Berlioz, who had taken the city by
storm only a few years before with his *Fantastic Symphony*. Paris
was brilliant in these years with the breath-taking piano technique
of the handsome Franz Liszt, and the exquisite sounds which
Frédéric Chopin was evoking from the keyboard. It was Chopin
who predicted that Gottschalk would soon become a "king of pianists," as he actually did, for he became the first of America's matinee
idols, combining the role of pianist, composer, and beau ideal.

Gottschalk, through his grandaunt, the Marquise de la Grange,
was admitted to the most exclusive circles of French society and
quickly became a favorite of royalty. He began playing his own

compositions, some of which were published when he was only fifteen and which were built around many of the Creole tunes he knew so well. One of these, *La Bamboula,* was written about 1845, when he was recovering from an attack of typhoid fever, and was to become one of the most popular of all his piano pieces.

In 1850, and for the next two years, Gottschalk made a series of concert tours through France and Spain. It was while he was in Spain that he is thought to have composed *The Banjo,* "Fantaisie grotesque," about 1851. Other important works of these youthful years are *La Savane, Le Bananier, Midnight in Seville, The Siege of Saragossa,* and *Jota Aragonesa.*

When he returned to America in 1852, Gottschalk's debut in Niblo's Garden, New York, on February 10, 1853, was a sensation, equal to Lind's recital of a year and a half before. Barnum immediately tried to manage Gottschalk, offering him $20,000 a year, but the pianist wisely refused, knowing he could make more on his own. During the winter of 1855-56 he toured extensively, but managed to give no less than eighty concerts in New York alone! Then he began to tour the frontier towns of the West, where he would often have to endure the coarse jests and jibes from certain groups in his audiences. Gottschalk was actually a fine musician, and a superb pianist, but Americans were mostly interested in seeing how fast his fingers could move over the keys. He was idolized by the women of his audiences, who, like the twentieth-century bobby-soxers, would rush up to the piano and tear to shreds his white gloves, which he always wore onto the stage. In his home town of New Orleans, the ladies would line the steps up to the second floor where he practiced, hoping to hear and see their idol. Unfortunately, the audiences of the day clamored for the light salon music which Gottschalk featured on his programs, and he once told a friend that he dared not play the classics "because the dear public don't [sic] want to hear me play it." They much preferred such pieces as *The Last Hope* (still heard today as a hymn tune), *The Dying Poet,* and *The Banjo,* in which he used the melody of *Roll, Jordan Roll,* almost identical with Stephen Foster's refrain in *Camptown Races.* It was all music of the Victorian era, heard in London and Paris, as well as in America. It reflected the gay, lighthearted days before the dark pall of war hung over the country.

In between the hundreds of concerts he gave throughout the

United States and Canada, Gottschalk made several trips to Cuba, the first apparently in 1853. Six of the years before he sailed to South America, from whence he would never return, were spent as a vagabond. In his *Notes of a Pianist* he said: "I have wandered at random, yielding myself up indolently to the caprice of Fortune, giving a concert wherever I happened to find a piano, sleeping wherever night overtook me . . ."

In 1865 Gottschalk sailed for South America, where he was to receive perhaps the greatest adulation of his career, in Buenos Aires, and especially in Rio de Janeiro. It was here that the composer was stricken while conducting a great music festival. He was taken to Tijuca, a neighboring village, where he died a few days later, on December 18, 1869. His body lay in state in the auditorium of the Philharmonic Society of Rio de Janeiro, and after impressive tributes, was taken for burial outside the city, in the cemetery of St. John the Baptist. In 1870 Gottschalk's remains were brought back to New York, and he was buried in Greenwood Cemetery, Brooklyn.

There is a decidedly Latin-American flavor in the music of Gottschalk's last years, as a result of his sojourn in the Caribbean. They are effective piano pieces and include: *Di que si (Réponds-moi!), La Gallina, Souvenir de Cuba, Souvenir de la Havane.* A manuscript score was recently found in Cuba, comprising a two-movement symphony, *La Noche de los Trópicos (The Night of the Tropics).* It is now a part of the New York Public Library's Collection of Musical Americana. The first movement, an Andante, is romantic in type while the second is filled with Latin-American dance rhythms.

Gottschalk was the first American composer and pianist to make a foreign reputation; he achieved an international rank that would satisfy the most ardent propagandists for American music today. He was by necessity a composer of sentimental pieces, but these were salon pieces par excellence, and many still have the ability to please those who hear them. But far more important in the history of America's native composers is the fact that Gottschalk looms as one of our most significant figures because he was able to absorb and weave into his music the colorful and exotic melodies and rhythms of Creole and Latin-American song. The nationalistic movement would not appear until the end of the century, with the advent of Dvořák, yet fifty years before Gottschalk had already composed and was playing his Creole tunes in Paris. He was akin to Chopin in his romanticism, but more superficial and more shallowly sentimental. He also lacked Chopin's harmonic inventiveness and individuality. But whatever his music lacks in the light of present-day standards no way lessens the debt we owe Louis Moreau Gottschalk.

NEW YORK'S CONCERT LIFE

Louis Antoine Jullien

At the height of this era of fabulous American performers in 1853, there arrived in New York a man who was to show that similar feats might be accomplished with an orchestra, and who was to be as sensational as any of the keyboard magicians—Louis Antoine Jullien (1812-1860). He was a Frenchman, already well known on the Continent and in London, who besides being a fine musician, was such a showman that he might have taught Mr. Barnum a few tricks. It must be said in Jullien's favor that he gave New York an opportunity to hear orchestral music played with superb musicianship and brilliant virtuosity. He brought most of his players with him, but he filled out the orchestra with the best local players, among whom was a man destined to stand with the greatest in America—young Theodore Thomas.

Jullien aimed to popularize good music, so he spared no means to have the largest possible orchestra, the best players, and the most attractive programs. He often presented a complete symphony, even two, in one evening. This was a novelty not only in America, but also abroad. The performance of single movements of symphonies, or the mixing of movements, had long been a European custom, not only in the days of Haydn, but extending into Beethoven's time. More than once Beethoven would have to substitute a popular slow movement from a favorite symphony when the audience did not take to the one that belonged to the work he was conducting. By this time Europe was getting away from this practice, but in America whole symphonies were still a novelty, and Jullien did music a real service in performing them.

Jullien, real musician that he was, was nonetheless a poseur, and made the most of every public appearance. He had impressive whiskers, and his dress was in the latest fashion, with bright-colored vests and diamond studs. He used a jeweled baton and wore white gloves, yet all this display was not for Americans alone—it was part of his stock in trade, both here and abroad. While conducting, Jullien stood on a crimson platform studded with gold. Nearby was a white and gold chair, in which the musical monarch might rest between numbers. For Beethoven a page brought him a gold baton resting on a gold salver. Jullien's programs were made up of much light music, as well as the symphonies—quadrilles, pot-pourris of national airs and popular songs of the day.

A concert at New York's Crystal Palace marked perhaps the climax of Jullien's career in America, and will keep his name in the legends of music. The Palace, on the site of what is now Bryant Park, in back of the New York Public Library, was the scene of nightly concerts by Jullien's orchestra. On this occasion the program announced a piece called *Night, or the Firemen's Quadrille.* The ladies in the audience had been warned that something unusual might happen. The music started softly, mysteriously, like a nocturne. Suddenly the clang of firebells was heard outside. Flames burst from the ceiling as three companies of firemen rushed in, dragging their hoses behind them. Real water poured from the nozzles, glass was broken, women fainted as the ushers tried frantically to tell them this was part of the show. All the while the orchestra was playing fortissimo and when Jullien thought that they had had enough, he signaled for the firemen to go, and in a glorious blare of triumph, the orchestra burst into the Doxology. Those of the audience who were still conscious joined in the singing.

With all of Jullien's stunts, he gave New York the best music it had heard, and he was shrewd enough to play the music of American composers. It is wise to remember that such men as he were concurrently treating the supposedly sophisticated audiences of Paris to the same assortment of programs.

Academy of Music

While Jullien was holding forth uptown at the Crystal Palace in 1853, ground was being broken for the new Academy of Music at Fourteenth Street and Irving Place. This institution was to form a bridge between the early opera performances and the golden years of the Metropolitan Opera. The new Academy, which opened on

October 2, 1854, was grander than the older Astor Place Theatre, and it was conceived as a place for the wealthy and fashionable to see and to be seen. It was here that Ole Bull had his opera company when he offered a prize for an American opera. The new theater opened under the management of J. H. Hackett. The opera was *Norma,* with the great Grisi as the heroine and the magnificent Mario playing opposite her as Pollione. Unfortunately the house seemed to have a jinx on it, for in less than two months the company went bankrupt, and for the next forty years the Academy's life was troubled and turbulent.

Chamber Music Concerts

A most hopeful phase of New York's musical life, directly influenced by the German immigrants, was the development of public concerts of chamber music. Until now held only in the homes of well-to-do musical amateurs (or Pennsylvania Pietists), these concerts took place in the halls of the city, for the benefit of the public. The foreign musicians brought with them a rich heritage of court orchestras and chamber groups, and they merely transferred the scene of cultural activity from Europe to America. Theodor Eisfeld and Otto Dresel were devoted pioneers in introducing this type of intimate music. Eisfeld was a violinist, and for fifteen years he was the conductor of the newly formed Philharmonic Society of New York. Dresel, who had been a pupil of Mendelssohn and Hiller, was a pianist and played with Eisfeld when he formed a group which presented a series of chamber music concerts, giving New Yorkers the chance to become acquainted with the magnificent literature of the masters.

Another venture, even more important, was the attempt to take chamber music to various cities throughout the country. The Fries brothers founded the Mendelssohn Quintette Club in Boston in 1849, and for fifty years, with a changing membership, the club toured American cities. It was truly a voice in the wilderness, and its members were so dedicated to performing only the classical repertory, that it was not long before they had a large and devoted public.

GERMAN DOMINATION OF AMERICAN MUSIC

It was perhaps natural that the German-born musicians should be devoted to the European masterpieces of classic and romantic literature to the neglect of our few native composers. In these years Germany was looked upon so universally as the source of all great music that even our own young composers flocked there to study with master teachers.

The effect was inevitable; they came home thoroughly saturated with German ideas and it was only natural that these American composers would pattern their music after the German models. Although this denied individuality to their own work, at least the foreign influence produced music that was workmanlike, and it led to standards of craftsmanship which later composers must either follow or surpass. But this music was not the true voice of America, even though the composers were deriving their inspiration from the stories and poems of our great literary figures. Instead the broad stream of truly American music, which included the hymns of the camp meetings and revivals, the music of the minstrel shows, and the songs of Foster, was still like a great underground river. It would not join the main stream of American music until the twentieth century. Thus, the closing years of the nineteenth century were marked by a period of foreign domination, principally German, that stifled any musical qualities that were typically American. The earlier eighteenth-century composers, like their fellow artisans and craftsmen, had a confidence and assurance which left its mark on all that they created, whereas, after the Civil War, Americans, like their colonial ancestors, began the cultivation of all things European, and musically it was the Germans and Austrians who became the predominant influence in our musical life.

The power of the press began to make itself felt, and many of the writers of the day were themselves responsible for the worship of everything foreign in America.

DWIGHT'S "JOURNAL OF MUSIC"

One of the best examples of such a leader may be found in the critic John Sullivan Dwight (1813-1893), who, as editor of Dwight's

Journal of Music, molded public opinion, and as champion of the European composer had a wide following.

Born in Boston, Dwight was graduated from Harvard in 1832 and became a Unitarian minister. He was bitter in his denunciation of Foster's songs and became the friend of classic music to the extent that he was often assailed as a Germanophile by those who fought to give the American composer a better chance. Dwight, it might be said in all fairness and despite his mistakes, was needed just at the time he was most effective, for he greatly aided the cause for better music. But unquestionably the cause of American music suffered at his pen.

Dwight's heart was in music and teaching, and after a few years in the ministry, he became a teacher of music and Latin at the Brook Farm Community at West Roxbury, Massachusetts. When the Community failed in 1849, Dwight returned to Boston and in 1852, founded his musical journal, which became an arbiter of all things connected with music. It had correspondents in several cities and continued publication until 1881. Dwight was intolerant of anything that did not come up to his standards of excellence. He had no use for sham or artificiality, and the showmanship of Jullien disgusted him. He was scornful of native composition and felt that the works of the German classicists were the sum and substance of worthy music.

AMERICAN COMPOSERS DEMAND RECOGNITION

The reverence for German music made it difficult for native composers to gain a hearing. Jullien, it is true, did perform a few native symphonic works and the Philharmonic Society of New York gave an occasional playing of an American composition. These performances, however, were so scattered and rare that a small group began to make themselves heard, demanding that their music be played because it was American music.

Anthony Philip Heinrich

One of the first of those who sought recognition was foreign born —Anton Philipp Heinrich (1781-1861). Born in the north of Bohemia just over the German border, as a young man Heinrich fell heir to the extensive properties of his uncle, who had also been his foster father. In connection with this flourishing business was a large banking house, and in managing his newly acquired fortune, young Heinrich visited France and England, parts of Spain, Portugal, and Italy. We can guess at his interest in music from the fact that he purchased a superb Cremona violin on one of his trips to Malta. It was to become his most cherished possession and one of the greatest assets in the life that lay ahead of him. Undoubtedly neglecting his business in the general depression brought on by the Napoleonic Wars, and in the pleasure of visiting new lands, Heinrich suffered such severe losses that he felt only a trip to the New World could save his business. Fitting out a merchant boat with the beautiful glassware of his native Bohemia, Heinrich set sail for America in 1810. In Philadelphia he became the director of music at the Southwark Theatre, receiving no salary, but, like the many musical amateurs still to be found in the city, serving because of the great joy it gave him. But in 1811, with the Austrian government in bankruptcy, Heinrich's fortune was wiped out, and he turned to music for a precarious livelihood. Life still seemed good to him, for he married while in Boston, and in 1813 Heinrich and his wife left for a visit to the old country. It was not a happy trip, for the young wife, soon to become a mother, became increasingly ill and terribly homesick, and when their daughter, Antonia, was born, they planned to return to America at once. Circumstances forced them to leave "Toni" with a relative, and after a three-months' trip from Trieste, the Heinrichs were once again in Boston, but it was too late. The frail mother had been through too much, and once again Heinrich was in America—and alone.

It is 1816, and it is now that we begin to follow the almost incredible career of Anthony Philip Heinrich, a new citizen (even to the Americanization of his name), a dedicated musician and champion of American music. In the succeeding years Heinrich would travel to distant places and mingle with the great and near great. Penniless but unbowed, with a spirit that would not be broken, he was admired and loved and respected for his devotion to the finest in music. Receiving an offer with a regular salary to go to Pittsburgh as director of music at the theater there, Heinrich started on a journey which would eventually take him to Kentucky. With no money and only his violin as a companion, Heinrich walked all the way from Philadelphia to Pittsburgh, like the itinerant journeymen in the previous century. Bad fortune still pursued him, and with the loss of his position in Pittsburgh (the theatrical manager apparently had no money), Heinrich was once again free to follow his own adventurous spirit. It was quite natural that he should invade the West, taking a river boat down the Ohio River, eventually reaching Limestone (now Maysville), Kentucky, and arriving in Lexington in time to take part in a concert on November 12, 1817. This trip was to make an indelible impression on Heinrich the musician, for it was his first taste of American frontier life, and his first contacts with the American Indian. Continuing to play and direct concerts in Lexington and Frankfort, Heinrich also gave violin lessons, all with tireless energy. Small wonder that eventually the strain proved too much and he became seriously ill. By the spring of 1818 Heinrich's health began to improve, and he retired to a small log cabin in the forest near Bardstown (one of Kentucky's early settlements), where he might regain his strength and have the freedom to practice his beloved violin. It was here that Heinrich began to express himself—first through improvisations on his instrument, and later in writing down his musical inspirations. Never having had a lesson in theory or composition, nevertheless Heinrich was completely captivated by the ease with which he composed, and it is for his ability to picture native scenes that today we honor him for being the first to attempt to depict America as he saw it.

When Heinrich published his first collection of music, in 1820, he called it *The Dawning of Music in Kentucky, or the Pleasures of Harmony in the Solitudes of Nature,* and wrote in its preface that "should he be able, by this effort, to create but one single *Star* in the *West,* no one would ever be more proud than himself, to be called an *American Musician.*" In reviewing the *Dawning* the editor of the *Euterpeiad* in Boston called Heinrich "the Beethoven of America."

Heinrich went to Boston in 1823, where he took part in concerts and was for three months the organist in Old South Church. In 1826 he arrived in London, where he planned to concertize and have some of his compositions performed. He met with no success and was forced to play in the orchestra at the Drury Lane Theatre in order to live. He was back in Boston in 1831, but he returned to England two years later, and from there made several trips to the Continent, where at long last he finally managed to have some of his orchestral works played in European cities. When he came back to America in the fall of 1837, Heinrich settled in New York, where, save for a brief trip to Europe in 1857, he lived for the rest of his life.

Heinrich was an eccentric and was eager to compose in the grand manner and on a huge scale. When he died he left several large chests full of manuscripts and orchestral scores (now in the Library of Congress), which required at least a hundred performers. In his later years in New York he came to be called "Father Heinrich," and he was a colorful character in the city's musical life during the 1840s and 1850s. He was chairman of the first meeting of the committee that formed the Philharmonic Society, although he was never an active player in the orchestra. He soon protested that the group had ignored his request to play some of his music, yet when the Society told him it was ready to consider his work, he withdrew the score he had submitted.

The leading musicians of New York gave Heinrich testimonial and benefit concerts on at least two occasions. One of them, in 1853, was rendered by a "numerous and powerful" orchestra under the leadership of Theodor Eisfeld and the composer, and several prominent soloists. The program featured a number of Heinrich's major works: *The Wildwood Troubadour,* sub-titled *a musical Auto-Biography; The New England Feast of Shells,* a "divertimento pastorale oceanico"; National Memories, a "Grand British Symphony"; Quintette—"The Adieu," from the oratorio of the "Pilgrim Fathers"; and *The Tower of Babel, or Language Confounded.*

Unfortunately for his place in history, Heinrich lacked the talent to match and carry out his intentions successfully. He was short on genius, but if his gifts had equaled his energy and his boundless enthusiasm for anything that was American, he might have been one of our major composers. It is not for his extravagant, repetitious works that we remember "Father Heinrich," but rather as a musical pioneer who not only believed in the American composer, but fought fiercely for the hearing that he felt all American composers were entitled to have.

William Henry Fry

The most vocal of the mid-century chauvinists was William Henry Fry (1813-1864), composer, music critic, and lecturer. He was an important figure in his time, for he composed the first grand opera written by an American that was produced, he was one of the first lecturers on music, and an early apostle of the rights of the American composer.

Fry was born in Philadelphia on August 10, 1813, the son of William Fry and Ann Fleeson, both of fine old American stock. William Henry had an overwhelming love for music and composed an overture at the age of fourteen, while a student at Mount St. Mary's at Emmitsburg, Maryland. He then studied theory and composition with Leopold Meignen, a Philadelphia musician and publisher who had studied at the Paris Conservatoire. Before he was twenty, Fry had written three more overtures, one of which won him a gold medal.

It was in his home city of Philadelphia that Fry's first opera, *Leonora*, was produced in 1845. The libretto was adapted by the composer's elder brother, Joseph, from Bulwer-Lytton's novel, *The Lady of Lyons*, and the performance was given in English by the Seguin opera troupe on June 4, 1845, at the Chestnut Street Theatre. The production was lavish, for the composer paid for it himself. There was a chorus of eighty and an orchestra of sixty, and the sets by Russell Smith were the finest that could be built. The production had a run of twelve performances, and a vocal-piano score was published. It shows that the first American grand opera was merely a reflection of the Italian opera of the day, very much in the style of Bellini and Donizetti. It had no spoken dialogue, but was composed of recitatives and arias, skillful ensemble numbers, and choruses, with a melodramatic climax. But the opera was all the work of Americans, and as such it was unquestionably an event of the greatest importance in America's musical development.

Soon after the production of *Leonora* Fry went abroad for six years as foreign correspondent of the New York *Tribune*. He had chosen to be a journalist, with music as an avocation. While he was in Europe he tried, but without success, to have *Leonora* produced in Paris. At the end of his stay, he returned to America and settled in New York as music critic of the *Tribune*, ready to take up cudgels for the American composer. As the *Tribune*, during the 1850s, was the most powerful newspaper in the country, Fry's position could hardly have been improved upon.

As for his own music, several of Fry's orchestral works were played by Jullien; *Leonora* had a New York production at the Academy of Music, a revised version and in Italian, in 1858; and another opera, *Notre Dame de Paris,* was produced in Philadelphia in 1864.

When Jullien played Fry's *Santa Claus: Christmas Symphony* for the first time on Christmas Eve, 1853, R. S. Willis, editor of the *Musical World and Times,* gave the piece only a brief and rather derogatory and condescending notice. Fry was furious and wrote Willis a twenty-five-page letter of protest, saying that as an American he was certainly entitled to consideration in his own country. His work, he pointed out, was the longest unified instrumental composition that had ever been written on a single subject and was therefore deserving of an extended review. Moreover, any piece which began in Heaven "and then swings down to Hell, returns to Heaven and thence to earth to depict the family joys of a Christmas party" was certainly worth more than a passing notice.

In the season of 1852-53 Fry presented in Metropolitan Hall, New York, a series of lectures on music which was probably the first course on music appreciation offered in this country. Some two thousand persons subscribed to ten lectures, which quite thoroughly covered the fundamentals of music—the voice, orchestral instruments, larger forms—and ended with a blistering attack on the public taste of the day for its neglect of the American composer. Fry was reported as saying that there was no taste or love for art in this country. There was too much servility on the part of American artists. The American composer should not allow the names of Beethoven, Handel, or Mozart to prove an eternal bugbear to him; he should strike out manfully and independently into untrodden realms, just as nature and inspirations might incite him.

Until this Declaration of Independence in Art should be made—until American composers should discard their foreign liveries and found an American school—and until the American public should learn to support American artists, Art would not become indigenous to this country, and we should continue to be provincial in Art.

Strong words, these, which might well have been spoken in 1952, rather than in 1852, though they ironically came from a man who chose for his first opera an English story and patterned it after the traditional Italian opera of his day.

Fry's manuscripts are now a part of the Fleisher Collection in Philadelphia.

George Frederick Bristow

The third champion of the American composer was George Frederick Bristow (1825-1898). His opera *Rip Van Winkle,* produced in 1855, was the second American grand opera to have a hearing, and was more important to our music history than Fry's *Leonora,* for it was based on an American subject, Washington Irving's immortal story.

Bristow was born in New York and at the age of eleven was playing the violin in theater orchestras. He was one of the first violins of the Philharmonic Society from its beginning in 1842 until after 1880, and was one of the local musicians hired by Jullien for his New York concerts. It was in his relationship with the Philharmonic Society that Bristow had his say about the neglect of native compositions. While Fry was having his controversy with R. S. Willis of the *Musical World* Bristow wrote a letter to the magazine in which he made this statement about the Philharmonic:

> It appears the society's eleven years of promoting American art have embraced one whole performance of one whole American overture, one whole rehearsal of one whole American symphony, and the performance of an overture by an Englishman stopping here, . . . who, happening to be conductor here, had the influence to have it played.

This letter drew an official statement from H. C. Timm, who was president of the Society at the time. Timm listed eleven works by Americans "either native or adopted citizens of this country," that had been played by the Society in its eleven years, one of them an overture by Bristow. Bristow resigned at the next meeting of the Board, but he was soon forgiven and reinstated.

Bristow took a forward step in choosing a native subject and locale for his *Rip Van Winkle,* but he followed Fry's lead in composing an Italian-like opera, even though it was sung in English. J. R. Wainwright's libretto had taken liberties with Irving's story by having Rip's daughter fall in love with a British officer during the Revolution. These Revolutionary episodes gave opportunity, of course, for soldiers' choruses and a martial song by the heroine, closely resembling a similar scene in Donizetti's *The Daughter of the Regiment.*

Whether or not Ole Bull's prize offer was the stimulus for Bristow's *Rip Van Winkle* may only be conjectured, but it is interesting to note that another opera on an American subject, by a foreign visitor, would be produced at the Academy of Music the following spring, March 24, 1856. The composer was the Italian conductor Luigi Arditi, remembered today for his vocal waltz, *Il Bacio*, which he wrote in St. Louis while there with an opera company at the Varieties Theatre. The opera he produced in New York was entitled *La Spia*, an adaptation of James Fenimore Cooper's *The Spy*. Arditi conducted the opening performance at the new Academy, and remained in this country until 1856. Unfortunately only the libretto of his opera survives.

When Bristow's *Rip Van Winkle* was first produced in New York in September, 1855, it had a four-week run of nightly performances at Niblo's Garden. In 1870 it was revived in both Philadelphia and New York.

In addition to the overture that the Philharmonic performed in its first eleven years of existence, Bristow heard four of his six symphonies performed by the Society. Jullien, too, played his works, which included the oratorios *Praise to God* and *Daniel*, two cantatas, several string quartets, and numerous choral and vocal works. The manuscripts are now in New York Public Library's Americana Music Collection.

Besides his creative work, Bristow was the director of the New York Harmonic Society, a choral organization, and from 1854 until his death in 1898, he was a visiting teacher in the New York public schools.

None of these men—Heinrich, Fry, and Bristow—were great musicians, but they were most important because of the consciousness of nationality, in a day when America's musical life was dominated by the music and musicians from abroad. Many of their controversies were extreme and open to contradiction, but they were the first to utter a word in an argument that has never ended even to this day.

CHAPTER VII

From the Civil War through the 1880s

CIVIL WAR SONGS

The Civil War produced hundreds of songs that could be arranged in sequence to form an actual history of the conflict, reflecting its events, its principal figures, and the ideals and principles of the opposing sides.

"The Battle Hymn of the Republic"

Of the many songs that have come down from these sorrowful years, none is more beloved than Julia Ward Howe's *The Battle Hymn of the Republic,* her most famous poem and the most stirring and memorable of those that came from the war.

The tune had long been familiar in Sunday School songbooks. As early as 1856 it had been set to words "Say brothers, will you meet us?" The composer is supposed to have been William Steffe, and the song became popular around Charleston, South Carolina. The refrain—"Glory, glory, hallelujah"—has never changed in the many versions of the song. When John Brown was hailed as a martyr by the Abolitionists in 1859 (on being hanged for his raid on Harper's Ferry), he became almost a national figure, and in the North, when a soldier with the same name became the victim of the practical jokes of his buddies, they wrote new verses about John Brown to the Sunday School hymn tune. At Fort Warren, near Boston, a member of a soldiers' glee club composed these verses which coupled the identities of their own John Brown with that of the late Abolitionist crusader. New words were sung—"John Brown's body lies amouldering in the grave"—and the song soon spread like wildfire. Other regiments took it for their theme as they marched South. Attempts were made from time to time to save the fine tune from ribaldry, but no one succeeded until Mrs. Howe was inspired to write her poem. She was the daughter of a New York banker, and the wife of a prominent New England reformer. She had already gained a reputation in Boston for her essays and poems. She was an ardent Abolitionist, and with her husband was near the front when they stopped to review some troops outside the city of Washington. A sudden skirmish forced them to withdraw, and as they drove back to the city, they sang the popular war songs to while away the time. Having just heard the soldiers singing *John Brown's Body*, Mrs. Howe's minister, who was in the carriage with her, suggested she should write some good words for such a stirring tune.

The thought obsessed her, and, waking as usual in the gray light of dawn, the words suddenly came to her, so forcefully that she got out of bed, found an old pen, and wrote out her immortal verses which began:

Mine eyes have seen the glory of the coming of the Lord.

"Dixie"

Dixie, the fighting song of the Confederacy, was, ironically, written by the Northerner Daniel Decatur Emmett, and as we have already found was originally a walk-around song for his minstrel shows. The South loved the song, and when it was later played at the inauguration of Jefferson Davis, in Montgomery, Alabama, it became the symbol of the Confederate States.

The meaning of the word "Dixie" was for a long time a mystery. It was thought to have come from the Mason and Dixie line, symbolizing the South, but with the success of the minstrel shows, it soon became "Dixie Land," another name for the South. While the word "Dixie" probably was used for years by the slaves and the white showmen, it was Emmett who established and popularized its meaning as the name of a carefree land.

Dixie's Land, as the song was originally called, was presented for the first time anywhere by the Bryant's Minstrels at Mechanics' Hall on Broadway, April 4, 1859. It was performed as a Negro walkaround, sung and danced by a few soloists in the foreground, and the rest of the company of six or eight men at the back of the stage.

The jauntiness of the tune, so characteristically American, gives it a carefree spirit which seems to portray the eternal spirit of America. It is for that reason, perhaps, that *Dixie* has become a truly national song, even though it is so definitely associated with the South. It is a truly American song, for it represents a state of mind common to all parts of the nation.

Other War Songs

Historically, the most interesting of the war songs are those that refer to actual episodes, even though their musical value is doubtful, and as songs most of them are forgotten today. Southerners commemorated historic events, while Northerners celebrated victories—all with songs. Inevitably there were, of course, the groups who were shrewd enough to sense the commercial value of sentimental songs that could be sung on both sides.

One of the most famous composers of Northern songs was George Frederick Root (1820-1895). Before the years of the war he had made a considerable reputation as a writer of ballads, as well as gospel hymns. He was born in Sheffield, Massachusetts, in 1820, but when he was six his family moved to North Reading, a town rich in musical history, not far from Boston. From childhood his ambition was to become a musician, and, making the most of his opportunities and through the help of his Boston teacher, A. N. Johnson, he was soon giving lessons and teaching singing schools. He worked with Lowell Mason in music instruction in the Boston public schools, and about 1844 went to New York, where he became the music teacher at Abbot's School for young ladies. Going to Europe in 1850 for further study, he returned to New York in August, 1851, and when Lowell Mason came to New York, Root helped him organize the New York Musical Normal Institute in 1853. The West called, however, and in 1858 Root journeyed to Chicago, where his brother had opened a music store in partnership with C. M. Cady, under the name of Root & Cady. Joining the business, which was temporarily ruined by the fire of 1871, Root lived an active life in the city, and was awarded the Doctor of Music degree by the University of Chicago.

The vogue of Stephen Foster's songs caused Root to try his hand at song writing, so he had a former pupil, the blind Fanny Crosby, write a few verses for him, and he wrote the music to *The Hazel Dell, There's Music in the Air,* and *Rosalie, the Prairie Flower,* this last song paying him $3000 in royalties. His most successful war songs were his *Battle Cry of Freedom,* and *Tramp, Tramp, Tramp, the Boys Are Marching,* the former being taken all over the country by the Hutchinson Family with rousing success. His two most popular sentimental songs were *Just Before the Battle, Mother* and *The Vacant Chair.* Probably his most famous hymn was *The Shining Shore* ("My days are gliding swiftly by").

Henry Clay Work (1832-1884) wrote the words and music of his war songs with a fiery partisanship, for his father had been imprisoned for maintaining an underground railway station for runaway slaves. Born in Connecticut, Work was only a lad when the family moved to Illinois, where the elder Work's antislavery views soon got him into trouble. Young Henry became an ardent Abolitionist, and his songs include *Kingdom Coming, Babylon is Fallen, Wake Nicodemus,* and, in celebration of Sherman's march from Atlanta to the sea, *Marching Through Georgia.* Work also became known for his temperance songs, the best known being the classic *Come Home, Father,* and today there is scarcely a school songbook but has that favorite of children, *Grandfather's Clock.*

A song that was written before the war proved to be a powerful propaganda weapon for the Abolitionist movement in the North. This was *Darling Nellie Gray* (composed in 1856 by Benjamin Russell Hanby) which told the story of an escaped slave who learned that his sweetheart had been sold, chained, and taken to Georgia. Patrick S. Gilmore, the bandmaster who was to make an indelible impression on Boston with his Peace Jubilee, wrote the exhilarating *When Johnny Comes Marching Home* in 1863.

Maryland's State Song, *Maryland, My Maryland,* was written by one of her native sons, who was living at the time in New Orleans—James Ryder Randall. Maryland did not leave the Union, but it was a slaveholding state and Southern sentiment was strong among the people. When the Massachusetts troops were fired upon as they passed through Baltimore, Randall wrote the verses, hoping that the incident would swing his state to the Confederate cause. He set them to the old German song *O Tannenbaum.*

Many songs were adapted to new words during the war. *The Star Spangled Banner* was rewritten as *The Southern Cross,* and the French national anthem—*La Marseillaise*—was used in many versions. John Hill Hewitt's best known war song, *All quiet along the Potomac tonight,* was set to the poem of Mrs. Ethel Lynn Eliot Beers of Massachusetts, first published in *Harper's Weekly* for November 30, 1861, and was sung on both sides. Another favorite of the battlefields was Walter Kittredge's *Tenting on the Old Camp Ground.* Added to these were dozens of songs which honored generals and leaders, particularly Lincoln. In many ways the songs are historical documents, for they afford a study of the contemporary state of mind of both sides.

AMERICA BEGINS TO MATURE

After the Civil War, as America began to mature and her industries grew and developed, the stage was slowly being set for the development of the arts. In music the many threads of two and a half centuries were now ready to be woven into the final pattern of her musical destiny. The fine tradition of choral singing would soon be expressed in many music festivals, as well as in the twentieth century's phenomenal growth of public school music. To a rich opera tradition would be added the growth of fine orchestras, and American singers and instrumental virtuosi would compete with any in the world. The sentimental ballads and the unrealized potentialities of Negro music would soon find their way to the American stage, eventually sending the contagious rhythms of American jazz around the world. The small voices of pioneer American composers were starting to demand their right to be heard, and the many conservatories and schools would soon develop American-trained musicians of the finest types. The music trades would shortly grow to undreamed-of heights, and musical conventions and competitions would gather together the top musicians in the land. When in 1869 the transcontinental railroad was completed and the West was at last opened, the staggering growth of business was to give America the great fortunes which were later to subsidize the arts, and allow native musicians many advantages and encouragements.

THE FIRST MUSIC SCHOOLS

Some of the nation's most important music schools and conservatories were established in the years following the close of the war.

Music education had already been recognized by instruction in music at Oberlin College in 1835 when a Chair of Sacred Music was founded, while Harvard College offered its first music courses in 1862. George Peabody had given the initial impetus when he founded the Peabody Institute in Baltimore, but the war had delayed its opening until 1868. The college music department and the independent music school were first exemplified by the founding of Oberlin Conservatory, at Oberlin, Ohio, in 1865. This was followed two years later when the New England Conservatory of Music in Boston was established by Eben Tourjée (1867). This was the first large institution of its kind in America, and the school graduated its first class of thirteen in 1870. Also in 1867, Cincinnati climaxed many years of good music in the Ohio community with the establishment by Clara Baur of the Cincinnati Conservatory of Music. Chicago, as though not to be outdone by the older eastern cities, saw the opening of the Chicago Musical College during that same year, 1867. At last the Peabody Institute opened its doors in 1868, and later, in 1886, Chicago's American Conservatory was founded.

While scores of Americans would still go abroad to seek a background of European study, these schools would feed the smaller towns and cities with well-trained teachers and performers, which was to be of the most vital importance in the musical growth of the country.

PATRICK S. GILMORE'S PEACE JUBILEES

That the day of the colorful and flamboyant concert was not past was proved in Boston in 1869, when Patrick Sarsfield Gilmore put on one of the most colossal musical shows in history. Gilmore was an old hand at giving concerts, for he not only had his own band, but had served as a bandmaster during the war. Settling in Boston, Gilmore planned his Peace Jubilee to "commemorate the restoration of peace throughout the land." Boston, as well as Worcester, had seen the first American festivals given by the Handel and Haydn Society (1857) and the Worcester County Musical Association (1858), but these were puny in comparison to the thousands Gilmore attracted with his showman tactics. A coliseum to seat thirty thousand persons was built, a chorus of ten thousand and an orchestra of a thousand were assembled. Railroads ran special excursions to the city, and President Grant, his cabinet, and top-ranking army and navy officers were invited, and came. Governors of the states came too, with large contingents of their citizens. Five days were given over to programs of gigantic proportions, of which guest conductors, like Carl Zerrahn, were in charge, and nothing was spared to make the Jubilee the most spectacular musical event ever held. Cannon, fired by electric buttons on a table in front of the conductor, were used to mark the rhythm of the national airs, and as if that were not enough, Gilmore had a hundred firemen in red shirts pound a hundred anvils in a grandiose arrangement of Verdi's Anvil Chorus from *Il Trovatore*.

In 1872, Boston was still not done with Gilmore, who felt he must have another festival. The idea of peace in America was somewhat old by that time, but as Europe had just had a war—the Franco-Prussian—he thought nothing could better serve his purpose than a World Peace Jubilee. To add to the international idea Johann Strauss the Younger was brought from Vienna to conduct the *Blue Danube Waltz;* Franz Abt came from Germany; and the soloists were all world famous. The chorus was doubled—twenty thousand sang—but this time Gilmore met his match. No conductor could hold such a mob together and the results were almost calamitous. Some Negro singers from the South made a great hit, however, and were to travel extensively in America and Europe. Fisk University had been founded at Nashville, Tennessee, in 1866 (one of the first to educate the free slaves), and in 1871 George White took twelve members of his choir on tour. After their Boston appearance they became known as the Fisk Jubilee Singers, and raised more than $150,000 for their institution.

THEODORE THOMAS, SYMPHONIC PIONEER

Things were different in New York as its era of gaudy concerts faded into the past, for a dominant personality was bringing orchestral concerts to a growing public, and making an honest attempt to raise America's musical standards. Theodore Thomas (1835-1905) will ever remain an epic figure in the nation's musical growth, for it is largely due to his efforts that America developed an audience for orchestral music, with every major city maintaining a permanent orchestra, the best of them unsurpassed by any in the world. Thanks to Thomas' tireless efforts the citizens of our great cities take pride in their orchestras, and form discriminating audiences to listen to them. It was Thomas who finally proved to the wealthy business men that the only worth-while orchestra was the one where the players could devote all their time to playing together, led and guided by a permanent conductor who needed financial backing and support.

Thomas had been brought over from Germany in 1845, when he was a lad of ten. His father had been a town musician in Esens, but with a large family and a small income he soon looked to America, hoping to make more money. New York did not prove too receptive, and young Thomas had to tuck his violin under his arm and play where he could—for dances, weddings, and in the theater. He even toured the South, while still in his teens, billed as "Master T. T."

By 1851 Thomas was playing in New York in the orchestra of the Italian Opera Company, but an unusual opportunity came when Louis Antoine Jullien engaged him for the first violin section for the New York concerts. Although Thomas squirmed under Jullien's antics, he learned much that was to be of the greatest help to him later on. Thomas was elected a member of the Philharmonic Society (whose three concerts a year would not interfere with a steady job), and in 1855 he joined Lowell Mason's son William in giving chamber-music concerts.

William Mason

It will be well to digress for a moment, so as to fit William Mason (1829-1908) into the picture, for he and Thomas were two of the most important of the many musical missionaries who had a part in developing music in this country. Like his father, Lowell Mason, he had the spirit of a pioneer. He distinguished himself in several directions, and in at least two of them he was an influence of prime importance. He sacrificed much to bring chamber music to the public, and to play it so often that people would grow to like it. As a piano teacher, he is in a large part responsible for the really excellent piano playing in this country today. Added to these activities, he was a prolific composer of piano pieces that had considerable vogue for many years.

William Mason was born in Boston, January 24, 1829, and showed an early love for music. When he was twenty he went abroad and studied with Moscheles, Dreyschock, and Liszt, and also gained the friendship of some of the greatest musicians of the time—Rubinstein, Brahms, Wagner, and many others. Franz Liszt was delighted with one of Mason's early piano pieces, *Les Perles de Rosée,* and gladly accepted the young composer's dedication. Mason returned to America in 1854 and immediately made a tour as a concert pianist, as far west as Chicago, devoting himself to the best music of the day, as well as to the classics. But the demand for flashy fantasias and outright stunts which had been cultivated by Thalberg and Gottschalk and their generation, forced him to end his recitals with improvisations on themes suggested by members of the audience, or with *Yankee Doodle* played by one hand against *Old Hundredth* by the other.

Chamber Music with Thomas

Mason's fine musical training perfectly fitted Theodore Thomas' high standards, and for thirteen years they accomplished pioneer work in confining their programs to string quartets, trios, and quintets. After the first seasons, no vocal selections were included in the programs. Although this often left little in the cash box, their refusal to compromise with public taste was but one more victory in the cause of better music.

Thomas, the Conductor

Theodore Thomas had his chance to conduct one night at the Academy of Music. He had been given the position of concertmaster of the opera orchestra, and when the regular conductor refused to conduct until he was paid, Thomas took the baton and did so well with a score he had never seen that before long he became one of the regular conductors at the opera. Conducting soon was a passion with the young man, and sensing the need of better music in the concert halls (probably realizing from his own tours the potentialities in taking music to the people outside New York), he organized his own orchestra, and gave his first concert in New York in 1862.

Thomas became convinced that only a permanent orchestra could produce the best results. It must be so thoroughly organized that the players could devote all their time to rehearsals and concerts under the guidance and control of their own conductor. Without financial backing, the only way to accomplish this great task would be to have enough concerts each season to keep the members busy. This would mean traveling, and before long the "Thomas Highway" became a reality. He played in all the principal cities from New England to the Pacific Coast, anywhere he could, even in churches and railway stations. Knowing that the standards of the country needed raising, he carried out his ideas of progressive programs, using each time some works that were a little beyond the experience of most of his audience, but also careful to include some lighter music that they could enjoy.

By 1867, Thomas had made his orchestra truly permanent, and he could guarantee his men a full season's work. His concerts in the summer became famous and in 1868 he moved them to New York's Central Park Garden. He started a spread of musical culture which has never ceased, and in his tours, he kindled many a flame which was to burn brightly through the years. While other immigrant boys were making fabulous fortunes, Thomas was growing rich, but his wealth was of the mind and spirit, and may never be truly estimated.

On a November day in 1869, Theodore Thomas could not know that a concert he gave in Chicago would overshadow a praiseworthy musical effort in that city, and plant the seed which would lead to the crowning work of his life, not only in Chicago, but in America. The same Hans Balatka who had conducted the Saengerfest in 1857 had made such an impression in Chicago that he was persuaded to move there, and in 1860 he reorganized the local Philharmonic Society. For six years he gave concerts that were not only fashionable affairs but which offered also the best in music— eight of Beethoven's symphonies, two of Mozart's and those of Mendelssohn, Haydn, and Schubert. In the seventh season, the attendance fell sharply because of the young conductor from the East— Theodore Thomas, with his orchestra, gave new meaning to music, the like of which had not been heard before in Chicago. The music lovers of the city could not know, however, that in sounding the death knell of their own group, they were preparing the way for this same young man to return in a few years, to make Chicago's orchestra the finest in the country. It was when Chicago had its new Auditorium that the time seemed ripe for an orchestra, and a committee approached Theodore Thomas with the idea of creating a permanent orchestra. Thomas was delighted at the prospect, for he was very unhappy in New York at that time, and the Chicago Symphony Orchestra was organized in 1891. This organization brought to Thomas the realization of his fondest dreams and he was able to give the Middle West an opportunity to hear the best symphonic music possible. For the first time in many years Thomas had security, for the Chicago board, rich and powerful, wanted a good orchestra, and fifty citizens pledged a thousand dollars each to make up any deficit that the new venture might incur. Thomas was able to gather together the men from his old orchestra, which he had been forced to disband. He started a period of happy activity which was to last for fourteen years, until his sudden death in January, 1905.

SIDNEY LANIER: POET AND MUSICIAN

By 1871 Thomas' visits to important cities began to bear fruit. In Baltimore, for example, his concerts had so impressed local musicians that the new director of the Peabody Institute, Asger Hamerik, a Dane, was already urging the trustees of the school to allow him to form an orchestra worthy of the city. Hamerik was a fine musician and had been a pupil of Niels Gade, Von Bülow, and a protégé of Berlioz. He had not been in the city for long when he was asked to audition a young flutist, none other than the poet Sidney Lanier (1842-1881). Born in Macon, Georgia, Lanier had suffered greatly during the Civil War and the Reconstruction, and had finally left his Georgia home because of ill health, brought on by the war and his subsequent imprisonment. He went to San Antonio, Texas, in 1872, hoping to effect a cure, and it was at this time that he seriously began to play his flute (it seemed to strengthen his weak lungs) and compose. He was not long in realizing that he much preferred his music and poetry to the work in his father's law firm, and in April, 1873, he left Texas for Baltimore, where he was to have an interview with Hamerik at the Peabody. Hamerik was greatly impressed with Lanier's playing and offered him the chance to be first flutist in his new orchestra. Lanier was delighted. He went on, then, to New York where he soon appeared in concerts in various halls and fashionable homes, winning favorable comments from the critics. He was even persuaded to play for Theodore Thomas, and it would be interesting if we could know what Thomas thought of Lanier's playing. The opening concert of the orchestra in Baltimore on December 6, 1873, saw Lanier at his orchestra desk, and he remained in the city for several years, composing, writing poetry, teaching at Johns Hopkins University, and lecturing, all the while fighting a losing battle with tuberculosis. We have only Hamerik's eloquent tribute to Lanier's musical ability, but all America knows the poet.

Lanier's musical compositions include several flute solos: *Sacred Melodies* (1868), *Fieldlarks and Blackbirds* (1873), *Swamp Robin* (1873), *Longing* and *Windsong* (both 1874); and there are also groups of songs and three unfinished symphonies—*Choral Symphony, Symphony of Life,* and *Symphony of the Plantation.* His poem *The Symphony* (1875) is of particular interest with its allusions to musical instruments, metrical devices, and other musical elements.

As real American ingenuity began to be felt in the musical life of our nation, it was accompanied by a bolder literature, which began to show the possibilities inherent in the culture of our nation. Leaders emerged in all fields to speak of American ways and reflect her life. The mystic Walt Whitman, whose verse is the most memorable of the century, challenged the great writers of Europe in defense of America as a democracy and in the following century inspired many American composers to make settings of his poems. American sculptors, who had journeyed to Rome in the early years of the century, were beginning to use local subjects as inspirations for their work, modeling them according to America's growing taste.

THE PHILADELPHIA CENTENNIAL EXPOSITION

While Theodore Thomas was proving that American standards of musical taste could be raised, it was unfortunate that he had to suffer a major disappointment at the Philadelphia Centennial Exposition of 1876. The music for the Centennial had been put under Thomas' direction, but the concerts proved to be financially disastrous and he personally assumed the subsequent debts. His major disappointment was the *Centennial March,* which he had commissioned from Richard Wagner. It proved to be merely empty and pompous.

John Knowles Paine and John Greenleaf Whittier wrote the music and words respectively for the *Centennial Hymn,* and Dudley Buck and Sidney Lanier produced the *Centennial Cantata*. Chimes rang from Machinery Hall, and a salute of cannon made a mighty climax of the final great peroration of the Hallelujah Chorus from Handel's *Messiah*. With the attendance of an emperor, kings, and presidents, plus millions of ordinary citizens, the Centennial celebration at least helped to bring America before the attention of the world at large.

THE CINCINNATI MAY FESTIVAL

Meanwhile Thomas was in and out of New York, as he was called to first one city and then another. On one of his periodic visits to Cincinnati in 1872 he was asked to help establish a national festival of singers in the city's exposition hall, which had been built two years before for the Saengerbund. The festival was to feature mixed choruses, singing in English, and the orchestra was to be enlarged. Thomas liked the idea, and the first festival was held in 1873, May 6-10, with a chorus of about a thousand and a large orchestra of which the Thomas orchestra was the nucleus. The principal works were Beethoven's Ninth Symphony, Handel's *Dettingen Te Deum*, and scenes from Gluck's *Orpheus*. From this was to develop the Cincinnati Biennial Musical Festival, which has become one of America's major festivals. In 1878 the New York Philharmonic Society appointed Thomas as its conductor, allowing him to keep his own orchestra for which he made programs of a lighter nature than those of the Philharmonic.

LEOPOLD DAMROSCH: RIVALRY WITH THOMAS

One of Thomas' contemporaries in the New York scene was Leopold Damrosch, who had first come to America to conduct the New York Männergesangverein Arion, a male chorus. Damrosch was ambitious, and because he wished to take a more active part in the city's musical life, he consulted Anton Rubinstein, who toured America in 1872-73. The leading New York musical figure was of course Thomas, and it was difficult for anyone else to do much conducting. Rubinstein suggested the formation of an oratorio society as an opening wedge. Damrosch was able to carry out his plans and in 1873 the Oratorio Society of New York was founded, giving its first concert in a piano wareroom on December 3, 1873. The chorus numbered between fifty and sixty voices, and by its third season it gave its first complete oratorio with orchestral accompaniment—Handel's *Samson*. In 1874 Damrosch began the annual performances of Handel's *Messiah* that he conducted until his death in 1885.

In 1878, Damrosch, by that time a bitter rival of Thomas, founded his own orchestra, and the Symphony Society of New York (later to merge with the Philharmonic) gave its first concert in old Steinway Hall on East Fourteenth Street, on November 9, 1878. The seventy musicians under Damrosch gave six concerts in their first season. Each was preceded by a public rehearsal, actually an afternoon concert preceding the evening performance. This was an innovation begun by the Philharmonic. It became the custom with the major American orchestras.

Opposition to Damrosch was of course forthcoming from the Thomas forces, and it undoubtedly gave much excitement to New York's concert life. By a clever bit of maneuvering, Damrosch was able to obtain through a pupil the score of Brahms's First Symphony, and so gave the New York première before Thomas.

MAPLESON STIMULATES OPERA IN NEW YORK

New York's opera life began to match the brilliance of its orchestral music, for in the same year that Damrosch started his new orchestra, James Henry Mapleson (1830-1901) came from London's Drury Lane to conduct opera seasons at the Academy of Music, and to take his company on tour. He produced the finest operas of the day, and the great singers of the world passed through the doors of the various opera houses, among them Giulia Grisi, Giuseppe Mario, Adelina Patti, Christine Nilsson, Clara Louise Kellogg, Minnie Hauk, Emma Nevada, Etelka Gerster, Lillian Nordica, Italo Campanini, Francesco Tamagno.

Already New York had had its taste of German operas, which were quite modestly given, often in the smaller East Side theaters that today would be called neighborhood playhouses. Wagner's operas were being heard, for sometimes *Lohengrin* would be given (in Italian), and both it and *Tannhaüser* were performed in New York in 1859, in German. By 1878 even *Rienzi* and *The Flying Dutchman* were attempted. These were rather haphazard ventures, for fine German performances were not to be given until the eighties (and uptown), but New York was at least matching the European opera houses of the day and audiences were becoming familiar with what was being heard across the ocean.

JOHN KNOWLES PAINE: FIRST TEACHER-COMPOSER

Boston was still the hub of American culture in the 1870s and it was logical that the signs of America's maturing as a serious nation, interested in the best music, should come from that city. Harvard, the very school that had been America's first college (and was still one of her most important), created a full professorship of music, and in so doing put the study of music once and for all in the same position as the study of the other arts. It was also fitting that the man who was responsible for this forward step—John Knowles Paine (1839-1906)—was the first important native composer who not only wrote in the larger forms, but created works that were recognized abroad. It is also heartening to know that Paine lived to see himself the dean of American composers, one who was responsible for a long line of important and prolific pupils. Today Paine's music is neglected, for our present-day composers are more competent and imaginative, but in his day he was outstanding (in comparison to men like Fry or Bristow), and a man of great vision in his belief in the value and need of music education.

Paine was born in Portland, Maine, on January 9, 1839, and studied music with Hermann Kotzschmar, one of the many Germans who came to America (1848) and remained. Paine had become a proficient organist by the time he was eighteen, and in 1857 he went to Berlin to study with Karl A. Haupt, where he gained a reputation and toured successfully. He returned to America in 1861, and a year later was appointed instructor of music at Harvard. It had been Paine's own idea that he teach at Harvard, for, after being named chapel organist and choirmaster of the university, he saw the need of acquainting more students with the fundamentals of music. He offered to give a series of lectures on musical form, and, after overcoming opposition to such a radical idea, he was allowed to lecture. No credit was given toward a degree, and at first only a handful of students came to hear him.

When Charles W. Eliot became president of the university, the lectures were resumed in 1870. Paine offered a course in harmony which proved so successful that one in counterpoint was added, and as the classes grew his work gained official recognition. In 1873 he was made assistant professor, and two years later he had the honor of becoming the first professor of music at Harvard. This led gradually to the development of the Music School at Harvard, where today there are courses in applied music, and in music as one of the arts. The Harvard curriculum has been a model for other universities to follow; and in the same way that Lowell Mason made the Boston public schools and those of the nation aware of the value of music, so John Knowles Paine was the pioneer in establishing organized music courses in the American colleges.

Paine's works were published and played both here and abroad. When he was not yet thirty he returned to Europe and conducted his Mass at the Singakademie in Berlin, and in 1873 he directed the first performance of his oratorio *St. Peter* in his native town of Portland, Maine. All through his life his compositions were performed often. Theodore Thomas gave the première of his First Symphony in 1876 in Boston, and as we have discovered, he also commissioned Paine to write the music of the *Centennial Hymn* for the Philadelphia Exposition in 1876.

Paine's music was in the style of the German romanticists, and although it may seem pedantic and dry today, in his own time, and compared with much that had been written, it had a certain amount of imagination. He composed chamber music and two symphonies, as well as program music suggested by paintings or by literature. His *Ocean Fantasy* was inspired by the legend of Poseidon and Aphrodite; a symphonic poem told of Shakespeare's *The Tempest* and an overture of *As You Like It*. His *Island Fantasy* was drawn from two paintings of the Isle of Shoals off New Hampshire. The contrasting themes suggest the dangers and beauty of the sea, in a manner somewhat reminiscent of Mendelssohn's *Hebrides* music.

The Second Symphony, bearing the title *Spring,* was first heard in Boston in 1880 and was published by Arthur P. Schmidt, who deserves a monument for publishing the larger orchestral works of our early composers. This symphony was another attempt at program music, and its first movement, *Nature's Awakening,* is rather like that of J. J. Raff's spring symphony (which Paine could hardly have known), written one year before Paine's. There are two motives, one "Winter" and the other "Awakening." The two conflict, and the strength of Winter fails. The second movement is *The May Night Fantasy* in which the bassoon adds to the merriment. Then comes a Romance, *A Promise of Spring*, in rondo form; and the finale is a sort of hallelujah on *The Glory of Nature*. Thus our American composers were echoing the German romanticists.

Perhaps Paine's finest music was that composed for a performance of Sophocles' *Oedipus Tyrannus*, which was played at the Sanders Theatre in Cambridge, Massachusetts, in 1881. The Prelude was awarded a gold medal when it was played at an international concert in Berlin in 1903, commemorating the unveiling of a monument to Richard Wagner. It includes a Prelude, six choruses, and a Postlude. (There is a recording by Howard Hanson and the Eastman School Orchestra of the Prelude.) Paine's opera *Azara* was produced twice in concert form, but never came to performance in an opera house.

The craftsmanship and inventiveness of Paine's scores are considerably in advance of those of the earlier American composers who worked in the larger forms, yet it is not only as our first successful symphonic composer that Paine was important; he was the teacher of many of our leading composers, some of whom appeared as the century closed and others in the early twentieth century— Arthur Foote, Frederick Converse, Daniel Gregory Mason, John Alden Carpenter.

OTHER COMPOSERS

Three other composers who came to the front in Paine's lifetime are important enough to mention here.

William Wallace Gilchrist (1846-1916)

Born in Jersey City, Gilchrist lived most of his life in Philadelphia, training under Hugh A. Clarke, the teacher who was appointed professor of music at the University of Pennsylvania in the same year Paine was awarded similar honors at Harvard (1875). Gilchrist was the organizer, and for forty years conductor, of the Philadelphia Mendelssohn Club, and led the old Philadelphia Symphony Orchestra, the ancestor of the present Philadelphia Orchestra. His other activities included vocal teaching and choir directing.

Gilchrist won a thousand-dollar prize offered by the Cincinnati Festival in 1882 for his *Psalm 46*, written for soprano, chorus, and orchestra. He also composed a *Christmas Oratorio, Psalm 90, Song of Thanksgiving, Easter Idyl, The Rose* (a cantata), as well as two symphonies and chamber music. He had a facile technique, and despite his success in choral fields, Gilchrist was in happier vein when he wrote for instruments. An exception in his day for not having studied in Europe, Gilchrist nevertheless reflected the conventional German music of his day.

Frederick Grant Gleason (1848-1903)

Another New Englander was Frederick Grant Gleason, who was born in Middletown, Connecticut, and taken to live in Hartford while still a boy. His father, who was a banker, was an amateur musician, but it was not until the son, at sixteen, had written a *Christmas Oratorio*, without any instruction in harmony or counterpoint, that he was allowed to prepare himself for the profession of musician. He was put to work with Dudley Buck, and later went abroad to study with Moscheles, Richter, and others. He came back to Hartford, but when he was thirty he moved to Chicago, where he spent the rest of his life as one of the city's prominent organists and musicians.

A prolific composer, Gleason's music was tinged with Wagnerisms, and he used the Wagnerian system of leitmotifs in many of his larger works. Among his important works were a piece for the World's Fair concerts, a *Processional of the Holy Grail;* a symphonic poem, *Edris,* based on a novel by Marie Corelli; and the orchestral tone poem *Song of Life.* He made a setting of *The Culprit Fay* for chorus, and wrote a number of operas. Most of these have never been known, for he left a clause in his will that their scores should not be examined until he had been dead fifty years. One opera, *Montezuma,* was never produced, although its soprano arias were sung in concert on several occasions. The opera *Otho Visconti* was produced at the College Theatre, Chicago, in 1907. Probably Gleason's handicap was that his intellect was not properly balanced by his emotions. He was more of a harmonist than a melodist, and his harmonic combinations, so influenced by Wagner, were the product of his mind rather than of his feelings. Once again the American composer was merely following the inevitable trend of his day in the imitation of the German writers.

Dudley Buck (1839-1909)

Dudley Buck and John Knowles Paine were close contemporaries, for they were born in the same year, studied in Europe at the same time, and both returned in 1862 to take up their work at home. Theodore Thomas commissioned both men to write music for our important expositions—Philadelphia in 1876 and Chicago in 1893— and each lived to see the twentieth century.

In the larger forms of choral writing Dudley Buck stands out as a pioneer, just as Paine rises above his colleagues as the first of our symphonists to achieve success. Born in Hartford, Connecticut, March 10, 1839, the son of a shipping merchant, Buck showed an early taste for music. His father, however, intended that he should become a businessman, and it was not until he was sixteen that young Dudley had any music lessons. He made such rapid progress that his father changed his plans and permitted his son to become a musician. Only the finest teaching would suffice, and so Dudley was sent to Europe in 1858, where he settled in Leipzig and studied with Hauptmann, Richter, Plaidy, and Moscheles. Later he had organ lessons with Johann Schneider in Dresden, spent some time in Paris, and came home in 1862 to become organist of Hartford's Park Church.

After years of organ playing in Chicago and Boston, Buck settled in New York in 1875, at the invitation of Theodore Thomas, as assistant conductor of the Central Park Garden Concerts. Already Buck had done missionary work in giving organ recitals, which were as educational as the work Thomas was doing with his orchestra. His musicianship was combined with the ability to catch and hold popular attention. As a choir director and composer he helped to develop our literature for the church, and since he was fond of the mixed quartet that has been a feature of American worship, and sometimes its curse, he had a profound influence on our choir music. His larger works include the *Centennial Meditation of Columbus* (1876), to the poem of Sidney Lanier, *The Nun of Nidaros* (1879), and *Scenes from The Golden Legend*—for which he won the $1000 prize at the Cincinnati Festival in 1880—both texts from Longfellow, as had also his *King Olaf's Christmas*, for male chorus with solos.

Buck turned to Washington Irving and adapted a libretto from the *Life of Columbus* for his cantata *The Voyage of Columbus.*

In *The Golden Legend,* Buck attempted the use of the leitmotif for identifying characters and emotions; yet he never became particularly Wagnerian, for he loved too well the Italian style of declamation and *bel canto.* His agreeable melodies were almost too suave at times, yet there was generally substance behind his facility. Buck wrote for his market, and his work as a whole represents a compromise between the public taste and the composer's own ideals. Yet he constantly worked to raise standards, and he succeeded.

EVENTS OF THE 1880s

The 1880s were to become even more musical than the preceding decades, as Boston became the chief center for American composers. Those that led the creative activity were known as the Boston group, and they will be discussed in our next chapter. At the same time we will watch New York enter her memorable golden era of opera, which is still a tantalizing memory, even to those who can only read about it. As the 1870s drew to a close, it was no mere coincidence that other parts of the nation were developing, for Thomas and his orchestra, and Mapleson and his opera company, had touched all the major cities of the country and there was a veritable ferment of activity everywhere. By now, musical institutions which are still in existence were already founded. The Ann Arbor Festivals of the University of Michigan were inaugurated (1879), and in 1881 at Bethany College in Lindsborg, Kansas, the annual performances of Handel's *Messiah,* which by now have developed into a festival week, had their start. Important musical periodicals began to be issued in these years, whose names are familiar to every musician and most music lovers today—the semi-monthly *Musical Courier* (1880) published in New York, and *The Etude* (1883) published monthly in Philadelphia.

Boston Symphony Orchestra

Boston's own particular glory, and the pride of the entire nation —the Boston Symphony Orchestra—came into being as the dream and through the efforts and support of one man, Henry Lee Higginson, who was born in New York on November 18, 1834. It would be idle not to admit that the years had been slowly but surely building to this great event, but thanks to Major Higginson that dream became a reality. He had a passionate love of music, and had planned a concert career for himself by going to study in Vienna. An injury to his arm, however, caused by overpractice after he had been bled for an illness, forced him to give up his beloved piano and eventually to become a banker. A man of great vision as well as a practical financier, he planned his new venture carefully, and he became the first of many great men of wealth who subsidized American music at a time when it meant the most to the nation. In the spring of 1881 he published the following statement:

> My original scheme was this, viz: To hire an orchestra of sixty men and a conductor, paying them all by the year, reserving to myself the right to all their time needed for rehearsals and for concerts, and allowing them to give lessons when they had time; to give in Boston as many concerts of classical music as were wanted; and also to give at other times, and more especially in the summer, concerts of a lighter kind of music, in which should be included good dance music; to do the same in neighboring towns and cities as far as is practicable, but certainly to give Harvard University all that she needs in this line; to keep prices low always, and especially where the lighter concerts are in question, because to them may come the poorer people; fifty cents and twenty-five cents being the measure of prices.

The first concert in this altogether amazing new venture occurred on Saturday evening, October 22, 1881, in the Boston Music Hall, which had been erected in 1852 in Hamilton Place. George Henschel was the conductor, and the program included Beethoven's Overture *Dedication of the House*, an aria from Gluck's *Orfeo*, Haydn's Symphony No. 12, in B-flat, Schubert's ballet music from *Rosamunde*, Bruch's scene, *Odysseus*, and Weber's *Festival Overture*. Annie Louise Cary was the soloist. Henschel led the orchestra until 1884, when public opinion forced another man to take over. Major Higginson chose Wilhelm Gericke, whom he had heard conduct in Vienna, and Gericke proved not only to be an expert musician, but also to have those subtle qualities in conducting that Henschel had lacked and which immediately brought a distinction to the performances. When Arthur Nikisch, then Leipzig's leading Municipal

Opera conductor, succeeded Gericke in 1889, his magnificent interpretive qualities built the orchestra to the heights it was to maintain, almost continuously, to the present day.

New York's Metropolitan Opera House

New York's pride—the Metropolitan Opera House—was first conceived, not as a great musical venture, but as the whim of a few millionaires to satisfy the social ambitions of the city's new and ostentatious society. The industrial revolution, the Civil War, and the seemingly inexhaustible mines of the West had created a large group of newly rich individuals, who thought that they could buy culture and social standing if they paid enough for it.

The fine old Knickerbocker stock of the older New York society began to be filled with a new blood stream that had far too much gold in it. The old Academy on Fourteenth Street could not take care of all the dowagers, each of whom wanted a box at the opera as she wanted a mansion on Fifth Avenue and a villa at Newport. The committee that met to consider plans for the new opera house certainly did not have the great love of music that Boston's Major Higginson had had when he planned for a symphony orchestra. The erection of the new building uptown, on Broadway, was first and foremost planned for the convenience of the rich, and last of all for artistic reasons. James Roosevelt, William K. Vanderbilt, Robert Goelet, and Joseph W. Drexel—to cite but a few of the names—commissioned the architect J. Cleaveland Cady to plan the new house. Cady had never had any previous experience in building an opera house. Many unfortunate defects resulted and have remained through the years to trouble the opera company. The new building was rapidly finished, and the first season got under way on October 22, 1883, with a gala performance of Gounod's *Faust*, sung in Italian by a cast that included Christine Nilsson, Sofia Schalchi, Italo Campanini, Giuseppe del Puente, and a Signor Novara, all of them well-known from their performances downtown at the Academy of Music. Two nights later Donizetti's *Lucia di Lammermoor* was given, with a new singer, Marcella Sembrich, who was destined to make operatic history in New York. *Il Trovatore*, *I Puritani*, and *Mignon* finished out the first two weeks, performances of which were practically no different than the city had been accustomed to.

The new house was a declaration of war for Colonel Mapleson and the board of the Academy of Music, and the ensuing battle was a furious one. The Metropolitan's first season was managed by Henry E. Abbey, and to show him and his sponsors that they meant business, the Irving Place house announced another season, which began on the same night. Mapleson had lost some of his brightest stars to the Metropolitan, but he still had Patti and Etelka Gerster, and in the next month he introduced a new Marguerite, Mme. Norton-Gower, who soon sang under the proud name of Lillian Nordica. When that first season was over, both sides faced a devastating and ruinous defeat. Mapleson was used to this, but poor Abbey was not, and could only withdraw in disgrace, and while he offered to serve the next year without pay, the board was not interested. They were businessmen and they did not take kindly to losing money. While the Metropolitan board pondered what they might do, Leopold Damrosch came to their aid, suggesting something so unusual and unprecedented that little could anyone dream it would forever after influence the destiny of the Metropolitan Opera Company. Dr. Damrosch suggested a season of German opera, sung in German, and by the best German artists. His offer was immediately accepted, and in the summer of 1884 he left for Europe to get singers and to make his plans as conductor and manager of the new season. The new repertoire was to be, of course, mainly Wagnerian opera, but to those would be added works by other Germans, as well as the best French and Italian operas. Damrosch saw his season commence auspiciously, but his sudden death in 1885 left the subsequent execution of his plans to his son, Walter. The German years at the Metropolitan enriched the repertoire with many masterpieces which New York might not have otherwise seen for many years, and brought singers who would have had no other reason to come to America for many years, if at all. Wagner's original Brünnhilde and Kundry—Amalia Materna—was engaged, as well as the master's protégé, the conductor Anton Seidl. Soon the audiences were hearing the great European singers, such as Albert Niemann, Emil Fischer, Max Alvary, Lilli Lehmann, and Marianne Brandt, and Wagner's greatest works—*Tristan und Isolde, Die Meistersinger, Das Rheingold, Siegfried* and *Die Götterdämmerung.* Thus New York unwittingly had its own share in upholding the German traditions which were the nation's dominating influence as the century drew to its close.

Touring Opera Company and a National Conservatory

Mrs. Jeanette Thurber (1851-1946), a patron of music in New York, is one of the unsung heroines in the history of America's music, for out of her enthusiasm and farsightedness, there were started in New York, in 1885, two ventures of the utmost importance. One, a touring American opera, ended in failure. The other, a conservatory which had a distinguished international faculty, would have as its head for three years the eminent Bohemian composer Antonin Dvořák.

New York had become so opera conscious with its new Metropolitan Opera House and its rivalry with the older Academy of Music, that the idea of a touring American opera company seemed a good one. That it failed was unfortunate, but that it proved a costly mistake for a man who did not deserve to have such a setback at that time was a calamity. Theodore Thomas, then at the height of his popularity in New York, was given the artistic direction of the American Opera Company, which was made up of fine artists, and designed to encourage American composers of opera by giving their productions in English, and to take opera to various parts of the country. The repertoire included Hermann Goetz's *The Taming of the Shrew;* Otto Nicolai's *The Merry Wives of Windsor;* Léo Delibes' *Lakmé;* Mozart's *The Magic Flute;* and Wagner's *The Flying Dutchman* and *Lohengrin.* A feature of the organization was the large chorus of fresh, young voices, and the old Academy of Music was attractively renovated for the opening on January 4, 1886. Thomas had been led to believe that the public would welcome an American venture in opera producing, and he was induced to become conductor of an enterprise which he thought was sponsored by the wealthiest men of the country. When he found that as soon as the company lost money on tour the backers withdrew in a panic, he was left with a surpassingly artistic venture, but with all the bills unpaid, and as though that were not enough he was blamed for its failure, although his only sin was that he had done a fine job. When he returned to New York he found that his prestige had greatly lessened, for he not only had to bear the unfair stigma of his opera failure, the bitter rivalry of the factions who were the followers of the Damrosches, but a new conductor, Anton Seidl. These were bad years for Thomas, and he was to know no peace until Chicago beckoned a few years later.

The National Conservatory of Music of America is unique in the annals of our nation's music schools, for not only did Mrs. Thurber obtain a charter from New York State, but as she also founded the school for Washington (as well as New York City), she also received a charter from the United States Congress, the only one of its kind in America. Until 1915 tuition was free, maintained from funds Mrs. Thurber and a few others gave. The first director was Jacques Bouhy (1885-89), followed by Antonin Dvořák (1892-95), and Emil Paur (1899-1902). Its distinguished faculty included Mme. Fursch-Madi, B. O. Klein, Adele Margulies, Raphael Joseffy, James G. Huneker, Henry T. Finck, Victor Herbert, Horatio Parker, Anton Seidl, and Max Spicker.

CHAPTER VIII

Last Years of the Nineteenth Century

THE BOSTON GROUP

The flowering of America's art music was the result of a group of composers active in New England—a few men who are generally grouped together because they lived and worked side by side, and because they had something in common artistically. Yet the relationship is one of sympathy and background, rather than of any particular traits of style that mark their music. They were all the product of the same age—coming at a time when the American composer was first having a respectful and interested hearing—and when all the musical world was under the spell of the German romanticists. These New Englanders are often called the Boston classicists, or the New England academics, yet neither term is quite accurate. None of them departed far from accepted paths, or ventured into startling experiments. Time has shown that their work is most important historically, as a part of America's musical evolution, for they are the first "school" of composition to appear within the nation, and as a group, these New Englanders set the standard for and dominated America's symphonic writing up to World War I.

George Whitefield Chadwick (1854-1931)

Paine's mantle as dean of American composers fell to George Whitefield Chadwick, who was born in Lowell, Massachusetts, on November 13, 1854. The son of an amateur musician, Chadwick's significance lies in the fact that he not only took over from Paine in carrying on the tradition of fine teaching, but his own work, while somewhat academic, had a spark of genuine inspiration, flavored with a sense of humor, and Philip Hale perfectly described his music when he wrote that it had "a certain jaunty irreverence, a snapping of the fingers at Fate and the Universe."

Chadwick was of New England stock on both sides of his family —orthodox, devout Congregationalists. His father was a good musician, who in his spare time, like his eighteenth-century musical ancestors, taught a singing class and organized a chorus and an orchestra in the neighborhood. He prospered in his business; first as a farmer, then as a machinist in Lowell, and finally, when George was six, the family moved down to Lawrence, where the senior Chadwick started a life and fire insurance business. Music always held George Chadwick in its spell. The musical gatherings of his relatives were high spots during his childhood, as he learned to play the piano and the organ. When he was graduated from high school George was allowed to take regular trips to Boston for piano lessons, all the while working in his father's business. When he was twenty-one, George knew that he must answer the call of music, and quitting his father's firm, plunged into serious study at the New England Conservatory, the school which he was to direct many years later.

Deciding to teach music himself, Chadwick secured an appointment as music professor of Olivet College in 1876, and had a part in one of the most important projects of his day, one that was to still further America's music in the twentieth century. A young musician, Theodore Presser, whose name would become known to millions throughout the world as a music publisher and benefactor, called a meeting of a small group of music teachers in Delaware, Ohio, for the purpose of "mutual improvement by interchange of ideas, to broaden the culture of music, and to cultivate fraternal feeling." This meeting alone can give some idea of the almost incredible growth of the private teacher in America, for the Music Teachers' National Association, which grew out of this meeting, is still one of the vital forces of America's music today. Eben Tourjée, who had founded the New England Conservatory of Music, was named the first president, and with him had come several outstanding musicians, one of whom was George Chadwick, who read a paper at the first meeting.

Perhaps this was the very stimulation that George needed at that time, to convince him that study abroad was what he needed. He had saved enough money from his teaching to cover his expenses, but he had not counted on the opposition of his God-fearing father. Teaching was one thing, especially in a college, but to have an out-and-out professional musician in the family was quite a different matter. But George was firm in his resolve to go, and he went to Europe.

Arriving in Berlin in the fall of 1877, Chadwick first studied with Karl August Haupt, but not receiving the training in orchestration that he felt he needed, he went on to Leipzig where he worked with Salomon Jadassohn. The teacher took a personal interest in Chadwick, and it was while he was with Jadassohn that he wrote the *Rip Van Winkle* Overture and two string quartets. Craving additional study after two years, he chose Rheinberger in Munich, rather than Franck in Paris, and from Rheinberger he learned the power of self-criticism.

Chadwick came back home in 1880, where he rented a studio in Boston and started to teach. Horatio Parker was one of his first pupils, and soon Sidney Homer and Arthur Whiting joined his class. In 1882 Chadwick was made instructor at the New England Conservatory, and fifteen years later he was asked to be its director. He held that position until his death, April 4, 1931. In the meantime he continued to compose, and also played a church organ and conducted choral societies.

Chadwick was one of the foremost orchestral composers of the Boston group, and wrote some twenty major works for orchestra. There were symphonies, one a sinfonietta, but it was the overture that offered him the happiest chance to express his ideas. He composed six of them: *Rip Van Winkle* (1879), *Thalia* (1883), *The Miller's Daughter* (1887), *Melpomene* (1891), *Adonais* (1898), and *Euterpe* (1906). The works that show his jauntiness and carefree spirit most effectively are *A Vagrom Ballad* (No. 4 of his *Symphonic Sketches,* 1907), and the symphonic ballad *Tam o'Shanter* (1917). The *Suite Symphonique* won first prize in the 1911 competition of the National Federation of Music Clubs. The *Symphonic Sketches* are in four movements consisting of *Jubilee, Noël, Hobgoblin,* and *A Vagrom Ballad.*

Chadwick attempted opera, but his dramatic powers were more suitable to the narratives of his orchestral ballads. The lyric drama *Judith* was performed in concert form at the Worcester Festival in

1901, and *Tabasco,* a comic opera, was given its première at the Boston Museum in 1894. Among his major choral works is the setting of Harriet Monroe's *Ode* for the opening concert of the World's Fair in Chicago (1893), *Viking's Last Voyage* (1881), *The Dedication Ode* (1886), *Phoenix Expirans* (1892), and *Noël* (1909). He published considerable chamber music, and over a hundred songs, of which his setting of Sidney Lanier's *Ballad of Trees and the Master* is perhaps the best known. In many ways Chadwick was typically American in his music, not from his use of folk songs or historic subjects, but by something far subtler, something he could never have avoided even if he had tried. His delicious impertinence is genuinely American, the dry humor of the Yankee. He added life to the forms he used, and gave us something vital. There is a freshness in his music that is a matter of spirit rather than of style or idiom.

Arthur William Foote (1853-1937)

Unlike his contemporaries, Arthur William Foote did not go abroad to study; in fact, it was not until he had been graduated from Harvard, when he was twenty-one, that he definitely made up his mind to be a musician. Born in Salem, Massachusetts, he had taken John Knowles Paine's music courses in college, and had been conductor of the Harvard Glee Club. After his graduation he decided to pass a useful summer before going into business, so he had some organ lessons with B. J. Lang, who so encouraged him that Foote decided that music should be his profession. The next two years were spent in studying organ and piano with Lang, and in 1876 he started on his own as a piano teacher, and was one of Boston's prominent teachers for over sixty years. From 1878 until 1910, Foote was organist of the First Unitarian Church in Boston, and he helped found the American Guild of Organists. He died April 9, 1937.

Foote's style was derived from the composers he had admired in his formative years, notably Brahms, and his Quintet for piano and strings is definitely Brahmsian in its melodic and harmonic flavor. He called himself a conservative, but admiration of Brahms was by no means a conservative matter in the late Victorian era, especially in Boston. In his writing, Foote seems chiefly concerned with harmonic rather than with contrapuntal patterns. He wrote many works in the larger forms, including *In the Mountains,* an overture, which was first performed by the Boston Symphony under Gericke in 1887. His *Serenade in E,* for strings, and his *Suite in D,* had been played a year earlier (1886). Foote took the episode of *Francesca da Rimini* from Dante for his Symphonic Prologue, probably his most distinguished work, somewhat programmatic in its development. It was first played in Boston in 1893, the same year in which Theodore Thomas played the *Serenade* for strings at the World's Fair. In 1894, Thomas conducted a performance of his Concerto for cello and orchestra at one of the concerts of the Chicago Symphony Orchestra, then in its fourth season. After 1900 he composed only two works for orchestra: a *Suite in E,* for strings (1910), and *Four Character Pieces after Omar Khayyám* (1912).

There are a number of choral works with orchestra—*The Farewell of Hiawatha,* for men's voices (1886), *The Wreck of the Hesperus* (1888), and *The Skeleton in Armor* (1893). Most of Foote's chamber music had its first performances at concerts of the Kneisel Quartet, and the large body of his smaller pieces includes a great deal of church music, almost one hundred and fifty songs (many from the English poets), some thirty piano pieces, and over thirty pieces for organ.

Horatio William Parker (1863-1919)

If Horatio Parker had been as successful in his symphonic works as he was in his choral writings, he might in his time have been the greatest of our American composers. Parker was born of a cultured family. His mother, Isabella Parker, the daughter of a Baptist minister, was a scholar and a musician, organist of the village church at Auburndale, Massachusetts, the town where Horatio was born September 15, 1863. His father, Charles Edward Parker, was an architect. As a child Horatio disliked anything connected with music, but suddenly, when he was fourteen, he seemed to wake from his musical sleep, and had his first piano lessons with his mother, and then with local teachers. He started to compose, and at sixteen he was made organist of a church in Dedham, and for its services he wrote hymn tunes, anthems, and choir services, as his Puritan ancestors might have done. About this time Chadwick returned from Europe, and Parker became one of his first pupils. Of course he must follow the inevitable trend of the day by studying in

Europe, and in 1882 he became a student of Rheinberger in Munich, at the Royal School of Music. By placing himself wholly in Rheinberger's hands, he acquired a contrapuntal mastery that helped him later to reach the summits of choral writing.

When he came back to America he settled in New York, and was put in charge of the music teaching at St. Paul's School in Garden City. He was organist at St. Andrew's and later at Holy Trinity, and he joined the faculty of the National Conservatory, where Antonin Dvořák was to be the director. Seven years later, in 1893, he had a chance to return to his native Boston as an organist and choirmaster of Trinity Church, then famous for the sermons of Phillips Brooks. In 1894 he was invited to head the music department of Yale University, the year its now-famous School of Music was founded. The Battell family had supported music at the University for many years, since 1854, when Joseph Battell had provided a fund for sacred music. This, with gifts from various members of the family, led to the creation of the Battell Professorship of Music in 1890, with Gustav J. Stoeckel as the first Professor. Dr. Parker followed Stoeckel in 1894, and held that position until his death in 1919. While at Yale, Parker organized the New Haven Symphony, subsidized by the University, and through the years commuted between New Haven, New York, and Philadelphia.

David Stanley Smith, Parker's assistant at Yale and later his successor, wrote: "It seems incredible, but through this period Parker composed incessantly. There was always a score in the making." He wrote nine pieces for orchestra, chamber music, and numerous piano and organ pieces, but it is for his choral music and operas that he is best known. He first achieved fame, both in England and America, for his cantata *Hora Novissima*, composed in 1891-92, and first performed in 1893 by the Church Choral Society of New York. Written for chorus and orchestra, the text Parker used was the Latin hymn of Bernard de Morlaix, his mother having made the English translation. After performances in Boston and Cincinnati, in 1899 it was performed at the Three Choirs Festival at Worcester, England, and it made such an impression on the English audience that Parker was commissioned to write a new work for the Hereford Festival—the *Wanderer's Psalm;* and the *Star Song* was written for the Norwich Festival in 1902. By this time his fame was almost greater in England than America, for the English had had, since the days of Handel, a predilection for good choral music, and they liked what Parker wrote. *The Legend of St. Christopher,* sung at Bristol, completed all that was needed for an award of the Doctor of Music degree by Cambridge University in 1902. In New York Parker had submitted both *Hora Novissima* and a cantata, *The Dream King and His Love,* in a prize contest at the National Conservatory. He won the prize, not for *Hora Novissima*—the judges, including Dvořák, liked *The Dream King* better.

Like many of Parker's works, the opera *Mona* was written for a definite purpose. Parker was able to do this, generally without sacrificing quality. Commissions, or prize contests, never drew hack work from him. The directors of the Metropolitan Opera House in New York offered a prize of $10,000 for an opera by an American composer, with an English text. Parker heard of the offer and was tempted. His friend Brian Hooker, professor of English at Yale, wrote the libretto—the tale of *Mona,* princess of Britain in the days of the Roman invasion, torn between her love for the son of the Roman governor and her hatred of the Roman conquerors. The opera was produced at the Metropolitan Opera House on March 14, 1912. This was the third American opera to be sung at the Metropolitan—Frederick Shepherd Converse's *The Pipe of Desire* had been performed in 1910 and Victor Herbert's *Natoma* a year later, by the Philadelphia-Chicago Company—but neither had made as profound an impression as *Mona.* Another opera, *Fairyland,* set to a libretto by Hooker, also won a $10,000 prize, in 1915. The prize was offered by the National Federation of Music Clubs, and the opera was performed six times in Los Angeles at the Federation Biennial in 1915.

Parker was a composer with a heritage of Puritan hymn singing, with an instinct for fine choral texture, for massed effects, and for full development of hymnlike themes. On this his German training was superimposed, yet this influence never prevented him from being individual. He clearly showed that America no longer had to be ashamed of her music, and at this particular time, this was of paramount importance in the nation's slow but steady maturing.

Mrs. H. H. A. Beach (1867-1944)

Mrs. Beach was one of the youngest of the Boston group, and her activities continued well into the twentieth century. Like Chadwick, she was one of those commissioned by Theodore Thomas to compose for the Chicago World's Fair in 1893. Her *Festival Jubilate* was performed at the dedication of the Woman's Building. She was born Amy Marcy Cheney in Henniker, New Hampshire, and moved with her family to Boston at the age of eight. Her parents were New Englanders of colonial descent, and she was musical from babyhood. She played the piano at four, and two years later she insisted her mother give her lessons. In Boston, her instruction continued under various teachers, and Amy also began to compose, training herself without outside help. She made her first public appearance at sixteen, and in a year played with the Boston Symphony and the Thomas Orchestra. Later, after her husband's death in 1910, she spent four years abroad, playing in concerts and introducing her own works in Germany. She achieved international standing and became the outstanding composer among American women.

Although she was best known to the public for her songs, particularly her settings of Browning's *Ah, Love but a Day* and *The Year's at the Spring,* she composed a number of larger works, among them a *Gaelic Symphony* (made from Gaelic themes) and a piano concerto, both of which the foreign critics received with enthusiasm. In 1898 she wrote a *Song of Welcome* for the Trans-Mississippi Exposition at Omaha, and in 1915 a *Panama Hymn* for the Panama-Pacific Exposition in San Francisco.

DVOŘÁK'S RESIDENCE IN AMERICA

By inviting Antonin Dvořák to head the National Conservatory Mrs. Jeanette Thurber indirectly exerted a strong influence on much of the American music that was composed during the next quarter-century. For although the composers who are discussed in this chapter (the Boston group and MacDowell) were either little affected by or were opposed to Dvořák's views on nationalism in music, there were many, as we shall see in our next chapter, who were inspired by them.

When Dvořák received an invitation from Mrs. Thurber to head her school, he was already a world figure, the recipient of many honors, a man secure in his position. The University of Cambridge had given him an honorary degree in music, and the University of

Prague one in philosophy. The Austrian government had decorated him with the Order of the Iron Crown, the Czech government had elevated him to the Academy of Arts and Sciences, and he was a professor in the Prague Conservatory of Music. Small wonder that he debated the worth of pulling up his roots and coming to a new country and a new world.

We know today how vitally stimulating was Dvořák's presence in America, for he was a composer of great talent and a fine musician, and he quickly recognized the worth of both American Indian and Negro music. He came just at the right time, for in his work at the National Conservatory he tried to develop a nationalistic school of music among his American pupils, and if he did not completely succeed, at least some of his students and other composers became aware of the possibilities inherent in American folk song.

Arriving in New York in 1892, Dvořák installed himself in an apartment on East Seventeenth Street, and almost at once threw himself into the musical life of the city. His days were filled to overflowing with teaching, conducting, composing, and hearing music. He discovered that his own outlook was broadening, and because he was well paid he was earning enough to give him financial security for the rest of his life.

One of his students at the school was a young Negro baritone, Harry Thacker Burleigh (1866-1949), who later became an arranger of spirituals as well as a song composer. As Dvořák became more and more interested in the great body of Negro song, young Burleigh became a constant visitor to his apartment. Manuscripts were pored over, discussed, and the music sung with the greatest enthusiasm. At the same time Dvořák had long talks with James Huneker, the music critic and essayist, and in about two months after his arrival, he began working on the Symphony "From the New World." The work was continued through the summer vacation in Spillville, Iowa, at a Czech colony, and shortly before the première of the New World Symphony, Dvořák made the following statement to the press: "These beautiful and varied themes are the product of the soil. They are American. They are the folk songs of America, and your composers must turn to them. In the Negro melodies of America I discover all that is needed for a great and noble school of music." A further significant statement was made in Berlin, when the Symphony was given in Germany for the first time: "Omit that nonsense about my having made use of 'Indian' and 'American' motives. That is a lie. I tried only to write in the spirit of those national American melodies." He had, of course, done the same with the Bohemian and Moravian folk music in his own country— not literally copied them, but rather had written his own music in the style and spirit of the native tunes he knew so well. So had his colleague and countryman Smetana, and his contemporary in Norway, Edvard Grieg.

In 1895, despite his great success and many excellent financial offers, Dvořák turned down the renewal of his contract and sailed for Prague. He could not resist the call of his homeland, and his last years, until his death on May 1, 1904, were spent in composing and teaching. The other works which date from his American sojourn include a cantata, *The American Flag* (1893); and two chamber works—a String Quartet and a Quintet—in which he used themes suggestive of the Negro spirituals, as he had done in the *New World Symphony.* America can never thank him enough for being among the first to help her to recognize the tremendous possibilities which were as yet latent within herself.

EDWARD MACDOWELL

It was in 1888 that Edward Alexander MacDowell, a native son who had been trained abroad and had won recognition there, returned to this country to practice his profession among his fellow Americans. He was born in New York December 18, 1861, in a decade which produced some of the most brilliant men of the latter nineteenth century: in 1860, Gustave Charpentier, Gustav Mahler, Hugo Wolf, and Isaac Albeniz; in 1861, MacDowell and Loeffler; in 1862, Claude Debussy and Frederick Delius. Pietro Mascagni was born in 1863, Richard Strauss in 1864, and Erik Satie in 1866.

MacDowell, of course, was a contemporary of the Boston group, but outside of the fact that he had lived abroad for years, in fact during the formative years of his life, spiritually he was never part of it, nor was he in sympathy with Dvořák's views on nationalism. He was an individualist. He had been active in Europe during the years of his residence there, and under the patronage of Franz Liszt he had been one of the first American composers to be truly recognized, for his compositions had much more substance than the showy display pieces of Gottschalk. His early works in the larger forms, written and published in Germany, brought him fame as an American who composed "serious" music.

Early Training

MacDowell had every advantage from his earliest years. His talents were given every opportunity to develop, and he had the best training possible. He was the third son of Thomas and Frances Knapp MacDowell. The father was of Scotch ancestry, the mother Irish. There was a Quaker background, and probably the fact that he himself had not been allowed to become a painter made his father sympathetic with his boy's extraordinary talents for music. Edward had his first piano lessons when he was eight—principally from a South American, Juan Buitrago. When Edward was fifteen it was decided that he should go abroad for study, and his mother took him to Paris. For a year he worked privately with Antoine François Marmontel, and then his teacher urged him to enter the competition for a scholarship at the Conservatoire. He won it, and became a regular pupil in 1877. One of his fellow students was a lad with queer ideas—named Debussy. By the summer of 1878, Edward had had enough of the Conservatoire. After hearing Nicholas Rubinstein in a concert, he told his mother that he could never learn to play like that if he stayed in Paris. In Germany, at the Stuttgart Conservatory, things were no more to his liking, and when a friend suggested Karl Heymann in Frankfort, it seemed an excellent idea. After a few lessons during the summer with Louis Ehlert in Wiesbaden, he entered Heymann's class at the Frankfort Conservatory in the fall. Here MacDowell was happy, for he began to study composition seriously with Joachim Raff, who was at that time the director of the Conservatory. Raff saw the possibilities of Edward's gifts, and it was through his influence that MacDowell eventually decided to become a composer. He also formed a friendship with his teacher that was to be one of his fondest memories.

Recognition Abroad

By 1880 MacDowell was a thoroughly trained musician, a gifted pianist, and, as he was very content in Germany, with no desire to return home, he began to take pupils himself. He was also beginning to compose. The *First Modern Suite* was written between lessons, and the *Second Modern Suite* on the train rides between Frankfort and his teaching in Darmstadt, at the Conservatory. When MacDowell was twenty-one, Raff, who was much pleased with his student's progress (especially with his First Piano Concerto), urged him to call on Franz Liszt at Weimar. The great man was most cordial, and with Eugène D'Albert, who was there also, he had MacDowell play the concerto for him. Leaving some manuscripts with Liszt, MacDowell was elated to have a letter from Liszt, saying that he liked his work, and had recommended the *First Modern Suite* to the General Society of German Musicians and that MacDowell was invited to play it at their meeting on July 11, 1882. Through Liszt's recommendations the Suite and the Concerto were published by Breitkopf & Härtel. With Liszt's encouragement (Raff had just died and the young man was heartbroken) MacDowell gave all of his time to composition, and the conductors of the little bands at the health resorts tried his new works at their rehearsals. All this was valuable experience. He returned to America in 1884 to be married in Waterford, Connecticut, to a young lady he had taught in Germany—Marian Nevins. The couple returned to Germany, living first in Frankfort (where MacDowell started his Second Piano Concerto), and moving to Wiesbaden in 1885, where in another year they bought a small cottage near the edge of a wood. MacDowell wrote well in his new surroundings, and his reputation grew. Back in America the great pianist Teresa Carreño, his good friend, whom he had first met through Buitrago, was making audiences familiar with the young composer by playing his works in her concerts.

Return to America

MacDowell had another blow when Liszt died in 1886, and it caused him to turn his thoughts to coming back to America and making a permanent home. He first considered living in New York, but was finally persuaded to make his home in Boston, where for the next eight years, from 1888, he lived in the Hub as a composer, teacher, and concert pianist. He disliked taking time from his composing to play the piano, but he was made to realize that he would have to make his works known by playing them, and that if he wanted pupils, it was imperative to establish his reputation as a concert pianist. Within three years his studio became a mecca for pupils.

MacDowell had a poetic insight and an imaginative temperament that made the later German romanticism his particular medium. He did not like to be classified as an American composer, feeling that he might be listened to only because America was still so young in the musical life of the world, and he wanted only to be heard if his music was worth while. It was in the 1890s that he began to show the real MacDowell as a composer for the piano. He was a tone poet, and perhaps his finest writing is in the field of the miniature, his small and effective piano pieces: the *Twelve Virtuoso Studies* (1894); the *Woodland Sketches* (1896), containing *To a Wild Rose* and *To a Water Lily*, whose exquisiteness made them immediately popular and thus caused the music to haunt him the rest of his life; and the *Sea Pieces*, issued two years later, 1898. Here is MacDowell at the height of his powers, lyric and dramatic. The last two works on his list were the *Fireside Tales* (1902) and the *New England Idyls* (1902).

MacDowell wrote several major works for orchestra, and though the orchestra was not his best medium, his early works were often performed, such as the symphonic poem *Hamlet and Ophelia* (1885); *Lancelot and Elaine* (1888); *Lamia*, after Keats (written 1888-89, published 1908); *The Saracens* and *The Lovely Alda*, two fragments after the *Song of Roland*, published in 1891.

Teaching at Columbia

The years in Boston were punctuated with concert tours, since his playing, especially of his own music, was much in demand. He enjoyed his independence, and was loath to tie himself down to a regular routine position when he was invited by President Seth Low and the trustees of Columbia University to come to New York and take charge of the new department of music, in 1896. Giving the invitation careful consideration, he finally accepted it. Not only was there a guaranteed income, he had a chance to put into effect some of his ideas for the education of American youth, and an opportunity to give musical training of the first order to some who could not afford to pay for it elsewhere.

The first years at Columbia went well enough. Seth Low wanted him because he was an individualist, and it was to the glory of the University to have him there. MacDowell worked intensively—lecturing on the history and aesthetics of music, and teaching classes in harmony and composition—correcting exercises with meticulous care, consulting students, and attending to matters of routine. In a year he had an assistant—Leonard McWhood, who had been his pupil—and in 1899 Gustav Hinrichs was engaged to conduct the student orchestra and chorus. And all the while MacDowell was planning and dreaming of what a university music department should be, especially in its relation to teaching other branches of the fine arts.

When MacDowell was absent on his sabbatical year in the season of 1902-03, Nicholas Murray Butler succeeded Seth Low as president of the University and started a reorganization according to his own ideas as to how the fine arts should be taught. MacDowell had visualized a department of fine arts at Columbia that would embrace not only belles-lettres and music, but architecture, painting, and sculpture. There was a conflict of views and President Butler announced in February of 1904 that MacDowell had resigned because he wanted more time to compose. MacDowell retorted publicly that he was leaving because he felt that his work had been futile, and that he could see no chance for conducting the kind of department he would care to be associated with at Columbia.

The Columbia affair is almost forgotten today, but at the time and because of MacDowell's indiscretion in talking to two student reporters, the news made the headlines in the New York papers with a fury that rocked the musical world. In retrospect, the events at Columbia are important chiefly as they throw a light on the character of the composer and its reflection in his music. Impulsive, hasty, yet generous and sensitive, MacDowell sometimes lost his sense of perspective. His music reaches out for great heights. It often achieves them, yet it frequently stops for breath on the way to the summit. There was no compromise, either in his music or in MacDowell. He had to be himself. He could not adapt his ideas to the ways of others, even though both were seeking the same object. They must take the same road, or one of them must stay at home. Columbia University is now proud of the fact that MacDowell was its first professor of music, and the position he occupied has been named the Edward MacDowell Chair of Music.

Last Years

MacDowell left Columbia in 1904, brooding over the controversy.

To make things worse, he was knocked down by a cab on the streets and injured. For a year he tried to do some private teaching, but in the spring of 1905 the strain had so told on his health that he suffered a mental breakdown from which he never recovered. For over two years his was a body without a mind, until he quietly passed away at the Westminster Hotel in New York, January 23, 1908. His body was buried at Peterboro, New Hampshire, where he and his wife had bought a house and farm on which they had spent their summers during the years at Columbia. Here he had built a log cabin, where he went early in the summer mornings to write those last pieces—his *Fireside Tales,* his *New England Idyls,* as well as the third and fourth piano sonatas, the *Norse* and *Keltic.* He often thought of having other artists share his retreat, and he and his wife talked of the artist colony they would some day found at Peterboro.

Mrs. MacDowell made the fulfillment of this idea her life work. Her concert tours, playing her husband's music, were undertaken for the distinct purpose of raising funds to maintain the colony at Peterboro. Today it is the summer refuge of artists, composers, poets, and writers who come to do their work in the spot where MacDowell wrote his last pieces, a monument to the memory of Edward MacDowell.

Estimates of His Music

It is not an easy matter to appraise MacDowell fairly in his relation to American music, or to the music of the world, even though he has been dead nearly a half century. Shortly after MacDowell's death, Lawrence Gilman, who later became the music critic for the *New York Herald Tribune,* wrote in his revised edition of the biography he had first written in 1905 that he knew of no piano sonatas since the death of Beethoven that could compare with the four of MacDowell for passion, dignity, and breadth of style.

Paul Rosenfeld, writing in 1929 on American music, said:

> Were it not for MacDowell's celtic descent, one might almost be tempted to attribute this group-wide weakness for the odors of sanctity to a racial strain, so many instances arising in which saxondom and snobbery . . . seem almost synonymous. . . . In music, this weakness took the form of sentimentality. The feelings entertained about life by him seem to have remained

uncertain; and while fumbling for them he seems regularly to have succumbed to "nice" and "respectable" emotions, conventional, accepted by and welcome to, the best people. It is shocking to find how full of vague poesy he is. Where his great romantic brethren, Brahms, Wagner, and Debussy, are direct and sensitive, clearly and tellingly expressive, MacDowell minces and simpers, maidenly, and ruffled . . .

Somewhere between these two views there must be a middle ground. It is too much to term MacDowell the composer of the greatest piano sonatas since Beethoven, nor can he be dismissed lightly and patronizingly. He is probably the first of our creative musicians for whom we need make no allowance for lack of early training. None of his limitations was caused by his being an American. Whether he is judged great or small, he may be considered simply as a composer, a musician, who was among the first of our Americans to be recognized as a composer of art music.

His Views on Nationalism

MacDowell was never in sympathy with Dvořák's nationalistic movement, but he was never for one moment ashamed of his own American nationality, and was always eager to advance the interests of native artists. But he made his stand very clear in one of his later lectures at Columbia University when he said: "nationalism, so-called, is merely an extraneous thing that has no part in pure art. For if we take any melody, even of the most pronounced national type, and merely eliminate the characteristic turns, affectations, as mannerisms, the theme becomes simply music, and retains no touch of nationality. We may even go further," he continued, "for if we retain the characteristic mannerisms of dress, we may harmonize a folk-song in such a manner that it will belie its origin." When MacDowell used Indian themes, as he did in his second *Indian Suite* for orchestra, he was careful to point out that he did not feel he was writing American music just because he used these melodies. He made one attempt at using American ragtime, in the Scherzo of his Second Piano Concerto, but he told his pupils that this idiom was not enough a part of his background to make it indigenous to his own music, although they were free to experiment with it themselves, if it came naturally to them. MacDowell felt, and time has proved him right, that Americanism in music was something more subtle and intangible than the mere use of native songs. "What we must arrive at," he explained to a friend, "is the youthful optimistic vitality and the undaunted tenacity of spirit that characterizes the American man." Herein lies the paradox of MacDowell, the American by birth, the composer who was German by study and environment. Markedly original, he guarded his manner of speech jealously, for in his latter years he often told his friends that he avoided hearing music, so that he would not be in danger of showing its influence. This possibly explains the limitations of his own music, for almost all composers derive from some source. His formative years in Paris and Germany and his subsequent residence in Boston, where his colleagues were steeped in the German post-romanticism, gave him no opportunity to come to know or understand American ways of life. And even America herself was at that time unaware of the great potentialities that lay within her own borders, that great body of song, which, although there were faint stirrings of interest in it, would not be completely recognized until after the first World War. Undoubtedly MacDowell, during the years at Columbia University in New York, began to sense, perhaps through his contacts with his students, what America needed and did not yet have. "Before a people can find a musical writer to echo its genius it must first possess men who truly represent it—that is to say, men who, being part of the people, love the country for itself . . . and in the case of America it needs above all, both on the part of the public and on the part of the writer, absolute freedom from the restraint that an almost unlimited deference to European thought and prejudice has imposed upon us." Thus, in one of his lectures at Columbia he unknowingly bared his own weaknesses and limitations, and at the same time spoke words that were not only prophetic, but would be fulfilled in the twentieth century in America.

Piano Pieces; Orchestral Music

It is for his piano music that we know MacDowell best. There are four sonatas: the *Tragica*, Opus 45 (1893); the *Eroica*, Opus 50 (1895); the *Norse*, Opus 57 (1900); and the *Keltic*, Opus 59 (1901). The last two were dedicated to Grieg. The *Tragica* is thought to have come out of his grief over Raff's death, for he said that in the first three movements he aimed to express tragic details, and in the Finale "to heighten the darkness of tragedy by making it follow closely on the heels of triumph." The *Eroica* Sonata (dedicated to William Mason) concerns the legend of King Arthur, while in the *Norse* Sonata MacDowell attempted to paint the barbaric feeling of the Norse sagas through the extended span of his phrases and wide chord formations. The *Keltic* Sonata, he wrote, "is more of a 'bardic' rhapsody on the subject than an attempt at actual presentation of it, although I have made use of all the suggestion of tone-painting in my power." There has been a new interest in these sonatas recently, and they have had much success on recital programs both in America and Europe. The *Tragica* and *Eroica* sonatas, with the concertos, have been recorded, and perhaps that deciding factor in all music—that of time—will allow a better estimate of their worth.

Besides the two piano concertos—No. 1 in A Minor (1884) and No. 2 in D Minor (1890)—MacDowell's finest orchestral work is his Second *(Indian)* Suite, Opus 48, which was first played by Emil Paur and the Boston Symphony Orchestra (to whom it was dedicated) in New York City, January 23, 1896. After that he wrote no more for orchestra, and this seems a fitting climax to his list in this field. The five movements are: I. Legend; II. Love Song; III. In War-time; IV. Dirge; V. Festival. MacDowell's own views on nationalism in music show clearly that he did not intend to write American music by using Indian themes, nor did he think that such material could be harmonized in a manner that would make it sound like the originals from which it was taken. He chose the themes from Theodore Baker's thesis on Indian music, which he knew, but he said to Hamlin Garland: "I do not believe in 'lifting' a Navajo theme and furbishing it into some kind of a musical composition and calling it American music. Our problem is not so simple as that." He may, of course, have been experimenting; but he was no doubt content to catch the spirit of his theme, the joys and sorrows of a vanishing race. This he did most eloquently, and in this case he seems more effectively American than ever before.

Although he was never satisfied with music's ability to match the syllables and inflection of a poem, MacDowell's songs, which should be mentioned, show a rare ability to interpret the spirit and mood of the verses he chose for a setting. He was happiest writing his own poems, and he published over forty songs, some of which are of a very high standard. They include *Menie, Thy Beaming Eyes, The*

Swan Bent Low to the Lily, Fair Springtide, Confidence, and *As the Gloaming Shadows Creep.*

Paine, Chadwick, Parker, and MacDowell represent a final maturing of the American composer, who, still learning his craft, could scarcely be expected to compete with the European musicians who had a rich heritage of hundreds of years. At last the American composer could look the world squarely in the face, and the twentieth century would see him take his rightful place in the world's music.

NATIONALISM AND IMPRESSIONISM ABROAD

The last quarter of the nineteenth century was most important in America's musical development, first because of the emergence of a group of serious composers who brought recognition to America throughout the world, and secondly because of the arrival of a world-famous composer—Antonin Dvořák—who made American composers and musicians aware of the value and importance of the great body of American folk music, which up to the closing years of the century had lain dormant and neglected. These same years were portentous ones in Europe, particularly in Russia and France: years which would be of the greatest influence on twentieth-century American composers. In order to understand the awakening of national feeling in Europe, or the nationalistic movement, we must pause and consider briefly its earliest manifestations, in the years in which the German traditions of the Boston group were at their height.

After the invasions of Napoleon and as one European country after another suffered enslavement and oppression, it was not long before some of these nations became aware of their national folklore. Russia's upsurge of nationalism had affected all the arts—literature, drama, criticism, as well as music. The musical revolt had been started by Glinka and Dargomizhsky. Glinka's operas, *A Life for the Czar* and *Russlan and Ludmilla,* were so thoroughly national in character that their composer is regarded as the real founder of Russia's national school. The movement was further aided by the Russian "Five," a group of composers consisting of Rimsky-Korsakov, Cui, Borodin, Moussorgsky and Balakirev. Time has proved that Moussorgsky was the most important figure of the "Five," writing music years ahead of its time, and the father of the contemporary music of today. His use of Russian folk music—the modal melodies, characteristic rhythms, as well as the harmonic idiosyncrasies—was to influence countless future composers. When his opera *Boris Godounoff* met with devastating criticism and official protest in 1874 and was dropped from the Russian State Theaters (and at one time banned by the Czar), it was the younger generation who realized its worth. Moussorgsky's stature as a composer would not be realized until well into the next century, but his influence was already at work. Through his hatred of all that was conventional in method, expression, and feeling, he aimed ruthlessly at truth, and thus became the first musical expressionist.

In the same year that saw the failure of *Boris* there appeared in Paris an article in the French paper *Charivari* (April 25, 1874) of the utmost importance to the future of music. No one could have possibly known how far-reaching this article would be, for at the time it was no more than a criticism of certain pictures which had just been exhibited in a Paris art gallery. Claude Monet's picture *Sunrise: An Impression,* using a new technique which such French painters as Monet, Manet, and Renoir had been experimenting with, was ridiculed and scorned, and Louis Leroy called them all "impressionists." Claude Debussy, greatly influenced by these painters, as well as by the contemporary group of poets known as symbolists and including such men as Verlaine, Baudelaire, and Mallarmé, tried to adapt their ideals in his music. In his orchestral piece *Prelude to the Afternoon of a Faun* (1892) he realized for the first time what all the impressionists had sought—the ability to suggest or evoke a mood, rather than to state it openly. Debussy used pastel-like instrumental colors, and the titles of his pieces suggested programs or pictures. He was as much of a radical as Moussorgsky, whom he greatly admired, richly hating convention and tradition. While his influence may have waned by the mid-twentieth century he eventually broke the long domination of Germanic tradition, giving to the music of France a new meaning and a greater momentum. As different as both movements were—nationalism and impressionism—each had its part in changing the course of musical history. They had one thing in common and that was the breaking of the strangle hold of the German post-romanticists. America, at that time merely an outpost of this very tradition, would not shake it off until the twentieth century, but in Europe there were currents of activity, of renewed life, which soon spread through all of the important countries.

The last decade of the nineteenth century continued the amazing cultural growth of America. Important events were taking place throughout the nation. Chicago's opera, which after the Fire had to move from house to house for some eighteen years, finally had its Auditorium opened on December 9, 1889. Adelina Patti sang *Home Sweet Home*, and President Benjamin Harrison came to see this new creation of Ferdinand W. Peck and his group of public-spirited citizens. The Auditorium was designed by Louis Sullivan, and dominated Chicago's skyline along the lake. It made an impressive setting for both opera and concerts, and happily its acoustics were excellent. Theodore Dubois, at that time one of France's leading composers, wrote a *Triumphal Fantasy* for organ and orchestra, which, like Wagner's *Grand March* for Philadelphia's Centennial, proved quite ineffectual. During the next years every important opera company in the country appeared in Chicago.

Elsewhere, New Orleans never missed her opera season, even though the productions during the Civil War years had been rather unimportant. San Francisco maintained, too, her love of opera, and tried even German opera in the 1870s. All kinds of companies, good or bad, appeared there, and the Tivoli soon grew from a beer garden into a real center of opera. In St. Louis, meanwhile, there was more interest in choral and orchestral music. In 1880 the St. Louis Choral Society was founded, made up of the singers from the various Saengerbunds, Maennerchors, and other choruses throughout the city. They were accompanied in their performances by the orchestra of the St. Louis Musical Union. By 1890, a consolidation was effected when the Choral Society merged with the orchestra. Given a new name—the St. Louis Choral Symphony Society—it was incorporated in 1893 with Joseph Otten as its conductor.

The Gay Nineties were the glorious years for New York's Metropolitan Opera House, a decade of amazing achievements largely due to the brilliant artists added to the company's roster. A fire in 1892 forced the cancellation of one season, but it later proved to be a boon. Society boxholders had become increasingly bored with German opera, and although it had proved popular, Wagnerian opera was not fashionable. The remodeling of the house gave it much the appearance it has today, and with an Italian system once more inaugurated, its life took on new meaning. This was the period of Jean and Edouard de Reszke, Pol Plançon, Victor Maurel, Lillian Nordica, Emma Eames, Ernestine Schumann-Heink, Emma Calvé, and Nellie Melba—to name but a few who made operatic history at the Metropolitan.

New zest was given to New York's concert life in 1891 when Music Hall, seating about 3000 persons, was opened with a five-day music festival, May 5-9. The New York Symphony Orchestra and the New York Oratorio Society combined for the concerts, and Peter Ilyitch Tchaikovsky was the guest of honor, conducting several of his works. In 1898, the name was changed to Carnegie Hall, in honor of Andrew Carnegie, who had provided the funds for its construction.

The Chicago World's Fair of 1893 (the music was in charge of Theodore Thomas, and a musical tempest in a teapot nearly destroyed that gallant figure) had an assembly of music clubs in attendance, and from the group came an organization, with Mrs. Theodore Thomas as its honorary chairman, which would hold its first biennial meeting just before the turn of the century as the National Federation of Music Clubs. The tiny seed which was planted in Chicago was to grow into a powerful, well-knit, and important musical organization in the twentieth century, one which would make invaluable contributions to the cause of music.

Cincinnati and Pittsburgh founded their present orchestras in 1895 (the latter was to have Victor Herbert as its second conductor —1898-1904), and in 1897 the Library of Congress organized its Division of Music, which has since become one of the largest and most important in the world. And in the West, in one of America's youngest cities, musically speaking, occurred one of the most important premières of the century. On October 14, 1897, in Los Angeles, the Dal Conte Opera Company of Turin, Italy, gave the first performance in North America of a new opera—La Bohème—written by a talented young composer, Giacomo Puccini.

SPANISH-AMERICAN WAR SONGS

In 1898 the Spanish-American War, which lasted for only a few months and which caused the civilian population little if any inconvenience, left in its wake hundreds of songs, of which only a few were to prove enduring. There were songs about Admiral Dewey and the sinking of the battleship *Maine*, but the war was over before these were actually widely known. The song which was most closely associated with the war was composed several years earlier: *A Hot Time in the Old Town*, its authorship claimed by Theodore Metz, one time bandmaster for the MacIntyre and Heath Minstrel Troupe and copyrighted on July 2, 1896. By account, a train stopped near a station called Old Town, and a number of Negro children put out a fire near the tracks. Someone remarked: "There'll be a hot time in the Old Town tonight," and Metz had the idea of a song. Published in 1896, it came into historic significance two years later, when Theodore Roosevelt's Rough Riders sang it during their attack on San Juan Hill. Roosevelt later renounced the song, deploring its playing at his public appearances. Close in popularity were *Goodbye Dolly Gray, Just Break the News to Mother,* and *On the Banks of the Wabash Far Away;* but the soldiers were also heard to sing *When Johnny Comes Marching Home,* just as they had done during the Civil War, and would do again in the first World War.

That year of the war saw the establishment in New York of one of the world's most important trade magazines, *Musical America* (1898). America was at last on the eve of her greatest era in music, and, in spite of the devastation of two world wars within the next half-century, she would become a leader of music. She had long since won her political freedom and more recently that in belles-lettres, painting, sculpture, and architecture. In the new century she would at last appreciate the value of her great musical heritage, and, as new currents were set in motion by the appearance of ragtime and the development of jazz, her thoroughly trained composers would keep pace with the ever-expanding nation, whose resourcefulness and activity would seem to know no bounds.

CHAPTER IX

First Decade of the Twentieth Century

STATE OF MUSIC IN 1900

In Europe the upsurge of nineteenth-century nationalism had swept through most of the countries like a breath of fresh air, bringing with it a sense of liberation and creative activity which could not be denied. Russia and France had already challenged the supremacy of German music and national schools of writing began to emerge on all sides. America was moving in step with Europe, and her music, while outwardly continuing a growth similar to that of English music in the last decade of Victoria's reign, was in fact far closer to European currents than it had ever been before.

While Italy was hearing the first performance of Puccini's *Tosca*, Paris, already familiar with the impressionism of Debussy, was seeing Charpentier's *Louise*. Both *Tosca* and *Louise* were further examples of the effective Italian *verismo*, which had emerged in 1890, with the première of Mascagni's *Cavalleria Rusticana*, produced in Rome. The new term *verism* (from *vero*, meaning true) as applied to opera was the integration of many of the best aspects of nineteenth-century opera. Accepting the continuity of Wagner's music drama, the flowing melodies and theatrical effectiveness of Verdi, and Moussorgsky's speechlike prosody—these became the components of a realistic opera, whose libretto was based on historical or topical subjects, rather than those that were legendary.

In Paris, the opening of the Exposition Universelle brought demonstrations of Oriental music, with its exotic scales, which fascinated such composers as Debussy, and would change the entire course of French music. England, discovering her own vast store of folk song, was also carrying on her great tradition of fine choral singing with the performance of Edward Elgar's oratorio, *The Dream of Gerontius,* which he wrote for the Birmingham Festival. In the far north, *Finlandia,* the work of a young composer named Jean Sibelius, was having its première in Helsinki, and in nearby Russia, Rimsky-Korsakov's opera *Tsar Saltan,* and Scriabin's First Symphony were heard for the first time in Moscow. The lush Wagnerian melody was still in evidence, but two scales new to art music were being employed—the whole-tone and the pentatonic—and there were parallel movements of triads and asymmetric rhythms.

With the completion in Paris of Debussy's impressionistic opera, *Pelléas et Mélisande* (first performance April 30, 1902), what might be termed a second phase in music set in, one which would last until 1913 when Stravinsky's startling new ballet, *Le Sacre du Printemps (The Rite of Spring),* would be the final straw in the breaking down of the older order and the beginning of what we today term modern music. During the intervening years Russian music would be influenced by Scriabin's mysticism and theosophy; trends would be of a primitive nature as a reaction against the too refined impressionism; futurism, heralding the music of the noisy machine age would have its first manifestations in Italy; while in Germany, neoromanticism was tinged with philosophic implications; and through it all, both in harmony and melody, chromaticism became so very extreme that tonality, as practiced up to the twentieth century, was soon to be abandoned by some composers, and "atonality" would be the new harmonic conception of Arnold Schoenberg.

A NEW ERA FOR AMERICAN MUSIC

In the United States, still for the most part under the domination of foreign-born performers and leaders, the stage was being set for the final emergence of the great orchestras and new and elaborate auditoriums and opera houses which would soon be the scene of brilliant performances, equal to any in the world. In 1900, America had few more than a half-dozen orchestras of major importance, but in the next fifty years the number would grow to at least thirty, supplemented by from six hundred to a thousand secondary groups. Audiences were growing, and the younger generation—thanks to the many excellent music schools and conservatories—was more musically inclined. The growth of music in the public schools had been nothing short of amazing, and at the turn of the century thousands of schools included musical instruction of some type, if only a period devoted to singing, several times a week. American composers, accepting Dvořák's challenge that they investigate and experiment with the vast treasure of American folk song, became more and more venturesome and audacious in their attempt to write music which could easily be recognized as "American."

And yet America, at the beginning of the twentieth century, was on the brink of one of the most extraordinary cultural conflicts in her whole history. The entire musical world, in fact, faced a change that would soon seem cataclysmic. The great tide of romanticism was on the ebb, its decorous traditions out of fashion, while at the same time another stream—the music of the future, new and unknown—was on the rise. By mid-century American music and musical life would reach great heights of brilliance and her composers would at last stand before the world with pride. Through the years each composer worked out his own particular salvation and found his own special mode of expression as a creative artist, and only time will tell how well each has done. At the turn of the century both music and literature were broadening, and they soon became more powerful and daring. As science, religious skepticism, and new ideas of psychology grew in strength, it was inevitable that earth-shattering changes would take place. The final blow to the old traditions came with the devastation of World War I, but even before that time, during the seemingly happy and carefree Edwardian period, there were rumblings and mutterings—voices speaking in the wilderness, to which only a few would listen.

ORCHESTRAS AND CONDUCTORS

Philadelphia Orchestra

The first major orchestra to be founded in the new century, and destined to become one of the glories of the United States, was the Philadelphia Orchestra, under the direction of Fritz Scheel, the German conductor who had been active in New York, Chicago, and San Francisco since his arrival in America in 1893. The Philadelphia Orchestra grew out of two groups in the city to which the Musical Fund Society and the visiting Germania Orchestra had given an initial impetus. The larger group—the Philadelphia Symphony Society—was an amateur one, led from 1893 to 1900 by W. W. Gilchrist; while the smaller ensemble of professional musicians, known as the Thunder Orchestra, had been directed by Henry Gordon Thunder from 1896 to 1899. The latter group was incorporated into the new Philadelphia Orchestra in 1900. Scheel had been brought from San Francisco to Philadelphia to conduct summer concerts at Woodside Park. His work was so impressive that a guarantee fund of $15,000 was raised in the spring, and with this backing the new orchestra gave its first concert on November 16, 1900, with Ossip Gabrilowitsch (who was to be one of the later conductors) as soloist in Tchaikovsky's Piano Concerto in B-flat Minor. In the second season the Philadelphia Orchestra Association was formed, and the group started to tour, going to nearby Pennsylvania cities, and by the third season (1902-03) giving concerts in Baltimore, Washington, and New York. It still maintains this schedule, and has added other cities in the course of years. In the early years of the orchestra Richard Strauss and Felix Weingartner were among the prominent guest conductors.

Boston Symphony

In Boston, Major Higgingson's orchestra was growing in splendid fashion, and when the 1899-1900 season concluded, the Boston Symphony left its old home in the Boston Music Hall (the original home of the group) for the new Symphony Hall that was formally opened on October 15, 1900. The Bostonians, too, started to tour, giving smaller cities and communities a chance to hear their excellent playing. Wilhelm Gericke conducted the Boston Symphony from 1898 to 1906 and in that year the orchestra acquired Karl Muck as its conductor. Muck was a superb musician, a veritable genius, and under him the orchestra rose to the greatest years in its history. At that time he could only stay two years, because Kaiser Wilhelm commanded him to return to Berlin's Royal Opera. He left his stamp upon the group, and would return in 1912 to carry on his memorable work.

New York Philharmonic

The year 1901 found the New York Philharmonic Society in the process of reorganization. Its programs had become so routine and the playing so mediocre in comparison with that of the Boston Symphony that the move was imperative. The cooperative policy which had been in effect since its organization in 1842—when the profits were divided among the members of the orchestra—was altered and the players paid guaranteed salaries. A board of directors was assembled. Emil Paur was the conductor at that time. He was followed in 1902 by Walter Damrosch for one season.

Minneapolis Symphony

In the Midwest, in 1903, the Minneapolis Symphony Orchestra was founded, and would become one of the major American orchestras. With Emil Oberhoffer as director, the orchestra first played in large churches, but in March, 1905, it took up its permanent home in a newly built Auditorium. It had played concurrently in Minneapolis and St. Paul, but when Northrop Auditorium was built on the campus of the University of Minnesota, the orchestra confined its concerts to that building.

Stock in Chicago

Chicago had a new concert hall in 1904, built with money raised by donations, and located on Michigan Avenue, across from the Art Institute. Theodore Thomas dedicated Orchestra Hall on December 14, and the Apollo Musical Club and the Mendelssohn Club sang with the orchestra "Hail, Bright Abode" from Tannhaüser and the Hallelujah Chorus from Messiah. In three weeks the great man was dead, and his assistant conductor, Frederick Stock, finished the season. In 1895 Thomas had brought over from Germany a young violinist, Frederick August Stock, who had been a member of the Cologne Orchestra. Stock had enjoyed several rare experiences in Europe, which he described vividly to Thomas. One of these was playing under the baton of Richard Strauss, whose orchestral tone poems were a novelty in those days. Stock and Thomas became close friends, and admiring his fine musicianship, Thomas soon made Stock his assistant conductor, allowing him to conduct on some of the tours. Upon Thomas' death Stock became permanent conductor and raised the orchestra to one of the finest groups in the country. He built an extensive repertoire, especially of American compositions, and for many years he gave more first performances of native works than any other one conductor. With his death in 1942, America lost one of her greatest and most beloved musicians.

Cincinnati Calls Stokowski

The nation first became aware of Leopold Stokowski (soon to become one of the country's most vital and forceful personalities) as an orchestral conductor when the Cincinnati Orchestra called him to become its director in 1909. Born in London in 1882, the son of a Polish father and an Irish mother, Stokowski was talented as a child, and later studied with Hubert Parry and Charles Villiers Stanford at Queen's College at Oxford. He also studied in Germany (where he met his first wife, the pianist Olga Samaroff, who was a student in Berlin), conducted concerts in Paris, and after playing the organ at St. James in Piccadilly, London, came to New York as organist and choir director of fashionable St. Bartholomew's Church on Park Avenue. But conducting was his prime interest, and he accepted Cincinnati's call with pleasure. Assembling seventy-seven men, in November, 1909, he inaugurated a new series of ten pairs of concerts.

Russian Symphony Orchestra

At the turn of the century a Russian-born cellist named Modest Altschuler came to New York and in 1903 organized an orchestra. He called it the Russian Symphony Orchestra and made its principal objective the introduction of works by modern Russian composers. The first concert was held in Cooper Union Hall, January 28, 1904, and during the fifteen years that the orchestra played (it finally disbanded in 1919) it did more to acquaint the American public with contemporary Russian music than any other organization in the country. In addition to its concerts in New York the Russian Symphony made several extensive tours, throughout the United States and into Canada. Among the works that received American premières at the hands of these players were Scriabin's *Poem of Ecstasy* and his *Prometheus* (1915), in which the part of *Luce* (Light) was played on a "color organ," called for in the score, and pieces by Ippolitov-Ivanov, Liadov, Rachmaninoff, Vassilenko, and Spendiarov.

When the *Poem of Ecstasy* was played for the first time (December 10, 1908) a young violinist from Russia, not yet sixteen years old, a pupil of Leopold Auer, made his New York debut as soloist with the orchestra. His name was Mischa Elman. Introduction of Russian soloists was another part of the Altschuler's program and among others who made their American debuts with his orchestra were the pianist Josef Lhévinne (1906) and the composer Scriabin himself (1906).

GOLDEN YEARS OF OPERA

The Metropolitan in New York

The autumn of 1903 marked the beginning of Heinrich Conried's five-year term as director of New York's Metropolitan Opera House. Conried had come from Germany in 1878 and after being engaged in various managerial enterprises became director of the Irving Place Theatre from 1892 to 1903. His regime at the Metropolitan has often been criticized for being so much in the old tradition that it invited the competition that Oscar Hammerstein was to give it in 1906, but he nevertheless did give New York its share of thrills. The first of them occurred on November 23 of that first autumn of 1903—the debut of Enrico Caruso. Strangely enough, the debut itself did not attract as much attention as did Caruso's subsequent performances of the season.

Conried's second sensation was exhibited on the following Christmas Eve, when he produced, against the wishes of Cosima Wagner and the Bayreuth authorities, the first performance ever given outside the hallowed Festspielhaus of Wagner's *Parsifal*. The affair caused much bitterness in Germany, but New Yorkers took *Parsifal* to their hearts, and its performances have become a yearly tradition at Easter time.

Three years later, another Conried bomb burst when Olive Fremstad sang the title role in Richard Strauss's *Salome* on January 22, 1907. Despite the great artistry of Fremstad she was unable to rise above the sensuousness of the plot, especially the famous dance and the closing scene in which Salome caresses the head of the dead prophet. The conservative subscribers of the Metropolitan were outraged and considered the work immoral and degrading. The scandal reached such proportions that on January 26, the Directors of the Opera protested to the management, and the opera was hastily withdrawn after one performance. *Salome* was not returned to the Metropolitan repertory until 1933 (although, as we shall see, it was performed at Hammerstein's Manhattan Opera House). In the 1940s it was to become one of the New York City Center's most popular productions.

The golden years moved on as 1906 brought the lovely Geraldine Farrar to the Metropolitan in her debut as *Juliette*, and the first performance of Puccini's *Madama Butterfly*, on February 11, 1907. Yet all was not serene at the Metropolitan, brilliant as the season was, because of the new rival opera house of Oscar Hammerstein.

Hammerstein's Manhattan Opera House

December 3, 1906, was a date of great artistic significance for New York opera, when Hammerstein opened the Manhattan Opera House. There had been an earlier Manhattan Opera House, also established by Hammerstein, on part of the site where Macy's store is today. That house opened on January 23, 1893, and had probably the most incredible season in the operatic history of America. Exactly two operas, Moszkowski's *Boabdil* and Beethoven's *Fidelio*, were produced before it closed its doors. The new opera house on West Thirty-fourth Street, between Eighth and Ninth avenues, however, was a direct challenge to the Metropolitan, and as much as the Metropolitan disliked the idea, the truth was that New York was the richer by hearing new and unusual works, many with their original casts, at a time when they otherwise might never have been sung. Hammerstein became a powerful figure, but eventually the wealth of the Metropolitan was too much for him. He lasted four years, and then agreed to sell his interests, and by contract, promised not to give further operatic performances in New York City. His company, while it prospered, brought lyric drama to life, and made New York really opera conscious. Among his important ventures was his importation of almost the entire Parisian cast of Debussy's *Pelléas et Mélisande*, and performances of Charpentier's *Louise*, Massenet's *Thaïs* and *Le Jongleur de Notre Dame*, Offenbach's *The Tales of Hoffman*, Strauss's *Elektra* and *Salome* (which of course was not being given at the Metropolitan). These were operas that were new even to Paris, and the singers who came in the leading roles were among the greatest: Mary Garden, Luisa Tetrazzini (who had already been a sensation in San Francisco in 1904), Charles Dalmorès, Lucien Muratore, Alessandro Bonci, as well as the conductor, Cleofonte Campanini, the brother of the great tenor, Italo Campanini.

Gatti-Casazza Comes to the Metropolitan

In 1908, the Metropolitan brought Giulio Gatti-Casazza from Italy as its new manager. With him came the conductor Arturo Toscanini, who was to become one of the great musical figures in America's history. During Gatti-Casazza's regime such singers were added to the star-studded casts as Emmy Destinn, Feodor Chaliapin (although he had long been in America), Frieda Hempel, Frances Alda, Maria Jeritza, Florence Easton, Giovanni Martinelli, and Giuseppe de Luca. During all these years the Metropolitan Opera Company had been touring, in the best American tradition, and its stars were known all over the country. There was the fateful visit to San Francisco, when on April 17, 1906, Caruso and Fremstad sang a memorable *Carmen,* and early the next morning were, with all of the city, shaken out of their beds by the terrifying earthquake. Caruso and others fled to the open parks as the city burned all around them.

Grand Opera in Chicago

In 1908 Chicago's own opera was on the downward trend, but it still had the chance to have a part in Gatti-Casazza's first season during the Metropolitan tour, when it heard the incomparable Toscanini conduct Emmy Destinn in *Aïda.* By 1910 opera lovers in the Midwest metropolis were demanding a new opera company, and chance played into their hands as a result of the Metropolitan Opera's feud with Hammerstein. Through the great patron of the Metropolitan, Otto H. Kahn, the opportunity came to take over Oscar Hammerstein's complete company from the Manhattan Opera House, as that redoubtable figure had just signed his contract promising not to produce opera in New York. Chicagoans were elated, and the board accepted the proposal with alacrity. On November 3, 1910, the new Chicago-Philadelphia Opera Company opened in the Auditorium with *Aïda,* Campanini conducting. On the second night local history was made when Mary Garden and Edward Warnery sang *Pelléas et Mélisande,* and five days later Garden did her immortal *Louise,* with Dalmorès. Another triumph was hers on November 25, when Chicago saw her unforgettable *Salome,* and from then on Mary Garden's name was forever to be associated with Chicago and grand opera. For a quarter of a century the Chicago opera was in every way the equal of the Metropolitan in New York, touring the nation and taking its place as one of the foremost opera companies in the world, becoming in the 1920s the Chicago Opera Association, then the Chicago Civic Opera Company, and finally, in 1928, the Chicago Civic Opera Association, with headquarters in the newly built Civic Opera House.

Boston Opera Company

Bostonians wanted their city to be as eminent in opera as its orchestra had made it in the symphonic field. During the first decade of the century a number of prominent citizens, led by Eben Jordan, raised sufficient funds and subscriptions to erect the Boston Opera House. It was opened November 8, 1909 with a performance of *La Gioconda*, with Lillian Nordica and Louise Homer in the cast. The director was Henry Russell, the impresario-son of Henry Russell, the ballad singer and composer we met in chapter 5. The younger Russell had become known to Americans when he toured the country with an opera company of his own, after managing seasons at London's Covent Garden in 1903-04.

Although everything seemed to augur well for the Boston Opera Company the annual expense was too great, and the deficits too large, for its continuance for more than five years. After 1914 it suspended operations and since that time the opera house has been used for visiting companies and for large dramatic productions.

GREAT VIRTUOSI

These were years of activity in America's concert halls and the stars of opera undertook extensive tours throughout the country. There were great violinists to match the golden voices, players already known to many through their recordings, men like Kreisler, Elman, and Zimbalist. There were also brilliant chamber ensembles, such as the trio comprising Alfred Cortot, piano; Jacques Thibaud, violin; and Pablo Casals, cello; or string quartets of the caliber of the Flonzaley and Kneisel. There were also the titans of the keyboard, carrying on the touring tradition of the last century, including Ferruccio Busoni, Vladimir de Pachmann, Josef Hofmann,

Leopold Godowsky, and Paderewski (who always traveled in his private Pullman car, with a piano for his daily practice). Women also played their part, although fewer were instrumentalists, but the name of Maud Powell, violinist, stands with the great women pianists such as Teresa Carreño, Adele Aus der Ohe, and Olga Samaroff.

In 1909, on November 4, Sergei Rachmaninoff made his first appearance in America when he gave a piano recital at Smith College in Northampton, Massachusetts. On the following November 28 he played for the first time anywhere his Third Piano Concerto with the New York Symphony Society, Walter Damrosch conducting. In 1917 Rachmaninoff was to return to America and eventually to make it his home.

FIRST PHONOGRAPH RECORDS

The Columbia Phonograph Company, a pioneer in the recording industry, in announcing its records for sale, inaugurated an era of great prosperity for many musicians. Almost as soon as the phonograph had become a reality, its potentialities were recognized, but in those early years no one could have dreamed what a great service it was to become in the cause of the native composer by mid-century. All the great and near great made records. Gladstone, Bismarck, P. T. Barnum, Florence Nightingale, and Edwin Booth, to name but a few, had their voices recorded by the wax cylinders which Thomas Edison had perfected in 1888. It was in this year that Josef Hofmann, then only a boy of twelve who had made his American debut the year before, paid a visit to the Edison laboratories so that he might see this marvelous new invention. In engraving some cylinders, Hofmann was the first serious artist to record. Soon after, Hans von Bülow made a recording of a Chopin mazurka, but this record has entirely disappeared. The great scientist himself had produced a record the year before (1877), of his own voice reciting "Mary had a little lamb," on a cylinder made of tin foil. But it was the invention of disc recording (patented September 26, 1887) that surmounted all the problems of mass production. The invention was the work of Emile Berliner, whose factory was to be the beginning of the Victor Company, the largest producer in the field. In the early years many records of unusual interest were made. Sigrid Arnoldson, the Swedish soprano, re-corded about 1889; Brahms played one of his own compositions into a phonograph in Vienna; but Adelina Patti, despite rumors to the contrary, never made commercial recordings during the decade of the 1890s. Neither was Jenny Lind's voice ever captured, nor that of Richard Wagner or Etelka Gerster. However, in England in 1888, one of Edison's phonographs was placed in the press gallery in London's Crystal Palace in an attempt to record the annual Handel festival. From an account in the *Illustrated London News*, the machine "reported with perfected accuracy the sublime strains, vocal and instrumental, of 'Israel in Egypt.'" But actually it would not be until records could be made in large quantities that good recordings would become a certainty. The early attempts were more like the present-day tape recordings, done on the spur of the moment, often at parties or social gatherings. When the flat disc record became obviously more practical than the cylinder (1893), it was the recording of the human voice that sounded more natural and lifelike than anything else.

Edison, of course, had actually planned literally a "talking ma-chine," and in his wildest dreams could never have foreseen the role which the phonograph was to play in the history of American music. What printing had done for language, so the record was to do for music, although it would take many years of research and experimentation. The first records were mostly of vaudeville sketches, monologues, and sentimental songs. Band music included marches by Gilmore's Band as well as Sousa's Grand Concert Band, piccolo and banjo solos, and the famous "Casey" series of dialogues by Russell Hunting. But by 1900, Europe had become aware of recording from the purely commercial standpoint. It was the celeb-rity recordings, announced early in 1903 by Columbia, which set off the business of serious recording in America. These "Celebrity Discs" offered the great voices of the day, such as Marcella Sem-brich, Ernestine Schumann-Heink, Francesco Tamagno, Mattia Bat-tistini, Pol Plançon, Edouard de Reszke, and Antonio Scotti. In England, London's Gramophone and Typewriter Ltd. soon added to its list such figures as Edvard Grieg, Pablo Sarasate, Joseph Joachim, and many others. Victor Maurel (Verdi's original Iago in his opera *Otello*) sang the "Dream of Cassio," and Emma Albani gave her famous interpretation of "Angels Bright and Fair." The

Victor Talking Machine Company (or simply Victor), which had already imported matrices from abroad, began to make its own recordings (with red labels) and by 1904 forged ahead with the fine recordings (now collector's items) by such singers as Louise Homer, Johanna Gadski, Giuseppe Campanari, Scotti, and Caruso. There were also the brilliant records of a young man who hailed from Brooklyn by the name of Emilio de Gogorza, who became one of the greatest of all recording artists. All these records, despite the imperfections of early recording, were notable for their evidences of excellent singing, and from the beginning these "red seals," as Victor called them, proved conclusively the value of the new medium—artistically as well as educationally. In a year's time other great voices were added, and just as no history of the American theater would be complete without some mention of its great stage figures, so records have preserved for us the voices of those illustrious operatic figures who helped to mold one phase of America's music. Some of the more familiar names (whose recordings are now being reissued on modern long-playing records) included: Emma Eames, Marie Michailowa, and Marcel Journet. In Berlin even the incomparable Lilli Lehmann forsook the privacy of her studio to make about thirty-four records between 1905 and 1907, and these are still among the treasures of recorded music. In her castle in Wales the aging Patti succumbed to the lure of recording and sang a number of songs and arias.

In these early vocal recordings only the piano had accompanied the singers, but in 1905, attempts were made to record the accompaniment of a small orchestra. As the range of many of the instruments was beyond the possibilities of the recording apparatus, the results were flat and unnatural. But many of the voices had an amazing clarity. It was in 1906 that Enrico Caruso made his first records accompanied by an orchestra, the year Roland Gelatt calls "the flowering of the Victor Company." By 1910 there was hardly a singer of note who could not be heard on records, and even a few instrumentalists had the courage to invade the field. Among these, all great favorites in the concert hall, were Eugène Ysaÿe, Mischa Elman, Fritz Kreisler, Jan Kubelik, Efrem Zimbalist, Vladimir de Pachmann, and Paderewski.

THE APPEARANCE OF RAGTIME

Concurrent with the growth of the recording industry, and starting in the 1890s, there was yet another manifestation of America's music: the introduction and growth of ragtime. In the twentieth century its catchy rhythms became the rage until about 1910, when the singing of the "blues" took over, from which would develop both jazz and swing. In the 1920s and 1930s, the recording industry would have its share in the spreading of this typically American phenomena.

Backgrounds of Ragtime

In the decade known today as the Gay Nineties there was a new group of itinerant musicians, thousands of them—both Negro and white—who spread the infectious rhythms of a new syncopated music. A few were singers, but most were pianists, and as they wandered from the many towns which lined the banks of the Missouri and Mississippi Rivers, they were welcomed by a people who hungered for any kind of entertainment that might let them forget the miseries of lives which seemed to know nothing but hunger and heartache. This new music (soon to be known as ragtime), was the natural outgrowth of the older minstrel shows, with their "plantation melodies" and "coon songs," which, as we already have discovered, were usually sung to the accompaniment of the banjo or guitar. The dances of that period also had their share in the evolution of ragtime, for by 1880 the cakewalk, buck-and-wing, and jig were invariably featured in the elaborate minstrel shows. And yet a newer medium was, of course, the wax cylinders of Edison's phonograph, and by the end of the 1890s the increasingly popular player piano appeared.

Soon ragtime would sweep the nation and gain great popularity in Europe. Its rhythms were gay and exciting, honest, and they were American to the core. It was music that came from a people, its appeal was universal, and it would prove to be the most revolutionary musical force that had yet come out of America. By the turn of the century all songs except waltzes and two-steps were written in ragtime, and nothing could have better expressed to the whole world the spirit of the American people.

Ragtime had its strongest impetus from such pieces as Krell's

Mississippi Rag, the first instrumental rag to be published in sheet music (January, 1897), which was followed in December with Tom Turpin's *Harlem Rag,* the first published Negro rag. These pieces set off an almost incredible publication of ragtime sheet music, thousands of pieces, which had their own share in the spread of the music from coast to coast and border to border. And when in September, 1899, John Stark's firm in Sedalia, Missouri, issued Scott Joplin's *Maple Leaf Rag,* the name of the most important man in the history of ragtime would soon become a household word. Despite later controversies, Scott Joplin still retains his title as "King of Ragtime."

It must not be forgotten that ragtime was primarily a pianistic art, which had already gained great popularity as early as 1895. In those days piano players who could "rag" authentically were in great demand both professionally and in amateur circles. In that year Ben Harney had published in Louisville, Kentucky, his ragtime song *You've Been a Good Old Wagon* (1895), and with his great success at Keith's and Tony Pastor's in New York had started the acceptance by the public of this new and exciting music.

While early ragtime was very simple, the serious or classical ragtime, as played by Scott Joplin or Tom Turpin, James Scott or Joseph Lamb, was extremely difficult. Its distinguishing feature was, of course, the use of syncopation (already used by the masters of European music), but its uniqueness was in the way the pianists of the day would oppose the regular accompaniment of the left hand with a right-hand melody whose accents fell on the weak, rather than the strong, beats. The excitement and stimulation of an almost continuous syncopation had a propulsive drive that carried a terrific emotional impact, which, although common to the Negro musician had never been used so effectively by traditional musicians, European or American, up to that time. Ragtime melodies were rarely singable and most often had no words. It was a music that emerged from earlier Negro folk songs and the syncopations of the banjos as played on the southern plantations or along the rivers, and, thanks to the genius of both Negro and white performers, was carried to new creative heights. It was Negro secular music at its best, a genuine, original creation and tremendously powerful.

The emergence of ragtime paralleled the national craze for the cakewalk, and persons from all walks of life in America and Europe fell under its spell. It was John Philip Sousa's band, playing Kerry Mills' *At a Georgia Camp Meeting* (1897), that was one of the first groups to popularize the syncopations of the cakewalk on both continents.

Ragtime's Pioneers

Scott Joplin (1868-1917), the greatest composer of ragtime, believed to his dying day that his own syncopated compositions could stand the test of being compared with classic European music. Throughout his life his creative fire burned with a bright, steady glow, and because of his great faith in what he was doing and because of the vision he had as to its importance in the history of American music, he had the wisdom and courage to withdraw from a life of active playing, to compose and teach. But without the assistance of John Stark in publishing his superb piano rags (and those of other great composers), Joplin's life might have been very different. His first work, *Original Rag*, had been published in Kansas City, Missouri, by Carl Hoffman, in March, 1899, but with the appearance in September of *Maple Leaf Rag*, by John Stark & Son, there began a partnership which was to have the greatest possible influence on the development of the so-called classic ragtime. It was because of their belief in each other and their common belief in the greatness of this new music that we today have so many permanent scores, without which the history of this phase of ragtime might ever remain just a memory.

Besides the many rags which Joplin composed, he also ventured into the realm of a rag opera. Copyrighted in 1903 (although never published), *A Guest in the House* was given a concert performance in St. Louis. The original score has disappeared, more's the pity, for it could not have come at a better time than in those years when all that America had in her theaters were the sentimental light operas of men like Victor Herbert and Reginald De Koven. Once again, in 1915, when Joplin had moved to New York, his other opera, *Treemonisha* (published in 1911), was given one performance (with no scenery or costumes) with the composer at the piano. Its failure left Joplin a broken man, both mentally and physically, and he died not long after, on April 1, 1917.

Some of the other important figures were Thomas M. (Tom) Turpin (1873-1922), the Negro pianist who was unofficially called the "Father of St. Louis Ragtime," whose *Harlem Rag* had been published in 1897 and featured in his Rosebud Cafe; James Sylvester Scott and his *Climax Rag* (1914); Louis Chauvin, for his *Heliotrope Bouquet* (1907), in which he collaborated with Scott Joplin; Arthur Marshall; and Scott Hayden. Ragtime centers were St. Louis and New Orleans with Antony (Tony) Jackson, and Ferdinand Joseph (Jelly Roll) Morton. In the same class with these great Negro composers were the five white men who are considered the most important of their day: Charles H. Hunter, Charles L. Johnson, Percy Wenrich, George Botsford, and Joseph F. Lamb.

Eventually· the scene shifted to New York, where the leading figures were James P. Johnson and Thomas (Fats) Waller.

All the while Tin-Pan Alley (the popular name for New York's sheet-music publishers) was issuing great quantities of music and gradually killing the true spirit of ragtime in their greed for money. By the time such songs as Irving Berlin's *Alexander's Ragtime Band* (1911) appeared, it was only a modified version of ragtime, not an authentic rag at all, for ragtime's popularity was on the wane as the newer "blues" caught the fancy of Americans. But looking back, ragtime was of the greatest importance, for it was a music of the people, deep-rooted in popular tradition, unique and original. It was a vital force in the first years of the century, one whose influence was far-reaching and enduring.

Ragtime Gives Way to the Blues

The period of transition from ragtime to jazz was marked by another singular manifestation of popular Negro-American song when W. C. Handy (born November 16, 1873) wrote his *Memphis Blues* in 1909, published in 1912. Ragtime was on the wane and it was Handy who first popularized the type of Negro song known as the "blues," from which was to come one of America's greatest contributions to twentieth-century music—jazz. The spiritual had originated in group singing, often improvised by a leader at religious services, and answered and elaborated upon by the congregation. The blues was a solo song, whose origins are lost in the dim past, but which had certainly developed along with all other types of Negro folk song, especially after the Civil War. It was Handy, however, who made the blues popular, and in 1914, when he published his famous *St. Louis Blues,* blues songs came to the height of their popularity. The blues was typically a slow, sustained lament, whose text most often bewailed a lost or absent lover, but with an undercurrent of philosophic resignation, sometimes humorous, which is altogether peculiar to the Negro race. The blues had a basic structure of twelve measures and gradually developed its own type of scale, which was our diatonic scale in which the third and seventh degrees were flatted ("blue"). The accompanying harmonies made frequent use of seventh chords rather than the simple triads of the average folk song. Usually three basic chords were used—the tonic, subdominant, and dominant seventh—and there were progressions of close harmony which we think of today as "barbershop harmony." The singer made much use of the blue notes by sliding or wavering with the voice (portamento) between the natural and flatted tone. Another feature, of great importance later, was the introduction of the "break" (a long established practice in both English and American folk song), which came at the end of each line as the text paused and the voice (and later the accompanying instruments) interpolated a bit of improvisation, which lasted about two measures. The blues continued as a popular type of song, but also developed into an instrumental style, which led directly to the emergence of jazz. In both his *Memphis Blues* and *St. Louis Blues* Handy introduced a rhythmic pattern in the bass line which had been common to Latin-American music, the habanera or tango. In addition to using the conventional three-line form of blues verse, Handy, in the *St. Louis Blues*, also used a four-line strain (in the second part), from which was to develop the typical thirty-two-bar popular American song of later years, that was, and still is, ground out by Tin-Pan Alley.

The greatest of the blues singers, who may still be heard on records, especially those of Folkways Records, included Gertrude "Ma" Rainey (1886-1939), Bessie Smith (*c.* 1900-1937), and Bertha "Chippie" Hill, (1905-1950).

One of the most important figures in this whole period of transition from ragtime to jazz was Ferdinand "Jelly Roll" Morton (1885-1941), already mentioned as one of the leading ragtime pianists. He was a creative force in the evolution of piano blues, which moved on to instrumental jazz. In 1938 the Library of Congress had Morton record all the many phases of ragtime, blues, and jazz that he knew

so well, and thus preserved for posterity one of America's most
unique and lasting contributions to music.

INVENTIONS AND EVENTS

Wireless

The year of McKinley's assassination, 1901, witnessed an event
which was obviously a boon to mankind, but which seemed at the
moment to have little connection with music. This was the year
in which Marconi sent by wireless telegraphy (later to be known
as radio) a message from Newfoundland to Wales. Then, on December 17, 1902, the first radio message was sent across the Atlantic.
Later in the decade the invention was applied for the first time to
music. On March 5, 1906, Lee De Forest transmitted a performance
of Rossini's *William Tell* Overture from a New York concert hall to
a radio receiving set in the Brooklyn Navy Yard.

That event, however, received little or no attention from music
lovers, and it was not for another quarter-century that radio broadcasting of music became a fact. Similarly, another event of 1902
seemed to have little connection with music, but heralded an institution that several decades later was to become one of the great
mediums for bringing music to the masses. It was in that year
that Los Angeles had its first theater exclusively for motion pictures.

Flying Machines

The year 1903, when Caruso made his sensational debut at New
York's Metropolitan, saw several events that seemed to have no
direct bearing on music but were nonetheless in the decades to
come to inspire American composers, both those who write popular
songs and those who compose concert music and operas. This was
the year in which Wilbur and Orville Wright made a success of
their first airplane. The reader does not need to be reminded of the
seemingly innumerable airplane songs that were written (*Come
Josephine in My Flying Machine, Come Take a Trip in My Airship,*
etc.), and he is also, we hope, familiar with the larger works that
were inspired by developments in the air in later years, such major
compositions as Marc Blitzstein's *The Airborne* (1946).

Ford's Model T

Henry Ford established the Ford Motor Company in 1903 and later his Model T, the "flivver," was to become the subject of many friendly jokes and songs, the latter taking their place with the hundreds of general automobile songs (*Get Out and Get Under*, etc.). In 1927 the ten millionth "flivver" was honored by the symphonic composer Frederick S. Converse in his orchestral tone poem, *Flivver Ten Million*, which seemed a worthy companion to Arthur Honegger's locomotive piece, *Pacific 231*, which had been heard first in Paris in 1924 and soon became widely known in America.

Baseball

1903 was also the year in which baseball's World Series was launched. Lest it seem that only popular songs have been written to memorialize baseball (*Take Me Out to the Ball Game*, etc.) we may know that a half-century after the World Series started, in 1953, William Schuman's opera *The Mighty Casey* was produced at the Juilliard School in New York. The libretto was based on the immortal baseball saga, *Casey at the Bat*.

GROWTH OF MUSIC FESTIVALS

It is no novelty today when opera stars appear in light operas and musical comedies, but in 1904 Ernestine Schumann-Heink broke all tradition when she appeared briefly in a light opera, *Love's Lottery*. It was, however, customary and usual for all the famous singers of the day, once the opera season was over and before vacationing in Europe, to tour the land and sing at the many American festivals which were rapidly emerging. There was a close link between this golden era of song and the festivals of music. The first major festival to have its start with the new century was at Bethlehem, Pennsylvania, where once again the fine Moravian tradition was renewed. Growing out of Bethlehem's Choral Union of 1880, J. Fred Wolle founded the annual Bach Festival, which today brings together musical pilgrims to hear, among other works, Bach's great Mass in B Minor. Performances were given in the Moravian Church until 1905, then with Wolle's removal to California, they were discontinued until 1912. In that year the Bethlehem festivals were resumed with the help of Charles M. Schwab. Held in the Packer

Memorial Chapel on the campus of Lehigh University, the chorus is accompanied by members of the Philadelphia Orchestra and outstanding soloists are featured.

The early festivals in various smaller towns and cities were developing into extraordinary events. Large choral groups rehearsed all winter to prepare for the gala concerts. Week-long schedules included symphonies, concertos, and excerpts from operas. In New England, the Worcester (Massachusetts) Festival was started in 1866 by Carl Zerrahn. It is still held annually each fall. In 1898 a more intimate, but delightful festival had started at Cornell College in Mount Vernon, Iowa. It is still an annual event, held in the College Chapel, with the Chicago Symphony Orchestra assisting.

MUSIC EDUCATION

New York's Institute of Musical Art

In 1904 a new and important addition to New York's music life came with the founding of the Institute of Musical Art by Frank Damrosch (Leopold's son and Walter's brother). It had an initial endowment of $500,000 from James Loeb. With Dr. Damrosch as its director the Institute had a notable faculty and became one of New York's major music schools. In 1926 it merged with the Juilliard School of Music.

Music Educator's National Conference

Another event of great educational importance was the meeting in Keokuk, Iowa, in 1907, of a group of musicians interested in the growth of progressive music in the public schools. They met to discuss ways in which they might cooperate and to enjoy the stimulation of discussions. From this meeting was to come the Music Educator's National Conference, founded largely through the efforts of Frances Elliot Clark, who subsequently became Educational Director of the Victor Talking Machine Company.

Music Division of the Library of Congress

Although it is in no sense a school, the Library of Congress in Washington has become in the years after 1902 one of the gold mines for research in music as well as in all other branches of learning and information. The year 1902 is mentioned because it was in that year that Oscar G. Sonneck became Chief of the Music Division. Under his direction as well as by his own efforts what had been merely piles upon piles of uncatalogued music which had been deposited with the copyright office were classified and catalogued. Funds were appropriated for the purchase of rare books, music, and manuscripts so that the institution has become one of the great music libraries of the world, possessing research material and facilities for study which have been unequaled in any other part of the country.

REVISION OF COPYRIGHT LAW

In his message to Congress in December, 1905, President Theodore Roosevelt wrote in part: "Our copyright laws urgently need revision. They are imperfect in definition, confused and inconsistent in expression; they omit provision for many articles which, under modern reproductive processes, are entitled to protection." It was more than three years later that Congress finally took action and the general revision of our copyright laws was enacted on the last day of Roosevelt's administration, in 1909.

The clause in President Roosevelt's message about "modern reproductive processes" referred to phonograph records. Prior to 1909 no phonograph record manufacturer had to pay anything to the copyright owners of the songs and pieces they recorded. The new law provided for a two-cent royalty per record, with the stipulation that once the copyright owner has licensed one manufacturer to record a composition, he must issue similar licenses for that composition, on the same terms, to all other manufacturers who desire it. This law is still (1957) in effect, and the coming of long-playing records has caused considerable confusion, for while a major work would require several records of the 78 RPM variety (each entitled to a two-cent royalty) it is now possible to record a half-hour work on a single record side.

Among the clauses of the new act that were of the greatest concern to composers of music and their publishers were those pertaining to performing rights. In that department the 1909 law represented a setback, for twelve years earlier, in 1897, Congress had for the first time recognized the performing right in music and had granted to the copyright owner the exclusive right of public performance. The 1909 law limited that right to public performance *for profit*. The effect of this provision and the efforts of composers and publishers to protect their interests through performing rights societies is told in our concluding chapter.

Another limitation of the performing right in the 1909 law seemed innocent enough at that time but has since come to plague copyright owners of music and has proved a bonanza to a half-billion-dollar industry. Not only were religious and educational groups exempted from paying for performing rights, but also what were described as "coin-operated" phonographs. In those days such instruments consisted of machines in penny arcades and similar places through which the listener could hear a phonograph record, generally a cylinder, by inserting a coin and putting a pair of hearing tubes in his ears.

Who could have foreseen that the descendants of these coin machines would be the juke-boxes of mid-century, representing one of the largest and most direct "for profit" uses of music of all times? Continued efforts to amend the law and remove the exemption have been made since the early 1940s but as late as 1957 no relief has yet been granted by Congress.

<h2 style="text-align:center">RUMBLINGS OF A REVOLUTION IN MUSIC</h2>

While these events were taking place in the United States musical affairs were fermenting in Europe. The first in a long chain of reactions was the publication in the Paris *Figaro* of Emilio Filippo Tommaso Marinetti's "Futurist Manifesto," on February 12, 1909. It aimed to annihilate all accepted forms in favor of a music that would have a machine-like precision, but the music that resulted was rather a pale imitation of impressionism, using primarily the whole-tone scale. On February 20 of that year Arnold Schoenberg actually made a decisive break with tradition when he wrote the second piece of his three *Klavierstuecke*, Op. 11, which marked his final departure from any tonality and created what we generally refer to today as "atonality." Twenty-five days later Schoenberg composed another piece (published as the first of the three in Op. 11) whose idiom was still further removed from tonality. As though this were not enough, the following May, Richard H. Stein completed a detailed exposition of his new system of using quarter-tones, instead of the traditional half-tones. Maurice Ravel had already, as far back as 1906, according to Nicolas Slonimsky, affirmed "his priority in evolving new piano technique," having previously replaced the traditional sonata form in his String Quartet (Paris, 1904) with "principles of continual thematic mutation."

Such declarations as these betokened the radical liberation of the traditional harmonic system; a liberation that was already in process of realization and which would bring with it the emergence of what today is still referred to as "modern music." Wagner, in his use of chromaticism, had, of course, started the destruction of the older harmonic concepts and principles. Debussy, too, had swept aside tradition and created a new era of harmonic freedom, with Schoenberg following shortly after and breaking with the principle of tonality altogether. A further innovation was polytonality, as used by Stravinsky in his second ballet, *Petrouchka* (1911), as well as by Darius Milhaud, and before either of them, around 1904, by the then-unknown American composer, Charles Ives. Polytonality, or the simultaneous sounding of several tonalities, was at first often confused with atonality because both sounded strange to contemporary ears. But actually it was a direct antithesis to atonality, reaffirming all that tonality had implied.

RECOGNITION OF THE AMERICAN COMPOSER

But what of the American composer during these eventful years? At last he was beginning to hear some performances of his works and there were indications that he would find encouragement. One of them was the establishment in 1900 by Ignace Jan Paderewski, the piano virtuoso who had made his American debut in 1891, of a fund of $10,000 the income from which was to provide cash prizes every three years to composers of American birth.

As yet native composers were not free from the Old-World traditions, but some were becoming bolder in experimentation.

The era following Dvořák's residence in America and MacDowell's term at Columbia was increasingly productive, and in the stimulation which followed there were unmistakable signs of a minor revolution among some of the younger composers, particularly against the domination of the German classicists, which all along had been the model for most of the American composers.

The desire for freedom and a genuine American expression was both natural and healthy, and even though some of the methods that were used to gain artistic independence were artificial and synthetic, the mere fact that our composers wanted it was wholesome and stimulating. These composers at the turn of the century were a serious and considerably talented lot. In Arthur Farwell's words they "broke the ice, so to speak, for American nationalism in music." That many of their early attempts were quite self-conscious is now apparent, and some of them failed to realize that nationalism is a subtle ingredient in an art product. It is more than just borrowing tunes from the Indians and Negroes.

It was still difficult for these men to get their works performed, for there were not as many orchestras in those years to play their works as there were to be later, and only a few publishers could afford to issue major works. Perhaps the most significant figure at the turn of the century was this same Arthur Farwell, who became the voice for this ardent group of American nationalists.

Arthur Farwell (1872-1952)

When the Wa-Wan Press was founded by Arthur Farwell in 1901, he and his colleagues let it be known that the Press would particularly welcome works that developed in interesting fashion any folk music found on American soil. Farwell's interest in folk music came from the fact that he was a spiritual descendant of the tribe of Tom Sawyer and Huck Finn. He always, in his own words, got "a great kick out of a rip-snorting development of a good old American tune." In his early years he concentrated on Indian themes, which were the basis of his orchestral work *Dawn*, played for the first time at the St. Louis Exposition in 1904.

Born in St. Paul, Minnesota, April 23, 1872, it was not until after his graduation from the Massachusetts Institute of Technology, when twenty-one, that he decided to become a musician. He had had violin lessons as a boy, but his first great inspiration came in Boston, when he heard Nikisch conduct the Boston Symphony. He plunged into the study of composition, and four years later went abroad to study with Engelbert Humperdinck and Hans Pfitzner in Germany and Alexandre Guilmant in Paris.

Returning to America in 1899 to lecture at Cornell University, he also began his first experiments with Indian music, and after founding the Wa-Wan Press at Newton Center, Massachusetts, the next years were spent in lecturing and study, and the raising of funds to support the Press. In 1927 he went to East Lansing, Michigan, where he conducted the theoretical courses and lectures on music history at the Michigan State College until his retirement in 1939. He died in New York City on January 20, 1952.

The other Indian compositions of Farwell's, besides his *Dawn*, included: *The Domain of Hurakan* (the wind god of the Central American Indians), 1903, and *American Indian Melodies*, 1901. He also made settings of Negro tunes, and cowboy and prairie songs, *From Mesa and Plain*, 1905, and composed incidental music for masques and pageants and several works calling for participation by the audience—*Symphonic Hymn on March! March!* (1917), *Symphonic Song on Old Black Joe* (1923), and *Mountain Song* (1924).

Henry Franklin Belknap Gilbert (1868-1928)

Henry F. B. Gilbert came as close to writing a typically American music as any of the composers of this period. It was not only that he chose American subjects and used native folk material, he treated them in an individual manner that was racy and spontaneous. Born in Somerville, Massachusetts, September 26, 1868, he was trained at the New England Conservatory in Boston and had private lessons with MacDowell. He became interested in the works of the Russian nationalists, particularly those of Rimsky-Korsakov, and in his own way he became an American counterpart of the founder of the Russian nationalist school, Mikhail Glinka. Many years later when Gilbert learned that Charpentier's *Louise* was to have its première in Paris, and that its score tended toward the use of popular themes, the young American worked his way to Europe on a cattle boat so that he could hear the first performance.

Gilbert was forty-two when he first gained substantial recognition. In April, 1911, the Boston Symphony played his *Comedy Overture on Negro Themes*, and even though some of the audience was disturbed by this new-sounding music, it caught their attention. The piece was based on the *Uncle Remus* tales of Joel Chandler Harris (1880), which had been an example of the marked growth of America's literature after the Civil War. The Overture's first theme was a Negro melody from the Bahamas, the second a Mississippi boat-song *I'se Gwine to Alabammy, oh,* and the middle section a witty, rollicking fugue on *The Old Ship of Zion*.

In 1913 Gilbert was commissioned to write a work for the Litchfield County Festival in Norfolk, Connecticut. The result was his *Negro Rhapsody*, which pictures first a Negro "shout," alternating a savage dance tune and a spiritual, with a final glorification of the spiritual in which the barbaric falls away to give place to nobler elements.

Gilbert's *Dance in the Place Congo* was first composed as an orchestral piece, but the composer later devised a dance scenario and it was produced in 1918 as a ballet at the Metropolitan Opera House in New York. The score uses five Negro Creole songs from Louisiana, and the plot is based on slave dances which were permitted in the Place Congo of New Orleans. The tropical grace of the Creole tunes is subtly drawn, but the gloomy, tragic background is weird and fantastic. The piece starts with a Bamboula, then the gaiety rises to frenzy until a bell summons the slaves back to their quarters.

Gilbert wrote a number of works not based on folk material, the most notable being a Symphonic Prelude to Synge's *Riders to the Sea*, composed in 1904 for small orchestra, and later expanded for full orchestra. It was, however, in his more American works that Gilbert was the most vital. His temperament responded to things that were spontaneous and unstudied and they became an integral part of his own expression. His other works include *Americanesque*, an orchestral work composed in 1903 and based on three minstrel tunes—*Zip Coon* (*Turkey in the Straw*), *Dearest Mary*, and *Don't Be Foolish, Joe*; and his *Three American Dances in Ragtime*, 1911.

Edgar Stillman Kelley (1857-1944)

One of the best-established and active composers at the turn of the century was a man who was four years older than MacDowell, Edgar Stillman Kelley. His works reflected the German influence of his student days in Stuttgart, but he was venturesome for his time. When he composed his Chinese orchestral suite, *Aladdin* (1915), he studied native music in San Francisco's Chinatown, and used oboes, muted trumpets, and mandolins to imitate Chinese instruments. His *New England Symphony* (No. 2, 1913) contained Indian songs and Puritan psalm-tunes. The incidental music he composed for the stage production of *Ben Hur* (1899) was based on Greek modes. This play, with Kelley's music, was performed five thousand times in English-speaking countries.

Kelley was fond of composing program works. His First Symphony, begun in his youth but not finished until 1937, was entitled *Gulliver,* and was descriptive of episodes from Swift's *Gulliver's Travels.* There was a Symphonic Poem based on Poe's *The Pit and the Pendulum* (1925), and a Symphonic Suite, *Alice in Wonderland* (1919). His oratorio *The Pilgrim's Progress* (1918), has been performed frequently in this country and in England. Kelley believed that in developing his own individuality a composer shows the traits and tendencies peculiar to his European ancestry as they are modified by his American environment.

Charles Martin Loeffler (1861-1935)

Charles Martin Loeffler was one of the picturesque figures in American music. There are many who denied his Americanism; not because he was born in Alsace (January 30, 1861), but because his music is so akin to the French music of Debussy's time that it is really not American at all. He first came to America in the summer of 1881, a fine musician with an unusual background. He had lived for a while in Russia, had been one of Joachim's favorite violin pupils, studied in Paris with Massart (pupil of Kreutzer), and played in Pasdeloup's orchestra. Loeffler was in New York for about a year, playing in Damrosch's orchestra, and sometimes with Theodore Thomas. Then Major Higginson asked him to come to Boston to play in the Boston Symphony, which had just finished its first season. He shared the first desk with Bernhard Listemann, the concertmaster, and when Franz Kneisel succeeded Listemann, Loeffler played side by side with Kneisel until 1903. Then he resigned, gave up playing the violin in public, and, living the life of a recluse at his farm at Medfield, Massachusetts, devoted the rest of his life to composition. He died there on May 20, 1935. Loeffler's residence in America, and the fact that he became a citizen in May, 1887, provided the basis for his being classed as an American composer. He was the first of many subsequent composers who were in the same position, yet such musical refinement and brilliance as Loeffler possessed were not any too common among the American composers of those decades. Paul Rosenfeld believed that Loeffler's many years in Boston made his work sterile, that the brilliant musician succumbed to the correct manners and inhibitions of New England. Yet Loeffler wrote with exquisite perfection, and seemed to turn everything he touched to jewels and gold. There were many who were dazzled by Loeffler's jewels, and who felt the pulse within.

Loeffler published practically nothing until he had finished his career as a violinist. Many of his works had been performed from manuscript during the years with the Boston Symphony, such as his Suite for violin and orchestra *Les Veillées de l'Ukraine* (after Gogol), in 1891, his *Fantastic Concerto* for cello and orchestra in 1894, and in 1895 his *Divertimento* for violin and orchestra.

His first published works (1905) were the dramatic poem *La Morte de Tintagiles* (after Maeterlinck), and a symphonic fantasy based on a poem by Rollinat, *La Villanelle du Diable*. Loeffler's most frequently played work was his *Pagan Poem*, based on the eighth Eclogue of Virgil, in which a Thessalian girl tries to become a sorceress, to draw her truant lover home. Written first in 1901 for piano and chamber orchestra, Loeffler remodeled the work and expanded it to symphonic proportions for piano and large orchestra. It was first played by the Boston Symphony in 1907. Three trumpets are treated obbligati, suggesting the refrain of the sorceress: *"Ducite ab urbe domum, mea carmina, ducite Daphnim"* ("Draw from the city, my songs, draw Daphnis home"). First they are heard off stage, then nearer and nearer until they finally come onto the stage, and the orchestra voices the triumph of the sorceress in an outburst of exultant passion. Loeffler's dark, brooding music brings the odor of strange incense and magic incantations.

Gregorian plain chant influence is apparent in the *Music for Four String Instruments* (published in 1923); and in the Symphony *Hora Mystica*, written for the Norfolk (Connecticut) Festival of 1916. The Library of Congress, under the provisions of the Elizabeth Sprague Coolidge Foundation, commissioned and published Loeffler's *Canticum Fratis Solis*, a remarkable setting for solo voice and chamber orchestra of the "Canticle of the Sun" by St. Francis. It was first performed in Washington at the first chamber music festival at the Library of Congress in 1925. In 1930, for the Cleveland Orchestra, Loeffler composed an *Evocation* for orchestra, women's chorus, and speaking voice. It was first performed in Cleveland, February 5, 1931, and was published in the same year by the Juilliard Foundation.

Spiritually, Loeffler was a mystic, a deep student of medieval culture and thought. Living in the twentieth century in America, he seemed a wanderer searching for a place where pious mystics would speak his language. Not finding it, he lived in his dreams. There, away from the currents of contemporary life, he polished his music until it was refined to a purity that would satisfy his sense of the exquisite.

Henry Kimball Hadley (1871-1937)

Henry Hadley was one of the most prolific composers of this period, a descendant of the Boston group. He was born in Somerville, Massachusetts, on December 20, 1871, and was a pupil of Chadwick at the New England Conservatory. He had much in common with his teacher, for in addition to a thorough command of musical resources, he had a fluency and buoyancy that made his music attractive and spontaneous. His list of works is a long one and includes five symphonies, five operas (one of them, *Cleopatra's Night,* was produced by the Metropolitan in 1920), tone poems, overtures, extended choral works, and much chamber music.

Before assuming his duties as conductor of the San Francisco Orchestra, Hadley had been active as a conductor of the Laura Schirmer-Mapleson Opera Company; the Stadt Theater in Mayence, Germany, in 1909; and on the Pacific Coast, the director of the Seattle Symphony. In 1920 he was made associate conductor of the New York Philharmonic and in 1929 organized a Manhattan Symphony Orchestra in New York, which he directed for three seasons. He died in New York in 1937.

It was in his role as conductor that Hadley had his share in furthering the cause of his fellow composers, and he did much to promote the recognition of their works. During his last years he founded the National Association for American Composers and Conductors, which has functioned since his death as a practical instrument for advancing the cause of American music. Among its varied activities this Association sponsors the Henry Hadley Memorial Library of works by contemporary composers, deposited in the New York Public Library.

Daniel Gregory Mason (1873-1953)

Daniel Gregory Mason is a composer who experimented with folk songs, but who came to the conclusion that American music is necessarily eclectic and cosmopolitan—that its distinctiveness must be individual rather than national. Taking little spontaneous pleasure in the impressionism of Debussy and Ravel, the mysticism of Scriabin, or the primitivism of Stravinsky, he turned in his own music to the classic-romantic type of beauty worked out by Beethoven, Schumann, Brahms, and Franck.

Mason was a member of the famous Mason family, the grandson of Lowell Mason, and a nephew of William. His father was Henry Mason, one of the founders of the piano house of Mason & Hamlin. He was born November 20, 1873, in Brookline, Massachusetts. When he was a student at Harvard, he attended the music classes of John Knowles Paine, but he found Paine so uninspiring that he virtually dropped his music while he was in college, except for writing the music for the Hasty Pudding Club shows. When he was graduated from Harvard he studied with Chadwick in Boston and Percy Goetschius in New York. Then he went to Paris to work with Vincent d'Indy. From 1900 he was active as a lecturer and teacher. In 1910 he joined the music faculty of Columbia University, and in 1929 he was made the MacDowell Professor of Music. In 1940 he retired from the chairmanship of the Music Department at Columbia, and was succeeded by Douglas Moore. Although he remained in New York, he was by descent and musical tradition the embodiment of all of the qualities that are today associated with the Boston group.

In the larger forms, Mason composed three symphonies, and in 1937 the New York Philharmonic-Symphony introduced the third, known as the *Lincoln Symphony*. Perhaps his best-known orchestral work is his *Chanticleer Overture* (1928), introduced by Nikolai Sokoloff and the Cleveland Orchestra in 1931. His inspiration was a passage from Thoreau's *Walden,* which he quotes in the score: "All climates agree with brave Chanticleer. He is more indigenous than the natives. His health is ever good, his lungs, his spirits never flag."

Mason experimented with folk songs, as in his *Suite after English Folk Songs* (1924), for orchestra; and two string quartets, Folk Song Fantasy, *Fanny Blair* (1929) and Quartet on Negro Themes (1919). From the 1920s came the Prelude and Fugue, Opus 20, for piano and orchestra; three pieces for flute, harp, and string quartet; and Variations on a Theme of John Powell, for string quartet.

Mason was widely known as a writer on music, as well as a lecturer. *From Song to Symphony* (1924) was an official textbook for the National Federation of Music Clubs, and *The Dilemma of American Music* (1928) and *Tune In, America* (1931), are analyses of the state of America's music. Mason has been called a "humanist in tones." In 1938 he wrote his recollections, called *Music in My Time.*

Edward Burlingame Hill (1872-   )

Edward Burlingame Hill is of New England parentage and of the Harvard tradition. His grandfather was president of the university, and his father a chemistry professor. He was born in Cambridge, September 9, 1872, and was graduated from Harvard with the highest honors in music, a student of John Knowles Paine. He later studied with Charles Widor in Paris, and Chadwick in Boston. In 1908 he became a teacher at Harvard—first as an instructor, then as an assistant professor, and from 1928 until his retirement in 1940, as chairman of the Division of Music. Unlike his colleagues in the Boston Group, instead of venerating the German music of his day, Hill's specialization was French music. His book *Modern French Music* was the outgrowth of his lectures at the Lowell Institute in Boston, as well as those for the universities in Lyon and Strasbourg.

For many years Hill was known most widely for program works, particularly for his two *Stevensoniana* suites for orchestra, based on poems from Robert Louis Stevenson's *A Child's Garden of Verses.* These were composed in 1917-1922, and the scoring is rich and colorful, with a leaning toward the French impressionists. He also composed three symphonies, two sinfoniettas, a violin concerto, a concertino for piano and orchestra, in addition to chamber music. Other of Hill's descriptive pieces are *Lilacs,* inspired by Amy Lowell's poem, a symphonic poem based on Poe's *The Fall of the House of Usher,* and *The Parting of Launcelot and Guinevere.*

When Hill's Third Symphony was introduced for the first time by the Boston Symphony, December 3, 1937, the composer announced that the work had "no descriptive background, aiming merely to present musical ideas according to traditional forms." By this time most American and European composers had foresworn the descriptive music of the post-romanticists and returned to the strict forms of the classic period.

CHAPTER X

The Second Decade and World War I

It was in Paris in 1910, that musical interest in Europe centered around a young Russian composer, Igor Stravinsky (1882-   ), whose first ballet, *The Fire-Bird,* was performed by Serge Diaghilev's fabulous Ballét Russe at the Paris Opéra on June 25. Still under the influence of both romanticism and impressionism, Stravinsky nevertheless showed many traces in his first major work of the innovations which were to culminate in his third ballet, *The Rite of Spring.* This was the beginning of a decade of unforgettable ballets by men who were among the world's greatest composers. Many of them, as well as the dancers and choreographers, would soon come to America to conduct, teach or perform, and some to become American citizens. Their list is more than impressive, not only because it sums up this great era of ballet's finest commissioned scores, but also because these composers represent the climax of classical ballet to which Tchaikovsky had given new meaning in the last years of the nineteenth century.

The decade of ballets included such important works as Stravinsky's *Petrouchka,* 1911; Ravel's *Daphnis et Chloé,* 1912; Stravinsky's *Le Sacre du Printemps,* 1913; Richard Strauss's *Josephslegende,* 1914; Béla Bartók's *The Wooden Prince,* 1916; Erik Satie's *Parade,* 1917; Milhaud's *Le Boeuf sur le Toit or The Nothing Doing Bar,* 1919; Stravinsky's *Pulcinella,* 1920; and Prokofiev's *The Buffoon Who Outwitted Seven Other Buffoons* (known also as *Chout*) in 1921. America's most significant contributions to ballet would not come until the 1930s, but American dancers and composers were soon to become aware of the significance of this new medium, and by mid-century, there would be an impressive array of commissioned works and great dancers.

Stokowski Moves to Philadelphia

With Leopold Stokowski's leadership of the Philadelphia Orchestra in 1912, the way was paved for America to hear the works of the most important contemporary composers for the next twenty years. These would be works that were the subject of controversy in Europe's leading music centers, many of which have today become part of the repertory of all major orchestras. Once again Philadelphia would assume musical leadership, this time in the field of symphonic music. The years under Stokowski had not seen the like in music since the bold experiments of Johann Stamitz and his court orchestra in the eighteenth-century town of Mannheim. The heavy, plodding mediocrity, so typical of many German leaders, entirely disappeared under Stokowski, and with his love of a beautiful tone above all else, the orchestra developed into the almost-perfect instrument it is today. Pure sound fascinated him to the extent that he was tireless in his experiments in reseating the orchestra to effect better balance, and if he thought sound might be improved, he had no hesitation in altering the scores of composers to suit his own purposes. Many of his interpretations were erratic and questionable, but under his direction the Philadelphia Orchestra became the most dynamic and brilliant the world had ever known. America was at last free of the domination of the Germans, and Stokowski became the first of the three great conductors (Koussevitsky and Toscanini were to follow) in the history of America's symphonic orchestras in the twentieth century.

Detroit and Baltimore

The Detroit Symphony Orchestra was established in 1914 by Weston Gales, who conducted until the 1917-18 season when Ossip Gabrilowitsch took over. Gabrilowitsch, also remembered as an excellent pianist, organized the orchestra and conducted it until his death in 1935. Baltimore, remembering the fine orchestra of

Hamerik's day, desired its own orchestra, and in 1916 the present orchestra was formed, the first in the country to have municipal support. Gustave Strube, who had been concertmaster of the Boston Symphony and was at that time teaching composition at the Peabody Conservatory of Music, became its first conductor. The opening concert—with the well-known violin teacher, J. C. van Hulsteyn, as concertmaster—was on February 11, 1916, and Mabel Garrison, a native of Baltimore and at the time a soprano with the Metropolitan Opera Company, was the soloist. The composer George Siemonn (in private life the husband of Miss Garrison), became the second conductor of the orchestra in 1930. The city's taxpayers also backed a Negro orchestra and chorus.

Cleveland and Los Angeles

Two more major orchestras were founded immediately after the war, that of Cleveland, Ohio, in 1918 (under the auspices of the Musical Arts Association, with Nikolai Sokoloff conducting the first concert in December), and in 1919 that of Los Angeles (when William Andrews Clark, Jr., announced his intention of forming a group, of which he would assume all of the financial obligations). Clark was a fine amateur violinist, anxious to see better music in the city, and he contributed $100,000 each year, doubling the amount as the orchestra grew. Walter Henry Rothwell (who had been the leader of the St. Paul Symphony for several years) became the conductor of the new Los Angeles Philharmonic Orchestra. He had worked under Gustav Mahler in Hamburg and Vienna, and he was given a free hand in building the new orchestra, which was to have a twenty-eight-week season. Rothwell had great success, and remained with the orchestra until his sudden death in 1927.

New Symphony Orchestra in New York

With the arrival of many composers of all types from Europe, it was natural that a movement soon got under way to provide an opportunity for Americans to hear the latest contemporary music. In the spring of 1919 in New York, Edgar Varèse, who had arrived from Paris in 1916, organized the New Symphony Orchestra. Dedicated to the performance of modern music, the first concert was given on April 11.

Artur Bodanzky later conducted this orchestra. Unfortunately, it did not survive for long and after a short career it was absorbed by the New York Philharmonic.

In these years America was busily cultivating her newest phase of popular music—jazz. Ragtime was still a popular word, and would be until the end of the war, but as the blues had become more and more popular with its inevitable transference to the piano and instruments, jazz as we know it today was gaining great favor. Dance bands appeared in the larger cities—New York, Chicago, San Francisco—from about 1912 on, and spread so rapidly that on October 27, 1916, the trade journal *Variety* printed the following item: "Chicago has added another innovation to its list of discoveries in the so-called 'Jazz Bands.' The Jazz Band is composed of three or more instruments and seldom plays regulated music. The College Inn and practically all the other high-class places of entertainment has a Jazz Band featured, while the low cost makes it possible for all the smaller places to carry their Jazz orchestra." On January 5, 1917, *Variety* marked the progress of "jaz" (so spelled) in the Chicago cabarets. Thus we know that jazz was being talked about even before America entered the war, although many people were not quite sure just what jazz really was.

Origins

One thing is certain, and that is that jazz had been developing for many years, long before its first appearance in the larger northern cities. There are many fanciful theories as to the derivation of the word "jazz," which at first was spelled *jas, jass, jazz,* or *jasz.* The first appearance in 1915 in Chicago of "Brown's Dixieland Jass Band" (according to the billing) might prove the word to be a northern one. However, many authorities claim that the word had long been familiar in New Orleans, just as the music we now call jazz had been in existence for many years. From the brilliantly colorful parades and processions, especially in the celebration of Mardi Gras, brass bands had long been popular, and when these bands began playing for dancing, especially when they got "hot," our modern conception of jazz was on the way. Contrary to popular belief, jazz did not start in the cheap saloons of the red-light district of New Orleans (although it was popular there); its sources go back for many years and were the expression of the people.

Dixieland Jazz

The white musicians who attempted to imitate the classic jazz of New Orleans' Negro musicians created what is known today as "Dixieland Jazz." The style had been drawn from Jack "Papa" Laine's Ragtime Band. When Tom Brown's "Dixieland Jass Band" (already mentioned) was brought from New Orleans to the Lamb's Cafe in Chicago in 1915, Dixieland jazz launched a vogue that soon swept the country. By 1917 another group, also called "Dixieland Jass Band," created a sensation in New York at Reisenweber's Restaurant, and that same year was the first band to make recordings of Dixieland jazz.

Sources of Jazz

The pioneers of jazz frankly admit the importance of the piano rags of Scott Joplin. Soon a small group of instruments would take over, consisting of a guitar, banjo, and mandolin, with sound effects on a washboard. Gradually the cornet, trombone, and clarinet were used, with an added string bass and drums. These early ragtime bands (as they were called) were really jazzing the piano rags long before jazz, as a term, became known. As the blues became increasingly popular, the instruments accompanying the singer gradually became more important and independent. The dance bands began to feature the instruments that most nearly approximated the human voice—the saxophone, cornet or trumpet, clarinet, and trombone. By the end of World War I the classic jazz band had become standardized, with reeds (saxophones and clarinets) and brasses (cornets or trumpets and trombones) taking care of the melodic line, while piano, banjo or guitar, string bass, and drums provided the rhythmic accompaniment. The final emergence of jazz was to become a mighty force, one of the most potent influences music had ever experienced.

MODERN TENDENCIES CONTINUE

In the years just before the first World War, America continued to go about her business, unaware of the momentous years ahead.

On the West Coast, San Francisco had overcome her disastrous earthquake, and on December 28, 1911, established her Symphony Orchestra with Henry Hadley, already one of the nation's outstanding composers, in charge. Much of the groundwork for the new orchestra had already been laid by the orchestra of the University of California, which J. Fred Wolle had led in the years he was absent from Bethlehem's Bach Festival.

Today it seems quite remarkable that while Europe was in the throes of the musical revolution led by such innovators as Debussy, Schoenberg, and Stravinsky, an American businessman—Charles Ives—was quietly writing in his spare time in New York and his native Connecticut music that was years ahead of his time. Music was his very life, and although his work would gain neither recognition nor understanding until nearly a half-century later, his ideas were as revolutionary as any of those in Europe, and in many cases anticipated the work of the European writers, who at the time got all the credit for what they were doing. Long before Stravinsky gained the spotlight, Ives was writing polyrhythms in a sketch, *March 1776*, which he was to incorporate in the second movement of his orchestral work *Three Places in New England* (1904). He did considerable experimentation with polytonality, (as had his father before him) many years before it became an accepted practice in Europe, which was just before World War I. Because Ives was such an isolated figure at this time, it is perhaps better that we wait until the 1940s to evaluate him as a composer, for it was in this period that his work finally gained understanding and approval.

Another American composer, full of new ideas, would become in the 1920s one of the most forceful figures of those turbulent years. He was Henry Cowell, who in 1912 played for San Francisco's Music Club and performed for the first time in public tone-clusters on the piano by using his forearm. His later experiments were to startle many audiences and he would become one of the first American composers to have a definite influence on certain European musicians. Slowly but inevitably, the pattern was reversing.

The first violent shock of the musical revolution hit the world in 1913, a little over a year before Kaiser Wilhelm threw the nations into the titanic convulsions of the first World War. The ferment and occasional bubblings, had there been anyone to notice, might have prepared the musical world for the explosion that was to follow, but life had been calm and seemingly peaceful in those early years of the century. Italy had warned music lovers of the impending change when on March 11, 1913, Luigi Russolo issued his manifesto in Milan, proclaiming the music of the future, which, he said, would be based on the "Art of Noises." But it was Stravinsky's ballet *The Rite of Spring*, conducted by Pierre Monteux in Paris on May 29, 1913, which actually seemed to draw the line of demarcation, marking the end of both impressionism and neoromanticism, and the beginning of modern music as we know it today.

Many European musicians were already familiar with the possibilities of new instrumental colors, especially in the extreme high or low registers of the different orchestral instruments. The musical impressionists had led the way, practically abandoning the group orchestrations of romantic music. Influenced by the Paris Exposition earlier in the century, more exotic percussion instruments were being utilized and the piano began to be used as an instrument of percussion. Neoromanticism had embraced all the trends that had prevailed in the post-Wagnerian era, with pictorial representational music, large and involved programs, and huge symphonic and operatic dimensions.

But at the première of *The Rite of Spring*, Stravinsky's score did not seem to be like anything ever heard before, and from the opening bassoon solo to the frenzied climax of the sacrificial dance, the ballet seemed to create music whose values were so startling, so revolutionary, that the audience hissed and booed, and made such a din that the dancers could not hear the orchestra. It had been difficult enough for them to try to learn the choreography of such a complex score, with its constant change of beat and polyrhythms, and strife had been rampant in the company for weeks. Now with the audience completely out of hand, the result was a scandal that rocked the musical world. In the days and weeks which followed, musicians had to decide whether or not Stravinsky was insane and therefore best ignored, or whether this new music was a foretaste or what was to come, and, if so, whether they must accept it.

But Stravinsky was not the only pioneer. Schoenberg, too, had finally broken with his early idealism of Wagner (as seen in his *Verklärte Nacht (Transfigured Night)* (1899), and having already made considerable departure from tradition with his *Three Piano Pieces*, Op. 11 (already mentioned), reached his most radical period so far in the melodramatic composition *Pierrot Lunaire* (1912). Demonstrations in Vienna had been hostile, yet this score with its themes of wide intervals, chords built in fourths, and the many contrapuntal devices he was to become known for was to become as important to the music of the future as was Stravinsky's ballet.

As though this were not enough, four days after the Paris première of *The Rite of Spring*, in Modena, Italy (June 2, 1913), the first concert of noise instruments was given. As wild as the idea seemed at the time, the use of percussion instruments would seem quite natural in the jazz bands and concert halls of America, and within a very few years.

CRUMBLING OF OLD VALUES

War in Europe—the news spread like wildfire, yet many refused to believe that such a catastrophe could be possible. Americans on the whole took the situation lightly, yet hundreds of them were caught in the capitals and cities of European countries that summer of 1914, as August was the peak of tourist travel.

The cataclysm of war brought about the total collapse of the traditions and decorous life of the nineteenth century, and a spirit of pessimism and futility that came to pervade peoples' lives gradually crept into all the arts. Modern painting had already created a stir in New York, when in 1913 at the Armory Show the works of Pablo Picasso, Henri Matisse and many other of Europe's moderns were exhibited for the first time as a group. The year before America entered the war further evidence of the disintegration of the old values was expressed by Tristan Tzara when he invented the word "Dada." Nicolas Slonimsky explains that Dada was "expressive of utter mental nihilism in the domain of art, literature, and music." It stood in opposition to impressionism as well as to neoprimitivism (which had been the attempt to recreate the elemental power of primitive music). Its primary intent was to destroy all values, and its votaries admitted their intention was "to spit in the eye of the world."

On April 4, 1917, the dance world witnessed an "abstract" dance recital at the Metropolitan Opera House, presented by Valentine de Saint-Point, with Pierre Monteux conducting an orchestra. The works of a French-American composer, Dane Rudhyar, who had been greatly influenced by Stravinsky, were played for the first time, and were entitled *Poèmes Ironiques* and *Vision Végétale*.

AMERICA IN THE WAR

On April 6, 1917, the United States declared war against Germany and the anti-German sentiment that had been spreading throughout the country included a reaction against German music and musicians. In 1918, violent protests arose from all sides over the performance of German music of any kind, and German musicians, many of whom were most loyal and law-abiding, were often persecuted in the most heartless fashion. In January the directors of the Philharmonic Society of New York issued a statement that no compositions by living German composers should be performed by the orchestra. But many persons insisted that neither Wagner nor Beethoven should be heard either. In Boston, Mrs. William Jay directed countless letters to Major Higginson over the presence of Karl Muck as conductor of the orchestra. Muck had returned to Boston and the splendid ensemble that it had been under his first seasons had continued. But how quickly in the hysteria of war could all that he had done be forgotten! As Muck was entirely innocent of any intrigue, the public sentiment that was roused against him was nothing short of the most cruel persecution. In March he was arrested as an enemy alien and interned at Fort Oglethorpe, Georgia, for the duration of the war, his spirit completely broken.

Songs of World War I

The war itself produced hundreds of songs, many of which were trivial, but others have lasted and are still to be found in the popular song collections of the day. From the Spanish-American War on, American soldiers have had to fight away from their homeland, which may account for the subtle difference that can be traced in the quality of some of the songs of each of our various wars. Of all of the war songs, those of the Civil War are still among the best, for just as it and the Revolutionary War were wars of survival, fought on home ground, their songs had a spirit and vitality that caused many of them to be sung long after the wars were finished.

Many of the Civil War songs were among the most popular with the American soldiers in France in 1917-18.

The earliest war songs of 1916 and onward seem silly because of their pacificism—*I didn't raise my boy to be a soldier, I don't want to go to war, Don't blame the Germans*. But other songs there were, for raising funds through Liberty Loans, encouraging knitting articles for soldiers, and the like. Perhaps the following may be considered the most representative and outstanding of the songs from World War I: *Goodbye, Broadway, Hello France; Over There; Dear Old Pal of Mine; Mademoiselle from Armentieres; Just a Baby's Prayer at Twilight; K-K-K-Katy; Keep the Home Fires Burning; Pack Up Your Troubles; Roses of Picardy; 'Till We Meet Again; Oh! How I Hate to Get Up in the Morning; Tipperary; Smiles;* and *The Long, Long Trail*.

Most of these are friendship songs, or pep songs, actually of the music-hall variety, good for marching as well as dancing in the precious hours of a treasured furlough. Each song tells its own particular story.

After the Armistice

A chance incident on the very morning that the Armistice was signed is of more than passing interest. It was then that Igor Stravinsky completed his score of *Ragtime* (for eleven instruments), whose rhythmical influences came of course from the highly popular American rag. Six days later Paris heard its first jazz band, at the Casino de Paris. Already American jazz was exerting a strong influence on music everywhere.

Musicians of importance were gradually emigrating to America, especially from Russia as the Revolution drew to its climax. Many became citizens, never to go back to their native countries, and once again, as in 1848, the foreign musicians were to have a decided influence on America's music. American composers were by now more certain of themselves and were therefore stimulated rather than overshadowed by these newcomers. Rachmaninoff left Russia forever in December, 1917, and a year later Serge Prokofiev, one of Russia's foremost composers, reached New York by way of Japan for a visit. On December 10, 1918, he appeared as soloist in his Second Piano Concerto, with the Russian Symphony Orchestra, Modest Altschuler conducting.

ENCOURAGEMENT AND FINANCIAL AID

The status of the American composer at the conclusion of the war was definitely improving, as far as performances of his works was concerned. The day when conductors and performers would seek out the composer for a chance to perform something new for the first time was yet to come, but about a dozen composers were represented in performances by the major orchestras and opera houses of the country.

Equally as difficult as getting performances of his work was the composer's attempt to secure publication in these years. For this reason the formation in 1919 of the Society for the Publication of American Music was most important. Founded by a group of musicians and music lovers in the New York home of the late William B. Tuthill, an architect, the Society's purpose is to issue for its subscriber members one chamber music work each year. Compositions are submitted anonymously and the winning composition is chosen by a group of judges. By 1957 the Society has been in existence for thirty-eight years, issuing annually a work of distinction and significance.

Juilliard and Eastman Bequests

Since both the Juilliard and Eastman bequests have been used in part to subsidize publication of American symphonic works, it is appropriate to mention them here, although this has required only a small part of these vast sums bequeathed to the advancement of music.

Augustus G. Juilliard, dying on April 25, 1919, left an endowment of some twenty millions, to be used to aid the development of music in the United States. Almost at the same time, George Eastman, inventor of the Kodak and great patron of the arts, gave a gift, equally generous, of three million dollars (to which he added later), for the purpose of founding the Eastman School of Music in Rochester, New York, which was to become a part of the University of Rochester. Thus, two of the three great schools that opened in the 1920s were made possible. Their influence on future generations of American musicians proved incalculable.

POSTWAR ART AND MUSIC IN EUROPE

Violent reaction was everywhere, with painting and literature reflecting the newer trends just as much as the music. The world seemed to fall apart as far as the arts were concerned, and anarchy and primitive brutality seemed the order of the day. Pessimism and futility found their outlet in prose and poetry, as men like H. L. Mencken cried out against the stupidities of the age, while Sinclair Lewis poked fun with his brittle wit in *Main Street*. Gertrude Stein (who would soon collaborate with Virgil Thomson in the field of opera) influenced many of the writers with her play of words that seemed to make no sense or to have any relationship with each other. The poets no longer spoke to the common man, as Longfellow had done, but instead men like Ezra Pound were writing in such a manner that even their contemporaries among the poets had difficulty in understanding what they were trying to say.

In music, the expressionism of the German composers, rejecting all tonality and using the twelve-tone system, was a dominant influence. New terms were created: *urbanism* (the music of the city), *neoclassicism, machine music.*

Neoclassicism was a return to the simplicity and the forms of the eighteenth century, a reaction against program music and inflated orchestral works, as well as against the impressionism of Debussy. The harsher instruments of the orchestra were cultivated, and percussion instruments became more and more important, thanks to the coming of the jazz band. The pictorial titles of the impressionist composer disappeared, and the younger composers began to use the more impersonal forms of the classical period—such as the suite, sonata, and symphony. *Machine music* took over, and replaced the older romantic concepts of melody and harmony.

COMPOSERS AT HOME

In America, at the end of the war, our composers embarked on a new era. Scores of them began writing in their own individual ways, accepting the stimulation and challenge of untried paths. They drew from the new jazz idiom, folk music, and the best of traditional music, and, as their own nation had done with her people, made them into music that was peculiarly American.

The Dvořák Influence

The influence of Dvořák might still be noticed in the work of some of his students and their contemporaries. By this time some of the more perceptive composers had recognized just how important had been the emergence of ragtime and the blues, while others were already utilizing materials which they had taken from the music of the American Indians. That many of these composers fell far short of being great creative geniuses is beside the point. What is important to remember is that they were significant at this time because they were not afraid to take up Dvořák's challenge and, in turning to the wealth of native material at hand, they slowly but surely turned the tide away from the domination of Europe, and prepared the way for future generations of American composers.

Rubin Goldmark

It was quite natural that from the circle of Dvořák's pupils at the National Conservatory the figure of Rubin Goldmark (1872-1936) should dominate New York's musical scene for many years, for he early manifested an interest in American nationalism. Although born in New York, his uncle was the well-known Austrian composer Carl Goldmark, and the young man had his early training in Vienna at the Conservatory. But when one considers the titles of some of his more important compositions it is obvious that he heeded the words of his New York teacher, Dvořák, and concerned himself with the American scene. There is an overture, *Hiawatha*, and a *Negro Rhapsody*, as well as *The Call of the Plains*, for orchestra, in which he successfully caught the American locale. Goldmark's best-known work was his orchestral *Requiem* suggested by Lincoln's Gettysburg Address. But perhaps even more important than his own creative work was his ability to impart his knowledge of musical fundamentals to others, and soon Goldmark was one of the leading teachers in Manhattan, first privately, and then as head of the composition faculty of the Juilliard School of Music (1924-36). His pupils included such men as Aaron Copland, George Gershwin, Vittorio Giannini, Frederick Jacobi, and Paul Nordoff. Within a few years the names of Gershwin and Copland would be ones to reckon with and a truly authentic American music would emerge in the decade of the 1920s.

Use of Indian Music and American Folk Songs

Meanwhile there were men who were exploring the vast body of American folk music, which was just beginning to be recognized. We have already spoken of the importance of Arthur Farwell and Henry F. B. Gilbert, but there are others who should be mentioned in the chronicling of America's steadily growing body of native composers. Today many of their pieces merely reflect the period in which they were composed, and strike us as sugar-coated and superficial, conventional and out of date when judged by present-day standards. But they served their purpose in those years and had their share in the ultimate liberation of American music.

Three composers might be cited, in the first two decades of the twentieth century, for their use of American Indian materials—Charles Wakefield Cadman (1881-1946), Arthur Nevin (1871-1943), and Charles Sanford Skilton (1868-1941). Time has faded this "Indianist movement," as Gilbert Chase calls it, but it once had a great attraction for many composers who felt that they had discovered something that was genuinely American.

Charles Wakefield Cadman

Cadman, born in Johnstown, Pennsylvania, established his reputation, after years of struggle, with two songs—*At Dawning* and *From the Land of the Sky-Blue Water*. The first was composed in 1906 and sold outright for cash to a publisher. For several years copies of it lay undisturbed on the publisher's shelves until it was discovered by the tenor John McCormack who started it on its way to a sale of over a million copies by singing it in his recitals. (Later the publishers voluntarily gave Cadman a royalty contract for the song.) *From the Land of the Sky-Blue Water,* published in 1908, also achieved wide popularity largely through a phonograph record sung by Alma Gluck. This was based on an actual Indian melody and legend.

The success of these songs helped Cadman to devote himself to composition and to continue his interest in Indian music, particularly in his opera, *Shanewis* (produced by the Metropolitan in 1918 in New York), and *The Sunset Trail* (an operatic cantata), presented in Denver in 1925 and a year later in Rochester by a troupe that became known as the American Opera Company. A number of

Indian melodies appear in the score of *Shanewis: The Spring Song of the Robin Woman* is based on a Cheyenne melody recorded by Natalie Curtis, and the Intermezzo uses an Omaha song from Alice Fletcher's collection. There is also an Osage ceremonial song, collected by Francis La Flesche, in the pow-wow scene near the close of the opera, and two of the narratives of Shanewis (the Indian maiden) were inspired by scenes described in Frederick Burton's book, *American Primitive Music*.

Cadman's *Thunderbird Suite* for piano (which he later orchestrated) is from the music he wrote for the production of a drama by Norman Bel Geddes. In its original form the score first presented Omaha themes in unaltered form, sung with Indian vocables by the actors during the action of the play. Between the acts the melodies were heard in idealized form, harmonized and developed. Another opera, *The Witch of Salem* (1924), was produced by the Chicago Civic Opera Company in 1926 and dealt with the witch-burning days of the Massachusetts colony. There was but one Indian character in the opera. Interest for Indian material was on the wane generally, and after 1925 the majority of Cadman's works were on a variety of American subjects.

Arthur Nevin

Arthur Nevin (the younger brother of Ethelbert Nevin, 1862-1901, who composed *The Rosary*) based his principal works on his experiences with the Blackfeet Indians. Spending the summers of 1903 and 1904 on the Blackfeet Reservation in Montana, he heard the story of *Poia*, and used it as the basis for his opera of the same name, for which Randolph Hartley wrote the libretto. Despite the fact that President Theodore Roosevelt had the composer give an illustrated talk on his work at the White House in 1907, the opera was not performed in an American opera house, but in Germany, at the Royal Opera in Berlin in 1909.

Charles S. Skilton

Charles Sanford Skilton, a graduate of Yale University and a pupil of Otis B. Boise in Berlin and Dudley Buck in New York, is remembered largely for his *Two Indian Dances (Deer Dance* and *War Dance)*, originally written for string quartet, and later expanded to orchestral form to make up the first part of his *Suite*

Primeval (1920). He published the second part four years later, four movements, all based on primitive songs: *Sunrise Song* (Winnebago), *Gambling Song* (Rogue River), *Flute Serenade* (Sioux), and *Moccasin Game* (Winnebago). Becoming head of the music department at the University of Kansas in 1903, Skilton spent much time at a nearby Indian School, Haskell Institute, learning many tribal melodies from the pupils. He also composed Indian operas, the three-act *Kalopin* (1927), and the one-act *The Sun Bride* (1930), the latter given a radio production by NBC in 1930.

Percy Grainger

One of the strongest champions of neglected American folk song has been the Australian-born Percy Grainger (1882-) who has long since become an American citizen. Trained in Europe, Grainger came to America in 1915 as a concert pianist with an established reputation, and it was through his attractive settings of English and American folk songs that audiences as well as composers gradually became aware of what riches lay within the boundaries of their own country. Grainger's work recalls Dvořák's pioneering of the previous generation, and he remains a significant figure for his share in liberating the music of the people.

John Powell

Perhaps the most important of these composers who believed in the fundamental importance to the cultural life of the nation of American folk music, especially that derived from Anglo-Saxon sources, was John Powell (1882-) of Richmond, Virginia. He had first been interested in Afro-American material, and had established his reputation as a composer (and pianist) with his *Rhapsodie Nègre*, for piano and orchestra, composed in 1919. It was widely played both in Europe and America, and it was chosen by Walter Damrosch as the representative American work to be featured by him as conductor of the New York Symphony Society on its European tour, with Powell as the soloist. Powell was careful to point out that in his *Rhapsodie* he was seeking to interpret the Negro as a race; he was not voicing America. The work begins and ends on a primal note—pagan, orgiastic. The idealization that creeps in during the middle section cannot maintain itself against the primitive instinct.

As Powell's Virginia antecedents and environment had given him a sense of profound nearness to the forerunners and founders of the nation, it was quite natural that his interests shifted from Afro-American material to the Anglo-American tunes and ballads as found in the Appalachian Mountains. In using these tunes in his own compositions Powell has preserved the modal nature of the material and has developed his idiom from the innate character of the melodies themselves, avoiding incongruous progressions and extraneous chromaticisms. As founder of the Virginia State Choral Festival, Powell has been a moving spirit in the annual White Top Mountain Folk Music Festival. Monday, November 5, 1951, was celebrated by the Commonwealth of Virginia as John Powell Day, culminating in the evening with a performance in Richmond by the National Symphony Orchestra of Powell's Overture *In Old Virginia* (1921) and his Symphony in A (1937). The latter work had been commissioned in 1932 by the National Federation of Music Clubs, but did not have its first performance until 1947, by the Detroit Symphony Orchestra. In many respects this Symphony was the culmination of the composer's life work, for it included in its thematic structure many of the Anglo-American folk tunes in which Powell had been absorbed and into which he had conducted extensive research.

Others of Powell's works in which he utilizes Anglo-American folk material include: *Natchez on the Hill* (1931) and *A Set of Three* (1935), both for orchestra and using Virginia country dances and folk tunes, respectively. Choral works include *The Babe of Bethlehem*, a folk carol (1934), and *Soldier, Soldier,* folk song (1936).

Two Nationalists: John Alden Carpenter and Ernest Bloch

On the concert programs of the day there appeared the names of two composers who, although they came from completely different musical backgrounds, nevertheless became nationalists in the finest sense of the word—John Alden Carpenter (1876-1951) and Ernest Bloch (1880-). The former, a gifted amateur, recalled the pre-Revolutionary War days when such amateurs as Francis Hopkinson were to be found in the leading musical centers. The latter, Bloch, was typical of the many European composers who had come to America through the years and who not only remained as a permanent resident, but who also promptly absorbed the finest aspects of the American spirit into their music, despite their European style and background.

When Carpenter completed his Suite *Adventures in a Perambulator* in 1914, he neither had to fight to get a hearing nor be ashamed of his fervid Americanism. His Suite was performed on March 19, 1915, by the Chicago Symphony, and was soon played all over America, as well as in the important cities of Europe. The American composer was slowly coming into his own. Of course, even though Carpenter was to employ many phases of the American vernacular, his style of writing was still predominantly European. He had been a student of Paine's at Harvard, but went to England to work with Edward Elgar, and while in Europe came under the influence of Debussy. But he had been quick to see the musical importance of ragtime (and later jazz) and was one of the first serious native American composers to employ their infectious rhythms in his compositions. His Concertino for piano and orchestra (1915) employs ragtime rhythms and he experimented with jazz elements in his two ballets, *Krazy Kat* (1921) and *Skyscrapers* (1926), all a number of years before the general acceptance by composers of these elements. *Skyscrapers* attracted much attention when it was first presented at the Metropolitan Opera House in New York (February 19, 1926), for it was Carpenter's most radical score to date. The ballet had been commissioned by the great Diaghilev, who desired a score which would "reflect some of the many rhythmic movements and sounds of modern American life." Today many musicians feel that Carpenter's works are superficial and merely reflect an earlier era, but in his time he was an important musical figure. Walter Damrosch once called him the most American of composers, and in drawing attention to the American composer and getting European performances and commissions, Carpenter made his own particular contribution to the development of America's musical culture.

When Ernest Bloch arrived in America in 1916, unheralded and unknown, he was already a professional musician and an expert craftsman. Bloch was to become one of the world's greatest composers, and since he won recognition here and American publishers were the first to publish his scores, he has become one of the first and best examples of America's ability to attract and hold first-class composers. In seeking to interpret our nation in his epic rhapsody

America, Bloch's figure looms high on our musical horizon as one of the first composers who might be classed as a nationalist, at a time when the nation, well on the road to musical maturity, needed just such stimulation. Born in Geneva, Switzerland, in 1880, Bloch came here as the conductor of a small orchestra playing for the dancer Maud Allan. Unfortunately the 1916 tour left him stranded in Ohio, and he returned to New York, penniless, without either backing or friends. Yet others had come to America and made good against great odds, and Bloch's quick recognition and later achievements are but another typical American success story. Fortune almost at once smiled on Bloch, for that very winter the superb Flonzaley Quartet played his Quartet in B Minor at a concert on December 29, 1916. The work made such a remarkable impression that Karl Muck, then conductor of the Boston Symphony Orchestra, invited Bloch to conduct his *Trois Poèmes Juifs (Three Hebrew Poems)* (1913), at two concerts in Boston, March 23-24, 1917. Still greater recognition came on May 3, when the Friends of Music gave a concert devoted to his works, Artur Bodanzky conducting. Musicians were struck by Bloch's individuality and the mastery of his medium, for his was a passionate temperament, and he seemed perfectly to combine the music of the East with the traditions of Western European music. A violin pupil of Ysaÿe in Brussels, Bloch had also studied at the Hoch Conservatory (Hoch'sche Conservatorium) in Frankfort. His ability was at once recognized, and he was asked to join the faculty of the David Mannes School in 1917, and in 1920 he became director of the Cleveland Institute of Music.

Chamber music in the United States had been greatly stimulated when Mrs. Elizabeth Sprague Coolidge, a patron of the arts, had opened her estate in the Berkshires, near Pittsfield, Massachusetts, for the performance of concerts of classical and modern works by American and European composers. This Festival, which was given irregularly after 1924, was almost at once the scene of many first performances, and American composers were soon commissioned to write for the concerts, as well as the later ones sponsored by Mrs. Coolidge in the Library of Congress in Washington.

It was not surprising that in 1919 Bloch's Suite for viola and piano won the Coolidge Prize. Before long students sought him as a teacher, first in Cleveland, and later when he went to head the San

Francisco Conservatory (1926) and held summer classes in composition at the University of California.

In his earlier years Bloch was something of a Hebrew prophet in his music, one of the sons of ancient Judea, moved, in his own words, "by the vigor and ingenuousness of the Patriarchs, the violence that finds expression in the books of the prophets, the burning love of justice, the desperation of the preachers of Jerusalem, the sorrow and grandeur of the Book of Job, the sensuality of the Song of Songs." The works that express this spirit most eloquently are the *Trois Poèmes Juifs* (1913), three *Psalms* for voice and orchestra (1914), *Schelomo,* a rhapsody for cello and orchestra (1915), and the Symphony *Israel* (1916).

In 1926, Bloch paid tribute to his adopted country by writing a symphonic work entitled *America.* It won a $3000 prize offered by the magazine *Musical America,* was performed by the New York Philharmonic in 1928, and soon after by major orchestras throughout the nation. The work had a mixed reception and has not had many performances since, but it was noble in spirit, of excellent craftsmanship, and deserves more than passing mention.

America, "an Epic Rhapsody in Three Parts," as Bloch explained, is built upon the concluding anthem (sung by a chorus and the audience), which appears "from the first bars . . . dimly, slowly taking shape, rising, falling, developing, and finally asserting itself victoriously in its complete and decisive form" in the last bars of the final movement. Throughout the score Bloch inserted various references (at the bottom of the pages) which he thought might clarify his intentions. Part I, *1620—The Soil—The Indians—(England)—The Mayflower—The Landing of the Pilgrims.* Indian themes, the trumpet "Call of America," *Old Hundred,* a sea chanty, all combine to tell of the country before and after the Pilgrims landed in Plymouth. Part II, *1861-1865—Hours of Joy—Hours of Sorrow.* The drama of the North and South: happiness, war, distress and agony. Negro songs; a bit from Stephen Foster; *Pop Goes the Weasel;* then war songs—*John Brown's Body; The Battle Cry of Freedom; Tramp, Tramp, Tramp.* Part III, *1926—The Present—The Future.* Speed, noise, jazz, the pomp of material prosperity. The Finale builds to a mighty climax, "The Fulfillment Through Love," as the audience rises to sing the anthem that "symbolizes the Destiny, the Mission of America."

Bloch's most widely played works, many of which are now recorded, are his *Concerto Grosso* for strings (1925); a Violin Concerto, introduced by Joseph Szigeti in 1938; a Suite for violin and piano, *Baal Shem* (1923), which was subsequently scored for violin and orchestra and first played by Szigeti in 1941; a Sacred Service (1934); and a work for cello and orchestra, *Voice in the Wilderness* (1936). There is also considerable chamber music and an opera *Macbeth*, produced in 1910 at the Paris Opera.

Charles Tomlinson Griffes, Eclectic

The many promising composers who appeared in the 1920s had a freedom in their writing that was due in no small part to the upheaval of the years during and after the World War. Many like Henry Cowell and Aaron Copland have become eclectics, drawing freely from all sources, yet the earlier Charles Tomlinson Griffes, dying in 1920 at the age of thirty-five and leaving a comparatively small number of works, has in the course of the years gained for himself a permanent place in American music. Griffes drew freely from the German romanticists, as well as the newer impressionism in France and the revolutionary tendencies of the Russians. His music toward the end of his short life was tinged by the newer freedom that was already being felt in American music. Griffes had a distinctive imagination, a rich sense of color, and his death cut short one of the most promising careers among the younger native composers.

Griffes was born in Elmira, New York (September 17, 1884), and showed early a decided talent for the arts and crafts, as well as music. But music was his choice, and he went to Berlin (as was the custom of that day) to study piano. While a student there, he was enrolled in composition with Humperdinck, and it was then that he decided to become a composer. His first musical influence was naturally romantic, but he was soon exposed to French impressionism and showed a fondness for Russian Orientalism that was to appear as the mysticism of his later works. He returned to America in 1907, taking a position at the Hackley School for boys in Tarrytown, New York, which he held until his death, April 8, 1920.

One of the first important performances came in February, 1917, when his dance-drama *The Kairn of Koridwen* was presented in New York. His largest (and most important) orchestral work, *The*

Pleasure Dome of Kubla Khan (after Coleridge, was given its première on November 28, 1919, by the Boston Symphony Orchestra, only a few weeks before the composer's death. He had started composition on this piece in 1912, and he gave his imagination free rein in his description of the palace and the revelry that might take place there. The result is colorful music, as is that of Griffes' Poem for flute and orchestra (1918), originally written for flute and piano. This is the most mature of his works; it starts in a gray mood and merges into a dance movement of strange tonality, with a suggestion of Oriental rhythm and color. Its first performance was masterfully played by the flutist Georges Barrère. Griffes played his piano pieces, *Four Roman Sketches,* for the MacDowell Club in New York in 1918. The most famous of these is the exquisite *The White Peacock,* which he also orchestrated. Based on the poems of William Sharp, others of the pieces in the Suite are *Nightfall, The Fountain of Acqua Paola,* and *Clouds.*

Griffes' growth had been amazing, and his last works had a definite modern trend, as he groped for something less rigid than the tempered scale and tried to create a medium which would sound the overtones he wanted to hear. His Piano Sonata (1918, revised 1919) belongs to this period and shows the intellectual consistency of a Schoenberg, a pursuit of tonal logic without the sacrifice of poetic conception. The themes are well defined, but it is their development that is interesting rather than the themes themselves.

The Philadelphia Orchestra gave a performance in its 1918-19 season of *Three Songs of Fiona MacLeod,* with Marcia van Dresser as the soloist, and in the same year, the Flonzaley quartet played his *Two Sketches Based on Indian Themes* (published posthumously as *Two Indian Sketches*). Already the American composer—once he proved his ability—was winning performances of his most important works. Although Griffes' output was comparatively small, he lived to see practically all of his major works performed, and those by the finest groups and orchestras that the nation could boast. In this respect Griffes becomes all the more important, for he proved through his sensitive music that at last the American composer might compete with his European colleagues. While he lived he was considerably in advance of his time, but now his works seem to have a permanent place in the repertoire.

CHAPTER XI

The Twenties

The decade of the 1920s, nowadays almost affectionately called the Roaring Twenties, was to be a period of conflict in all of the arts, which in itself would be a clue to the era's great vitality. The music seemed more noisy than ever, frequently primitive, and designed to shock the conservatives. From the many manifestoes, the isms, the revolts, there emerged what gradually came to be known as the "modern." Dadaism formally died about 1922 in Paris, but soon the French capital would be the center of the surrealist movement.

Jazz

With the coming of Prohibition came the era of the speakeasy, the flapper, and the growth of jazz. These were restless years and the younger generation seemed constantly to be searching for the unattainable. New dance steps and rhythms appeared, as the popularity of jazz brought with it a realization of the potency of rhythm. Sentiment all but vanished. The earlier breakdown, a noisy type of Negro dance, soon had a variant in the one-step that Irene and Vernon Castle made popular from 1913 on (the Castle Walk). The fox trot of Negro ancestry was a marchlike ragtime, and by 1920 the shimmy became immensely popular and was as peculiarly American as Zez Confey's piano piece *Kitten on the Keys*. The Black Bottom was another lively dance, and by 1925, still another variety of the fox trot (and once popular among the Negroes)—the Charleston— became the rage of the younger set.

In certain small American communities, however, jazz was already in disgrace and was considered wicked by minority groups. In

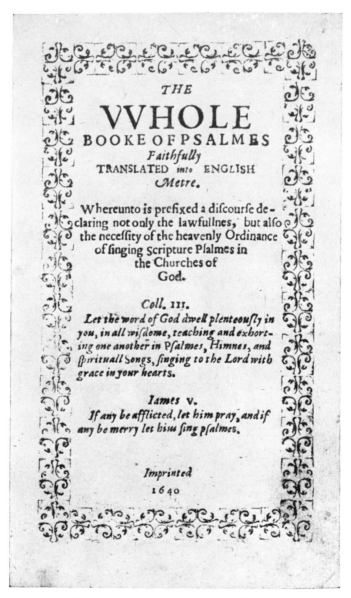

THE
VVHOLE
BOOKE OF PSALMES
Faithfully
TRANSLATED *into* ENGLISH
Metre.

Whereunto is prefixed a discourse de-
claring not only the lawfullnes, but also
the necessity of the heavenly Ordinance
of singing Scripture Psalmes in
the Churches of
God.

Coll. III.
*Let the word of God dwell plenteously in
you, in all wisdome, teaching and exhort-
ing one another in Psalmes, Himnes, and
spirituall Songs, singing to the Lord with
grace in your hearts.*

Iames V.
*If any be afflicted, let him pray, and if
any be merry let him sing psalmes.*

Imprinted
1640

Title page of *The Bay Psalm Book,* the first full-length book published in the Colonies. *New York Public Library*

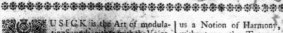

First page of Thomas Walter's *The Grounds and Rules of Musick Explained; Or An Introduction to the Art of Singing by Note* (1721). *New York Public Library*

Page twelve of William Billings' *The Singing Master's Assistant* (1778), his second book. *New York Public Library*

"Old Hundredth" as it appeared in Thomas Walter's book. *New York Public Library*

Oliver Holden's *Coronation* printed in shape notes in Smith and Little's *The Easy Instructor* (1802)

Manuel Garcia   Maria Malibran

Father and daughter who gave New York its first season of grand
opera (1825). *New York Public Library*

Broadway, New York, about 1830. Many concerts were held at the
City Hotel. J. L. Hewitt's music store is at the right. *Knickerbocker
Photo Service*

Stephen Foster's purse. *Foster Hall Collection*

A typical mid-century minstrel performer. *Foster Hall Collection*

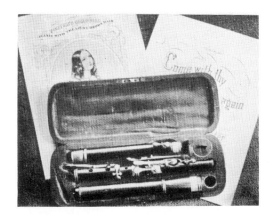

Stephen Foster's flute. *Foster Hall Collection*

EDISON'S
PARLOR SPEAKING
PHONOGRAPH.

THE MIRACLE OF THE 19th CENTURY.

It Talks. It Whispers. It Sings. It Laughs. It Cries.
It Coughs. It Whistles. It Records and
Reproduces at Pleasure all
Musical Sounds.

The first recorded attempt to make a Talking Machine was 2600 years ago though diligent efforts have been making ever since, it remained for Prof **THOMAS ALVA EDISON**, of Menlo Park, New Jersey, to finally solve the problem, and place within the reach of every one a machine that not only talks, but will record sounds of all kinds, and **REPRODUCE THEM INSTANTLY**, with **FIDELITY** and **DISTINCTNESS**

The adaptation of this wonderful invention to the practical uses of commerce not having, as yet, been completed, in all its mechanical details, this company is now prepared to offer to the public only that design or form of apparatus which has been found best adapted to its exhibition as a novelty

THE "**PARLOR SPEAKING PHONOGRAPH**" is intended for use in the parlor or drawing room, and will hold 150 to 200 words. The cylinder is so arranged that the foil can be taken off and replaced at any future time, thereby reproducing the same sounds that have been imprinted upon it. It speaks loud enough to be heard in any ordinary room. We have a limited number now ready which we will sell for $10 cash, packed for shipment, with all needed appliances ready for use.

E. H. JOHNSON, Sec'y,

Edison Speaking Phonograph Co.

P. O. Box 2702, NEW YORK CITY.

An early phonograph advertisement. *New York Public Library*

George Gershwin. *Vandamm*　　　Aaron Copland. *ASCAP*

Scene from the original production of *Porgy and Bess. Vandamm*

Charles Ives. *Wide World Photos*   Howard Hanson.   *Bryan Morgan, Rochester, N.Y.*

Leonard   Bernstein.   *Whitestone Photo, courtesy ASCAP*   Norman Dello Joio.   *ASCAP*

January, 1921, the city authorities of Zion City, Illinois, banned any further jazz, condemning it along with such sinful practices as smoking. But jazz persisted as such composers as Carpenter, and later George Antheil and Aaron Copland, began to tap its resources.

Radio

The great news of 1920 was the amazing new invention—radio. On July 20 music was broadcast from a ship, the SS *Victorian*, on her way to Canada. One month later, August 20, America had its first radio broadcast from a studio, when Detroit's WWJ opened. Eleven weeks later Pittsburgh's KDKA station had the honor of being the second American station to broadcast. Radio was to become one of music's most potent forces, and excitement over the new discovery ran high. Almost at once the majority of musicians, sure that their days were numbered, set up a hue and cry over this new "canned music" which came over the air waves. Gloom was felt on all sides, yet could these performing artists have seen into the future and realized what was yet to come their lamentations would have turned to joy.

Noisemakers in Europe

Quite another type of concert was given in Paris in June, 1921, when the Italian futurist Luigi Russolo conducted an orchestral concert entirely given over to noise instruments. He sought to reproduce the spirit of the machine age, and he used every type of noisemaker he could get. Nicolas Slonimsky lists some of them: Thunderclappers, Exploders, Crashers, Splashers, Bellowers, Whistlers, Hissers, Snorters, Whisperers, Mutterers, Gurglers, Screamers, Screechers, Buzzers, Cracklers, Shouters, Groaners, Howlers, Wheezers, and the like. This was extreme, to say the least, but it did show how rapidly the interest in the use of percussion and noise instruments alone was growing. In many cases it stemmed from the rhythmic sound effects of the jazz bands.

NEW MUSIC SCHOOLS

Eastman School of Music

The Eastman School of Music opened in 1921, with an additional gift of a million dollars from Mr. Eastman so that the school might be completely endowed and not have to be run for profit. The Sibley Music Library, started in 1902 as a public circulation collection, was attached to the school in 1922. In 1924, Howard Hanson was offered the directorship of the school. He has held the post ever since. The school has become justly famous for its outstanding composition students, as well as for its sponsorship of an annual series of orchestral concerts which feature the works of American composers. A fund was also made available for the publication of such works as were qualified, making it considerably easier for the most promising compositions to be circulated and performed.

The First Graduate Schools in Music: Juilliard and Curtis

When on February 22, 1923, Frederick A. Juilliard bequeathed ten million dollars to the Juilliard Musical Foundation (which had been incorporated in 1920 with the twenty-million bequest of Augustus D. Juilliard, with Eugene A. Noble as secretary-manager), the second great music school of the twentieth century had its birth. Its trustees sought at once to gather together a faculty of the best musicians with the finest reputations, who could give young American students the advantage of their wide and valuable experience on the operatic and concert stage. There was already many fine schools in America, as well as excellent teachers, but the rich and varied musical background which could only come from an international faculty, could no longer be denied the many talented young students. An institution unique in America, the Juilliard Graduate School was set up to aid the well-prepared applicant in a manner comparable to the graduate school of a university. Its first home was in a six-story house which had been built by one of the Vanderbilts, and its faculty included the pianists Ernest Hutcheson, Alexander Siloti (who had been a pupil of Liszt), Josef and Rosina Lhévinne, Olga Samaroff Stokowski, Carl Friedberg, and James Friskin. Violinists no longer needed to go to Europe in order to study with Leopold Auer, for he became a member of the faculty. Singers had the advantage of studying with the great Marcella Sembrich, cellists with Felix Salmond, and composers with Rubin Goldmark.

Juilliard had specified that the fellowship holders must be Americans, but a year later, when Mary Louise Curtis Bok (the daughter of the famous publisher, Cyrus H. K. Curtis, and the wife of Edward Bok) created the Curtis Institute in Philadelphia (1924), its students were chosen from all over the world. The first director of the Curtis Institute was John Grolle, who was succeeded in 1925 by William E. Walter, and in 1927, Mrs. Bok appointed Josef Hofmann, who had been the head of the piano department. By 1928 tuition fees were abolished, and entrance could be had only on a scholarship basis. The faculty, like that of the Juilliard, contained some of the finest artists of the day. Violinists included Efrem Zimbalist, Carl Flesch, Leopold Auer. Marcella Sembrich, Elizabeth Schumann, and Emilio de Gogorza made up the voice department. Moriz Rosenthal and Isabelle Vengerova taught piano; Carlos Salzedo, harp; Fritz Reiner, conducting; Rosario Scalero, composition; and musical criticism was under the supervision of Samuel Chotzinoff.

Both the Juilliard and Curtis schools gave the young American student the rare opportunity to develop musically under an artist-faculty steeped in the finest European traditions. For the first time America had schools of music which could rank with the great universities. The musicians who made up the faculties soon did what earlier musicians from Europe had done—they took root and became a powerful influence in molding the artistic standards of America. As they took part in the life of a fast-maturing nation, this was but another forward step toward the musical independence of the United States. The aspiring student no longer had to go to Europe to study, but could work in the surroundings that were a part of his heritage.

When John Erskine became president of the Juilliard Foundation, plans were made for a new building, and in 1926, taking over the Institute of Musical Art, the Graduate School was housed in a new building adjoining the Institute, overlooking the Hudson River. A theater, fully equipped for operatic performances, was a welcome addition, and many unusual operatic performances produced by the school have since become a welcome feature of New York's musical life.

CONTINUED INTEREST IN OPERA

There had been no lessening of interest in opera in America after the war, and New York and Chicago were still the two great opera centers of the nation, alternating in giving seasons in each other's home town. In 1920, the Chicago Grand Opera Company had an interesting visitor at a New York performance of Debussy's *Pelléas et Mélisande,* at the Lexington Theatre, with Mary Garden singing Mélisande. In the audience was Maurice Maeterlinck, author of the drama, who was hearing it for the first time, nearly eighteen years after its première in Paris. He had publicly denounced Debussy's music and had consistently refused to attend the opera. His reason was the fact that Debussy had insisted on having Mary Garden as Mélisande, instead of Maeterlinck's preference, his common-law wife, Georgette Leblanc.

Opera in Chicago

At its home in Chicago the opera company continued to give the finest productions of opera, sparing no expense, for it was richly subsidized by Harold McCormick and his wife, Edith Rockefeller McCormick. Serge Prokofiev was brought over from Russia in 1921 to conduct the world première of his witty and brilliantly written opera, *The Love for Three Oranges,* on December 20. Based on Carlo Gozzi's fantastic tale, the opera was heard no more until New York's City Center revived it in the 1950s. It was this type of novelty, plus the standard repertory sung by artists of the first magnitude, that gave Chicago its golden years, which, unfortunately, ended during the depression. When Mary Garden became artistic director of the Opera in the 1921-22 season, she created a scandal both with her realistic performance of *Salome* and the deficit of over a million dollars for the twelve-week season. McCormick withdrew his financial support, and a new company was formed under the guidance of Samuel Insull, who was able to obtain a guaranty fund of half a million dollars from a group of businessmen. Giorgio Polacco became the director of the Chicago Civic Opera, and for the next ten years the performances were among the greatest in the history of American opera. Besides Miss Garden, the galaxy of superb singers included Edith Mason, Rosa Raisa, Claudia Muzio, Tito Schipa, Charles Hackett, Vanni Marcoux, Lotte Lehmann, Frida Leider, and Alexander Kipnis. The great Amelita Galli-Curci, Toti dal Monte, and Feodor Chaliapin were shared with New York's Metropolitan Opera.

Chicago also had an excellent summer opera, which lasted for about twenty years, having been started in 1911 under the sponsorship of Louis Eckstein. The ten-week season (whose deficit Eckstein made up many times) was given in lovely Ravinia Park on the north shore, with the Chicago Symphony in the pit and many leading singers, including those of the Metropolitan Opera, appearing in the rustic pavilion, which was unbelievably kind to their voices. Memorable performances were given, such as *L'Amore dei Tre Re*, with Lucrezia Bori and Edward Johnson; *Manon*, with Bori and Schipa; and by Elizabeth Rethberg, then at the height of her career.

Metropolitan in New York

New York's Metropolitan Opera Company matched the Chicago performances in these years with its illustrious roster of singers. Toscanini had become unusually popular, but had resigned his conductorship in 1915. During the war, the German singers had their troubles and for a time all German opera was dropped from the repertory. Around 1920 it began to be heard again.

One of the greatest voices ever to be heard at the Metropolitan was that of Rosa Ponselle, who made her debut with Caruso on November 15, 1918, as Leonora in Verdi's *La Forza del Destino*. She became a sensation almost overnight, and in the course of years many operas were revived for her. In her first season she sang the role of Rezia, in the Metropolitan's first production of Weber's *Oberon*, and also created the soprano lead in Joseph Carl Breil's *The Legend*, an American opera. With Caruso, she sang *La Juive* the next season, scoring a triumph, and their performance of December 24, 1920, was Caruso's last public appearance. His illness and forced retirement was a severe blow to the Metropolitan, and his death at the early age of forty-eight, in August 1921, was a tragedy that saddened the world. After his departure from the Metropolitan his roles were sung by Giovanni Martinelli and Beniamino Gigli. Chaliapin returned to score a personal triumph which had not been his some years before, and Clarence Whitehill and Friedrich Schorr greatly strengthened the German wing with their sensitive and musical singing of the important Wagnerian roles. Giuseppe de Luca was one of the most popular baritones in these years, and John Charles Thomas won critical acclaim although his repertoire was limited. A young singer of secondary roles, Lawrence Tibbett, skyrocketed to stardom overnight, when he made a sensational success as Ford, in a revival of *Falstaff*, provoking one of the greatest demonstrations in the history of the opera house. Ponselle again achieved a personal triumph in Spontini's *La Vestale,* which was first sung at the Metropolitan on November 12, 1925. But it was Ponselle's interpretation of the tragic title role in *Norma* in 1927 that will cause her name to last in operatic history. She has become a legend, for her voice was indisputably one of the greatest America has produced, with its rich low notes, and her brilliant dramatic high voice. Her trills were superb and her florid passages matchless. Her eventual retirement to private life in Maryland seemed to close yet another era with an abrupt finality.

San Francisco Opera Company

On the West Coast, San Francisco created an operatic institution which has come to be one of the most important in America. In 1906 an enterprising young man had been fascinated with his first acquaintance with that lovely city. He was Gaetano Merola, who had first arrived as a pianist for Lillian Nordica and a concert troupe. As he returned to the coast city from time to time he listened as his friends spoke longingly of the glories of past opera performances, and as the years passed, with both the New York and Chicago companies bringing their finest productions, Merola still knew that this was not enough—San Francisco must have its own opera company. In 1922 he organized three outdoor productions of *Carmen, Faust,* and *Pagliacci,* using guest stars, and giving the performances under a full moon in the football bowl of Stanford University. The venture lost money, but Merola soon got enough patrons to organize a permanent company—the San Francisco Opera Company. Its first season was in the autumn of 1923, in an improvised theater in the Civic Auditorium. With guest stars taking the leading roles, local singers were trained for the secondary parts and a chorus was rehearsed. The orchestra was made up of players from the San Francisco Symphony, and the repertoire included *La Bohème, Andrea Chénier, Mefistofele, Tosca,* and *Romeo and Juliet.* The singers were of the best: Claudia Muzio, Queena Mario, Beniamino Gigli, Giuseppe de Luca, and Adamo Didur, and the season was a triumph. To the present day, the San Francisco Opera Company has become a symbol of the city's cultural leadership of the Pacific Coast, as it tours each season to all the principal cities.

Summer Opera in Cincinnati

In the East, Cincinnati, with its long history of the finest in music, began summer operas at the Cincinnati Zoo. Mrs. Charles P. Taft and Mrs. Mary Emery, both patrons of the arts, were the leading spirits in the founding and supporting of this project for many years. For years the Cincinnati Orchestra had been losing its best players to better-paying positions. It was obvious that some plan must be devised to keep these players in Cincinnati, and after much discussion, in 1920 an open-air theater was built in the Zoological Gardens, where bands had been hired to give daily concerts to entertain the visitors. Ralph Lyford, at that time an outstanding member of the Conservatory faculty and head of its opera department, hearing of Mrs. Taft's interest in summer opera, told her of his dream to give Cincinnati its own opera group.

Thus, in 1921, Cincinnati had its first grand opera season, opening with a performance of *Martha*. Each year the season, in June and July, has become increasingly important, for it is a serious professional training ground, comparable to the smaller European opera houses where young and promising singers may gain the experience that is so important to a professional career, and where more experienced artists may try out roles for the coming winter. Many of America's top-ranking singers have been glad of the opportunity to sing new roles at a time of year when they are free from their tension of the winter season. It was at the Zoo that Grace Moore sang her first *Tosca*, and three *Carmens*—those of Gladys Swarthout, Risë Stevens, and Blanche Thebom—were also given their initial tryouts there. James Melton was but one of many other singers, now well known, who made their first operatic appearance on Cincinnati's stage. From its establishment, the Cincinnati Opera Company has not missed a season of opera, except in 1926, when Ralph Lyford died.

ORCHESTRAL MERGERS IN NEW YORK

The decade of the twenties saw a series of orchestral mergers in New York. We have already learned, in chapter 10, of the absorption by the New York Philharmonic of the short-lived New Symphony Orchestra founded by Varèse. Another orchestra had been started about this time in New York—the National Symphony—and

Willem Mengelberg was brought from Holland to conduct it. But New York could not seem to support three orchestras, and the National Symphony also was short-lived. It was merged with the Philharmonic in 1921 and Mengelberg became one of the Philharmonic's conductors. Another attempt to have a third orchestra came soon after, when a City Symphony was organized with the Dutch conductor Dirck Fock at its head. This too succumbed and again the Philharmonic took over.

The most important merger came in 1928. The previous mergers had been with newly-organized orchestras that could not compete with the well-established Philharmonic and New York Symphony. This time, however, it was the New York Symphony itself which could continue no longer, and by merging with the Philharmonic to form the Philharmonic-Symphony Society left New York with but one orchestra. Some of the New York Symphony players joined the Philharmonic, while others followed their beloved Walter Damrosch to the National Broadcasting Company, where they played in the "house orchestra" and continued to follow their former conductor's baton in his Music Appreciation broadcasts for school children, as well as other broadcasts. A number of the players eventually became part of the NBC Symphony that was formed for Arturo Toscanini in 1937, which played for seventeen years until it was officially disbanded by NBC when Toscanini retired in 1954 and then became the Symphony of the Air.

GREAT ORCHESTRAL MUSIC

Koussevitzky, Stokowski, Toscanini

When Serge Koussevitzky arrived in Boston in October, 1924, as the new conductor of the Boston Symphony, he and Arturo Toscanini and Leopold Stokowski were to make musical history in America. Never had there been such a brilliance of performance, such magnificent sounds, as each was to evoke from his ensemble. Frederick Stock had been conducting superbly in Chicago, but at his finest he was still the personification of the German tradition as it was known throughout Europe and which Theodore Thomas had brought with him to America. The same was true of the Damrosches, Gustav Mahler, Anton Seidl, and Felix Weingartner in New York; while Boston had been dominated by Henschel, Paur, and

Muck. Only the brilliant and dynamic Russian, Arthur Nikisch, had broken this heavy tradition. Stokowski was the first conductor to make America orchestra conscious, and his perfection of such a matchless instrument as the Philadelphia Orchestra, and his programs of the most dissonant contemporary music in the 1920s gave Philadelphia a leadership it had not had before. While Stokowski often brought down the wrath of his board as well as his audiences upon his head, the opposition in no way dimmed his pioneering instincts. The finest as well as the newest music was heard in America, sometimes when the ink was scarcely dry on the manuscript paper.

Toscanini was the acme of musical integrity, respecting the composer's wishes above all else, and in his tenure of almost a decade with New York's Philharmonic-Symphony he made that period the most spectacular in its history. His interpretations of the classic repertory were models of artistic perfection, and when he resigned in 1936, the orchestra lost its greatest inspiration.

Koussevitzky had early shown his diligence when he learned to play the double bass as a virtuoso. His orchestral concerts in Europe had shown him to be a fine conductor, and within three years of taking over the Boston Symphony Orchestra, he taught it to play with a cleanness and precision that was only matched by Stokowski's Philadelphia Orchestra. As time went on, Koussevitzky began to seek out young American composers, playing their works and commissioning new ones. Stock had done this in Chicago, but in those days the American composers were not of the caliber that they were ten and twenty years later. Koussevitzky's encouragement of native composers did more to improve and develop our native talents than that of any other one person. These men—Stokowski, Toscanini and Koussevitzky—were giants whose influence can never be forgotten. For the first time in its history America had orchestras that matched (and often excelled) the finest in the world.

ELECTRICAL RECORDING

As radio developed rapidly, the momentary eclipse of the record industry ended, and with the discovery of the value of the radio microphone for recording purposes, electrical recording became a reality. With such fine symphony orchestras and brilliant operatic performances as America was beginning to hear, it would not be too long before albums of complete symphonies and operas would be issued, bringing great music within the reach of every man.

England had for many years been the world's leader of orchestral recordings, for as early as 1909, Hermann Finck had conducted the London Palace Orchestra in the first major orchestral recording— Tchaikovsky's *Nutcracker Suite*. Within the year the same group recorded Mendelssohn's incidental music to *A Midsummer Night's Dream*. These were issued by the English branch of Germany's Odeon Company, and it was natural that the Gramophone Company would not be outdone. In January, 1910, Landon Ronald and the New Symphony Orchestra (founded in 1907 by young Thomas Beecham) recorded a condensed version of the first movement of Grieg's Piano Concerto with Wilhelm Backhaus as the soloist. By 1913 Germany challenged England by obtaining the services of the Odeon Streich-Orchester (conductor unknown) and put out Beethoven's Fifth and Sixth symphonies, uncut, the first complete symphonies ever made. To offset this recording the Gramophone Company signed Arthur Nikisch and the Berlin Philharmonic Orchestra in February, 1914, to perform Beethoven's Fifth in its entirety.

In the United States both Victor and Columbia were much more concerned with the latest rage—the dance—and soon the country was flooded with tangos and hesitation waltzes, one-steps and turkey trots, many of which Vernon and Irene Castle had helped to make popular. As for the serious repertory, there was still the constant battle between the artists and the recording companies as to what they should play or sing. The serious musicians naturally wanted only the best music, with no lowering of standards, while the record companies insisted on cut versions of pieces that they thought would appeal to a wide and rather uncultivated commercial audience. Columbia, by 1917, issued condensed versions of single movement of symphonies played by the New York Philharmonic under Joseph Stransky and by the New York Symphony with Walter Damrosch, while Victor had a contract with Stokowski and the Philadelphia Orchestra for abridgments that would fit one side of a twelve-inch record, and also made a few recordings of the matchless Boston Symphony under Karl Muck.

In the course of the next years, in fact until electrical recording became an actuality, little serious art music was recorded. But that same period was a boon to the newest musical element—jazz—and countless bands carried the infectious rhythms around the world through their recordings. No other medium could have taken American jazz to so many people so fast. It was one of the principal recorders of popular music, Paul Whiteman, who was to introduce a new idea to the world, as well as a talented musician, George Gershwin. Whiteman was a Victor feature, as was Fred Waring, while Columbia had such big names as Ted Lewis and Fletcher Henderson. The impact of the appearance of American jazz, especially in the music of Gershwin, was staggering. Its rhythms, so well suited to the spirit of those mad, restless days and the glitter of the nights spent in some plush speakeasy, circled the globe. From this new element was to come a resurgence of rhythmic vitality which the Western composers of the last generations had all but forgotten in their concentration on harmony, counterpoint, and pieces of mammoth proportions. It was the millions of records that captured the spirit of jazz and made it the voice of America. Perhaps it was brash and a little impudent, but it spoke a language that all could understand.

By 1924, it was the Bell Telephone Laboratories (the research department of the American Telephone and Telegraph Company) and not the record companies, that perfected the process of electrical recording. The complacence of the record companies all but lost them the one development that was to revolutionize and reanimate their industries, and it was not until late in the spring of 1925 that both Victor and Columbia issued their first commercial electrical recordings. Again, however, they were still single records, the first Red Seals of Victor being Alfred Cortot playing the piano and Stokowski conducting the Philadelphia Orchestra in Saint-Saëns' *Danse Macabre*. It was England who was once again the pioneer in issuing the first full-length electrically recorded symphonic work —Symphony No. 4 by Tchaikovsky, with the Royal Albert Hall Orchestra under Sir Landon Ronald, an HMV label (December, 1925). In March, 1926, Arturo Toscanini made one recording with the New York Philharmonic for Brunswick (which the maestro did not like). It was Victor that issued the first electrically recorded symphony in America—Dvořák's *New World* Symphony, with Stokowski and the Philadelphia Orchestra, listed as Album M-1. This was the first in a series which was to set a standard throughout the world for sheer tonal beauty and put both orchestra and conductor in a class by themselves.

Gradually all the major orchestras of the nation began to record for Victor—Stock and the Chicago Symphony; the San Francisco with Alfred Hertz; Detroit's orchestra under Ossip Gabrilowitsch; and in 1929, Toscanini and the New York Philharmonic-Symphony and Koussevitzky and the Boston Symphony. The best conductors, especially the great three—Stokowski, Koussevitzky, and Toscanini— became the stars in the musical firmament, replacing the earlier idols of the century, the singers. It was undoubtedly a revolutionary step forward, entirely in keeping with the decade of the Roaring Twenties. It could not last, for circumstances beyond the control of mortal man would bring about another digression before the recording industry would come into its own by mid-century.

GEORGE GERSHWIN SYMBOLIZES THE GROWTH OF JAZZ

Perhaps no name the world over is more a symbol of American music than that of George Gershwin (1898-1937). There can be no doubt that he has made a greater impression on America's twentieth-century musical life than any other single composer. The concert in 1924 that introduced his *Rhapsody in Blue* to the world has become as important in its way as Stravinsky's *The Rite of Spring* had been a little over ten years before.

Early Career

Gershwin, born in Brooklyn, New York, on September 26, 1898, had little musical training. He started work when he was only sixteen, and he chose music, which already had become his very life. He was a demonstration pianist for the firm of J. H. Remick & Company in New York, and he quickly learned the idiom of Tin-Pan Alley and began to write tunes of his own. They were good tunes, and as they had an unexpected twist of rhythm, or a slightly different harmony, it was not long before some of his songs were published.

Gershwin's first real success was with the song, *I Was So Young, You Were So Beautiful,* which was interpolated in a musical comedy called *Good Morning, Judge!,* produced in 1919. But during the year that his own show was on Broadway *(La, La, Lucille)* it was the song *Swanee* that brought him real fame, for Al Jolson used it in *Sinbad*. From 1919 until 1933 Gershwin wrote one hit after another, a series of musical comedies, each filled with incomparable tunes. He came to maturity just in time to catch the real spirit of the Roaring Twenties, and his melodies and rhythms are the embodiment of the restlessness and endless searching for the unattainable, which are a part of any decade of readjustment and transition.

Whiteman and Gershwin

In the early 1920s, Paul Whiteman had recorded Gershwin tunes, and both names were as familiar to jazz devotees in London and Paris as they were in countless American cities. Whiteman had been one of the first serious musicians to become fascinated with jazz, and he gave up his position as violist with the San Francisco People's Orchestra to learn the new idiom. He formed a small band, which was interrupted in its development by World War I, when Whiteman enlisted as a bandleader. His actual career started with his postwar engagement at the Alexandria Hotel in Los Angeles, and from there he went to New York. Soon he was appearing at the Palais Royal, which was in its heyday at that time, and before long he was hailed from all sides as "The King of Jazz." His trips to Europe (by that time he was playing and recording Gershwin's music) were a sensation. Houses were sold out far in advance, and people could never seem to get enough of this music. Whiteman, as an orchestra man and a trained musician, realized from the beginning that it was most important to have proper scores for his performances, not leaving them to the excitement of the actual concert, which the older bands had done. True jazz, of course, depended on the improvisation of the moment. But Whiteman was preparing the way for the fusing of the jazz element with serious music. In February, 1924, Whiteman planned a gala concert at Aeolian Hall, New York, in which he planned to show the development of modern jazz. The affair was called an "Experiment in Modern Music," and he gathered together some of the great names of his day, including Victor Herbert and George Gershwin.

Gershwin had tasted success and made money, for by 1924 he had written the scores for four of George White's *Scandals,* as well as the musical comedies *Sweet Little Devil* and *Lady Be Good.* But his creative spirit would not rest and he was constantly thinking of writing serious music in the larger forms, music that would gain him the respect of musicians. This was understandable, for in those days Carnegie Hall and the Palais Royal were miles apart, artistically speaking. The day was yet to come when a young American composer might have a work played by the Philharmonic, while nearby a Broadway audience might be enjoying his latest musical score.

Whiteman needed a special piece with which to climax his program, and in seeking the help of Gershwin (who was only too willing to cooperate), they hit upon the idea of a concerto that would feature Gershwin's excellent piano-playing with an orchestral background. Gershwin put off writing his new piece until almost the last moment, but once started, he finished his *Rhapsody in Blue* in ten days. Whiteman turned over the score to his excellent arranger, Ferde Grofé, whom he had first met in 1919 in San Francisco, and who stayed with him for over a dozen years. Grofé was born of a musical family, and it was he who wrote Whiteman's carefully planned and thoroughly worked out symphonic arrangements, which had been of the greatest help for both performances and recordings. In orchestrating the *Rhapsody*, Grofé was to gain his own particular fame as a result.

"Rhapsody in Blue"

A most distinguished audience gathered on February 12, 1924, to see and hear this new "Experiment," as well as to be seen. The program went as scheduled. Jazz was presented in its native form, then current tunes were given jazz treatment, popular melodies were played in "semi-symphonic" arrangement, and Victor Herbert appeared as guest conductor for a suite of *Serenades* he had written for the occasion. But it was the performance of Gershwin in his *Rhapsody in Blue* that was the hit of the program, and the music's success was immediate. It contained all the elements of Tin-Pan Alley as to tunes and rhythms, but it also showed that young Gershwin had written a piece of serious music of high order, combining the jazz he knew so well with a highly romantic slow section, with its Tchaikovskian theme, its effectiveness greatly enhanced by Grofé's brilliant and colorful orchestration. The *Rhapsody* established Gershwin's fame overnight, and by now it has become a modern classic. Although it has been played possibly more than any other one piece of contemporary music, with both good and bad performances, it has stood the test of time.

Later Works

A year later, in 1925, Walter Damrosch commissioned Gershwin to compose a Piano Concerto for the New York Symphony Society. This meant that he was recognized as a serious composer, and on December 3, 1925, Gershwin played the piano part in his Concerto in F. This time he wisely chose to do his own orchestrating, and sought the advice of Rubin Goldmark, knowing that he must work in terms of a symphony orchestra and not a jazz band. As Gershwin could afford to make sure his score sounded as he wished it to, he hired the Globe Theatre and an orchestra of sixty musicians to play the piece over for him for several hours, so that he might listen and study the effects of various combinations. Opinion still varies as to which is the better piece, the *Rhapsody in Blue* or the Concerto, but the fact remains that both have become a part of the standard repertory, and the choice would seem to be a personal one.

Gershwin's next symphonic piece was *An American in Paris,* first performed by the New York Symphony in 1928. Its humor and gaiety are infectious and its orchestration is colorful, with a touch of realism in its use of taxi horns. Its depiction of an American three thousand miles from home gave opportunity for the use of a blue mood and a blues theme which Gershwin could handle racily and authentically.

A *Second Rhapsody* based on a five-minute sequence composed for a motion picture, *Delicious,* has not enjoyed the popularity of the *Rhapsody in Blue.* It is perhaps more self-conscious when it tries to portray the din of rivets on the streets of a metropolis. Gershwin first called it *Rhapsody in Rivets,* but changed the name to *Second Rhapsody,* and it was played first by the Boston Symphony in 1932, just a year after the satirical musical comedy *Of Thee I Sing* (which won its authors the Pulitzer Prize) was first produced. With a book by George S. Kaufman and Morrie Ryskind, lyrics by Gershwin's brother Ira, and the music by George, this was an attempt at a Gilbert and Sullivan treatment of government officials. It was highly successful, but when it was revived in 1952 it seemed that the satire had somehow lost its poignancy and the allusions were not as pointed as they had once seemed.

No such fate has met Gershwin's major work, the opera *Porgy and Bess*, which will be discussed in a subsequent chapter. The years have shown that what Gershwin accomplished had a far deeper meaning than could have been imagined in his own time. Gershwin's music became the music of the people and his tunes were sung everywhere, just as Foster's had been sung by the popular entertainers of his day, the minstrel troupes, and were then taken up by high and low alike. The only difference was that Foster's songs reflected the sentimental ballads of a simpler day, while Gershwin's music pictured his own sophisticated era. Yet Gershwin was able to go farther than Foster, and in fusing art music with popular music, he was to influence composers all over the world.

When Gershwin died in Hollywood on July 11, 1937, one of his greatest tributes came from Arnold Schoenberg—when he said over the radio the next day: "Music was to him not a mere matter of ability, it was the air he breathed, the dream he dreamed. I grieve over the deplorable loss to music, for there is no doubt that he was a great composer."

LEAGUE OF COMPOSERS

In 1921 Edgar Varèse founded in New York the International Composers' Guild to champion the cause of contemporary music by giving performances of new works. American composers hailed this organization as an outlet for their music but in a short time several composers became dissatisfied and withdrew to form the League of Composers, which would have the avowed purpose of giving equal representation to all phases of modern music.

At the first concert of the League on November 11, Ernest Bloch's Piano Quintet had its first performance. Bloch had finished this composition in Cleveland the preceding March, using quarter-tones to create emotional tension. The League soon commissioned works, especially from native composers, and gradually extended its influence throughout America and even in Europe with its magazine, *Modern Music*. Eventually it was to sponsor stage productions, radio programs, and to establish exchange concerts with European countries. Its value was quickly recognized and it became one of the strongest influences of any musical group in the nation. Leading symphony orchestras, chamber music ensembles, choruses, and soloists began to offer to perform the commissioned works. Only in America could so much be accomplished in so short a time. In 1954 the League of Composers merged with the International Society for Contemporary Music, with Roger Sessions as the first chairman of the board.

AMERICAN COMPOSERS STUDY IN PARIS

Once again the younger composers, whose works were soon to be heard throughout the land, were going to Europe to study, but this time there was a difference. They were wiser, more mature than their fathers and grandfathers had been, and their attitude had changed radically. Until the first World War Germany had been the country where one must study, and at the turn of the century, even though Paris was equally important, singers sought to be heard at the Berlin Opera, and no pianist with any self-respect would dream of a concert career without making a Berlin debut. During the war, with the Germans as our enemies, there was much sentiment in America against anything Teutonic. The quantity of French and Italian music that was heard as a consequence was amazing. Many Russian musicians and the great Ballet Russe had to leave Russia after the Revolution, and some of this talent ultimately found its way to America. While abroad, many American soldiers were able to get to Paris on leave and they never quite forgot its charm. As schools of music were set up to promote the study and practice of the arts, as in Fontainebleau, many of the awards were made possible by American foundations, like the Juilliard, or were sponsored by leading universities, such as Harvard and Yale. In Paris in the 1920s, young American composers found a favorable and stimulating atmosphere conducive to music study, where teachers seemed able to teach the necessary craftsmanship and still allow the student to keep his own individuality and personal ideals. The great figure for the American composers was Nadia Boulanger, who taught in this manner, and was responsible for a large number of our composers who became well-known in the thirties and forties.

AARON COPLAND

One of Boulanger's first outstanding American pupils to appear in New York was Aaron Copland, who had been born in Brooklyn on November 14, 1900, of Russian-Jewish parents. Copland had studied in New York with Rubin Goldmark, but found the composer too pedantic and academic. He went to Paris to study at the Fontainebleau School of Music and was equally dissatisfied. In 1921 he began studying with Mlle. Boulanger, whom he had met as a member of the school's faculty. Copland became her first full-time American pupil. He returned to America in 1924, and on January 11, 1925, Walter Damrosch and the New York Symphony performed his Symphony for organ and orchestra, with Mlle. Boulanger (who had commissioned it) as soloist. Copland later revised this work and it had many performances in both Europe and America.

Copland's real recognition came within the next two years, with his suite *Music for the Theatre* and his Piano Concerto. The former, written for small orchestra and piano, was commissioned by the League of Composers (its first commission), and had its performance on November 20, 1925, in Boston, with Koussevitzky conducting. Eight days later it was heard in New York's Town Hall, at a concert of the League of Composers, under the direction of Koussevitzky. Copland had remarked that he "was anxious to write a work that would immediately be recognized as American in character," and it was natural that he adopted the currently popular jazz idioms and rhythmic patterns in the second movement, *Dance*. Earlier in the year Copland had been honored with the first Guggenheim Fellowship in musical composition, and had composed most of his suite in the peaceful atmosphere of the MacDowell Colony in New Hampshire actually completing it in September, at Lake Placid. The Piano Concerto was given its first performance in Boston on January 28, 1927, with Copland as the soloist and Koussevitzky conducting. Continuing his use of jazz rhythms, Copland wrote the Concerto in two connected movements, with the second movement using both a "slow blues" and a "snappy number," within the larger symphonic framework. The Concerto was the last of Copland's experiments with symphonic jazz. He felt that its emotional scope was too limited and that he had done all he could do with its idiom.

In 1929 Copland was able to make profitable use of a score which he had originally written in Paris—music for a ballet, *Grogh*. He had started work on a *Symphonic Ode* for a contest announced by the RCA Victor Company, but he realized that he did not have time to finish it before the closing date. Instead, he extracted a set of three dances from the score of *Grogh*, called it a *Dance Symphony* and entered it in the contest. It shared equally with four other works which together won the total prize of $25,000.

Since his jazz period Copland has become a composer of what the Germans would call *Gebrauchsmusik*, or translated literally, music for use. He has considered carefully the modern composer's widening market—motion pictures, radio, the phonograph, ballet, schools, and colleges. For high school use he composed an operetta, *The Second Hurricane* (1936), and for young orchestras *An Outdoor Overture* (1938).

For motion pictures Copland has written background music for a number of Hollywood films: *Of Mice and Men* (1939), *Our Town* (1940), *North Star* (1943), *The Red Pony* (1948), *The Heiress* (1948), as well as the documentaries *The City* (1939) and *The Cummington Story* (1945). In composing film music Copland has equaled the achievement of several foreign composers who have avoided the flamboyant clichés of Hollywood and have provided genuinely creative music which can be heard apart from the picture, yet never distracts the audience's attention from the action when heard with the film.

Several of the film scores have been adapted by the composer to concert uses. *Quiet City* is a work for trumpet, English horn, and strings which is derived from his incidental music for Irwin Shaw's play (1940). The music from *Our Town* has been played frequently as a concert suite of that name, and the *Children's Suite* is taken from the music for *The Red Pony*.

Similarly, three of Copland's widely played concert pieces were originally music for ballets—the suite *Billy the Kid* (1938), Four Dances from the ballet *Rodeo* (1943), and *Appalachian Spring* (1945). For broadcasting Copland composed *Music for Radio* (1937) on commission from the Columbia Broadcasting System. Suggestions from radio listeners led to the adoption of another title for the piece, *Saga of the Prairie*.

The foregoing titles suggest that Copland's locale as a composer is definitely American, as do his *John Henry* (1940) for small orchestra and his *Lincoln Portrait* (1942) for narrator and orchestra, and his selection of *Twelve Poems of Emily Dickinson* as the text for a a song-cycle for voice and piano (1950). He has also made new arrangements of a group of *Old American Songs* (1950, with a second set in 1954), and paid tribute to Latin-America in his orchestral *El Salon Mexico* (1936) and *Danzón Cubano* (1942). The latter piece was originally written for two pianos, and was transcribed for large orchestra in 1945.

Copland's catalog of chamber music includes his early trio, *Vitebsk* (1928), his one attempt to use Jewish material; a Sextet for strings, piano and clarinet (1937, actually a reduction of the Short Symphony); and a Quartet for piano and strings (1950). His Piano Sonata (1941) has become well known and his opera *The Tender Land* was performed in 1954 by the New York City Center Opera Company.

Copland is also active as a lecturer and teacher, particularly at the Berkshire Music Center, Tanglewood, Massachusetts. As an author his books include *What to Listen for in Music* (1939), *Our New Music* (1941), and *Music and Imagination* (1952). In the history of twentieth-century American music, he will ever remain an important musical figure, an eclectic who draws freely from every available source, and writes both effectively and well, with a command of his mediums and his materials.

HOWARD HANSON

A little over a month after George Gershwin's *Rhapsody in Blue* was introduced, another important event took place, this time at the Eastman School of Music in Rochester, New York. The Rochester Philharmonic Orchestra, founded by Mr. Eastman in 1923 (succeeding the Rochester Symphony of 1922) and having Albert Coates and Eugène Goossens as the conductors for its first season, had chosen Goossens as its regular conductor. On March 19, 1924, Howard Hanson appeared as guest conductor, as the new director of the Eastman School, as well as a composer. Hanson would soon make Rochester a vital music center for American music, presenting on his programs more American music than any other living man. On this occasion he conducted the initial performance of his *Nordic* Symphony (his first). Born in Wahoo, Nebraska, on October 28,

1896, of Swedish parents, Hanson studied at Luther College, Nebraska; Northwestern University in Illinois; and in New York, at the Institute of Musical Art. In 1921 he won the American Prix de Rome, and lived abroad for three years. Upon his return in 1924, he took up his duties at the Eastman School, and was at once put in a position of leadership in the cause of "the new in American music"—a position he has held for over thirty years.

In 1925 the Eastman School presented the first of what was to be an annual series of concerts devoted to the works of American composers. These concerts had an enormous value from the outset, for the Eastman School would not only perform the works of composers from all parts of the country, but would also delve into the past and present symphonic works from earlier generations of American composers.

There could be no question but that the nation was on the verge of a period of great creative activity and the American composer would soon stand on his own merit. As a summing up, and as a matter of record, it will be of more than passing interest to quote a list of American orchestral works which, in the seven years after World War I, had the greatest number of performances in the United States. Compiled by Howard Hanson and read in a paper to a Music Teachers' National Association Conference, the list is the best testimony to the rapid growth of native composers, as well as a key to the outstanding composers of 1919-1926. Many of the pieces are dated and no longer heard, while others have never been dropped from the orchestral repertory. Still other composers, like MacDowell, have had their music revived with much success. All are the evidence of America's gradual maturing. Dr. Hanson's list included:

Carpenter—*Adventures in a Perambulator; Concertino*
Chadwick—*Anniversary Overture*
Eichheim—*Oriental Impressions*
Goldmark—*Negro Rhapsody*
Griffes—*The Pleasure Dome of Kubla Khan; The White Peacock*
Hadley—*The Ocean*
Hanson—*Lux Aeterna; Nordic* Symphony
Hill—*Stevensonia Suite*
MacDowell—*Woodland Sketches;* Second Piano Concerto; *Indian Suite*

Mason—First Symphony; *Russians;* Prelude and Fugue
Powell—*Negro Rhapsody*
Schelling—*Victory Ball; From an Artist's Life; Fantastic Suite*
Skilton—*Indian Dances*
Sowerby—*King Estmere; Comes Autumn Time; From the North-land;* Piano Concerto
Taylor—*Through the Looking Glass*

As a composer, Hanson's *Nordic* Symphony showed him to be a romanticist, and its rather austere writing revealed his Scandinavian background, his spirit akin to that of Sibelius. In spite of his devoted interest in the development of American music he is no chauvinist demanding a national idiom; to him American music is music written by Americans, whether they are descendants of the settlers of Plymouth or Jamestown, or sons or daughters of newly arrived immigrants.

Hanson's list of orchestral works includes three other symphonies: the Second, *Romantic* (1930), the Third (1937), and the Fourth, *Requiem* (1943). Five symphonic poems bear the titles *Before the Dawn* (1919), *Exaltation* (1920), *North and West* (1923), *Lux Aeterna* (1923), and *Pan and the Priest* (1926). There are also a Concerto for organ and orchestra (1926); a Fantasy for string orchestra (1939); a Serenade for harp, flute, and strings (1948); *Pastorale* for oboe and strings (1949); and a Suite from his one opera, *Merry Mount,* which had its first performance at the Metropolitan in 1934. *The Lament for Beowulf* (1925) and *Three Poems from Walt Whitman* (from "Drum Taps"), composed in 1935, both for chorus and orchestra, are among his better-known choral works. There are also chamber music works, piano pieces, and songs.

THE GUGGENHEIM MEMORIAL FOUNDATION

Young American composers had an added stimulus in 1925, when the John Simon Guggenheim Memorial Foundation was set up to improve the quality of education and the practice of the arts and professions, as well as to foster research and to provide for the cause of international understanding. Former United States Senator and Mrs. Guggenheim created this trust in memory of their son, who had died in 1922. The first grants were for work abroad, but some were granted in the United States. Citizens from other Americas

were also to share in the grants, and were allowed to work in the
United States, while citizens of the United States had the chance
to work in Latin America. Fellowships were awarded regardless of
sex, color, or creed.

AMERICA'S AUDIENCES GROW

Organized Audience Plans

The composer is by no means the sum total of American music.
He must have an intelligent audience. As the composer was at last
coming into his own in the 1920s, there was developing at the same
time an "organized audience plan" which by mid-century would
cause no less a person than Clifford Curzon, the English pianist, to
say: "American culture has been libeled. Every city abounds with
people of good taste. That's not true in other countries, once you
get away from the capitals. In America, every audience knows why
it is there."

What is known to the trade as the "organized audience plan" was
started in the fall of 1920 by Harry P. Harrison of the Redpath
Chautauqua and Lyceum Bureau in Chicago. He was a clever and
an enterprising man, and to create further demand for musical audiences, groups of outstanding artists were offered to clubs, Lyceum
and Chautauqua audiences in a manner that was almost foolproof.
In 1920, an All-Star Series included Ernestine Schumann-Heink,
Charles Marshall, and other well-known artists. The Lyceum circui'
had flourished nearly a century before, when men like Ralph W?'.o
Emerson lectured, and in the closing years of the nineteenth ce .tury
the Chautauqua had become the chief source of entertai ment,
especially for smaller cities and remote or isolated commι aities,
presenting both musical and nonmusical attractions. Harrison promised no financial risk to those who were interested in taking his
artists, for salesmen were sent out in advance to set up the necessary machinery for collecting subscriptions, so that the series and
the communities would be assured of having the money in hand.
The idea was so successful that in 1921 Harrison created the firm
of Harrison and Harshberger, to make the project entirely musical,
rather than keeping it a part of the Chautauqua series. The new

firm sold memberships in the Civic Music Association and the idea spread rapidly. The local units were nonprofit groups, whose concerts could be attended only by those who were members, and all moneys were banked at the end of an advance campaign before the artists' contracts were signed. Under the old system, local appearances of the important artists were only possible through a manager in a big city, or by the sponsorship of a local club. Artists were grouped as "box-office attractions" or "legitimate artists," and often had to sing and play the popular pieces demanded by the audiences, as had the earlier traveling virtuosi. The big stars had their own press agents, but few important managerial offices had their own publicity departments.

These great stars were expected to travel in state, and the singers and string players engaged their accompanists for the entire season, while the pianists always had a tuner who looked after the instruments they played. In the days before the war, two or three concert grands were assigned to an artist for the season, and were shipped ahead to the various cities. This expense was met by the piano firms whose instruments were used, and it was considered a part of good advertising. With changing conditions after the war, Harrison's idea caught on so fast that in 1922 he was joined by Ward French. The venture fared so well that in 1925 Samuel Insull, the utilities magnate, was attracted to the enterprise, and bought controlling interest, incorporating it as the Civic Concert Service. Insull was keeping in mind the singers of his Chicago Opera Company, and he saw a good way to keep them content while they were in the city for their season. By getting them additional concerts in nearby cities, he not only added to their income, but the Middle West was opened up to fine music.

In the East, it was not long before several independent New York managers saw the possibilities of organized audiences, and in 1928, seven of them—including Arthur Judson and Daniel Mayer—formed the Community Concerts Corporation. Sigmund Spaeth was the first president, and fifteen cities and communities within a large radius of New York were organized in their first season. This was but another manifestation of American ingenuity, and by the 1930s organized audiences became a big-time business, as well as a potent force for the dissemination of music throughout the country.

Aid for the Talented Young Performer

The strength and vitality of the 1920s set many musical currents in motion, each of which in its own way was of prime importance. The composers were already being helped through the foundations and groups like the League of Composers; audiences were growing who craved good music; the record industry took on new life; and radio was beginning to reach the farthest corners of the nation. These were good years for America, so different from the depression and reconstruction period in Europe after the war, where life seemed to be at its lowest ebb. With the establishment of the excellent graduate schools, the continued growth of the conservatories and music departments in the colleges and universities, it was natural that there would be a large group of young people who were seriously planning for a professional career. They poured into New York and Philadelphia, and in a few years they were ready to take the big step toward public recognition. It was at this time that Olga Samaroff Stokowski, as a faculty member of the Juilliard Graduate School (and for two years music critic of the *New York Post*), realized that these young performers, despite all the fine opportunities for training that had been created for them, still had an immense hurdle to surmount—gaining entrance to the "big field." While the composer might leave behind him the works which still could be performed and thus give future generations a chance to atone for the neglect accorded him while he lived, the rare abilities of a truly fine performer must die with him. Every young American facing the big chance to become known had already had much done for him. Musicians and music patrons had already created endless opportunities for such talents, and groups like the National Federation of Music Clubs had grown into a powerful organization in the twentieth century, with local clubs providing a valuable outlet for both amateurs and professionals. Many organized contests for the young aspirant had been set up, many with generous money prizes, and in New York the Naumburg Foundation (through the generous gift of Walter W. Naumburg) had made debut recitals possible for six American winners annually, who were chosen by a competent jury through public contests. The National Music League was established to get management for the young artists not yet established, and they had a chance to concertize for a modest fee.

Aware of all of this, Mme. Samaroff could not forget her own difficult years as she worked to establish herself as a pianist with two counts against her from the start—she was an American and a woman. Someone, therefore, must knock at the door of the "big field," for although a young musician might win the top prizes, he might soon be forgotten or relegated to the low-fee concert tour, which inevitably put a professional stigma on him in the eyes of the seasoned artist who had arrived and was established. The obvious solution was to gain for him a performance with an important symphony orchestra, for this immediately conferred a special distinction on the young player and gave him a new status in the professional world. Most young and unknown Americans had no chance whatsoever of getting this rare opportunity, yet to them, the symbol of the big field was an orchestral engagement. Only in this way could the old domination of a favored few be broken once and for all.

In 1928, there was a wide celebration honoring the genius of Franz Schubert, who had died a century before. It was Ossip Gabrilowitsch who suggested the Viennese composer as a champion for the young performer. Schubert's neglect while he lived, and his early death, made him a logical choice for a patron saint for such a venture. The undertaking was incorporated as The Schubert Memorial, and two institutions who were interested—the Victor Talking Machine Company and the Juilliard Musical Foundation—became charter members. The prize was to be a professional debut in New York with an orchestra, and the Artists' Advisory Board included all of the outstanding conductors of the nation's major orchestras. Of the three first contestants, Muriel Kerr, a piano pupil of Hutcheson at the Juilliard, is still a performing artist today, as well as a member of the Juilliard faculty. That the project was a sound one was attested by its rapid growth, for it soon reached such proportions that the National Federation of Music Clubs, under the presidency of Mrs. Ruth Haller Ottaway, took it over as a part of their organization. For many years the Schubert Memorial winners were given a chance by the big managers, which was yet another step forward and indicated a definite change in American attitude toward her own future artists.

GROWTH OF THE CONCERT BAND

One of the American institutions that is dear to the hearts of many is the brass band. It had long been a familiar sight in every city and town, at every summer resort since the Revolution. The bands had grown and developed along with the orchestras, and many, like those of John Philip Sousa and Arthur Pryor, were among the first musical groups to make phonograph records. With the advent of the twentieth century, cities like Baltimore and Kansas City had made their bands professional, and the wind-instrument symphony player, busy in the winter months, also had the advantage of summer work. Today, Chicago's Grant Park and New York's Central Park (to name but two locations), are visited by thousands of music lovers who gather to enjoy good band music. In New York, since 1924, the concerts of the Goldman Band have been underwritten by the Daniel and Florence Guggenheim Foundation, whose aim is "to promote the well-being of mankind throughout the world."

The Marine Band

The United States Marine Band dates from 1798, when it was merely a fife and drum corps. In 1800, when the national capital was moved from Philadelphia to Washington, the Marines, already known as the "Presidential Troops," arrived in Washington late in July. The grimness of life in the new capital was considerably lightened by the band's concerts given at their camp on a hill overlooking the Potomac and also furnishing the dance music for the Washington Assembly balls.

When President John Adams held a New Year's Day reception in 1801, the Marine Band furnished the music, not only making its official debut, but inaugurating the series of like receptions that have continued to the present day. President Jefferson sponsored the band and many subsequent Presidents had important roles in its illustrious history. It was President Van Buren who instituted outdoor concerts on the Capitol grounds, and President Tyler those on the White House lawn. In 1856 President Pierce approved the necessary legislation to provide extra pay for these outdoor concerts and in 1861 the Marine Band was made the chief band of the service by a bill passed by Congress with the approval of President Lincoln.

The bill provided for a drum major, one principal musician, and thirty musicians for the band, in addition to sixty drummers and sixty fifers. There was no further change in the status of the band until March 3, 1899, when President William McKinley signed the Act of Congress that increased the players' pay and enlarged the group to sixty performers, with a leader and a second leader. Today there are many army, navy, and air force bands, touring the country, Canada, and Europe, and broadcasting regular programs over the air. The value of band music in the public schools (and for the general public) as a means of musical development, was eventually recognized, and the League of Composers led the way in commissioning outstanding composers to write band music. So great has been the growth of America's bands that there is hardly a child that has not had his chance to belong to one during his school years.

John Philip Sousa

Sousa, the "March King," (1854-1932) started his career as a band-leader in 1880 when he was appointed director of the Marine Band. In 1892 he formed his own organization and was one of the principal figures in developing what is known today as the "concert band." His own compositions were mostly marches. One of them, *The Stars and Stripes Forever,* is so well known abroad, as well as in this country, that foreigners have thought it was our national anthem. Other famous Sousa marches are *The Washington Post, The High School Cadets,* and *The Gladiator.* He also composed the scores of three successful operettas: *The Bride Elect, El Capitan,* and *The Free Lance.*

Edwin Franko Goldman

In later years Edwin Franko Goldman (1878-1956) continued the development of the concert band to the point where it is a truly symphonic organization. The free summer concerts of the Goldman Band in the parks of New York City have been a leading attraction for more than a quarter-century. Goldman was also a prolific composer of marches. The most popular of them is *On the Mall.* Goldman's talented son, Richard Franko Goldman (1910-   ) was an assistant conductor of the band beginning 1937. He succeeded his father as conductor in 1956. A pupil of Nadia Boulanger, among his works for band are *A Curtain Raiser and Country Dance* and

Hymn for Brass Choir. Two of his books are *The Band's Music* and *The Concert Band.*

EXPERIMENTAL COMPOSERS

The 1920s became famous for its experimental composers who dinned the ears of their listeners with strange dissonances and noises that seemed to contemporary ears to have little to do with music. Two young men, one here and the other abroad, seemed to be leaders of the extremists. They were Henry Cowell and George Antheil, both of such talent that they outgrew their desire to startle their audiences and became recognized in their maturity as composers of substance and sincerity. It will be recalled that Cowell had started his career by using clusters of tones sounded on the piano by the use of his forearm. Leo Ornstein (1895-) used "note-clusters" as early as 1915, and Charles Ives had employed chords in his piano music that had to be played with a ruler.

Henry Cowell

Henry Cowell, making his reputation first as an experimenter, has always had an inquiring mind and a keen interest in the unusual. He worked with the inventor Leon Theremin in developing the "rhythmicon," an electronic instrument for producing intricate rhythmic combinations. He was also interested from the beginning in modern music, not alone for promoting his own works but in behalf of all contemporary composers. He founded the quarterly publication *New Music* to issue the works of American and European innovators. As a writer and critic he is friendly to all new music that he thinks is valid and sincere, not only that of the extremists but of conservatives as well. He is in much demand as a teacher, lecturer, and performer, and until 1956 divided his time between New York and Baltimore, where he taught composition and lectured at the Peabody Conservatory of Music.

Born in Menlo Park, California (March 11, 1897), Cowell taught himself through endless experiments on an old upright piano which he had managed to buy. His early, experimental works include *Communication* (1920), *Vestiges* (1924), *Synchrony* (1930), *Two Appositions* (1931), and *Four Continuations* (1934) for strings—all orchestral pieces.

In contrast to his experimental music, Cowell has written in recent years many works that seem almost naïve in their straightforward simplicity, many of them reflecting his Celtic ancestry. A number of them are devoted to an American background; for example, his series of pieces called *Hymn and Fuguing Tune*, which attempts to show how the old New England church music might have developed into a definitely American style.

By 1955 he had composed eleven symphonies, an *Irish Suite* (1933), a *Celtic Set* (1939), and such program pieces as *Tales of Our Countryside* (1940) and *Saturday Night at the Firehouse* (1947). At this writing he is greatly interested in the possibilities of tape recording, believing it to be one of the important mediums of the future.

George Antheil

George Antheil, the "bad boy of music" (as he called himself), was Henry Cowell's principal rival in writing unconventional music. Born in Trenton, New Jersey, in 1900, he studied at the Philadelphia Conservatory of Music and with Ernest Bloch. He lived abroad for many years, and came into the headlines when his *Ballet Mécanique*, first introduced in Paris, was produced in New York in 1927. Its score called for ten player-pianos, and all sorts of mechanical noisemakers. The next day the newspapers told how startled and uncomprehending most of the audience was, as hisses and cheers intermingled. The *Ballet Mécanique* was the most advanced type of abstract music. Antheil compared it (in a letter to Nicolas Slonimsky in 1936) to the painting of Picasso. The composer felt he might do anything he wished—such as repeating one measure "one hundred times" or having certain pianola rolls silent for "sixty-two bars"—as long as he felt the parts, in his mind, ultimately balanced. "My ideas," he said, "were the most abstract of the abstract." When he shortened his *Ballet Mécanique* for a revival at a concert of the Composers Forum in New York, which Carlos Surinach conducted on February 20, 1954, both Antheil and the conductor received an ovation.

In his years abroad Antheil's jazz opera *Transatlantic* was produced in Frankfort in 1930 and America heard that its plot concerned American presidential elections. The year before a ballet, *Fighting the Waves*, had been produced at the Abbey Theatre in Dublin.

In 1932 and 1933 Antheil was awarded a Guggenheim Fellowship.

He remained something of a legend to American stay-at-homes until 1934, when the Juilliard School produced an opera he had written to a libretto by John Erskine, *Helen Retires*. The music for this work was not the best Antheil had, or has since, produced, but from that time on Americans have had opportunity to learn more of his varied talents and to appraise him as a thoroughly sincere, poetic, and sensitive composer. For a number of years he has lived in Hollywood, where he devotes several months each year to composing scores for motion pictures and the rest of his time to writing music of his own choosing.

In addition to a *Jazz Symphony* which he wrote for twenty-two instruments in 1925, Antheil has composed six symphonies. The First and Second (1922 and 1926) were early works. The Third was composed in 1934; the Fourth introduced by the NBC Orchestra under Stokowski in 1942; the Fifth by the Philadelphia Orchestra in 1949; and the Sixth by the Manhattan School of Music in 1950. There is an early Piano Concerto (1926), a more recent Violin Concerto, and orchestral pieces and chamber music.

Carl Ruggles

Another independent thinker from this period is the atonal composer Carl Ruggles (1876-). Born in Marion, Massachusetts, but for many years a resident of Vermont, Ruggles has worked out his own system, influenced very little from the outside, and any similarity that his music may have to that of Schoenberg is one of chance. Lawrence Gilman once called Ruggles a "master of a strange, torrential, and disturbing discourse." As a composer he has chafed under the restrictions imposed upon him by the capabilities of orchestral instruments. Their limitations of range prevent his themes from extending themselves as far as the composer would like, and many added instruments are needed to achieve the massive sonorities he desires. Much of his music is austere, yet no one can doubt his honesty and integrity. His list of works is relatively small and they have not been widely played. It includes *Angels* (the second movement of *Men and Angels* [1920], rescored); *Men and Mountains* (1924); *Portals* (1926); and *Sun-Treader* (1933)—all orchestral—and *Toys* (1919), for soprano and piano; *Evocations* (1937-45), piano solo; and one opera, *The Sunken Bell*.

Edgar Varèse

Edgar Varèse, born in Paris in 1885 and resident in America since 1916, was one of the boldest experimenters of this era, frankly expressing himself in sonority and rhythmic complexity at the expense, and often to the exclusion, of all melody and harmony. His *Ionisation* is composed for two groups of percussion players, thirteen in all, using only sounds of indeterminate pitch. His music is predominantly percussive; for example, his *Equatorial* for organ, brass, percussion, theremin instrument, and bass-baritone voice. The titles of others of his orchestral works are *Espace, Amériques, Arcana, Metal, Integrales, Hyperprism, Octandre,* and *Offrandes.* Henry Cowell has written of Varèse: "if stirring auditors to an almost unendurable irritation be taken into account, then the music can be said to be highly emotional."

Carlos Salzedo

Seven days after George Antheil's startling concert at Carnegie Hall, on April 17, 1927, the celebrated French-American harpist Carlos Salzedo (1885-   ), who had created new effects and sounds on the harp, gave a performance for the International Composers Guild of his Concerto for harp and seven wind instruments. His invention of a modern harp, which was said to be as much of an improvement over the standard harp "as an ox to an airplane," and on which he devised percussive effects on the framework, as well as unique harmonies, made him an important innovator. In his own way he reflected the complexities of the machine age. His many compositions include *The Enchanted Isle* (1918), for harp and orchestra; *Four Preludes to the Afternoon of a Telephone* (1921), for two harps. Harp solo compositions (these have been recorded) include *Eight Dances, Short Stories in Music, Chansons dans la nuit,* and *Whirlwind Harp.*

EXPERIMENTAL INSTRUMENTS

New instruments began to appear in the 1920s. The August Foerster piano manufacturing firm obtained the first patent for a quarter-tone piano (March 18, 1924), which was to have a considerable vogue in the ensuing years. Two years later the League of

Composers sponsored a demonstration by the Mexican composer, Julián Carillo (March, 1926), in which quarter-, eighth-, and sixteenth-tone music was played on special instruments. The instruments included the octavina (eighth-tones), and an arpa citera (sixteenth-tones). Carillo played his Concertino, employing these special instruments, for the first time with Stokowski and the Philadelphia Orchestra on March 4, 1927.

THE FIRST SOUND PICTURE

The motion picture industry took a momentous step forward during the summer of 1926 with the first New York showing of a 100 per cent sound picture, *Don Juan,* which the Vitaphone Company issued and presented to an invited audience on August 5. The picture featured Henry Hadley conducting the New York Philharmonic Orchestra, and it at once demonstrated the strides electrical recording had made. The early sound tracks were made on special discs that played the length of a film reel.

ECLECTICISM THE NORM FOR AMERICAN COMPOSERS

Impossible as it is specifically to classify American composers (and many of them dislike being put into a narrow category), looking back on the 1920s, one easily becomes aware that many of the composers of that day were markedly eclectic in their compositions, a condition that would soon become the norm for the American composer. From the many composers of the period who might be cited, two men, already in their fifties in 1927, stood out above the others as the decade drew to its close—Ernest Henry Schelling (1876-1939) and Frederick Shepherd Converse (1871-1940).

Ernest Schelling

Ernest Schelling was a piano pupil of Moszkowski and Paderewski, and until he was injured in an automobile accident in Switzerland in 1919, was one of the leading American concert pianists. He turned to conducting in later years, appearing with many of the major orchestras and became well-known for his Children's Concerts with the New York Philharmonic-Symphony Orchestra. From 1935 to 1938 he was the conductor of the Baltimore Symphony. As a composer he wrote several works which were successful and widely played: the orchestral *Impressions from an Artist's Life* (1913), with piano; and *A Victory Ball* (1923), with a program from the poem by Alfred Noyes, in which vivid music, portraying the gaiety of dancers, is interrupted by the sounds of war in the roll of the drum. *A Victory Ball* was introduced by Stokowski in Philadelphia, and became one of the most popular pieces of the 1920s. Schelling also composed a *Legende Symphonique* (1906); a *Suite Fantastique* (1905); a Violin Concerto, played by Fritz Kreisler (1917); and a tone poem, *Morocco* (1927), the composer conducting the New York Philharmonic at the première.

Frederick S. Converse

Frederick Shepherd Converse, who had been a student in John Knowles Paine's classes at Harvard, was born in Newton, Massachusetts. He later worked with George Chadwick and then went to Germany to study with Josef Rheinberger. He enjoyed the distinction of being the first American composer to have an opera produced at the Metropolitan Opera House, his one-act *The Pipe of Desire* (1910). The titles of his orchestral works show his interest in American life: *Flivver Ten Million* (1927); *California,* tone poem (1928); *American Sketches,* a suite (1933). In *Flivver Ten Million* Converse's homage to that thoroughly American institution of that era, the Model T Ford (which had just passed its ten-millionth mark in production) amusingly depicts all of the experiences that came with riding in the old Ford car, including a collision from which the hero, righted and shaken, proceeds on his way with redoubled energy, "typical of the indomitable American spirit." In addition to the usual resources of the modern orchestra the score calls for a muted Ford horn, a wind machine, a factory whistle, and an anvil. Converse also composed three symphonies; a Concerto for piano and orchestra; incidental music for the stage and films; and several choral works. He also taught composition at the New England Conservatory of Music, and from 1931 to 1938 was the school's dean.

David Stanley Smith

Another composer who belongs in this group is David Stanley Smith (1877-1949), who was long identified with music in our colleges. Smith was a pupil of Horatio Parker and later became his assistant at Yale. In 1920 he succeeded Parker as dean and professor, as well as conductor of the New Haven Symphony Orchestra. Thus he bridged the work of the Boston group, with its European domination, and became one of the first important composers to anticipate the eclectic tendencies which, in a few years, would become almost a standard procedure for the younger native composers.

Smith left one of the most impressive lists of chamber-music compositions that has been credited to any composer. These include eight string quartets and several sonatas for piano and various instrumental combinations. His orchestral works include four symphonies; a *Prince Hal Overture* (1912); *Impressions,* a suite (1916); *Fete Galante,* for flute and orchestra (1920); *Cathedral Prelude,* for organ and orchestra (1926); *Epic Poem* (1926); and several large choral works including *Vision of Isaiah* (1927), *Credo* (1941), *Requiem* (1942), and *Daybreak* (1945).

Arthur Shepherd

Arthur Shepherd (1880-) might be chosen as a good example of the significant change that was taking place in the work of the American composers of this period. Despite the essentially Germanic training he had at the New England Conservatory in Boston, Shepherd's very eclecticism saved him from being a mere echo of his teachers and their environment. Born in Paris, Idaho, of English parents who had been converted to Mormonism and gone to the West in the 1870s, Shepherd taught in both Salt Lake City and Boston before settling in Cleveland, Ohio, as assistant conductor of the Cleveland Symphony Orchestra. He also became chairman of the Music Department at Western Reserve University, and music critic of the *Cleveland Press.*

As a composer, Shepherd has tried to avoid self-conscious attempts at modernism and has concerned himself only with the communicative power of his music. Some detect racial traits in his writing, chiefly Anglo-Celtic, resulting perhaps from his English parentage. But he also had an interest in French music, especially the work of Fauré and D'Indy, as well as the pioneering work of Arthur Farwell in American folk song. In his Symphony No. 1, which he finished in 1927 and called *Horizons: Four Western Pieces for Symphony Orchestra,* Shepherd based his score partly on frontier ballads—*The Dying Cowboy, The Old Chisholm Trail,* and the *Dogie Song.* It is full of the raciness, the adventure, and the spacious life of the plains. His other works include the *Overture to a Drama* (1919), which Virgil Thomson called in 1950 "still a vigorous and buoyant piece"; Symphony No. 2 (1938); *Fantasia on Down East Spirituals* (1946); a Violin Concerto (1946-47); three string quartets and a Piano Quintet; *Triptych* (1926) for soprano and string quartet; two piano sonatas; two cantatas—*City in the Sea* (1913) and *Song of the Pilgrims* (1934); and many songs.

TRENDS IN A CLOSING ERA

With the economic collapse of October, 1929, a vital era was to close. The period since the war had been one of trial and error, and as interest in the so-called machine music waned, American composers in keeping with their colleagues the world over turned more and more to the cold impersonal style of the strict forms of earlier periods. The American composer was drawing freely on all types of music, the best of each generation. As Curt Sachs pointed out, "such archaism was not entirely new." Bach had taken from all existing sources what he wished and imbued it with his own particular genius. Mozart and Beethoven in their later years marveled anew at the wonders of Bach's magnificent fugues; and Haydn had been stirred enough by Handel's mighty oratorios to write two of his own. Mendelssohn, in making the world aware once again of the greatness of Johann Sebastian Bach, was so inspired by the master's contrapuntal writing that he freely mixed it with the romanticism of his day. Brahms, too, in the midst of the program music of Liszt and Wagner, turned back to the earlier styles. In America, for over a quarter of a century there had been an avoidance of the larger forms, so popular with the romantic composer, but as the cycle completed itself, the late 1920s not only brought back a popularity for the older forms, but also a renaissance of ancient instruments. Organs, such as the one at Harvard University, were reconstructed to the specifications of Baroque instruments; recorders, viols, harpsichords, and clavichords were used again, as musicians sought to recreate the actual sounds of early chamber music. Contemporary composers began to write modern works call-

ing for these instruments, using the old variation forms of the passacaglia and chaconne, as well as the constantly recurring bass
motives (basso ostinato). Even Schoenberg's use of the twelve-tone
system was an attempt on his part to bring order out of the chaos
of atonality. Time has already shown what a tremendous upheaval
this era witnessed, yet it was to take nearly two decades, and a
second World War, before many of these forces would be traced to
their ends.

CHAPTER XII

The Thirties

THE FINANCIAL CRASH

Like the deluge from a great dam which suddenly bursts without warning, the economic collapse of October, 1929, brought ruin and hardship to millions. Yet out of the want and misery, and the many changes necessitated by such an upheaval, there was to come much of benefit as the air cleared and conditions once again took a more normal course.

Musically, the collapse seemed in many ways to have a therapeutic effect. There was less restlessness and the machine music of the 1920s gave way more and more to the pure neoclassicism that had first been noticed a few years before. The past years had been dominated by all types of revolutionary writing, with Stravinsky and Schoenberg in the lead, and as Virgil Thomson pointed out, "the so-called 'modern music' was obligatory for all right-thinking young composers." In Paris, where Thomson was living in the early 1930s, reaction set in among some of the younger composers, with the use of personal sentiment as a chief element. Some began to call this new trend "neoromanticism," but it at least showed that the rising group of composers had no intention of going backward. The years were bringing more commissions, and whereas the romantic composer of the nineteenth century would have scorned such a task for fear his creative spirit might be endangered, the young modern soon prided himself on the chance to show what he could do. Like Copland, many began to write music for a practical use, such as for the radio, motion pictures, and ballet. For the next twenty years some of the finest contemporary scores would be the result of such commissions.

Another type of music that emerged was the so-called "proletarian music," which was music that had a strong political content and was purportedly written for the workingman—the man in the street. It had a simplicity that was easily understood by the untutored, and had become more significant since the Russian Revolution in 1917. The Association of Proletarian Musicians, formed in Russia in 1924 to spread these doctrines, was disbanded by the Soviet government in April, 1932.

ORCHESTRAS

New Conductors

Despite the depression and hard times, orchestral music continued to grow. Eugène Goossens was appointed Director of the Cincinnati May Festival as well as the Symphony Orchestra in 1931, following the orchestra's nine successful years under Fritz Reiner. Eugene Ormandy, in the same year, began to make musical history for the Minneapolis Symphony, and would remain there until he was called to Philadelphia in 1936. St. Louis engaged for its orchestra Vladimir Golschmann, who had inaugurated the Concerts Golschmann in Paris, and under him the orchestra has had a steady and distinguished growth.

New Orchestras: Indianapolis, Washington

The new decade opened with the founding of two new orchestras, in Indianapolis, and Washington, D. C. Ferdinand Schaefer started the Indianapolis Symphony in 1930, with concerts given on a cooperative plan in which the players shared in the net receipts. Schaeffer conducted until the season of 1936-37, when Fabien Sevitzky was appointed and the players were engaged on a salaried basis. In the nation's capital in 1931, Hans Kindler founded the National Symphony Orchestra, which had been his dream after three successful concerts in 1930. Howard Mitchell, a talented young American, was the first cellist and assistant conductor, and would become the permanent director when Kindler resigned in 1949. It was a promising sign that the seat of American government should have its own orchestra at last.

Boston Symphony's Fiftieth Anniversary

The Boston Symphony Orchestra, in celebrating its fiftieth anniversary, commissioned many works from the leading composers of the world. Such memorable compositions included Howard Hanson's Symphony No. 2, *Romantic* (November 28, 1930), and Stravinsky's *Symphony of Psalms*, "composed for the glory of God and dedicated to the Boston Symphony Orchestra" (December 19, 1930). In Cleveland, for the dedication of Severance Hall, the new permanent home of the Cleveland Orchestra, Loeffler's commissioned work, *Evocation*—portraying the building of a temple dedicated to the Muses—had its première on February 5, 1931.

RADIO

In the early days of radio, the large corporations that were broadcasting music through their nation-wide networks sincerely believed that these programs of serious music would be of the greatest value, musically, to a maturing nation. The concerts of the New York Philharmonic were heard on the air, and Walter Damrosch retired from active conducting in the concert hall to give all of his time to the very popular music appreciation broadcasts designed for school children. There were many short recitals on national, as well as local, stations, and soon entire acts of an operatic performance might be heard from the stages of the Chicago and Metropolitan opera houses. By 1930 the two major networks—NBC and CBS—took over the field of concert management, the former having merged on January 1, 1929, with the Concert Bureau (from which was to come the National Concert and Artists Corporation—NCAC, as it is known in the business), while the latter created Columbia Concerts on December 12, with Arthur Judson as its head and Ward French as the General Manager. A third radio chain appeared in 1934, the Mutual Broadcasting System.

AMERICAN OPERAS

The opera companies had serious difficulties during the depression. In the mid-thirties the Chicago Civic Opera Association actually succumbed to its financial troubles and even the Metropolitan in New York was in danger of closing its doors. In 1933 the American public was called upon to "Save the Metropolitan," as the slogan of the fund-raising campaign urged, and it was only the gifts of the public, including thousands of listeners to its weekly radio broadcasts, which has kept the Metropolitan from bankruptcy, even to the present day.

When Edward Johnson took over the management of the Metropolitan Opera Association (its new name since the fund-raising in 1933) after the sudden death of the newly appointed Herbert Witherspoon in May, 1935, many new singers continued to make operatic history, although the repertoire was chosen principally from standard works. Lily Pons had made a spectacular debut as Lucia in 1931, and in January, 1956, would be the first singer ever to celebrate twenty-five years of continuous appearances at the Metropolitan. Kirsten Flagstad's debut as Sieglinde in *Die Walküre* on February 2, 1935, proved to be a sensation, and inaugurated a new and exciting era of Wagnerian opera. Radio had already broadcast its first opera from the Metropolitan's stage on Christmas Day, 1931, with a performance of *Hansel and Gretel*, and by the next fall, the Saturday matinee broadcasts were begun and they still continue, followed by the nation.

Deems Taylor

In spite of the expense of new productions the Metropolitan produced a number of American operas during these years. The first of these, in the 1930s, was Deems Taylor's *Peter Ibbetson*, first performed February 7, 1931.

Taylor's earlier score, with libretto by Edna St. Vincent Millay, *The King's Henchman* (February 17, 1927), had been the first American opera to be staged at the Metropolitan in ten years, and had been a great success, remaining in the repertoire three years. Its popularity brought forth a second commission from the Metropolitan, *Peter Ibbetson*, for which Taylor used a libretto that he wrote with Constance Collier, based on the play that she had written from Du Maurier's novel.

Taylor, born in New York City in 1885, was already well-known as an orchestral composer, having won first prize in 1913 for his symphonic poem *The Siren Song* in a contest sponsored by the National Federation of Music Clubs. But it was his orchestral suite

Through the Looking Glass that brought him recognition when it was performed by Carolyn Beebe and the New York Chamber Music Society in 1919. Taylor later rescored the work for full orchestra and from 1923 on, it has been played by almost every major orchestra here and abroad. *Peter Ibbetson* ran up sixteen performances in four seasons, a record which has not been broken by any other American composer at the Metropolitan. Taylor is a fluent writer, and has shown considerable feeling for the theater, but as his operas showed their derivations too apparently, they are neglected today.

Louis Gruenberg

Louis Gruenberg (1884-   ) provoked talk with his colorful opera (and perhaps his most arresting work) *The Emperor Jones,* based on Eugene O'Neill's play, which was given at the Metropolitan with Lawrence Tibbett in the title role on January 7, 1933. It had many productions both here and abroad, and at the time of its première Olin Downes wrote in the *New York Times* that it was "the first American opera by a composer whose dramatic instinct and intuition for the theater seem unfailing, and whose musical technique is characterized by a very complete modern knowledge and a reckless mastery of his means." Some argued whether any music would add to the effectiveness of the stark terror inherent in O'Neill's play, but it was generally agreed that Gruenberg's savage music, with its explosive detonations, its howls and outcries, provided the most finished and theatrically effective opera that the Metropolitan had yet produced. The Juilliard School of Music had already produced Gruenberg's earlier "fairy opera for the childlike"—*Jack and the Beanstalk*—with a libretto by John Erskine (November 19, 1931). The score of that work was modern, the orchestral instruments subtly suggesting the cow, the giant's falsetto, and the laying of the golden eggs.

Gruenberg has shown a preoccupation with jazz in some of his music. In his two major choral works, *Daniel Jazz* (1923) and *Creation* (1924), as well as in the *Jazz Suite* for orchestra (1925).

Hanson's "Merry Mount"

Merry Mount is Howard Hanson's only opera, and it was first produced in concert form at the Ann Arbor (Michigan) Festival on

May 20, 1933. The following February (1934) it was seen in full production at the Metropolitan Opera House in New York. The libretto by Richard L. Stokes, dealt with Thomas Morton and his Maypole which shocked his Puritan neighbors, and of the fatal love the Puritan pastor felt for one of the girls in Morton's company of cavaliers. Critical comment on the opera was not too favorable. Olin Downes wrote that the music was "at times conventional and noisily effective. Otherwise, it displays neither originality nor any special aptitude for the theatre." *Merry Mount* was given nine performances at the Metropolitan.

Thomson's "Four Saints in Three Acts"

The same February that saw the first opera-house production of *Merry Mount* brought the performance of a unique and controversial score by Virgil Thomson, a composer who is more fully discussed later in this chapter. The work was an opera, first heard in Hartford, Connecticut, on February 8, 1934. Its fantastic but intriguing libretto was by Gertrude Stein, and the cast, an all-Negro one, wore costumes of cellophane. Sponsored by the Society of Friends and Enemies of Modern Music, the opera appeared in New York at the 44th Street Theatre on February 20, 1934, where it had forty-eight performances. Lawrence Gilman described the music that Thomson set to Gertrude Stein's seemingly meaningless words as "deceptively simple, a little self-consciously candid and naïve, actually very wily and deft and slick, often subtly and wittily elusive, distinguished in its artful banality." The music was drawn from all types of religious music, from Georgian chant to the hymns and songs of the earlier revivals and camp meetings. Thomson has a wonderful feeling for prosody when it comes to setting it to music, and his score was a marvel of clarity and inspired imagination. In 1947, *Four Saints* was given a complete radio performance by CBS (May 25), and in the spring of 1952 it had a triumphant revival on Broadway, with Thomson conducting, going afterward to Paris for the Festival, where it created a sensation.

Gershwin's "Porgy and Bess"

It was not the Metropolitan, but Broadway, which saw the performance of a masterpiece, by now an American classic—Gershwin's *Porgy and Bess*.

On September 2, 1935, George Gershwin finished his last important work, and on the thirtieth, Boston heard its world première. The opera was based on Du Bose Heyward's novel *Porgy*. A play had been made from it by Du Bose and Dorothy Heyward, and the composer's brother Ira collaborated with the authors in writing the libretto for the opera. The New York opening was on October 10, at the Alvin Theatre under the auspices of the Theatre Guild. *Porgy and Bess* enjoyed a run of 124 performances and in 1942 was given a revival which had an equally long run. Since then it has been given by other companies, notably by one which toured extensively in America and Europe during the early 1950s.

Gershwin spent considerable time gathering material on the Negroes around Charleston, South Carolina, and studying the Gullah dialect. There can be no doubt that he produced something highly authentic in his recreation of life in Catfish Row, the Negro tenement section of Charleston's waterfront. The opera's arias were the embodiment of American jazz songs, just as earlier composers, like Verdi, had expressed the tuneful Italian songs of their day. Some of the most popular songs in *Porgy and Bess* are *Summertime* (Clara's lullaby in the opening scene); Porgy's happy, carefree song of love, *I Got Plenty o' Nuthin'!;* Porgy's and Bess's love duet, *Bess, You Is My Woman Now;* Sportin' Life's funny song at the picnic, *It Ain't Necessarily So;* and the wonderful blues song which Sportin' Life sings to Bess when he tries to persuade her to go with him, *There's a Boat Dat's Leavin' Soon for New York*. Gershwin wrote a well-integrated operatic score, one that was gripping and compelling in its drama and immensely sharpened by the Negro-like music he composed for it. It was an American opera which dealt with a group of American folk, and because of Gershwin's knowledge of the jazz idiom and popular song of his day, his music could not have been more appealing or appropriate.

Marc Blitzstein

Political left-wing operas made their appearance with Marc Blitzstein's *The Cradle Will Rock*, produced in New York on June 16, 1937. Following the trends of the writers of the day, Blitzstein (1905-   ) used his music to further liberal causes. The opera was originally intended for the WPA Theater in New York, but because of the leftish connotations it was produced instead by the

Mercury Theatre. The production had no scenery or costumes; the singers had to be placed in the audience in order to get around the union regulations which prohibited participation in an unlicensed production; and Blitzstein acted as pianist and narrator. It was a powerful and biting allegory about the labor movement, and it made a deep impression and ran on Broadway for several months. It was revived in 1947 with great success, Virgil Thomson writing in the *New York Herald Tribune* that *The Cradle Will Rock* was "one of the most charming creations of the American musical theatre. It has sweetness, a cutting wit, inexhaustible fancy, and faith."

Blitzstein's next stage work, *No For An Answer*, also concerned itself with trade-unionists, and was produced on January 5, 1941, at the Mecca Auditorium in New York. It portrayed a love scene, a labor-party meeting, an arrest, a fight, a fire, and the death of a union organizer. In reviewing this work Virgil Thomson found Blitzstein's musical style "pungent and deep, his dramatic sense strong, and his timing of dramatic points accurate." Much of this was due to the fact that the work's "locale is here and that its language is our own." Blitzstein further showed his talent for the theater in 1949, when he composed the score for *Regina,* the musical adaptation of Lillian Hellman's play *The Little Foxes.* This was produced on Broadway in 1949 and in 1953 it was performed in revised form at New York's City Center.

Gian-Carlo Menotti

Meanwhile in Philadelphia, under the sponsorship of the opera department of the Curtis Institute, one of the brightest and most promising of the young opera composers—Gian-Carlo Menotti (1911-   )—had his first opera produced at the Academy of Music on April 1, 1937. Born in Italy, Menotti had come to the Curtis Institute to study, and his little opera buffa, reminiscent of the great art of Rossini, was entitled *Amelia Goes to the Ball.* It was given in New York and Baltimore, and in 1938 was given a production by the Metropolitan Opera, where its success clearly demonstrated that America's lyric theater had a new talented and valuable composer. Menotti's subsequent operas will be listed and discussed in the chapter dealing with the 1940s.

Opera for the American Schools

It was Aaron Copland who recognized the possibilities of opera for production in the American schools when he composed *The Second Hurricane* especially for girls and boys from eight to eighteen. The libretto was based on a dramatic rescue during a flood, and the work had its first performance on April 21, 1937, at the Henry Street Music School in New York, with Lehman Engel conducting. Another highly successful work, written especially for school and amateur performance, was the "folk opera" by Kurt Weill (1900-1950), *Down in the Valley*, first performed at Indiana University on July 5, 1948. It was as simple and natural as the music of Stephen Foster, and just as American, although the composer was German-born. Weill had arrived in America in 1935, later became a citizen, and until his untimely death in 1950, he was to be one of the best and strongest writers for America's ever-growing light musical theater. He played a major part in the amazing growth and maturing of America's musical comedies.

Walter Damrosch

Our record of opera would not be complete without the mention of Walter Damrosch's *The Man Without a Country*, based on Edward Everett Hale's popular story. Damrosch (1862-1950) was seventy-five when he conducted its première at the Metropolitan Opera House on May 2, 1937, the grand old man of American music. This was followed in November, 1942, by *The Opera Cloak*, performed by the New York Opera Company. Both were old-fashioned, conventional operas (as were his earlier *The Scarlet Letter* and *Cyrano de Bergerac*) written in the style of a bygone day, but they indicated the interest of American composers, regardless of age, in the lyric theater.

RUMBLINGS IN EUROPE

In Europe there were ominous rumblings, which America, desperately trying to pull out of the depression, hoped would blow over. Hitler's influence was growing in Germany, and his followers were staging demonstrations whenever they disapproved of something out of the ordinary. As early as 1930, stink bombs were thrown at the Frankfort Opera House, as the Nazis vented their wrath against Kurt Weill for what they called his "immoral" opera, *Mahagonny*. Weill had used the American jazz idiom in this opera, a satire whose scene was laid in Alabama and whose story exposed the corrupt practices of evil and hypocritical men. There can be no doubt that it influenced Blitzstein's later operas of social injustice. But the Nazis did not like it, and as they marched in the succeeding months to the strains of the Hitlerite hymn, sung to new sets of words which praised the Nazis' fight for freedom, work, and bread, more bombs protested against all types of modern music, especially jazz. The situation got out of hand in Italy in May, 1931, when an enraged Fascist (aping the Hitler youths), struck Arturo Toscanini because the *maestro* refused to play the Fascist hymn at his Bologna concert. Within four days Toscanini was condemned as unpatriotic by Italian artists and musicians.

The real persecution began in Germany in 1933 when Carl Ebert, Director of Berlin's Civic Opera, and the conductor Fritz Stiedry, were dismissed from their posts by an order from Dr. Goebbels. The stated reason was that they did not meet the requirements of the Aryan section of the nationalistic statutes. Four days later "Negro jazz" broadcasts were forbidden, but the real climax came on March 16 in Leipzig, when a concert that Bruno Walter was to have conducted was canceled. The claim was that a performance by a Jew might be harmful to public morale.

American musicians immediately rallied in support of Walter, one of the world's truly great musical figures, and on April 1 protested by cable to Hitler. Germany's arrogant reply was the immediate banning of all music and performances by the men who signed the letter—Toscanini, Walter and Frank Damrosch, Koussevitzky, Bodanzky, Harold Bauer, Gabrilowitsch, Loeffler, Fritz Reiner, and Rubin Goldmark. By May, affairs were no better, and on the thirtieth, Arnold Schoenberg and Franz Schreker were dismissed from the faculty of the Prussian Academy of Arts, by the order of the German Ministry of Education. It was at this time that the leading figures of world music began to seek refuge in America, and this move on their part would once again (as it had in the past) completely change the destiny of American music. Schoenberg arrived in America in October, 1933, and joined the faculty of the Malkin Conservatory in Boston. In November, the League of

Composers honored him with a concert of his chamber music in New York.

GROWING IMPORTANCE OF RECORDED MUSIC

Another step forward in the dissemination of serious music came out of these depression years through the medium of recorded music. As various companies had begun to record the standard works in the orchestral repertory from 1927 on, Stokowski became one of the most important pioneers in this field through his endless experiments with sound, and his interest in all phases of recording and broadcasting. His records with the Philadelphia Orchestra became the best sellers of these years. Soon funds were available for gifts of records to public institutions; and Dr. Frances Elliott Clark, educational director of the Victor Company, did a magnificent job in having records made which were to be used in the public schools throughout the nation. By 1933, the Carnegie Foundation granted funds to purchase materials for music study, including record collections and phonographs. Wherever schools, colleges, and libraries were feeling the pinch of the depression this material was placed where it would do the most good. This was one of the highest functions of recorded music, because both students and musicians, as well as listeners, had the opportunity to hear the music which they could not perform, and in many cases not hear in live performances. Society sets of little-known composers were issued in 1932 in England, and thousands became acquainted for the first time with Delius; Hugo Wolf; Sibelius; Purcell; as well as with all of the sonatas of Beethoven; certain complete operas of Mozart; and many of the works of Bach. In 1936, the Gramophone Shop in New York (now no longer in existence) published the first *Encyclopedia of Recorded Music,* and newspapers began to have record columns. Great collections of inestimable value to the teacher and student were issued (most of them first recorded in Europe), such as *L'Anthologie Sonore,* edited by Curt Sachs (Parlophone-Odeon); Columbia's *History of Music by Eye and Ear* (edited by Percy Scholes); *Seven Centuries of Sacred Music* (Lumen).

The time was surely ripe for one of the most interesting educational movements in the history of music—that of training the layman or listener.

THE LISTENER'S MUSIC COURSES CREATED BY
OLGA SAMAROFF STOKOWSKI

If Olga Samaroff Stokowski had done nothing else (she had already won world recognition as a pianist, teacher, and critic), she would go down in musical history as one of the great educators of the twentieth century. Through her work with the talented young musicians who came to New York, she soon realized that the future of good music in America demanded the creation of larger and more intelligent audiences. Many appreciation courses had sprung up all over the country in the first flush of radio, yet many of them failed because they tried to pin a story on, or "explain" every bit of music heard. In many instances, especially in the schools, literally anyone taught music appreciation, and too often fixed opinions were forced upon the unwary layman, based on the likes or dislikes (or the ignorance) of the person in charge. Walter Damrosch had been doing a superlative job for the children through his radio broadcasts, but Samaroff knew that she must reach the older members of America's new and vast audience—persons who had once learned to play or sing, or the countless thousands who sincerely loved music, but had no way of learning "what made the wheels go round." As a critic in New York, she discovered that at some time or another everyone is a listener, even the trained musician, once he is outside his own particular field.

Samaroff soon realized that listening to music could be made an active and not a passive experience, and the layman could be trained just as much as a composer or performer. Experimenting with members of New York's Junior League, of which Mrs. Theodore Steinway was president, a course was designed that was entertaining, but did not shun technicalities, and taught fundamentals as it went along. At first both the musicians and the public were dubious, for a veritable cult still existed which insisted that America was not a musical nation, and the only way to enjoy music was to make it oneself. For years poor amateur performances were countenanced by persons who would not have dreamed of reading editions of the classics filled with misspelled words.

With the advent of radio, and the improvement of recorded music, when the finest music might be had in the remotest sections of the nation and children were growing up to the strains of Brahms or

Verdi, America as a nation began to be truly music-conscious for the first time. The phonograph was already doing for America's music what printing had done for language. The laymen in Samaroff's first classes began to learn their themes as thoroughly as they knew their favorite literary characters, and soon discovered what a new and rich musical life was theirs for the asking. Public classes were first given at the Mannes School in New York, through the belief and enthusiasm of Clara and David Mannes. A wide selection of slides gave a visual impression of certain basic forms and types, which greatly aided the layman. It was pointed out that the technique of the listener lay in his power to recognize, and to that was added the necessary background of information (with simple ear-training) that enabled him to listen intelligently to music in the concert hall or over the radio. The phonograph became his practice instrument, and many used the easier classic scores as they listened to records.

The courses grew so rapidly that they were moved to New York's Town Hall, where Samaroff conducted them, assisted by her talented students, until her death in 1948. The Juilliard Graduate School, realizing their value, engaged Mme. Samaroff to train students as teachers so that the work might be carried back to the students' home communities. In a very short time courses were being given in Philadelphia, Washington, and Baltimore, with Harriett D. Johnson (now music critic of the *New York Post*) as artistic director. She, with many other inspired young teachers, carried this new idea—along with Samaroff—all over the country, giving courses in private schools and colleges, with summer sessions in the Middle West and on the West Coast. Robert Lawrence, Rosalyn Tureck, Francis Madeira, Helena Zurstadt, and George Kent Bellows were among the first artist-teachers who had their share in this new phase of music education. The Peabody Conservatory of Music in Baltimore still continues to give the original Listener's Courses under Mr. Bellows, one of which has been designed for the students in the school music department—a workshop which trains them for future public school teaching. Thus Olga Samaroff Stokowski (American-born Lucy Hickenlooper and the first American woman to gain entrance into the famed Paris Conservatoire) became a unique educator, worthy of carrying on the traditions Lowell Mason had started a century before. In giving confidence to the American listener, she had her share in creating better audiences, on which the performer and the composer must perforce depend. Mme. Samaroff's death in 1948 removed a great figure from contemporary musical life, but the results of her work and her many talented students who are still performing bear witness to her stature as an artist and a teacher.

FEDERAL MUSIC PROJECT OF THE WPA

One of the most important projects of the 1930s was that of the Federal Music Project of the Works Progress Administration (WPA). This was created by the United States government under President Franklin Delano Roosevelt and was established on August 1, 1935, as a branch of the Emergency Relief Bureau, as a need growing out of the financial crash with its subsequent depression. It was aimed to preserve the skill of unemployed musicians who were on relief. Unemployment was at its height and the arts were hit the hardest. Nikolai Sokoloff was appointed national director of the music section of the WPA, with Ellen S. Woodward the administrator. Designed as a relief measure "to avoid the necessity for specially trained musicians taking manual assignments for which they were unfitted," the music project had given employment to over 10,000 persons by the end of the 1930s. The program was designed "to give such cultural values to communities that a new interest in music would be engendered and the audience base expanded." Programs and performances were planned for schools, hospitals, and various tax-supported institutions. Men were placed in bands, orchestras, and even in dance bands, as well as in choral and opera units, throughout forty-three states and the District of Columbia. In every community sponsors met part of the expense, either in money or materials, and among the backers were the great universities like Harvard and Columbia, as well as the large state universities. City and county boards were joined by schools and boards of education, and the National Federation of Music Clubs. Parks and recreation boards, musical unions, and chambers of commerce, all had their share in the work. American composers were encouraged, so that by 1938, nearly six thousand compositions by some fifteen hundred composers had been performed. Lending libraries were established, folk songs were collected, and tests of the therapeutic value of music were made in hospitals and corrective institutions. Instruction was given in the rural areas as well as in the congested cities. The WPA was yet another expression of American ingenuity in time of stress and need. As the second World War drew near, the project had already served its purpose and further activities were suspended in 1941.

AMERICAN COMPOSERS IN THE 1930s

As the caldron of war slowly came to a boil in Europe the situation in Germany and Italy grew more tense. Non-Aryans were not allowed to be employed by any German orchestras. Wilhelm Furtwaengler resigned his various musical and political posts on December 4, 1934, over the banning of Hindemith's music, but was reinstated on April 25, 1935. Italy retaliated against the stern criticism of her Ethiopian conquest by forbidding the music of all nations who dared to raise their voices against her actions.

In America the times never seemed better and her composers were busy with commissions, especially in the field of radio, now at its peak. It was this decade of the 1930s that saw the emergence of a young American school of composers, men who were intelligent and imaginative, fine craftsmen, yet blessed with American independence, unafraid of expressing themselves in whatever style and form that suited their purpose. The 1920s had promised American music of stature and competence; the 1930s saw the beginning of fulfillment.

There was also a subtle change in attitude of native composers, whether working at home or abroad. Residence in Europe and foreign travel, exposure to all types of music, were enabling the young American composer to grow and deepen with amazing rapidity, and many were already international figures. From the disillusionment of the first depression years there had come a mighty challenge when President Roosevelt told his fellow Americans that "we need not be frustrated by our misfortunes but could be masters of our future." All branches of the arts responded to the spirit of the man who had risen above his own handicap, and with the superb work of the WPA project in the succeeding years the musicians had the will to fight their way out of the morass of the depression.

When Roger Sessions had returned from Europe in 1933, he and his contemporaries had warned American composers that they could no longer remain isolationists, but must keep abreast of all musical trends and movements, especially in the field of music education and the growing musical public. Aaron Copland also repeatedly pointed out that the radio and phonograph were creating intelligent audiences and the composer of tomorrow must continually keep this in mind. "It makes no sense," he said, ". . . to continue writing as if they did not exist." Thus was to come, in the years before the second World War, an era of functional music, written for both old and new mediums.

Of the many fine composers who were writing during these years, and whose works were being heard both here and abroad, it is only possible to choose certain ones—those who most clearly exemplify the trends of the period or who most contributed, at that time, to the slow but definite maturing of America as a musical nation. The restless years, the experimental years, which had brought such changes to all the arts since the end of World War I, seemed over, and a new era was ushered in. Many of the composers remained conservative and traditional in their writing; others had predilections for musical Americana, getting their inspiration from the vivid pages of America's history or reflecting the accelerated tempo of contemporary life. A third group, some of whom might well fit into either category, refused to be held down and were therefore eclectics, choosing freely from various systems and divergent sources that which best suited them.

NATIONALISTS

As the nationalist composer began to become a significant figure and was recognized per se both at home and abroad through performances of his works in important musical centers, it will be well to start with those whose music was not only distinctively American, but whose very melodies and rhythms had their roots deep in the vast body of American folk music. The resources of this music, ignored for the most part for so long by those whose backgrounds were steeped in the European tradition, were just beginning to be tapped, and there was a wealth of gold to be found for the searching. At last the true spirit of America seemed ready to break the chains of bondage and find its rightful expression in the music created by her sons.

Roy Harris

One of the most controversial figures of this decade was Roy Harris, born in Lincoln County, Oklahoma, on February 12, 1898, in a log cabin, the son of Scotch-Irish pioneering parents. Many recognized in his work a vital force, a primal, rough-hewn vitality that seemed to derive its flavor from the Middle West of his birth. Others thought his melodic line distorted and unnatural and felt that he went to unnecessary extremes to avoid the obvious. But all those who admired and those who criticized agreed that the music Roy Harris composed was genuinely American in its spirit and flavor.

Harris was twenty-four years old before he decided that he wished to compose, but once his decision was made, he lost no time in going to Los Angeles to work with Arthur Farwell in harmony and with Modest Altschuler in orchestration. A tireless worker, Harris wasted little time on short pieces, but turned almost at once to the larger forms. His *Andante for Orchestra* was not only successful, but so impressed his teachers that they brought it to the attention of Howard Hanson at the Eastman School in Rochester, and Hanson conducted the première in the spring of 1926. It was then that Harris decided to go to Paris and study with Nadia Boulanger, who was having such success with her young American students.

It is clear that several of Harris' works entitle him to a high place among American composers even though many feel that the promise of his early pieces has not been fulfilled. His Piano Sonata (1928), composed in Paris while he was a member of the Boulanger group, is gaunt and homely, and its racy scherzo movement, with a theme that is reminiscent of *Turkey in the Straw,* is vivacious and decidedly American. A broken spine necessitated Harris' return to the United States for a major operation and weeks of convalescence. He then returned to Paris for another period of study, and when he finally returned to New York, Harris found that he was a firmly established composer. Enthusiastic praise sounded from all sides, and even his former teacher, Farwell, went so far as to open his article on Harris in the *Musical Quarterly* (January, 1932) with: "Gentlemen, a genius—but keep your hats on!" Despite the dissenting voices, Harris' success as a composer seemed definitely assured when his First Symphony (1933) was given its première by Koussevitzky and the Boston Symphony on January 26, 1934. But it was his Third Symphony, also introduced by the Boston Symphony (1939), that has been Harris' most consistently played work. When Toscanini and the NBC Symphony played it in 1940 Francis Perkins wrote in the *New York Herald Tribune* that it was "one of the most significant contributions of the last few years to the native orchestral repertoire, in breadth and scope, consequentiality of ideas and emotional force."

In addition to his prolific composing Harris has been active not only as a teacher of talented young composers but as an organizer of cultural events and of movements to benefit his fellow composers. He has enjoyed fellowships and grants-in-residence from the Pasadena (California) Music and Arts Association; he has been a faculty member of the Westminster Choir School in Princeton, composer-in-residence at Cornell University, Colorado College, and at the Pennsylvania College for Women in Pittsburgh. In November of 1952 he organized the first Pittsburgh International Contemporary Music Festival which presented ten concerts of music by composers from all over the world.

Harris' list of compositions is much too long to give in full. It includes seven symphonies, two of which have distinguishing titles —No. 4, the *Folk Song Symphony* (1939) and No. 7, the *Cumberland Symphony* (1951), so-called because it is derived in part from Harris' *Cumberland Concerto*. There is also a *Symphony for Band*, composed for the West Point Band, which played it at the International Festival in 1952 at Pittsburgh. In his overture *When Johnny Comes Marching Home* (1934), Harris uses the tune of *When Johnny Comes Marching Home* in a way that makes it seem to germinate its own treatment and development. Among the other symphonic works are *Farewell to Pioneers* (1935); *Time Suite* (1937), commissioned by CBS for their 1937 summer radio programs; *March in Time of War* (1943); a Concerto for two pianos and orchestra (1946); a Violin Concerto (1948-49); and *Kentucky Spring*, a scherzo (1949). He has written three string quartets and a Piano Quintet (1936), one of his finest scores. There is also a long list of choral works, piano music and songs.

Harris' style may be found in his long, flowing melodies, dynamic rhythmic patterns, richly textured harmonies, and fine contrapuntal writing. There is a challenge in what he has to say, an enthusiastic vitality which stems from the man himself. Like it or not, no one can deny the honest sincerity that is the essence of Harris' music. He has succeeded in vividly expressing the greatness and strength, the vastness of his country, America.

There are, however, several reservations that must be made in praising the work of Roy Harris. He is often repetitious, with persistent reiteration of rhythmic and melodic figuration akin to that of the Russian, Shostakovich. And, like Shostakovich, Harris is often his self-interpreter in explaining the inner meanings of his music—as in his *Symphony 1933*, in which the first movement, to quote the composer, attempts "to capture the mood of adventure and physical exuberance," the second movement "the pathos which seems to underlie all human existence," and the third "the mood of a positive will to power and action."

Furthermore, in spite of Harris' aggressiveness and resourcefulness in obtaining first performances of his works from major organizations, there are not as many repeat performances of the majority of his compositions as are given to those of a number of his colleagues. At the present moment (1957) the Third Symphony and one or two other pieces are the only Harris works from the past which have become part of the orchestral repertoire. Writing of the Third Symphony after a New York performance in 1957 (by the Philharmonic-Symphony) Paul Henry Lang remarked in the *Herald Tribune*: "If Mr. Harris had only continued in this vein instead of attempting to naturalize a native-born American, he would have retained the freshness as well as the individuality of his gifts; only good and unselfconscious composition is needed to produce genuine American music."

Douglas Moore

Among the composers who came into prominence during the depression years there are others who may be classed as nationalists. One of them, Douglas Moore, derives his inspiration from American literature and legend. Born at Cutchogue, Long Island, on August 10, 1893, Moore was educated at Hotchkiss School and at Yale University, where he studied music with Horatio Parker and David Stanley Smith. After service in the navy Moore went to Paris, where he worked with Vincent d'Indy and finally with Nadia Boulanger.

Later, when he became Curator of Music at the Cleveland Museum of Art, he studied with Ernest Bloch.

It was while he was in Cleveland, in 1922, that Moore composed an orchestral work, *Four Museum Pieces* (originally written for organ), first performed in 1923. Here, too, Moore first met the poet Vachel Lindsay, who was to open up to Moore new vistas of America's past and kindle his interest in the colorful pages of her history. Moore's next score, and the first based on a truly American subject, was *The Pageant of P. T. Barnum,* introduced in 1924 by the Cleveland Orchestra and later widely played throughout the nation and abroad. Its five movements depict various episodes and figures in Barnum's career and the music reflected the era of the country fiddle, the brass band, and rank sentimentality. First, *Boyhood at Bethel*—country dances, parades, and church hymns. Next, *Joice Heth* (the one-hundred-and-sixty-one-year-old Negro woman who was Barnum's first exhibit), followed by *General and Mrs. Tom Thumb,* a picture of the midgets. The last two movements were *Jenny Lind* and *Circus Parade.* In 1928, Moore produced a symphonic poem, *Moby Dick* (based on the Melville novel), and in 1931 his *Overture on an American Tune* (originally named after the source of its inspiration—Sinclair Lewis' *Babbitt*). Other works in the American vein included *Village Music* (1942), *In Memoriam* (1944), and *A Farm Journal* (1947).

The programmatic "Barnum" suite and the "folk opera" *The Devil and Daniel Webster,* first produced in 1939, would be sufficient to give Moore a high place among American composers. The libretto of the opera is the story by Stephen Vincent Benét which tells of the New England farmer who sold his soul to the Devil in return for material prosperity. When the Devil claims his payment during the farmer's wedding festivities, Daniel Webster wins with his oratory a verdict in favor of the farmer from a jury composed of famous scoundrels summoned from Hades by the Devil. The opera is splendidly integrated and has enjoyed numerous productions since it was first produced. In the summer of 1953 it was given nightly performances from July 18 to August 30, in an open-air theater at Sturbridge, Massachusetts. Other stage works include an earlier opera, *White Wings* (1935) to a libretto by Philip Barry; *Giants in the Earth,* using a libretto by Arnold Sungaard (based on a novel by O. E. Rolvaag), produced at Columbia University in the spring of 1951 and winning the Pulitzer Prize in Music that same year. Moore's most recent opera, *The Ballad of Baby Doe*, had its world première on July 7, 1956, at the Central City (Colorado) Opera Festival. For schools Moore has composed an operetta, *The Headless Horseman* (1936), with a libretto by Benét. He has also written incidental music for productions of *Twelfth Night* (1925), *Much Ado About Nothing* (1927), and Robert Sherwood's *The Road to Rome* (1927).

Moore has composed two symphonies, the first, *A Symphony of Autumn* in 1930 and the second in 1945. There are two orchestral suites, drawn from scores he composed for documentary films— *Power and the Land* (1940-41) and *Youth Gets a Break* (1940-41).

Moore's chamber music is traditionally written, distinguished, and individual. It includes a Sonata for violin and piano (1929); string quartets; two quintets—one for winds and the other for clarinet and strings; and *Down East Suite* (1944), for violin and piano.

In 1926 Moore joined the music faculty at Columbia University and in 1940 succeeded Daniel Gregory Mason as head of the Music Department.

William Grant Still

One of America's leading Negro composers, William Grant Still, has been highly successful in drawing upon the themes and the shifting moods of the music of his race. He started his career as an arranger of popular music for W. C. Handy, Paul Whiteman, Don Voorhees, and for such musical shows as Earl Carroll's *Vanities, Rain or Shine,* and the unforgettable *Shuffle Along.* Born in Woodville, Mississippi, on May 11, 1895, Still studied at Wilberforce University and Oberlin College, and later worked with Chadwick at the New England Conservatory of Music. After a stint in the navy, he continued to study composition, this time with Edgar Varèse in New York.

About 1925, Still decided to devote himself to the development of the Negro idiom and the treatment of Negro subjects in his programmatic works, which drew their inspiration from the folk music of his people. Three of his larger works form a trilogy: *Africa,* the *Afro-American Symphony,* and the Symphony in G Minor. *Africa* has been revised no less than five times, the first version appearing in 1930 and the sixth in 1935. After years of arranging and playing in night-club orchestras, it was not until his second major work, the *Afro-American Symphony,* was heard in 1930 that Still began to attract attention as a composer. The symphony was widely performed in the United States and Europe, and has proved the most enduring of the trilogy. A later work, Symphony in G Minor, was introduced by the Philadelphia Orchestra under Leopold Stokowski in 1937.

In 1935, Still became associated with radio as an arranger and director of programs for the Columbia and Mutual networks. From this period comes *Kaintuck* (1935), for piano and orchestra (commissioned by the League of Composers); and *Lenox Avenue,* commissioned in 1937 by CBS for its summer programs. Hans Lange conducted the broadcast première of *Lenox Avenue,* which paints a vivid picture of New York's Harlem.

One of Still's most arresting scores, *And They Lynched Him on a Tree,* for two choruses, contralto solo, and orchestra, based on a text by Katherine Garrison Chapin, was presented in 1940 by the New York Philharmonic-Symphony at its summer Stadium concerts. Another poem by the same author was used for *Plain Chant for America,* scored for baritone and orchestra, and introduced in 1941. In 1944, the New York Philharmonic-Symphony gave first performances of *In Memoriam* and *Old California;* and the Cleveland Orchestra gave the première of Still's *Poem for Orchestra,* based on a poem by Verna Arvey, the composer's wife.

Still has composed several works for the stage, including three ballets—*La Guiablesse* (1927); *Sahdji* (1930); and the rewritten radio piece, *Lenox Avenue;* as well as two operas, *Blue Steel* (1935) and *Troubled Island* (1938). The last was produced at the New York City Center on March 31, 1949. The libretto, with its setting in Haiti, was by the well-known Negro poet, Langston Hughes.

ECLECTICS

Roger Sessions

Of the many eclectic composers of this decade, there was no more impressive figure than Roger Sessions. A serious and uncompromising composer, dedicated to the cause of furthering American music, Sessions has consistently been one of the *avant-garde,* which possibly explains why some of his works have not been as popular as those of his contemporaries. Born in Brooklyn, New York, on December 28, 1896, Sessions came from a long line of New England ancestors. He was graduated from Harvard in 1915, and for two years studied under Horatio Parker at Yale. He joined the faculty of Smith College (1917-21), but went on to Cleveland with Ernest Bloch, with whom he was studying and who wanted him as his assistant at the Cleveland Institute of Music. When Bloch resigned in 1925, Sessions also left, and spent the next eight years in Europe on various fellowships awarded him by the Guggenheim Foundation, the American Academy in Rome, and the Carnegie Foundation. His residence in Florence and Rome, as well as Berlin, and his visits to France, Austria, and England, brought him in close touch with the music, the artistic life, and traditions of many foreign nations, all of which sharpened his natural eclectic tendencies.

When Sessions' Second Symphony was played by the New York Philharmonic-Symphony in 1950, Cecil Smith remarked in *Musical America* that "it would not be wrong, though it would be glib, to say that the symphony begins with Schoenberg (or, closer, Alban Berg) and ends with Stravinsky." In the course of his review, however, Mr. Smith gave it as his opinion that it was "one of the best symphonies any American has yet written." He also pointed out that the work was not heard in New York until it had already been played in San Francisco (1947), and Amsterdam. Similarly, Sessions' First Symphony, composed in 1926-27, was not heard in New York until it was played by the Juilliard School Orchestra in 1949. Mr. Smith's further remarks on the Second Symphony aptly sum up the way Sessions has always approached composition. "One feels," writes Mr. Smith, "that every measure is just as Mr. Sessions wanted it, and that he refrained from offering it for performance until he was sure it had assumed its whole form." This high standard of self-criticism no doubt accounts for the relatively short list of Sessions' works. It was obvious from the first, and caused Paul Rosenfeld to write that Sessions might become an "American Brahms," if properly developed. Of the First Symphony he wrote: "The material is stark and the outline strong."

The most widely played of Sessions' works is his orchestral suite from *The Black Maskers,* originally written in 1923 as incidental music to a play by Leonid Andreev. In 1928 he composed another orchestral Suite, in four movements. There is also an opera, *The Trial of Lucullus*, first performed at the University of California (1947); a Violin Concerto (composed 1931-35); two string quartets (1936, 1951); two piano sonatas (1930, 1946); and three Chorale Preludes for organ, written in Florence in 1924-26. After the Second Symphony (which won the Naumburg Award in 1949 and the New York Music Critics Circle Award in 1950) Sessions composed a Third Symphony (1948). He has also written two important books: *The Musical Experience of Composer, Performer, Listener* (1950), and *Harmonic Practice* (1951).

While on a visit to Paris, Sessions met Aaron Copland in the studio of Nadia Boulanger, and from this encounter came the Copland-Sessions Concerts, given in New York City from 1928 to 1931, which featured primarily the works of young (and often unknown) American composers. Presenting two programs a year in various halls and theaters, with more American works than European being represented, this unique series was of the greatest possible value to the cause of contemporary American music. Although Sessions returned to America to help launch the series, the concerts ultimately had to be abandoned because Sessions felt he should still remain abroad. As president of the International Society for Contemporary Music (and in fact throughout his career), Sessions has done much to advance the interests of his colleagues both in America and Europe. After years of teaching in New York, at Princeton University, and at the University of California, Sessions is a member of the music department at Princeton.

Virgil Thomson

Virgil Thomson was easily one of the most controversial American composers of the 1930s. That his music delighted many while it enraged others was, in the words of Peggy Glanville-Hicks (*Musical Quarterly*, April, 1949), "not because of its idiom, which is simple, direct, and free of innovation, but because of its content. . . ." Although Thomson might easily be called a nationalist composer because he has consistently drawn on the hymns and revival songs that were a part of his Midwestern background, it was the liberating atmosphere of Paris in the 1920s that freed his creative spirit from any provincialism, sharpened his judgment, and stimulated his excellent mind.

Thomson was born in Kansas City, Missouri, on November 25, 1896, and lived there until 1917, when he gave up his position as organist and choir-director to enlist in the United States Army. Out of the service in 1919, Thomson entered Harvard University, studying with Edward Burlingame Hill and Archibald Davison. Interrupting his studies at Harvard to go to Paris to work with Nadia Boulanger in 1921, Thomson returned to Harvard to graduate in 1922 and become a member of the music faculty. During the three years he lived in Boston, he was also organist at King's Chapel and conducted the chapel choir. But the call of Paris was too strong, and in 1925 Thomson returned to the city he loved so deeply, where he was to remain for most of the time until 1940, when the Germans arrived.

Paris, in these years, had become the musical center of Europe, and her cafés, studios, and salons were the gathering places for many of the important writers, poets, artists, and musicians of the day. Here Thomson felt the influence of Erik Satie, and came to know the group of young composers who had followed Satie. They had banded themselves together as *Les Six* and included Georges Auric, Arthur Honegger, Darius Milhaud, and Francis Poulenc. Thomson worked through the dissonant modernism of the period, observed the delight of composers like Honegger and Milhaud in American jazz, whose idioms they used, and himself followed the neoclassic tendencies of the day. His first mature piece was his *Sonata da Chiesa* (1926), whose three movements, patterned after the old church sonatas and calling for clarinet, trumpet, viola, horn, and trombone, were: Chorale, Tango, and Fugue. The insertion of a tango in what purported to be a traditional church sonata shows how Thomson had come under influence of Dadaism, a movement that debunked the older forms, all artifice and pompous devices, and allowed all styles and forms to be moved about and intermingled freely. But although Thomson's eclectic tendencies were being conditioned by all he saw and heard in Paris, his rich background of American hymnody came to the front when he essayed his next important work, *Symphony on a Hymn Tune* (1928). Using for his two themes the old hymns *How firm a foundation ye Saints of the Lord* and *Yes, Jesus Loves Me,* employing a meticulous sense of form and expert craftsmanship, Thomson not only showed his delightful wit, but nostalgically recalled his home and country.

It was at this time that Thomson completed the score of his opera *Four Saints in Three Acts* (1928), which we have already discussed, and which, when it was performed in America in 1934, established Thomson as a controversial composer.

Thomson has described himself as a neoromanticist, and it was in his two string quartets, written in Paris in 1931-32, that he turned his back on the "modern music" that as he has pointed out in his many lectures, had been "obligatory for all right-thinking young men." He was aware that music had reached a one-hundred-percent dissonant saturation point, a stone wall, and for him there was nothing to do but to go backward. Thus, the string quartets were in their own way a revolt on his part and are marked by an over-deliberate use of personal sentiment as their chief element. He did all of the things in writing them that were not supposed to be done in those days, but their bland sounds were a part of their truth-telling and they give a clue to just how far the composer was a reactionary. Originally written to develop his skill in writing for strings (much of the orchestral music of the day had turned from strings to winds and percussion instruments), their style and content were the antithesis of the abnormal psychological state which had been rampant in all the arts.

Like Copland, Thomson has used the music he has written for motion pictures as concert pieces—scores for the documentary films *The Plough That Broke the Plains* (1936), *The River* (1937), and *Louisiana Story* (1948). In these Thomson is at his best, powerfully objective, and the scores are masterly in their shifting moods and orchestral colors. He has also composed incidental music for productions of *Hamlet* (1936), *Antony and Cleopatra* (1937), and *Oidipous Tyrannos* (1941).

Other orchestral pieces are a Second Symphony (1931); *Twelve Portraits* (1937-1944); three landscape pieces—*The Seine at Night* (1947), *Wheat Field at Noon* (1948), and *Sea Piece with Birds* (1952); and a concerto for cello and orchestra (1950). His chamber music includes a Violin Sonata (1930), a *Serenade* for flute and violin (1931), a Sonata for flute alone (1943), *Stabat Mater,* for soprano and string quartet (1931). For organ he has written *Passacaglia* (1922), four sets of *Variations and Fugues on Sunday School Tunes*

(1926-27), and *Wedding Music* (1940). There are also many choral works, songs, and piano works, including four sonatas (1929-1940); two sets of Etudes (1943-44; 1940-51); and over a hundred *Portraits*, which he composed from life as the subject posed for him (1929-1951).

Thomson is also one of our most gifted writers on music and from 1940 to 1954, he was music critic of the *New York Herald Tribune*, succeeding Lawrence Gilman. His books include: *The State of Music* (1939), *The Musical Scene* (1945), *The Art of Judging Music* (1948), and *Music Right and Left* (1951).

Randall Thompson

Randall Thompson (1899-   ), now Professor of Music at Harvard University, is yet another excellent example of the eclecticism of the younger composers of the late 1920s and early 1930s. He has drawn freely from the past, experimented with jazz and folk music, yet his idiom is personal and constantly forward looking. A native of New York City, Thompson was graduated from Harvard in 1920 and received a master's degree two years later. He studied music under Walter Spalding and Edward Burlingame Hill at Harvard, and later worked with Ernest Bloch. From 1922 to 1925 he was a Fellow of the American Academy in Rome, and in 1929 and 1930 he was granted a Guggenheim Fellowship. It was while he was in Rome that a number of his early works were performed: the orchestral prelude *Pierrot and Cothurnus* (1922); *The Piper at the Gates of Dawn*, tone poem (1924); *The Wind in the Willows*, string quartet (1924); Piano Sonata (1923); and Suite for piano (1924). After his return to America Thompson's *Jazz Poem* for piano and orchestra was performed at the American Composers Concerts in Rochester in 1928, and in 1930 the same group played his First Symphony. But it was the performance of Thompson's Second Symphony (again in Rochester) in 1932 that established him as one of the nation's finest composers. When it was first played in New York in 1933, Lawrence Gilman remarked in the *Herald Tribune* that Thompson "has not been afraid to sound quite different from Schoenberg. His music has humor, and warmth and pleasantness; many will find it agreeable and solacing." The work is highly rhythmic, but Thompson has not used the obvious percussion devices in producing and emphasizing his rhythms. The music itself is intrinsically rhythmic, and rather than utilizing a modern battery of percussion, the score contents itself with cymbals and timpani. Thompson's Third Symphony was composed a number of years later and had its first performance by the CBS Orchestra at Columbia University's 1949 Music Festival.

Thompson is particularly felicitous as a composer of major choral works. Perhaps the most important is *The Peaceable Kingdom,* for mixed voices *a cappella* (1936), commissioned by the League of Composers. It is subtitled "A Sequence of Sacred Choruses—Text from Isaiah." The words are drawn verbatim from the Bible and the opposed choirs of the double chorus are used to carry out the dual idea suggested to the composer by *The Peaceable Kingdom,* a painting by the eighteenth-century American artist Edward Hicks. Satire is often the basis for Thompson's choral music, as in *Americana* (1932), which uses as a text excerpts from Henry L. Mencken's department in the old *American Mercury.* One of Thompson's most popular choral works is the *Alleluia* (1940), for mixed voices *a cappella.* His *Testament of Freedom,* for men's voices with piano or orchestra, was sung first by the University of Virginia Glee Club on April 13, 1943, for the two-hundredth anniversary of Thomas Jefferson's birth.

An opera commissioned in 1942 by the Columbia Broadcasting System in association with the League of Composers, *Solomon and Balkis,* had its première over the air on March 29, 1942, Howard Barlow conducting. It was given a stage production at Harvard University on April 14.

In 1941, Thompson, with Benjamin Britten and Alexandre Tansman, was awarded one of the three Coolidge Medals given for distinguished service to chamber music. This was when the First String Quartet in D Minor was performed in Washington, October 30, 1941.

Herbert Elwell

Herbert Elwell (1898-   ), now resident in Cleveland where he is music critic for the *Cleveland Plain Dealer,* first came into prominence with the orchestral suite he arranged from his ballet, *The Happy Hypocrite* (1925), for which he won the Eastman Publication Award. Born in Minneapolis, he received a fellowship from the American Academy in Rome (1926) and studied composition with

Ernest Bloch and Nadia Boulanger. His more recent works include *Introduction and Allegro* (1941); *Ode* (1952); and *The Forever Young* (1954)—all for orchestra; *Lincoln,* cantata for baritone, chorus and orchestra (1945); *Requiem Aeternam,* for chorus and orchestra (1947); *Pastorale,* for voice and orchestra (1948). There is considerable chamber music, including *Blue Symphony* (1943), for medium voice and string quartet; and songs and piano pieces. For many years Elwell taught at the Cleveland Institute of Music, and one of his most promising pupils was the young Negro composer, Howard Swanson, who will be discussed in a later chapter.

Mary Howe and Marion Bauer

Two important women composers belong to this group of eclectic composers—Mary Howe (1882-   ) and Marion Bauer (1887-1955). Mrs. Howe, a native of Richmond, Virginia, but for many years a resident of Washington, D.C., has composed numerous works including: *Dirge* (1931), *Sand* (1932), *Spring Pastoral* (1936), *Potomac* (1940), and *Whimsy.* Her recorded works include *Suite* (1923) for piano and strings, *Interlude* for flute and piano, and *Three Pieces after Emily Dickinson* (1941) for string quartet. Marion Bauer, born in Walla Walla, Washington, led an active life as a teacher, critic, and author of books on music. Her interest in Americana may be seen from the wide variety of titles she gave to her works, such as *A Lament on African Themes* (1928), for chamber orchestra; *Sun Splendor* (1936) and *Indian Pipes* (1929), for orchestra; a piano concerto, *American Youth* (1943); *Lobster Quadrille,* for chorus. Her large list of chamber works includes the *Fantasia Quasi una Sonata* (1928), for violin and piano; a Sonata for viola or clarinet (1935); and a Concertino, for oboe, clarinet, and string quartet (1929-43).

TRADITIONALISTS

Walter Piston: Twentieth-Century Classicist

That several composers of the 1930s have been grouped together and called traditionalists, does not imply that they were either unaware or withdrawn from the contemporary musical scene, but rather that their interest has been in such classic forms as the sonata and symphony, which they produced with all the care of the skilled artisans and expert craftsmen of an earlier century. Nor must it be assumed that the traditionalist composers in the years before World War II were isolated figures living in their own little ivory towers, for they were not. They were completely aware of every changing trend and movement, and freely exposed themselves to all styles and "isms," yet each charted his own course and was content to work within the larger forms of the earlier European masters.

Walter Piston is just such a composer, a writer of skill and imagination, one who has been happiest in the quiet atmosphere of a great university. Born in Rockland, Maine, on January 20, 1894, Piston studied painting before he decided to make music his career. After graduation from the Massachusetts Normal Art School in 1916 and enlistment in the navy as a musician, he entered Harvard University (where Virgil Thomson was a fellow-student) and was graduated with honors in all the music courses in 1924. He then went to Paris for two years and became a pupil of Nadia Boulanger, where he was soon immersed in all the music the French capital had to offer in those years. Upon his return to America he joined the Harvard music faculty and eventually succeeded Edward Burlingame Hill as chairman of the music department. It was here that Piston made one of his greatest contributions to twentieth-century music education. As a progressive teacher Piston was fully aware of the impact of contemporary music as well as the revival of interest in the music and instruments of earlier periods. In revising the university's courses in harmony and counterpoint in keeping with the tremendous developments music had made in the twentieth century, he produced three important textbooks: *Principles of Harmonic Analysis* (1933), *Harmony* (1941, rev. 1948), and *Counterpoint* (1947).

The materials to be found in Piston's music are the sum total of all that contemporary music had to offer, assimilated by him in his own fashion quite impartially. He naturally had a predilection for the culture of France, but at the same time his rhythms clearly showed that he knew thoroughly his native jazz. Because of his concern with form and the formality of his style, some have felt that Piston's music lacks emotion, but in some of his later works, such as the Second Symphony (1943), the melodies are more expansive and romantic in mood. Virgil Thomson wrote in the *New York Herald Tribune* that the Second Symphony was "a little thin of substance," the thinness resulting from Piston's academic method of composition, "in which formalities about workmanship, rather than the immediacies of personal feeling, are the main pre-occupation."

Piston's most widely played work is his music for a ballet, *The Incredible Flutist*, which proved to be a turning point in his creative life. Written in the spring of 1938 for the Boston "Pops" Orchestra, it was performed in November of the same year by the Hans Wiener Ballet with the Providence (Rhode Island) Symphony Orchestra. It concerns the coming of a circus to a village, the circus' featured attraction being a flutist who can charm the animals with his music. Piston's list of orchestral works includes four symphonies (1937, 1943, 1947, and 1950); a *Symphonic Piece* (1927); *Prelude and Fugue* for orchestra (1934); two suites for orchestra (1929, 1948); Concerto for orchestra (1933); Concertino for piano and orchestra (a 1937 CBS radio commission); Violin Concerto (1939); and a Sinfoniette (1941). His chamber music includes three string quartets (1933, 1935, 1947); sonatas for piano (1926), flute and piano (1930), and violin and piano (1939); a Suite for oboe and piano (1931); a Trio for violin, cello, and piano (1935); Sonatina, violin and harpsichord (1945); two quintets, one for flute and string quartet (1942), the other for piano and strings (1949); *Prelude and Allegro* for piano and strings (1934); *Divertimento* for nine instruments (1946); *Partita* for violin, viola, and organ (1944); and Duo for viola and cello (1949).

Samuel Barber: Neoromanticist

Samuel Barber's career is an excellent example of just how far the native American composer had come by the late 1930s. Not only was he one of the most widely played of any of the composers who were writing at the time, but he twice won the Bearns Prize from Columbia University, as well as the Pulitzer Scholarship in 1935 and again in 1936. Thus he was the first composer to receive this honor in two successive years. But that was not all, he had the added distinction of having two of his works—the *Adagio for Strings* (1936) and *Essay for Orchestra* (1937)—selected by Toscanini in 1938 as the first American pieces to be played under his leadership by the NBC Symphony Orchestra. Both the *Adagio* and the *Essay* had been written while Barber was in Rome on fellowship (1935-37), as was his *Symphony in One Movement*, which was first performed in Rome by the Orchestra of the Augusteo under Bernardino Molinari.

Barber was born in West Chester, Pennsylvania, on March 9,

1910, the son of a musical mother, whose sister was the famous contralto, Louise Homer. Barber received his training at the Curtis Institute in Philadelphia, a member of the first classes when the school opened in 1924. His composition teacher was Rosario Scalero and one of his classmates was Gian-Carlo Menotti. The works of this period include *Dover Beach* for voice and string quartet (1931); the delightfully humorous Overture to *The School for Scandal* (1932), and *Music for a Scene from Shelley (Prometheus Unbound)* (1932), both for orchestra. Other works followed, all getting repeated hearings, including his *Second Essay for Orchestra* (1942) and *Capricorn Concerto* (1944). The Concerto for violin and orchestra (1939) was played first in 1941 by Albert Spalding with the Philadelphia Orchestra and by Ruth Posselt with the Boston Symphony. Vladimir Horowitz introduced Barber's Piano Sonata (1949) in 1950 and played it on tour.

From the simple elegance of his early writing, tinged with neoromanticism, Barber has, in his later works, used more dissonance and polyharmonies, which are especially apparent in his ballet suite *Medea* (1947); *Knoxville, Summer of 1915,* for soprano and orchestra (1947); the Second String Quartet (1943); as well as the Piano Sonata, in which he employed the twelve-tone technique. *Prayers of Kierkegaard,* for soloists, chorus, and orchestra, is one of his most recent works, commissioned by the Koussevitzky Foundation. Charles Munch conducted the Boston Symphony Orchestra in the work's première on December 3, 1954, and the following spring it had a resounding success in Vienna under Massimo Freccia, conductor of the Baltimore Symphony Orchestra.

Leo Sowerby

Leo Sowerby, born in Grand Rapids, Michigan, May 1, 1895, had the distinction of being the first composer to hold a fellowship in the American Academy in Rome (1921). It was while he was resident in Rome that his *Ballad of King Estmere* for two pianos and orchestra (1922) and his First String Quartet (1923) were introduced there. Not long after his return to America he was appointed organist and choir director of St. James Episcopal Church in Chicago (1927), and in recent years he has become known as one of the leading composers of anthems and organ music. He still continues to compose in all forms. Among his better-known orchestral works are

Comes Autumn Time, an overture (1916); *Irish Washerwoman* (1916) and *Money Musk* (1917), both settings of traditional tunes. The last two were inspired by his period of study with Percy Grainger, who, as we have discovered, was at that time championing the cause of the neglected folk song. There is also the suite *From the Northland* (1923); *Medieval Poem,* for organ and orchestra (1926); *Prairie,* the tone poem based on Carl Sandburg's poem (1929); as well as symphonies and concertos. Of his choral works, two of the best known are the cantatas *The Vision of Sir Launfal* (1925) and *Canticle of the Sun* (1943). The latter won for him the Pulitzer Prize in 1946. Himself a pupil of the American Conservatory of Music in Chicago, Sowerby has been a teacher there and for a number of years the head of its composition department.

Bernard Rogers

Bernard Rogers has been associated with the Eastman School of Music in Rochester since 1929 and has numbered among his pupils many of the younger generation of composers, among them David Diamond, Gardner Read, Gail Kubik, Burrill Phillips, and William Bergsma. Born in New York City on February 4, 1893, Rogers attended the Institute of Musical Art, studied with Ernest Bloch 1919-21, and, after being awarded a Guggenheim Fellowship in 1927, worked with Nadia Boulanger in Paris and Frank Bridge in England.

Rogers' music is deeply personal and at times overpowering in its emotional impact. He is traditional in his classic style and expert workmanship. From the inspiring study with such great teachers as Bloch and Boulanger, the exposure to the modern music of England and France, and his great interest in painting, Rogers gradually evolved a technique that was as individual as it was colorful. Two of his most widely performed works are the cantata *The Raising of Lazarus,* completed while he was in Paris and first presented in 1930, and *The Passion,* which was first performed in part at the Eastman Festival in 1942, and which is considered his finest work. Rogers' interest in the art and music of the Orient may be seen in his tone poem *Fuji in the Sunset Glow* (1925) and *Japanese Landscapes* (1925). Other works with a Biblical derivation are the orchestral *The Supper at Emmaus* (1937), inspired by Rembrandt's painting; a cantata *The Exodus* (1932); *Dance of Salome,* for orchestra (1938). There are also four symphonies (1925, 1928, 1936, 1945); a Dirge, *To the Fallen* (1918); an Overture, *The Faithful* (1922); *Five Fairy Tales* (1934); *Once Upon a Time*, for small orchestra (1935); *Fantasy* for flute, viola, and orchestra (1937); *Pinocchio*, for small orchestra (1950); and *The Silver World*, suite for strings and woodwinds (1950). Influenced by his avocational painting, Rogers gave his orchestral suite *Characters from Hans Christian Anderson* (1944) the subtitle "Four Drawings for Small Orchestra."

Rogers' opera *The Warrior* was produced at the Metropolitan Opera House in New York in January, 1947. Its libretto, by Norman Corwin, was based on the story of Samson and Delilah, but despite the excellent reputation of both composer and librettist, the opera was not a success. Virgil Thomson wrote in the *New York Herald Tribune:* "His music is beautiful in texture and intensely expressive in detail, but it has no continuity. . . . Structurally the score is discontinuous; and expressively it lacks sustained feeling, as does the libretto." Rogers has written two other operas, the earlier *The Marriage of Aude*, produced at the Eastman Festival in 1932, and *The Veil* (1950).

Quincy Porter

When Quincy Porter became Professor of Music at Yale University, he completed his musical cycle, for he had graduated from that illustrious university in 1919, where he had studied with Horatio Parker and David Stanley Smith. Born in New Haven, Connecticut, on February 7, 1897, Porter went to Paris, where he became a student of Vincent d'Indy. Returning to the United States, he did further work with Ernest Bloch and was awarded a Guggenheim Fellowship in 1928. He was on the faculties of the Cleveland Institute of Music and Vassar College, and went to Boston to become the Dean of the Faculty at the New England Conservatory of Music (1938) and then its director (1942). A traditional composer, Porter leans toward the composition of chamber music, having written eight string quartets (the first in 1923), besides works for other combinations. His orchestral works include *Ukrainian Suite* (1925); Suite in C Minor (1926); *Poem and Dance* (1932); *Symphony* (1934), introduced by the New York Philharmonic-Symphony in 1938; *Dance in Three-Time* (1937); *Two Dances for Radio* (1938); *Music for Strings* (1941); Concerto for viola and orchestra, played by the

CBS orchestra in 1948; *Sextet on Slavic Folk Songs* for strings (1952); and the Concerto for two pianos and orchestra, which won him the Pulitzer Prize in 1954.

MUSICIANS FROM ABROAD

As the threat of war continued to loom over Europe, many of her composers came to America and continued to compose and perform their latest works throughout the country. Paul Hindemith arrived in the spring of 1937, making his first appearance in Washington at the eighth Festival of Chamber Music given at the Library of Congress under the Elizabeth Sprague Coolidge Foundation. On a program of his own works (April 10), he played his Sonata for viola alone. In Los Angeles Ernst Toch's *Pinocchio Overture*, drawn from the children's tale, was given its first hearing by Otto Klemperer and the Los Angeles Philharmonic Orchestra, on December 10, 1936.

In New York, with Toscanini's departure in 1936, young John Barbirolli became the conductor of the Philharmonic-Symphony. Fate had other plans in store for Toscanini, already a legendary figure, for he was back in New York a year later, with a radio orchestra especially created for him. The nation had a Christmas present with the maestro's first concert (1937) as the new musical director for the NBC Symphony Orchestra. Until 1954, this titan of music would bring great pleasure to radio audiences. For the memorable opening concert, the studio audience of a thousand was given satin programs, so that Toscanini would not be disturbed by the rustling of paper.

NEW MUSIC FESTIVALS

Two new music festivals appeared in this decade. On a private estate near Saratoga Springs, New York, the first Festival of Contemporary Music was given at Yaddo. Eighteen chamber works were performed in three concerts on April 30 and May 1, 1932. In 1934, Henry Hadley originated the first Berkshire Symphonic Festival at Stockbridge, Massachusetts, conducting three concerts with an orchestra made up of members of the New York Philharmonic-Symphony. The next year three more concerts were given, this time with an orchestra drawn from the principal orchestras in the East. In 1936, the Boston Symphony Orchestra with Koussevitzky was engaged, and three concerts in August were so successful that in 1937 the Tanglewood property in Lenox and Stockbridge (given by Mrs. Andrew Hepburn and her aunt Mary Aspinwall Tappan) became the permanent home of the Festivals. A large shed to house orchestra and audience was built in 1938 (until then the Festivals had been held in a tent). By 1940, when the Berkshire Music Center was opened, the annual affairs had become one of the great festivals of America, and included a summer school which attracts thousands of music lovers, students, and an outstanding faculty.

DEVELOPMENT OF SWING

By the late 1920s and the early 1930s the highly arranged, smooth type of jazz which Paul Whiteman popularized had gained the ascendency over the original "hot" variety that was true to its folk origins. Then, in the early years of the depression hot jazz burst forth once more with renewed vigor, this time with a new name— "swing." Perhaps the most accurate definition that can be given to swing is a free style of improvisation around a given tune, generally, at least in the so-called "jam sessions," improvised by the individual performers.

Benny Goodman

It was probably Benny Goodman, who formed his own band in 1934, who did the most to popularize swing. In New York, high school students gathered by the thousands to hear him when he played in movie theaters. These teen-age "jitterbugs" or "alligators" as they were called danced in the theater aisles, and added to America's vocabulary such pertinent expressions as "in the groove"; "boogie-woogie"; "jam sessions"; and "killer diller."

Soon the big names of swing included in addition to Goodman, the Dorsey brothers, Tommy and Jimmy; Harry James; Gene Krupa; Woody Herman; Glen Miller; and Artie Shaw, to name but a few. Large dance bands became the rage and were a commercial success, while the smaller "hot jazz" bands had rough going. The 1920s had already known the big Negro bands of men like Fletcher Henderson, Duke Ellington, and the trumpet playing of Louis Armstrong, but by the 1930s, musicians were "swinging" the classics as well as folk music. New instruments appeared, such as the vibraharp and the electric guitar, and pieces had elaborate arrangements and orchestrations. Many of the players had musical training, and some, like Goodman, were expert players of both classical and popular music.

AMERICA'S NEWIST MEDIUM: BALLET

As teen-age Americans were dancing as never before, there began to emerge a greater interest in ballet, but little could anyone dream that the fresh vitality of the younger generation would soon match the art of the Russian dancers of a quarter-century before. Yet it was this same age-group which turned to serious dancing, and through sheer hard work and much perseverance eventually made American ballet the envy of the world.

Stage dancing there had been, of course, such as that in the nineteenth-century minstrel shows, which had become an integral part of theatrical entertainment. Native composers had also used dances from both Europe and the Latin-American countries, but the possibilities of an American ballet was something quite new. It was when the Russian choreographers who had been with Diaghilev began to emigrate to America that the gap was slowly bridged between the older Russian ballet and the American product. All of this was the outgrowth of their schools and companies, which had started back as early as Adolph Bolm (1917) and Michel Fokine (1919), and was carried on in 1931 by Leonide Massine, and in 1933 by George Balanchine. Naturally their work was patterned after the Russian school, especially of the Diaghilev era, but by the late 1930s and through the 1940s, American ballet came into its own.

Such a development was not new in the history of music, for seventeenth-century ballet in France was basically Italian, just as in the eighteenth-century Russian ballet was inspired by France. Americans could also remember the excitement which followed in the wake of Diaghilev's 1915-16 tour, with the great Vaslav Nijinsky as the featured star. In 1932 Wassily de Basil founded a company of Russian dancers, brought them to America, and engaged Fokine, Massine, and Balanchine to create new choreography. It was this group—the Ballet Russe de Monte Carlo—which touched off America's interest. The years in between had had brief moments of brightness, as Pavlova toured, and in Chicago and the Middle West, Adolph Bolm and Ruth Page had already done pioneering work. America grew more sure of herself, and in New York, as a protest against the domination of the Russians, a new project was started by Lucia Chase and Richard Pleasant in 1939: Ballet Theatre. Placing the importance on new ballets by both American and English choreographers, in an incredibly short space of time many young dancers were trained and brought to star billing, including Nora Kaye, Alicia Alonso, Jerome Robbins, John Kriza, and Harold Lang.

In 1932, possibly as a relief from the drabness and gloom of the depression, New York had witnessed an amazing revival of puppet shows. Within a year, ballet and dance took the limelight, as many unusual companies toured the nation. Uday Shan-Kar and his Hindu dancers; the German company of twenty members, billed as the Jooss Ballet; and the international dancer, Serge Lifar; all competed with the Ballet Russe de Monte Carlo. One of the first ballets employing popular American tunes was Nicolas Nabokov's *Union Pacific*, based on the building of the transcontinental railroad, and danced for the first time in Philadelphia at the Forrest Theatre by the Monte Carlo Ballet on April 6, 1934. Other composers followed, as when on January 6, 1938, Virgil Thomson's *Filling Station* was given its première in Hartford, Connecticut, by the American Ballet Caravan. The music recalled familiar American tunes (though none are directly quoted), and brilliantly captured the spirit of the times. The same company danced Aaron Copland's *Billy the Kid* (based on the notorious bad man) for the first time in Chicago in October, 1938. Eugene Loring created the choreography and danced the title role. Copland used such cowboy tunes, often in fragmentary form, as *Git Along Little Dogie, Good-by Old Paint*, and *Oh, Bury Me Not on the Lone Prairie*. The first New York performance was in May, 1939. Stravinsky, conducting the world première of his ballet *The Card Party* at the Metropolitan Opera House (April 27, 1937), presented a score that was a mixture of romanticism, impressionism, and jazz.

In the years when ballet had been neglected in America, there had developed the so-called "free dance"—that is, dancing that did not follow the accepted laws of ballet technique so popular in Europe. Early in the century, Isadora Duncan (1878-1927) had created a new form of dance that rejected all formalized movement, employing instead the movements of her body in her attempt to show the "inner life of man which arises from the soul." Many of these same ideas were carried on by Ruth St. Denis and Ted Shawn in the company known as the Denishawn Dancers from 1915 to 1930. They reached and pleased a large audience, and kept the dance from passing out of the picture altogether.

Unquestionably the greatest exponent of the free dance is Martha Graham, who, after endless experimentation with all types of bodily movement, sought to avoid telling a story and instead used movement for its own sake and for the emotions she sought to project. Building a superb technique through the most rigorous discipline, she used her dancing to express ideas and emotions, never merely to look well. She was an innovator, and brought "modern dance" to its greatest heights in the 1940s. From 1928 on, Louis Horst composed her music, which in the early years, brought her recognition. His works included *Fragments: Tragedy and Comedy, Frontier, American Provincials,* and *Primitive Mysteries.* In succeeding years Miss Graham was to commission music from the leading contemporary composers, and we shall meet her again, as well as Ballet Theatre, in the 1940s, at the height of their successes.

Two other innovators who worked during the 1930s should be mentioned—Doris Humphrey and Hanya Holm.

WAR CLOUDS

As the clouds of World War II hovered threateningly, America's musical scene took on a decidedly cosmopolitan air, as the great influx of political refugees from Europe continued. Already the big three of modern music were residents—Stravinsky, Schoenberg, and Hindemith—and soon there would be added such men as Béla Bartók and Darius Milhaud. The stature and personalities of these men were an inspiration for our own composers, and the newcomers, too, were influenced by America. There was noticeable each year a higher level of skill, a finer craftsmanship, and an improvement in the quality of music composed.

In Chicago in September, 1938, an all-Negro jazz version of Gilbert and Sullivan's *The Mikado* was sponsored by the WPA at the Great Northern Theatre, with such success that the next season saw it in New York. This set a trend in adaptations of various kinds during the war years. Radio continued to furnish the best music as WOR, of the Mutual Broadcasting System, started weekly broadcasts of Bach cantatas and (1940) all of Mozart's piano concertos. NBC broadcast a new comic opera by Menotti—*The Old Maid and the Thief* (April 22, 1939), while in May, Douglas Moore's folk opera, *The Devil and Daniel Webster*, had its first radio hearing.

With the war actually starting with Hitler's declaration to Poland (September 1, 1939) and Great Britain and France taking Poland's side, America seemed a haven as two great expositions opened—the Golden Gate International Exposition in San Francisco and the New York World's Fair. Television, for some years in experimental stages, became more of a reality as NBC telecast the opening ceremonies of the New York Fair. America, musically, was in the healthiest state in its history, and the war seemed far away.

CHAPTER XIII

American Folk Music

INCREASED INTEREST IN FOLK MUSIC

Discussion of American folk music may logically follow our chapter on the music of the 1930s, for it was in the thirties and forties that scholarly and musicianly research into our musical folk heritage reached its apex, and expert specialists had delved into the neglected byways of folklore and had unearthed amazing treasures. It is true that collecting folk songs had started in a limited way almost a century earlier, with Negro spirituals in the 1850s and 1860s. In our century John Lomax issued this first volume of cowboy songs in 1910, Cecil Sharp his Appalachian ballads before 1920 (his first collection was published in 1917). These and other pioneer volumes were issued in the early 1900s, but it was in the years to follow that a constantly increasing number of folk song collections were issued which grew to such proportions (together with recordings of folk singers) that by 1951 Charles Haywood was able to compile his astoundingly voluminous *Bibliography of American Folklore and Folksong*, a work of 1292 pages.

It was in the 1930s and 1940s also that our composers came to make a truly valid use of folk music in their compositions. We have learned how a number of composers heeded the advice of Antonin Dvořák in the 1890s and early 1900s and turned to Negro spirituals and Indian music for thematic material. At that time, however, the result of the movement was a rather self-conscious adoption of extraneous ingredients which did not generally succeed in producing basically integrated art works. In a few years there was a strong reaction against seeking a nationalist expression by such obvious means, a reaction that was partly influenced by Mac-Dowell's views on the subject.

As the years passed and new sources of folk song were discovered, some of which were incorporated into our popular music, these folk elements began to be absorbed into our art music more spontaneously, until by the thirties and forties it became more natural for some of our composers to use an American folk melody or to compose a theme in folk manner than to write in traditional European styles, as their predecessors had done.

One of the amazing facts that modern folk-music research has disclosed is the existence of so many different groups of songs and tunes, most of them belonging to specific regions or to different types of people—Negroes, mountaineers, cowboys, frontiersmen, lumberjacks, and others. While these songs usually belong to each section alone, many may be found to overlap and to exist in different versions in several parts of the country. They may be sung by lumberjacks as well as mountaineers, cowboys, or Negroes. The songs themselves are of foreign as well as native origin, and frequently may be a combination of the two.

Before considering the various groups of our folk songs, it is interesting to note that New England is credited with the earliest recorded American folk ballad: *Springfield Mountain,* dating from 1761. A man named Nathan Torrey is supposed to have composed the words of this ballad (it has been fitted to several tunes, including *Old Hundredth*), and this attribution of authorship raises the question of whether a song may be considered a true folk song if it is known to have been written by a single person, rather than by a group or community. Phillips Barry, a noted authority, has perhaps solved this problem satisfactorily by speculating that the original creation is probably the work of an individual, and that it is then subjected to "communal recreation" by those who subsequently perform it. Thus, folk songs are altered in the course of oral transmission, and the result is often many different versions of the same songs.

TYPES OF AMERICAN FOLK MUSIC

Negro Music

The African music that the first slaves brought to this continent was just as primitive as the songs and dances of the native Indians.

The Negro slaves, with their close contacts with the white people, soon began to modify their native music, absorbing the music they heard their white masters sing. Thus it is that the Negro music which has developed in the United States is more in the nature of folk music than it is of primitive music. For this reason it has exerted a much greater influence on the works of American composers than has the music of the Indians.

Negro singing first became known in the country north of the Mason and Dixon Line through the travels of the Negro singing groups, first from Fisk University, then from Hampton, Tuskegee, and other industrial schools. Since the appeal of these singers was to the church groups that sponsored their recitals, most of the programs of these itinerant singers were devoted to the Negro religious songs or spirituals. As a consequence, it is these songs which became the most widely known of all the Negro folk songs. As a slave the Negro looked to the afterlife as a release from his earthly bondage, and because he was often forbidden by his master to sing of his own desire for freedom, he found a parallel to his own servitude in the Bible stories of the slavery of the children of Israel, and he hoped for the day to come when he might be led out of the wilderness by his own Moses.

Many of the spirituals are sad, expressing the resignation to the trials of everyday life and looking to the hereafter for deliverance. *Swing low, sweet chariot* (based on a pentatonic scale) is a typical example of this type, while *Go down Moses* uses the scale most often encountered in the songs of the Magyars of Hungary. The particular flavor of these songs was unique, and they had an immediate appeal. Others are exuberant and gay, optimistic and rhythmic, such as *I want to be ready*, and *Roll, Jordan, roll*. With their origins in the meetinghouses, where the leader (like the old Puritan precentor) would sing a line and the congregation of worshipers would answer him, they might start thus:

> *Leader:* I got a robe, you got a robe.
> *Congregation:* All God's chillun got a robe.
> When I get to heab'n, gonna put on my robe.
> Gonna shout all over God's heab'n.

The quartets and choruses from the Negro institutes sang in parts, using harmonies of their own improvisation. They were not as complicated as they sounded (in reality they were quite simple), but in the churches and campmeetings, there was much doubling and filling in of parts, which made them sound complex.

The origin of Negro melodies is still a matter of speculation, and a subject of much controversy. Some students have found that the African primitives and the American Negro have both used pentatonic scales, and that both have a tendency toward syncopation. Each has a talent for complicated, involved rhythmic patterns, which has set their music apart. Some authorities claim a white origin for many of the Negro songs we know today, feeling that the white evangelists and religious revivalists of the South were a great influence. George Pullen Jackson in his *White Spirituals from the Southern Uplands* (and other books), claims a white origin for many of the Negro spirituals, and shows many parallels between the songs of both races. The most tenable theory is that the Negro brought with him his own native musical idioms, and that his proximity to white men led him to repeat many white songs in his own way, with a personal variation. In other words, the Negro songs are an Afro-American product.

The emphasis on religious songs in the various collections of Negro spirituals that were issued shortly after the middle of the nineteenth century caused us to overlook for many years the secular songs of the Negro: his work songs—for cotton-picking, corn-shucking, stevedoring; railroad songs of the section gang; steamboat songs; prison songs of the chain gang and the rock pile; bad-man songs; and, of course, the blues. In recent years these secular songs have attracted the attention of many collectors and are being issued in a number of interesting volumes.

The Negro love of narrative balladry manifested itself by his versions of many of the Anglo-Saxon ballads sung by the Appalachian mountaineers. Yet many of his ballads were of his own making, songs in which revenge is absent and slavery is not mentioned—songs which show the gentle patience, often tinged with melancholy, which is characteristic of the race. The many bad-man songs include the tale of *Travelin' Man*, who made a living stealing chickens, or *Bad Man Lazarus*, who "broke in de commissary" and was finally shot down with a "forty-five." The most famous of the comparatively modern ballads is *Frankie and Johnny*, of which hundreds of versions are on file in the Archive of American Folk Song at the Library of Congress in Washington.

The blues, as we have already discovered, is a type of sorrow song altogether peculiar to the Negro race. The many transformations of the blues form through the years are an indication of its beauty and power. All of the Negro music, not only the blues, has exerted a great influence upon both America's art and popular music, as well as that of many other countries.

Anglo-American Folk Music

Although we have a record of only the psalm-singing of the first New England settlers, it can hardly be doubted that some of them brought with them the secular songs and ballads that had flourished for centuries in England. Many such ballads as *Lord Randal* and *Barbara Allen*, and songs like *Billy Boy* may have come over with the first settlers.

Maine, Vermont, and to a certain extent New Hampshire are the New England states in which most of the ballad survivals are found, and most of them seem to be of Anglo-Saxon origin. But many are also claimed as American, such as *Fair Charlotte*, which may be dated about 1835, and is supposed to have been written by a blind poet named William L. Carter.

New England is particularly distinguished for its country dances, the square dances in which a caller announces the various figures. From the beginning of time, music, poetry, and dance have been inseparable among the folk. Most of the tunes used for these dances are of British origin, but they were often given new names to associate them with local places and people. Thus *Lady Walpole's Reel* became *The Boston Fancy*. *Hull's Victory* was another popular tune, celebrating the battle of the *Constitution* and the *Guerrière* in the War of 1812.

The whalers of New Bedford and Nantucket have had their chanteys and the lumbermen of the Maine woods their lumberjack songs. A typical example of the interchange of songs among different sections of the country is found in the Maine lumberman's *Canaday-I-O*. This is based on an old English sea song, which is also the basis for the western ballad *The Buffalo Skinners*.

Appalachian Mountain Balladry

Folk songs are always best preserved in isolated regions, for in such places the refinements of civilization have not brought a more formalized and sophisticated culture. People who are denied communication with other communities rely on themselves for amusement and for the emotional outlet of singing. It is therefore in the mountainous sections of Kentucky, Tennessee, the Carolinas, and Virginia that a true art of folk song has survived. British settlers came early to these Appalachian highlands, and they and their descendants continued to live in places that were secluded and inaccessible. Few roads were built in the mountains, and the railroads were miles away. Each family was self-sufficient, raising its own food. Money was unnecessary, for bartering was the custom of the day. In the case of disputes with neighbors, justice was invariably a private matter, settled with a gun. Revenge would lead to blood feuds between families that were carried on for generations. Otherwise the southern mountain folk were a leisurely people, hospitable and kindly when their suspicions were not aroused. Any stranger was welcome, provided he was not a "revenooer" interested in illicit whisky.

The ballads these people sang were mostly of British origin, and of the many collected by Francis E. Child in his *English and Scottish Popular Ballads*, more than a hundred were found in America. The most widely known is *Barbara Allen*, of which nearly a hundred American versions have been preserved in recorded or written form in the Archive of American Folk Song in Washington. The songs and ballads have come down orally for generations, as parents have taught them to their children, and they have remained in remarkably accurate form. Sometimes the wording and the tunes will vary in different regions and in the singing of various singers, but many of the American versions were sometimes closer to the prototypal form than those heard today in England. It may seem incongruous to hear, in the highlands of America, of knights and ladies, of chivalrous courtship, of castles and ships, of days that were but a memory when our country was settled. Still sung in the mountains is *The Hangman's Song*, known as *The Maid freed from the gallows; Frog went a-courtin'; The Elfin Knight;* and *The Little Mohee*. Some, with their reference to comparatively modern events, are obviously of American origin, as when *Brother Green* speaks of the "Southern foe" (referring to the Civil War); and *The Wreck of the C. & O.*, and *The Boston Burglar*, are plainly mountain versions of American ballads.

Most of the tunes used by the mountaineers for their songs and ballads are cast in what Cecil J. Sharp has called "gapped" scales. These are the old pentatonic (five-note), hexatonic (six-note), and heptatonic (seven-note) scales (analogous to the white keys of the piano), which are found among all peoples in the world. There are six of these gapped scales each corresponding to one of the six medieval church modes: Ionian (C to C); Dorian (D to D); Phrygian (E to E); Lydian (F to F); Mixolydian (G to G); and Aeolian (A to A).

The mountain people usually sang without accompaniment, but occasionally a singer might use a fiddle or guitar, and in some sections, a dulcimer. This mountain dulcimer has no connection with the "piano" dulcimer of many strings, but is a long, shallow wooden box with sound-holes, and three strings stretched over it, two of them used as drones, the other for the melody. Usually it was plucked, although in the mountains it was sometimes bowed.

Cowboy Songs

The great interest in folk music in the second decade of the twentieth century led to the discovery of one of the most important groups of regional songs—those of the western cowboys. The cowboy's songs were collected just in time, for the coming of the railroad and other forms of modern transportation has greatly lessened the need for the old time-honored cowpuncher. The roundup has almost vanished, and the cattle trails to Kansas and Montana are overgrown with grass.

Most of the cowboy songs (they might well be the work of unknown individuals, rather than of a group in the manner of folk music) were parodies of old ballads and popular songs of English, French, Irish, Scotch, German, Spanish, and Negro origins. They all showed the essentials and characteristics of folk songs, as they were transmitted orally. They were simple with a personal point of view and a deep concern for the everyday life they depicted. In the 1870s and 1880s large groups of men were needed to take care of the cattle in the winter, as well as to round them up when spring came. Like all isolated people, the cowboys had to make their own entertainment to lessen their loneliness.

Many of the songs were sung by the cowboys to accompany their labors. The "dogie" (motherless calf) songs were usually soft, to quiet the restless cattle at night, or were sung to quiet stampedes. The day-herding songs were often loud and rhythmic yells to stir up lagging cattle and keep them on the move. The rhythms of all the cowboy songs are unique, for they must fit the rhythm of his horse, otherwise he could not sing them at all. Newton Gaines discovered three types: the rhythm of walking, trotting, and the lope— all with the simplest of melodies. The cowboy usually sang in the first person, and his songs showed him to be an intensely democratic person, mostly interested in himself and his experiences, some of which were vividly imaginative and colorful. There were songs of work and love, dirges, hymns, narratives, and even some humorous ditties. The songs which came from the Spanish Southwest, near the Mexican border, would frequently have Spanish verses and phrases. One of the bragging narrative type is *The Old Chisholm (Chizzum) Trail*, very simple as to structure, with a refrain (of probable Indian origin) to be sung by whatever group happened to be on hand:

> Coma-ti yi yippy, yippy yea, yippy yea,
> Coma-ti yi yippy, yippy yea.

The cowboy liked desperado songs and tales of bad men—*Jesse James; Billy the Kid,* and the ballad of the *Hell-bound Train.* He sang songs of lament for his dying comrades (*The Dying Cowboy*), as well as the sentimental *Home on the Range,* or the religious *Rounded Up in Glory.* The songs were often accompanied by a guitar, and at the dances were supplemented by a violin and an accordion.

In all folk music, it should be remembered that the ballad is impersonal and relates a story, while the song, which is subjective, deals with the emotions of the singer.

Tin-Pan Alley has long since become acquainted with mountain balladry and cowboy songs, and by mid-century it has come to cater to public demand with a curious mixture of "hillbilly songs" and "western songs." These have been so much the rage that a tabulation in 1952-53 of current songs shows a definite trend from the

Southland to the western prairies as the favorite locale of the up-to-date Broadway song writer for radio and juke-box appeal. Like the earlier minstrel songs, the hillbilly songs are caricatures, the city man's idea of a countryman's singing.

Lumberjack Songs

Collectors have gathered lumberjack songs from the woods of Wisconsin, Michigan, and Minnesota. Some of them are familiar to the Maine woodsmen also. The shanty boy, or lumberjack, rarely sings while he is actually at work. He is not by nature a gang-worker, so he does not sing the type of work-song in which the rhythm is concurrent with group effort. The lumberjack sings during his hours of leisure, for his own entertainment. Most of the woodsmen's songs were composed originally by individuals rather than by groups in communal fashion. New verses have of course been added by other bards as the songs have been sung around the campfire. As a song has grown older, it has gained a variety of anonymous contributions.

Creole Songs

Another important and influential group of songs came from the great population of early nineteenth-century Louisiana—the Creole songs. The term "Creole" is correctly applied only to the mixed Spanish and French people of Louisiana, the great landowners, but in recent years it has quite incorrectly been used for those of mingled white and Negro blood. Naturally the language of these songs is almost invariably French patois, with a little Spanish and African. The melodies are usually of French and Spanish origin or flavor, but the rhythms are often decidedly African in character. There is much syncopation, and the songs would often begin with a snap, or catch (a quick syncopation with an immediate return to normal). These songs were intended to be danced to, and naturally employed dance rhythms of both duple and triple time. The songs contained all the details of life among the miserable and despised Negroes, expressing the most elemental emotions of fear, love, and jealousy. They were usually accompanied by a banjo.

The dance-songs grew out of the custom of the colored population to gather in the Place Congo, which was a large, unpaved square, where they danced until the curfew gun was fired. The dancers and musicians, in the center, were surrounded by a circle of stamping, clapping, and shouting people, all keeping time to the music. The instruments were crude drums, empty barrels, gourds (filled with dried peas or corn), bones, marimbas, quills (a type of Panpipe), and, of course, banjos. The many love songs were chants of unrequited love or the sadness of separation; while the satirical songs often taunted a cruel overseer, but might as often be directed for or against the political candidates of the day.

The principal dance-songs were *Counjai (Coonjai, Coon jai),* a love dance; the Cuban *Hananera* (alternating between duple and triple rhythm, such as *Quande pata' la cuite [When the potato is cooked]); Bamboula,* no doubt named after the drum that was used with it. Of the love songs, the most familiar were *A, Suzette Chere; Clementine;* and *Suzanne, Suzanne, jolie femme.* The satirical songs were *Miché Préval, Msieu Banjo,* or *Loema tombe.* Some of the songs were sung at particular times—*Quand pata' la cuite* would announce supper in the plantation nursery; bedtime brought the lullaby *Gué-gué Solingaire;* and the work of sweeping and scrubbing might be accompanied by the tune of *Suzanne, Suzanne, jolie femme.* Many of these Creole songs have been forgotten, as few were recorded on paper. Even with their French and Spanish influence, they were basically Negro music, "a creation, not an imitation." We have already learned in chapter VI how Louis Moreau Gottschalk used Creole melodies in his early compositions.

Other Folk Songs

Two other great bodies of folk songs have been those of the French Canadians, and the Hungarian folk songs of America. The former group contains the genuine folk songs of Normandy and the Loire River, brought to Canada before 1680, with the first settlers; those dating after 1680, which for the most part have been transmitted by writing; and the native songs of French Canada.

The Hungarian-American folk songs belong to the coal miners, the steel workers, factory workers, and the like—all the heritage of the many Hungarian peasants who emigrated to America in large numbers. With these people came the Gypsy bands, who, in the homeland, had always interpreted their music. The resources of this phase of folk song have hardly been tapped, but there are signs of a revival of interest.

The Spanish influence in California and the Southwest, with its isolation, created a wealth of folk songs of Spanish origin. California nearly lost hers, but many may still be heard in New Mexico. The songs go back to the Old World, some with the versification of the fifteenth century. Still existing are the *alavados,* the traditional hymns sung during Holy Week, and the many songs of the three-hundred-year-old Nativity play, *Los Pastores.* Many are of local origin, with a flavor and wit characteristic of the people. One of the most famous of the love songs is *La Cucaracha (The Cockroach).*

With the increasing interest in folk songs has come the spread of folk festivals, aimed at promoting and preserving folk music, as well as American folk arts in general. The most important are: the American Folksong Festival, Ashland, Kentucky; the Asheville Mountain Song and Dance Festival, Asheville, North Carolina; the National Folk Festival; the Pennsylvania Folk Songs Festival; and the White Top Festival, White Top Mountain, Marion, Virginia.

Folk Hymns and Gospel Songs

Religious music has its folk songs and popular tunes. The gospel song is in many respects the popular "hit" song of hymnody. As a type, it has a long history, and has been the most stirring, even disturbing, phenomenon in religious music. It appeared as revival song, Sunday School song, or gospel hymn less than one hundred years ago and its production line is still moving rapidly.

Gospel songs are actually a side sprout from an older, sturdier stem whose roots reached deeply into the rich soil of both American and British folk song. This earlier music remained long unwritten and was unknown to the musically literate, and since it was purely "country" music, was completely strange to most urban ears. The late George Pullen Jackson in a quarter-century of research found that throughout the upland South there is still a rural community-singing activity carried on by the *Sacred Harp* singers, who took their name from the title of a thick, oblong, hundred-year-old volume of part songs that is still their only manual of music. Dr. Jackson characterized the songs of these people as white spirituals and he published a number of volumes which analyzed the songs and their origins. Through his discoveries he threw new light on the growth of country religious song, which began some two hundred years ago. He also claimed that in these white spirituals may be found the origins of countless of the Negro spirituals.

As has been pointed out in an earlier chapter on nineteenth-century hymn-tune composers, song innovation accompanied or followed a peculiar outburst, the "Great Awakening," which began with Jonathan Edwards and other religious ecstatics. It had become apparent that psalm singing was too sedate to suit this fiery upheaval of hell-fire and heaven-storming. The new songs had to be suited to the countryside and frontier. Under such circumstances it was natural that these religious leftists (rural Baptists, chiefly, then Methodists, New Side Presbyterians, and others) should begin to sing their favorite folksy hymns (Watts, Newton, Stennett, Cennick), as well as many homemade religious lyrics, to the well-known tunes of the old secular ballads—*Barbara Allen, Little Sir Hugh, Captain Kidd, Lord Lovel,* and scores of others. This process went on during the decades following the Revolutionary War.

About 1800 the all-denominational camp meetings took up these songs, enlivened them, filled out partially remembered texts with much repetition, refrains, and choruses, and thus made them over into a rather roistering type of song which took its place by the side of the comparatively quieter variety. The songs were known by various names—spiritual songs, camp meeting songs, and revival songs. These folk-song types grew in popularity throughout the first half of the nineteenth century, this despite the frowns and protests of the more cultured church folk and their musical leaders. For almost this entire period many of the songs remained "unwritten music," and when they did gradually appear in printed form from 1813 to the 1860s they were given in the Little and Smith shape notation, which had been introduced late in the eighteenth century.

There were exceptions, for as early as 1805 one musical enthusiast, Jeremiah Ingalls, had dared to publish a book containing revival songs—*The Christian Harmony*—in New Hampshire. According to Dr. Jackson it was shunned in its region as illegitimate, and it had no successors there. The really successful, and in time complete, recording of the unwritten songs occurred first in Pennsylvania, with *Wyeth's Repository of Sacred Music, Part Second* (1813), then in Virginia (*The Kentucky Harmony*, about 1815), and in still later and southern books.

This rural music had hardly come to light before commercial music publishers and song writers recognized in it a trend that could be exploited. The earliest commercial publications, such as J. W. Dadmun's *Revival Melodies* (1858), showed obvious adaptation of folk-melody ideas. Gradually the lighter gait of the march and the waltz, the refrain-and-chorus pattern, and the text repetitions of the earlier anonymous folk material followed further and naturally into the production of the gospel-song writers.

One of the oldest of them was Charles Crozat Converse (1832-1918), composer of *What a friend we have in Jesus.* William Howard Doane (1832-1915) achieved fame with *Saved by the blood, My faith still clings,* and *Sound the alarm.* Philip Bliss (1838-1876) contributed the music for *Pull for the shore* and *Rescue the perishing.*

One of the leading latter-century composers was Ira David Sankey (1840-1908), for many years the partner of Dwight L. Moody, one of the most famous revivalists of the day. "Moody and Sankey" songs became almost a generic term and two of the most widely sung were *The Ninety and Nine* and *A Soldier of the Cross.*

In the twentieth century there was Homer Rodeheaver (1880-1955), who for over twenty years (1909-1931) led the music at Billy Sunday's revival meetings. His song *Brighten the corner where you are,* became famous as the theme song of Sunday's mammoth tent meetings.

CHAPTER XIV

The Forties

WAR YEARS

As the decade of the 1940s dawned, and the conquests of Hitler alarmed the world, America was shocked out of the smugness of her isolationism. With the depression years a thing of the past, life seemed full of promise and the arts were flourishing as never before. New inventions appeared every year, and many would greatly further the cause of music. Such a one was the new radio without static (FM or frequency modulation), demonstrated near Worcester, Massachusetts, from station WIXOJ, by Major Edwin H. Armstrong (January 5, 1940). Television was beyond its experimental stage, and promised to be one of the most important mediums in the years ahead.

Songs of World War II

The hundreds of songs that came out during the years after America's entry into the war were vastly different from those of the same class of earlier years. Life for the American soldier had changed radically since the days of World War I and his musical outlet was not confined to the singing of songs. The principle of selective service was so widely accepted that there was no need for the old-type recruiting songs, and the many musical references to the draft were often facetious. Dozens of songs were commissioned, published, and copyrighted by the Treasury Department to aid in the selling of bonds.

Thousands of young men and women, stationed in or near large cities, or filling the coastal cities on a last treasured leave, flocked to the concert halls and opera houses to hear the great music they had come to know and love. New vitality was brought to America's concert life as the need for diversion grew, and nearly two thousand communities were aligned with the organized plans ("community" and "civic") for concerts, and music might be found in sections of the country which had never had much, if any, serious music. During the war years Americans spent more on music than they did on baseball.

The many overseas units and top-ranking stars who circled the globe to entertain troops often included the best singers and performers from the musical world, while in between these visits, there was always the radio and phonograph. Many songs were quickly forgotten and radio itself may have had a great deal to do with the impermanence of the World War II songs, for nothing can shorten the life of even a good song as effectively as excessive radio use. For the sake of the record it might be interesting to list the most popular songs of the war years. They were of all types and included: *White Christmas, The Last Time I Saw Paris, Don't sit under the apple tree, My Sister and I, Bell Bottom Trousers, The White Cliffs of Dover, There'll Always Be an England, Der Fuehrer's Face, Coming in on a Wing and a Prayer, Praise the Lord and Pass the Ammunition, Rodger Young, Waltzing Matilda, Lili Marlene,* and a song, written nearly fifteen years before the war, Irving Berlin's *God Bless America.* The song writers organized a committee which met regularly with representatives of the Armed Forces and of the civilian war effort, to learn what types of songs were needed, not only for the services, but for war plants and the many diverse activities and projects.

The very impermanence of these World War II songs undoubtedly had a deeper meaning. America as a nation was more mature and knew what a grim, sordid business war was and she was in deadly earnest. Radio and modern science had drawn the world closer together and world events and great battles could be followed almost hourly. There was no longer any glamor to war and all America was united in one effort—to get it over as soon as possible. As people sought comfort in their religions, so soldiers and civilians alike found solace in the great music that was performed. Music seemed to be everywhere as American orchestras developed and attained new heights of perfection, while American ballet and opera, the newest of the arts in the nation, saw their greatest years.

The war brought forth a long line of new music that, rather than the music of popular song (as in the First World War), might be said to be a catalogue of the war itself. Much of it was undoubtedly music for the moment, but the following list will show how diversified were the composers, and that all were native-born, new citizens, or permanent residents:

Barber—*Commando March*
Bennett—*The Four Freedoms*
Creston—*Fanfare for Paratroopers*
Damrosch—*Dunkirk*
Harris—*March in Time of War*
Martinu—*Memorial to Lidice*
MacDonald—*Bataan*
Piston—*Fugue on a Victory Tune*
Rogers—*Invasion*
Schoenberg—*Ode to Napoleon*
Wagenaar—*Fanfare for Airmen*

The American soldiers still sought music, when they were shipped overseas, and many will never forget the deep experiences of concerts by the great performers, such as Dame Myra Hess (to name but one), given in bomb-shattered halls, in cellars, or wherever a few hundred could gather. In all branches of the service, the best talents were gathered together for touring concerts and theatrical entertainment. None could forget the power of music at a time like this.

THE ERA OF GREAT BALLETS IN AMERICA

On January 16, 1944, Virgil Thomson made a prophecy in his Sunday column in the *New York Herald Tribune*. Thomson had become its music critic in 1940, following the late Lawrence Gilman, and had already established himself as one of the nation's most provocative writers on music. He wrote that "music's renewal will probably take place on this continent, where the ancient skills are less ingrown than they are in Europe. . . . What we need is . . . more of opera and ballet, and that is what we are apparently going to have after the war." We know now how right he was, for as we found in our chapter on the 1930s the stage was already set for the emergence of both a truly American ballet and opera.

Ballet Theatre

When Lucia Chase and Richard Pleasant formed Ballet Theatre in 1939, they were successful in breaking down the domination in the ballet field of the Russians. From the outset new ballets were commissioned from American composers, and soon a number of young American dancers became famous as stars. The war years were Ballet Theatre's most brilliant period and its success was due to the three outstanding men who were put in charge of the artistic productions. They were Eugene Loring, well-remembered for his brilliant choreography for *Billy the Kid* (Ballet Caravan, 1938), in charge of the American wing; Anthony Tudor, the talented English choreographer, responsible for the English division; and Anton Dolin, who was in charge of the classical ballets.

New York City Center Ballet

With the formation of the New York City Center Ballet in 1948, under the leadership of Lincoln Kirstein and George Balanchine, at the New York City Center (the old Mecca Temple on West Fifty-fifth Street), American ballet matured with amazing rapidity. Kirstein was very much like Diaghilev in his ability to inspire his workers, create outstanding ballets, and commission the best possible scores. He had been building toward this moment through a series of companies, starting in 1934, and including the American Concert Ballet of 1943 and the distinguished Ballet Society of 1946. Several of these companies, traveled on the road. It was Kirstein who gave particular emphasis to presenting American dancers in American ballets with American music.

Working with Kirstein was George Balanchine, who had been with Diaghilev, and his coming to America had a significant effect on the dance theater. Young and independent, he was a perfectionist, as well as having a genius for creation. Almost at once he inspired a talented younger group of choreographers, including Jerome Robbins, Todd Bolender, Ruthanna Boris, William Dollar, and John Taras.

As the City Center Ballet took the leadership in American ballet, the company was to grow to be one of the finest in the world, and, after its winter season, would tour Europe in the summers. Most of the dancers were Americans, with occasional foreigners who were notable. With a firm insistence on discipline Balanchine convinced everyone that only rigid schooling could create useful work habits, and he saw the potentialities in the young American dancers. Building good techniques was not enough, however, and Balanchine had the vision to find and train good choreographers, knowing that it is only through their creative work that the dance can grow. New blood is the only hope for all the arts—this ability to look ahead and not dwell on the greatness of the past.

As much of the modern dance tended to become stereotyped through too much imitation of Martha Graham by smaller groups who lacked the flame of her genius and so could never be artistically successful, the initial impetus given by Ballet Theatre in its greatest days seemed to merge, as the City Center group developed, into a distinctive style that was to make American ballet quite different from that in Europe. As this style crystallized in the closing years of the 1940s it included the best qualities of the older traditional ballet from Europe, intermingled with a strong national flavor, leading to a vitality and a farsightedness that augur well for the future.

Jerome Robbins

There were several personalities who left their mark on the dance theater in these years. Jerome Robbins, who danced with Ballet Theatre in 1940 (and did exceptionally fine work), showed his superior creative powers when his own ballet, *Fancy Free,* was given its première in April, 1944. It was a delectable bit of Americana, in which the plot concerned three sailors on leave, and it had a lilting score by Leonard Bernstein, a composer-conductor whom we shall meet in chapter XV. Robbins drew freely from contemporary composers from the beginning, rather than using the standard symphonic works as Anthony Tudor usually did.

Agnes de Mille

Another important member of Ballet Theatre's company was Agnes de Mille, who had her first important recognition with her ballet of the Southwest, *Rodeo* (October 16, 1942). First presented by the Ballet Russe de Monte Carlo, it had an admirable score by

Aaron Copland, who drew on the folk tunes of the region and skill-fully combined the folk feeling with a brilliant neoclassic technique. *Rodeo* was an immediate success, and as Miss de Mille was at her best in miming, a new quality was added to America's dance theater. She was to go even further through her venture into the musical comedy field.

In the 1920s, Michel Fokine had worked for Florenz Ziegfeld and other producers on Broadway, but these dances were actually a by-product. The real use of ballet in the theater came with Balan-chine's *Slaughter on Tenth Avenue* (music by Richard Rodgers), which Ray Bolger danced in the production *On Your Toes* (1936). Miss de Mille, in creating the dances for Rodgers and Hammer-stein's *Oklahoma!* (April 1, 1943), and later for *Carousel, Allegro,* and *Brigadoon,* so integrated them into the plot that they became part of the story, and a new era was inaugurated for musical pro-ductions. As the composers were beginning to write equally well for Carnegie Hall or Broadway, so the choreographers became adept in either the serious repertory or in the field of lighter entertain-ment.

Martha Graham

Martha Graham, once over her difficult years in getting started, continued to be the mainstay of "modern dance," producing new dance dramas, the scores for which were commissioned from the best contemporary composers. All her productions were excitingly effective. Isamu Noguchi, the sculptor, created *décors* which were actually three-dimensional and became a part of the dance patterns. Miss Graham sought to go beyond telling a story, as she tried to communicate the emotions of the mind and soul and the psycho-logical implications in the behavior of such legendary figures as *Medea, Judith,* and *Joan of Arc.*

Significant Ballets

A list of the most significant ballets of these years will bear testi-mony to the great stimulus they gave to all the related arts:

Rodeo—Copland; De Mille; (Ballet Russe de Monte Carlo, October 16, 1942)
Herodiade—Hindemith; Graham; (Library of Congress, October 30, 1944)

Imagined Wing—Milhaud; Graham; (Library of Congress, October 30, 1944)

Fancy Free—Bernstein; Robbins; (Ballet Theatre, April 11, 1944)

Appalachian Spring—Copland; Graham; (Library of Congress, October 30, 1944)

Serpent Heart—Barber; Graham; (Columbia University, May 10, 1946)

Facsimile—Bernstein; Robbins; (Ballet Theatre, October 24, 1946)

Night Journey—Schuman; Graham; (Harvard Symposium, May 3, 1947)

Minotaur—Carter; Taras; (Ballet Society, March 19, 1947)

Fall River Legend—Gould; De Mille; (Ballet Theatre, April 22, 1948)

Orpheus—Stravinsky; Balanchine; (Ballet Society, April 28, 1948)

Ballet Ballads—Moross-Latouche; Godkin; Litz; Holm; (Experimental Theatre, May 13, 1948)

Wilderness Stair—Dello Joio; Graham; (American Dance Festival, August 13, 1948)

Errand into the Maze—Menotti; Graham; (Ziegfeld Theatre, February 28, 1947)

OPERA

Opera, too, was reflecting the great change in America during the war years. Unusual productions marked the early years of the 1940s, such as the all-Negro production of *Aïda*, given in the Chicago Opera House on October 10, 1942. When, in 1944, the National Negro Opera Company presented a Negro cast in *La Traviata* to an audience of ten thousand in New York's Madison Square Garden (and later toured to Chicago, Pittsburgh, and Washington), it showed very clearly that there might be a future for Negro opera, provided there was a proper choice of repertory for the Negro's musical gifts and ability to sing. In South Carolina, at the Spartanburg Music Festival, Ernst Bacon conducted the première of his American flavored opera, *A Tree on the Plains* (May 2, 1942). It was among the first to be filled with homespun songs (some dealing with hitchhiking and chewing gum).

It was at this time that Gian-Carlo Menotti wrote a series of operas, composing both librettos and music, which were so successful that he took first place among living American opera composers.

Menotti Operas

After his first opera, *Amelia Goes to the Ball,* Menotti received a commission from the National Broadcasting Company for a radio work, and the result was the opera buffa *The Old Man and the Thief* (1939). In 1942 the Metropolitan Opera Company staged Menotti's tragedy *The Island God,* the première taking place on February 20. Full recognition came to him in 1946, with his tragic opera, *The Medium,* written as a commission from the Alice M. Ditson Fund of Columbia University, and given its first performance at the Columbia University Festival at the Brander Matthews Theatre on May 8. The following February (1947), after revisions, it was produced by Ballet Society together with Menotti's *The Telephone* as a curtain raiser. Both operas scored such a success that they reached Broadway the following May under commercial auspices at the Ethel Barrymore Theatre, where they had a long run. Later Menotti supervised a motion picture version of *The Medium.* The magnificent acting and singing of Marie Powers in the role of Madame Flora, the medium, greatly added to the success of the opera, and as late as the season of 1955-56, *The Medium,* with Miss Powers, was touring American cities.

Similarly, *The Consul,* another tragedy, was produced at the Ethel Barrymore Theatre in March, 1950, and immediately achieved such a "smash-hit" status that seats for it were sold at a premium. It was subsequently produced in numerous foreign cities. The plot of *The Consul* concerns the fate of a patriot in a European country behind the Iron Curtain and the frantic efforts of his wife to obtain a visa and escape to a free nation. Defeated by red tape and the inhuman routine of the consulate, she finally commits suicide. Menotti was hailed for his knowledge of and feeling for the theater, his excellent craftsmanship, and his boldness as a dramatic author.

Opera at the City Center

No one could have foretold in 1943, when the city of New York took over the old Mecca Temple, just how deeply its future productions would influence New York's cultural life, especially that of opera. When Lászlo Halász, the Hungarian-born conductor working in St. Louis, came to New York to produce three operas for a short season of three weeks as inexpensively as possible, another venture was on its way. Puccini's *Tosca* (February 21, 1944) was such a hit in the three-thousand-seat auditorium that in the fall a second season was given, and from then on there would be two seasons a year, before and after those of the Metropolitan. With a five-year lease taken in 1945, the New York City Center of Music and Drama became a nonprofit cultural center for the people of New York, where prices would be kept low, and which, it was hoped, would ultimately function all year round. In 1945 concerts of the New York City Symphony Orchestra were inaugurated by Stokowski. Later, Leonard Bernstein conducted them from 1946 to 1948, without pay. The concert season was abandoned as the other attractions became more popular. One, of course, was the ballet company, already mentioned, that grew out of Lincoln Kirstein's Ballet Society. The ballet performances have in every way equaled the opera productions. When a drama season started in 1949, with Maurice Evans as the artistic director, the theater needed only some summer project (and installation of air conditioning) to be open all year round. This came about in 1954, with a series of musical productions, such as *Carousel* and other revivals.

The grand opera performances were invariably rewarding, for they were given with all the care of a first-class stage production, and their quality was of the highest level to be had under the circumstances.

Singers were chosen with an eye to a well-integrated performance and not because they were stars, and soon it was the opera itself which drew the crowds. In this way New York at last had a house that could match the smaller European houses that are so important to singers for learning roles and for gaining the proper experience before going on to the world's larger houses. Many singers ultimately went on to the Metropolitan, but many more were well-suited to the more intimate type of production the City Center featured, and wisely remained.

Opera at Central City

Another annual opera season of importance, where the productions are first-class and in a superb setting, are those in the Rocky Mountains, at an altitude of over eight thousand feet, in the old mining town of Central City, Colorado. At the height of the great boom in the West—in the 1860s and 1870s—this town was a popular rendezvous for the miners, who flocked to see the many entertainments from *She Stoops to Conquer,* to *Ten Nights in a Barroom.* When the log theater was destroyed by fire, plans were made for a house that would be the pride of this wealthy boom town. Great artists like Joseph Jefferson and Sarah Bernhardt played on its stage, traveling from Denver on a narrow-gauge railroad which has long since vanished. When the ore in the surrounding mines was exhausted the Opera House was closed and locked, and the steep, narrow streets were silent.

In 1931, the abandoned Opera House was given to the University of Denver by three children of one of the original builders, Peter McFarlane. The University had no money to restore the house, but two Denver idealists, Ida Kruse McFarlane and Anne Evans, had the idea of making the theater a memorial project, dedicated to the pioneers of Colorado's early days. With the help of the citizens of Denver the theater was restored, and for several years its productions were either plays or light operas. In 1941, Herbert Graf of the Metropolitan Opera Company was engaged to put on Rossini's *The Barber of Seville* and Gluck's *Orpheus.* The quaint charm of the restored town brought many tourists to the festival. When the war intervened, the house was forced to remain dark until 1946, but it functioned once again, with Donald Oenslager as the designer. The Opera House seats some seven hundred persons, and is known to have fine acoustics, equaled by few opera houses in the world. As Graf returned to Europe each summer after the war, Elemer Nagy took over the productions in 1950 (he headed the Hartt College opera workshop in Hartford, Connecticut), and each season operas are sung in English, with casts of young singers. A legitimate play follows the season of opera.

Lemonade Opera

New York had a novel summer venture in 1947, when Max Leavitt directed a cooperative enterprise known as the Lemonade Opera. So-named because it filled the period between spring and fall (and lemonade was served outside), Lemonade Opera scored a great success, its artistic productions evoking the highest critical acclaim. Leavitt was a dynamo of energy, a creative genius, and with a small company and two pianos he gave New York audiences superlative summer productions of Mozart's *Don Giovanni,* Humperdinck's

Hansel and Gretel, Prokofiev's *The Duenna,* Haydn's *The Man in the Moon,* and Weill's *Down in the Valley.* The project had to be abandoned after the 1949 season, but it was reanimated in May, 1953, for one season, again in the Village Presbyterian Church on Thirteenth Street. Leavitt had secured the rights to *Don Pedro,* an opera buffa, which Hans Erismann (conductor and choirmaster of the Zurich Municipal Theater) put together from two unfinished Mozart operas, and a group of arias which Mozart had written for some of his favorite singers—a custom of the day. The translation was by Joseph Longstreth, who wrote the Lemonade version, and alternate casts sang, accompanied by two pianos, virginal, and lute (on stage). Once again, although an artistic success, the venture failed financially, and another chapter of opera history closed. It was a great pity, for it showed typical American ingenuity, and was one of the most imaginative enterprises ever attempted, a natural outlet for the young singer who not only needs experience but grows under artistic stimulation.

Other American Operas

New American operas came in quick succession and many have remained in the permanent repertory. Some were most advantageous to smaller companies and college opera departments and workshops, and in this respect more than served their purpose.

One of these was Virgil Thomson's opera, *The Mother of Us All,* in which he again collaborated with Gertrude Stein. Originally commissioned by the Alice M. Ditson Fund of Columbia University, it had its première at the Brander Matthews Theatre on May 7, 1947. Built around the life story of Susan B. Anthony, the nineteenth-century pioneer in the woman's suffrage movement, the cast is made up of historical figures—Daniel Webster, Lillian Russell, Ulysses S. Grant—and Virgil T. and Gertrude S. (the authors). Once again Thomson showed his rare ability in setting English words to music, his elegance in orchestral writing, and used all types of popular American song of the nineteenth century from revival and gospel hymns to folk songs.

Other operas of this year were Kurt Weill's *Street Scene,* based on Elmer Rice's play concerning life in New York's tenements (January 9, 1947); and Roger Sessions' *The Trial of Lucullus,* set to the text of Bertolt Brecht's radio play and first performed at the University of California on April 18, 1947, in Berkeley. The subject was a timely one, for it dealt with the defeat of an arrogant dictator.

With other operas like Kurt Weill's *Down in the Valley* (1948) and William Grant Still's *Troubled Island* (1949), already mentioned in earlier chapters, American opera composers were using all types of folk and popular music in their scores in the most sophisticated way, the songs seemingly simple in construction, and in English, for American singers to sing and American audiences to understand. Slowly the old cry against opera in English was being broken down. With their locales mostly in America, their stories about people we seemed to know and understand, their tunes close to the music America knew best, American operas seemed at last to have caught on.

MUSIC FOR SOUND FILMS

The coming of sound pictures in the late twenties and their development during the thirties and forties opened up a new medium for composers: writing background music to accompany the pictures. In the days of silent films the musical accompaniment had developed from the solo pianist of the nickelodeon to the organists and orchestras (sometimes of symphonic proportions) in the movie palaces of the large cities. Generally the music that was played was arranged locally for each presentation of the film. The producers supplied "cue sheets" designating the kind of music that should accompany specific episodes and action. Several enterprising music publishers issued large books of cue music, with pieces and themes arranged by subject and category—music for comedy scenes, to portray the gamut of emotions (sorrow, joy, love, etc.), music for the perennial chases, and for every type of situation in the pictures that were being produced.

The big theaters in the major cities maintained staff arrangers to write a complete score for each new picture, and during the twenties several pictures were issued for which scores were composed and furnished to exhibitors by the producers. One of these films was *The Thief of Bagdad* starring Douglas Fairbanks, Sr., for which the American composer Mortimer Wilson (1876-1932) was engaged to write an accompanying score, synchronized with cues to the picture. This score employed leitmotivs to identify characters and to emphasize underlying emotions.

Such ventures as this proved highly successful in the major cities where the orchestras were adequate and had time to rehearse the timing of the music with the film. But in smaller cities and towns the results were not so happy.

With sound pictures all this was changed. The music was now actually recorded on the film and there was no chance of any slip-up or mistakes when the picture was actually shown. Since the early thirties an entirely new branch of the composing profession has grown up in Hollywood. We have already learned and we will learn still further how various of our composers have written film scores on occasion—men such as Aaron Copland, Virgil Thomson, George Antheil, Louis Gruenberg, Leonard Bernstein, and others—but there are musicians whose principal efforts are devoted to this work. Among them are Adolph Deutsch (b. England, 1897), who wrote the scores for *The Maltese Falcon* and *Father of the Bride;* Franz Waxman (b. Germany, 1906), *Sunset Boulevard;* and Erich Korngold (Bohemia, 1897), *The Constant Nymph, Of Human Bondage.*

Two native Americans have been singularly successful in their film scores: Werner Janssen (b. New York, 1900), *The General Died at Dawn,* and Bernard Herrman (b. New York, 1911), *Citizen Kane, Anna and the King of Siam.* Janssen was a pupil of Frederick S. Converse and for three years (1930-33) a Fellow at the American Academy of Rome. From 1934-36 he was one of the conductors of the New York Philharmonic-Symphony, and in 1938-39 of the Baltimore Symphony. Among his symphonic works is his tone poem *New Year's Eve in New York.* Herrman, trained at the Juilliard Graduate School, is likewise a conductor, having become a staff conductor of the Columbia Broadcasting System in 1938 and that organization's symphonic director in 1943. Herrman's compositions include a dramatic cantata, *Moby Dick* (1940) and various symphonic works.

BROADWAY REFLECTS AMERICA'S CULTURAL GROWTH

Before we take leave of America's dance theater and lyric theater and the music of Hollywood, all of which went through a tremendous development in the 1940s, it is most important that we survey the impressive progress of the lighter form of entertainment as found on Broadway. It, too, was truly American in character. The quality of musical comedies had improved, for librettos were better, and songs and lyrics were frequently a triumph of collaboration. The scores were orchestrated with unbelievable brilliance by the best men of the day, and the choreography of the dances began to take an important place in the integration of the productions as a whole. By this time, many of the composers were men who were trained in the craft of writing music, having studied with outstanding teachers, either privately or at the many schools. So impressive has this development been that many look to the future for the final merger of Broadway and our opera houses and concert halls—in other words a *real* American opera.

BACKGROUNDS OF AMERICA'S MUSICAL COMEDY

"Broadway" has long since become the symbol of the popular entertainment field, just as "Tin-Pan Alley" has become the symbol of the production of commercial songs. During the last century American audiences had become familiar with the names, as well as the music, of Europe's incomparable group of comic opera composers. There had been a steady stream of the productions of Gilbert and Sullivan, Johann Strauss, Jr., Von Suppé, Lehar, and even adaptations of Offenbach. Now the procedure was being reversed, as the excellent musical comedies of America's "great" were playing in European capitals, those of Cole Porter, Jerome Kern, Richard Rodgers, and Gershwin. In between these comic operas and musical comedies was the popular type of light entertainment at the turn of the century—operetta, which was, of course, much nearer traditional opera than it was to the so-called "musical comedy." The dominating figure in this field was Victor Herbert.

Victor Herbert

Herbert (1859-1924) was a thoroughly equipped composer, who, although born in Ireland and trained in Germany, threw himself so quickly into America's musical life, particularly into helping the struggling native composers, that he seems today one of the greatest Americans of them all. Herbert, whose grandfather was the well-known Irish poet Samuel Lover, toured Europe as a cellist, and around 1880-81 played under Eduard Strauss, who had succeeded his brother Johann, Jr., as Vienna's Waltz King. When the season was over, Herbert again went on tour through Germany and Switzerland, and after an especially fine concert in Stuttgart, he was offered, and he accepted, a post in the court orchestra. It was then that Herbert fell in love with the Viennese soprano, Therese Förster, and they became engaged. The year was 1886, and the Metropolitan Opera Company had sent Walter and Frank Damrosch to Germany to engage singers for its second season of German operas. Frank was greatly impressed with Therese Förster, and offered her a contract. As she and Herbert had planned to marry in the fall, she would not accept unless both of them could come to America, and so it happened that Herbert arrived in America as a cellist in the Metropolitan orchestra while his wife was to be one of the leading sopranos. In between performances at the opera house, Herbert appeared as a soloist, often playing his own compositions, and winning a reputation as one of the foremost cellists of his day. His restless spirit soon carried him beyond orchestral playing and he turned to conducting and further composition. After much success as a band conductor, Herbert was appointed the Director of the Pittsburgh Symphony, a post he held from 1898 to 1904. Herbert's first operetta (it is called a "comic opera" on the score) was written for the popular touring company, the Bostonians. It was called *Prince Ananias,* and was first performed in New York on November 20, 1894, with great success. There followed in quick succession a series of almost forty works, the most lasting of which have been: *The Fortune Teller* (1898), *Babes in Toyland* (1903), *It Happened in Norland* (1904), *Mlle. Modiste* (1905), *The Red Mill* (1906), *The Rose of Algeria* (1909), *Naughty Marietta* (1910), *The Lady of the Slipper* (1912), *The Madcap Duchess* (1913), *Sweethearts* (1913), and *Eileen* (1917).

In his music for the light-opera stage, and in such instrumental pieces as *Badinage* (1895), *Punchinello* (1900), and *Indian Summer* (1919) Herbert had a sparkle and freshness that was individual and striking. Dozens of his songs are still popular today, and *Naughty Marietta* was made into a highly successful motion picture. The operettas themselves are still favorites with stock companies and amateur groups, and occasionally they are revived on Broadway. That nearly all suffer from dated (and inferior) librettos is now conceded, but they pleased a vast public in his day and Herbert achieved his distinction in spite of them.

Herbert's list of more serious works include two concertos, several orchestral suites, and two grand operas—*Natoma* (1911) and the one-act *Madeleine* (1914). None of these, however, have enjoyed the success accorded his light operas.

Reginald De Koven

Herbert's principal rival as a composer of operettas was Reginald De Koven (1859-1920), who produced almost twenty light operas, but whose works, except for his early *Robin Hood* (1890), have not proved as enduring as those of Herbert. *Robin Hood* has become a classic, but De Koven was never able to write anything which equaled it in popularity. Two of its numbers, *Oh Promise Me* and *Brown October Ale*, have become perennial favorites, the first at weddings and the other with lusty baritones. Like Herbert, De Koven was a well-trained composer (he had studied in Germany and with Delibes in Paris) who aimed at more ambitious targets. His two grand operas, *The Canterbury Pilgrims* (1917) and *Rip Van Winkle* (1920), with librettos by Percy MacKaye, were given major productions, but did not prove successful. De Koven's other light operas include *The Knickerbockers* (1893), *The Algerian* (1893), *The Highwayman* (1897), *Red Feather* (1903), *The Golden Butterfly* (1907), *The Beauty Spot* (1909), and *Her Little Highness* (1913).

George M. Cohan

Broadway's slowly changing scene became apparent with the remarkable career of George M. Cohan (1878-1942). Starting in the theater as a youth, with his father, mother, and sister, Cohan became one of the leading figures in the twentieth-century's popular music. In his lifetime Cohan was a song-and-dance man, actor, producer, director, playwright, and composer of words and music of songs which had a certain ragtime flavor even though they were never in the modern jazz idiom. Many of the songs from his shows are still popular: *I'm a Yankee Doodle Dandy, Give My Regards to Broadway,* and *Mary*. In addition to his show tunes Cohan composed the most widely sung of all World War I songs—*Over There*.

Rudolf Friml and Sigmund Romberg

Two composers who were born abroad had their share in the growth of American operettas and both of them based their works somewhat on European models. Rudolf Friml (1881-) was born in Prague, studied composition with Dvořák, and came to America in 1901 as accompanist for the violinist Jan Kubelik. Sigmund Romberg (1887-1951) was a native of Hungary who came here in 1909. Both composed scores for what may be termed romantic operettas to librettos written by such outstanding writers as Dorothy Donnelly (1880-); Otto Harbach (1873-); Oscar Hammerstein II (1895-); and Herbert Fields (1897-) and Dorothy Fields (1905-). As a rule the works were period pieces but their plots were better integrated and the introduction of musical numbers was more logical than in the books that were supplied to Victor Herbert.

Friml's most successful productions were the *Firefly* (1912); *High Jinks* (1913); *Katinka* (1915); *Rose Marie* (1924); and *The Vagabond King* (1925). Romberg's included *Maytime* (1917); *Blossom Time* (1921) based on an idealized life of Franz Schubert; *The Student Prince* (1924); *My Maryland* (1927); *The Desert Song* (1926); *The New Moon* (1928); and *Up in Central Park* (1945).

MODERN BROADWAY MUSICALS

Irving Berlin

While the light opera or operetta was to remain popular until around 1930, there was a noticeable change in the field of musical comedy (as we think of it today) which had grown out of such early and fabulously successful productions, as *The Black Crook* (first produced at Niblo's Garden on September 12, 1866); *A Gaiety Girl* (brought from London's Gaiety Theatre in 1894); and Ivan Caryll's *The Pink Lady,* in 1911. It was undoubtedly Charles Dillingham's "syncopated musical show" *Watch Your Step,* for which music and lyrics were written by Irving Berlin, that saw the beginning of an American musical comedy, which by mid-century was to be the finest of its type in the world. Berlin's career has been one of the complete American success stories. Born in Russia in 1888 (his real name was Izzy Baline) and brought to this country in infancy, he grew up on New York's Lower East Side and started early on a career that eventually made him one of America's leading popular-song writers, theater owners, theatrical producers, and music publishers. He was first a "busker" and singing waiter in Chinatown and on the Bowery, and his early songs, which were great hits, included *Alexander's Ragtime Band, Everybody's doin' it, When my baby smiles at me, A pretty girl is like a melody, What'll I do?, All Alone, Blue Skies, Remember,* to name but a few. Like Cole Porter, Berlin writes both the words and music of his songs.

From the two world wars came two soldier productions of Berlin's —*Yip, Yip, Yaphank* (1918) and *This Is the Army* (1942), both of which featured his early song, which was sung everywhere, *Oh, how I hate to get up in the morning.* Other well-known musical comedies included *Face the Music* (1932); *As Thousands Cheer* (1933); *Louisiana Purchase* (1940); and finally his greatest success, *Annie Get Your Gun* (1946), with Ethel Merman as Annie Oakley, the legendary sharpshooter of Buffalo Bill's Wild West Show. The show's great number of popular songs, some of Berlin's best, included: *The girl that I marry, They say it's wonderful, You can't get a man with a gun, Doin' what comes naturally,* and *There's no business like show business.* There was also *Call Me Madam* (1950). It was during World War II that Berlin's *God Bless America* (long associated with singer Kate Smith) and *White Christmas* were at the height of their popularity.

Jerome Kern

Jerome Kern, (1885-1945) born in New York, was blessed with a melodic gift that combined warmth and tenderness with gentle humor. He was first known to Broadway in 1911 through the score for *The Red Petticoat.* This was followed in 1914 with *The Girl From Utah* and later with a series of shows produced at the Princess Theatre in New York—*Oh! Boy* (1917), *Very Good Eddie* (1915), *Oh, Lady, Lady* (1918), and others written in collaboration with Guy Bolton and P. G. Wodehouse. Then came *Sally* (1920), with the collaboration of Victor Herbert, and which featured the lovely Marilyn Miller; *Stepping Stones* (1923), *Sunny* (1925), *Showboat* (1927), *Sweet Adeline* (1929), *The Cat and the Fiddle* (1931), *Music in the Air* (1932), *Roberta* (1933), and *Very Warm for May* (1939). Nothing that Kern wrote ever surpassed his score for *Showboat,* which has had several revivals since its opening in 1927. The libretto was adapted from Edna Ferber's novel of the same name by Oscar Hammerstein II, and seldom has any subject been treated with better taste, musical and dramatic, than this story of a theatrical troupe on board an old Mississippi River steamboat. Its incomparable tunes include such favorites as *Old Man River, Only Make Believe, Can't help lovin' that man of mine, Why do I love you?*, and *My Bill*. Authorities have differed as to whether *Showboat* is a musical comedy, an operetta, a play with music. But no matter. That it is one of the milestones in the American theater, all agree. Its tunes are beautiful and fresh, and in less than twenty years, it earned its own immortality.

Cole Porter

One of the most sophisticated of musical comedy composers, Cole Porter was born in Peru, Indiana, on June 9, 1892. He became a law student at Yale, then in 1915 went to the Harvard Music School for study in harmony. Later he went to Paris and studied at the Schola Cantorum, at the time Vincent d'Indy was in charge. Porter wrote both the words and music of his songs (and still does), and there can be no doubt that life in Paris was an education in itself, for Porter unabashedly wrote about sex in typical twentieth-century fashion in his very first show, *Fifty Million Frenchmen* (1929). His many successful musical comedies include: *The Gay Divorcee* (1932), *Anything Goes* (1934), *Jubilee* (1935), *Red, Hot and Blue* (1936), *Du Barry Was a Lady* (1939), *Panama Hattie* (1940), *Let's Face It* (1941), *Something for the Boys* (1943), and *Kiss Me Kate* (1948). The last show, based on Shakespeare's *The Taming of the Shrew,* was Porter's greatest success, and many feel that it is his finest score. Certainly the later production, *Can-Can* (1953) did not measure up to *Kate,* whose song *Wunderbar* once again showed Porter's subtle satire, while *So in love am I* has a tender, haunting poignancy. However, his newest production, *Silk Stockings* (1955) is another big hit. Of his other songs, *Night and Day, Rosalie,* and *Begin the Beguine* are as popular as ever.

Richard Rodgers

It was in the 1940s that American musical comedy reached its greatest heights, producing a new genre that combined all of the

best elements of the past, with the addition of imaginative choreography. This type at once showed the world that America had
no peer in this particular field. It was Richard Rodgers (1902-   )
who wrote the music for these musical comedies, and he was most
fortunate in having two of the finest lyricists America had yet
produced, first the late Lorenz Hart (1895-1943), and after Hart's
death, Oscar Hammerstein II. Rodgers was born in New York (June
28) and showed an early talent for music. It was while he was a
student at Columbia University that he met "Larry" Hart. They
joined talents for the 1918 varsity show at Columbia, *Fly With Me,*
which was the first of many collaborations, with Fate seeming to
move further away as each new show was born. When Rodgers was
about ready to give up music and take a job, success came to the
team in 1925 almost overnight, with *Garrick Gaieties,* written for
the Theatre Guild (1926).

The most successful Rodgers and Hart productions include *A
Connecticut Yankee* (1927), based on Mark Twain's story; *Present
Arms* (1928); *Jumbo* (1935); *On Your Toes* (1936), whose ballet
Slaughter on Tenth Avenue as we have already mentioned, was a
new and important departure; *Babes in Arms* (1937, written in
collaboration with George Kaufman and Moss Hart); *I Married an
Angel* (1938); and *Pal Joey* (1940). Based on John O'Hara's *New
Yorker* stories, *Pal Joey* might be said to be the first of the important
musical comedies of the 1940s. It has since then been successfully
revived. Its hit tunes, clever satire, superlative dancing and choreography touched a new level of proficiency. It was after their production of *By Jupiter* (1942) that Lorenz Hart suffered an extended
illness, and his untimely death in 1943 removed a vital and forceful
personality from the Broadway scene.

Rodgers was indeed fortunate in finding a collaborator in Oscar
Hammerstein II (born 1895), who was already established firmly in
the theater as a result of his librettos and lyrics for Romberg, Kern,
and others. Their first venture was *Oklahoma!* (1943), written for
the Theatre Guild and based on Lynn Riggs's play *Green Grow the
Lilacs,* which the Guild had produced in 1931. After playing in
New Haven and Boston (where the name was changed from *Away
We Go* to *Oklahoma!*), Rodgers and Hammerstein's new musical
opened at the St. James Theatre in New York on March 31, 1943.
The critics did not rave, but the public did, and *Oklahoma!* re-

mained in New York for almost six years (while second companies toured the nation), making musical history by having the longest run on Broadway of any musical production. It was a delectable bit of regional Americana, as clean and sturdy and fresh as the typical American youth. With Agnes de Mille's imaginative choreography and such songs as *O what a beautiful morning, People will say we're in love, Many a new day, The surrey with the fringe on top,* and *Oklahoma!*—it deserved every bit of its amazing success.

Except for *Allegro* (1947), which was not a success, all of Rodgers and Hammerstein's collaborations have enjoyed extended runs in New York and long transcontinental tours, with productions of many in the capitals of the world. *Carousel* (1945); *South Pacific* (1949); and *The King and I* (1951), (which was the incomparable Gertrude Lawrence's last show); *Me and Juliet* (1953); and *Pipe Dream* (1955) need no introduction to present-day readers. American musical comedy, like American music itself, had at last matured and reached its highest level yet.

Frederick Loewe

Another Broadway team has come to rival Rodgers and Hammerstein in producing expertly integrated musicals that merge all the elements of drama, comedy, lyrics, and music into an entertainment that is as valid artistically as it is successful. After *Brigadoon* in 1947, their first real hit, Frederick Loewe (1904-   ), composer, and Alan Lerner (1918-   ), librettist, collaborated on *Paint Your Wagon* (1951), which had a longer run in London than it did in New York. Then in 1956 they introduced to Broadway what promises to be one of the great hits of all time—*My Fair Lady,* their adaptation of George Bernard Shaw's *Pygmalion.* As this book goes to press (summer of 1957) *My Fair Lady* has been running at the Mark Hellinger Theatre for more than a year, and to obtain seats even those with influence must apply for them months in advance. The success is deserved; *Pygmalion* remains *Pygmalion* in its musical treatment, the songs are fresh and individual, and the cast with Julie Andrews, Rex Harrison, and Stanley Holloway is inimitable.

Loewe was born in Vienna and was a pupil of Eugène d'Albert and Ferruccio Busoni. He came to the United States in 1924 and started his career as a concert pianist. Lerner is a Harvard graduate who has written successfully for radio and for motion pictures, as well as for the Broadway stage.

Various Broadway Composers

The record, far from complete in so short a history, still must include a few other significant figures in the history of American theatrical entertainment. George Gershwin's contributions have been considered in an earlier chapter, but there is also Vincent Youmans (1898-1946) with his two hits—*No! No! Nanette* (1925) and *Hit the Deck* (1927); Kurt Weill's *Knickerbocker Holiday* (1938), and *Lady in the Dark* (1941), two of the best Broadway shows of the decade; and by Frank Loesser (1910-   ) *Guys and Dolls* (1950), based on the Damon Runyon stories, one of the cleverest and most brilliantly written American musical comedies. Loesser's newest score is *The Most Happy Fella* (1956). Julie Styne (1905-   ), from England, is best known for *Gentlemen Prefer Blondes* (1949) and *Hazel Flagg* (1953). Perhaps no composer has caught the Negroid spirit of the blues since Gershwin better than Harold Arlen (1905-   ), the son of a Buffalo, New York, cantor. He first wrote for the Cotton Club revues and Earl Carroll's *Vanities*, but his greatest success came with the song *Stormy Weather*. Nothing could be more American in spirit than his score for the motion picture *The Wizard of Oz* (1939), in which Judy Garland immortalized *Over the rainbow*, and his score for the 1944 production of *Bloomer Girl*. But he returned to his earlier idioms in *St. Louis Woman* (1946) and *House of Flowers* (1954), which many consider his finest score. He is at present working on a blues opera. Others who have gained distinction in the musical theater are Arthur Schwartz (1900-   ) with *Band Wagon* (1931), and *A Tree Grows in Brooklyn* (1951); Ray Henderson (1896-   ) with *Good News*; and Alec Wilder (1907-   ), for his sensitive and beautiful songs.

OUR COMPOSERS INTERPRET AND EXPRESS AMERICA

Virgil Thomson once remarked: "The United States is the one country in all the world that produces all kinds of music that there are. Only here do composers write in every possible style and does the public have access to every style."

These two sentences express more accurately than many a lengthy treatise exactly what American music is. It is not just jazz; it is not just hillybilly, country, or cowboy music; it is not just Negro spirituals, or the blues, or the music of the cities—it is any one or all of these and many other things. And just as America itself is made up of so many different kinds of people, with so many different racial origins, living in all kinds of places, its music, to be representative, must express them all. Whether a composition be a Broadway song with a thirty-two-bar chorus or an hour-long symphony, if it comes from the background and experience of the man who wrote it and that man belongs in some part of America, his work is authentically American.

General recognition of this fact has probably helped American music to mature in the past quarter-century more than any other stimulus it has received. Composers have become less self-conscious about nationalistic expression; they have relaxed and devoted themselves to composing whatever it is natural for them to write. Without their realizing it, their music has become more truly American for the very reason that they have thought less about making it so. Derivations from foreign sources have become unimportant and we hear much less today than we did a few years ago about styles, idioms, and formulas. The musical revolutions that swept the world in the early decades of the twentieth century seem remote, even though they have left an indelible mark on all music, whether American or European. Today there is no better sign of the maturing of American audiences than their ability to comprehend contemporary music, even though they may not always like it.

America's composers in the 1940s, although thoroughly aware of the styles and devices, the many movements of the last quarter-century, were rather wearied of much in the past, and began to fulfill Virgil Thomson's prediction of the ultimate renewal of music on American soil and by American composers. There were fewer experimental composers at this time and a mere handful who might fit into the classification we have already used—nationalists. More composers, led by men like David Diamond, Paul Nordoff, and the younger William Bergsma, followed the traditionalists of the preceding decades, while William Schuman, Paul Creston, and Norman Dello Joio had marked eclectic tendencies. Indeed, with upheaval of World War II, when American troops as well as civilians were sent to practically every country in the world. it became increasingly difficult to limit many of the composers to specific categories. America was maturing rapidly and again Virgil Thomson summed up the decade when he wrote in the *New York Herald Tribune* in January, 1948: "The way to write American music is simple. All you have to do is to be an American and then write any kind of music you wish. There is precedent and model here for all kinds. . . ."

Continuing our policy of grouping some of the most significant composers of the 1940s as either traditionalists, nationalists, or eclectics, it must be remembered that it is by no means possible, nor feasible, to mention more than a few in each grouping. Time alone can prove the worth of the amazing amount of music that was being written at this time, and many stars in the musical firmament who shone brightly during and after the war may in the next decade or two find their talents eclipsed by newer and brighter ones.

TRADITIONALISTS

David Diamond

David Leo Diamond was born in Rochester, New York, on July 9, 1915. He had his early training at the Institute of Music in Cleveland, where his family had gone when he was ten years old, but returned to Rochester and with the aid of a scholarship studied composition with Bernard Rogers at the Eastman School of Music. He was to become one of Rogers' most prominent students, working later on with Roger Sessions in New York and then with Nadia Boulanger in Paris. His first four symphonies (1940, 1943, 1945, 1945) clearly indicated the younger composers' interest in the symphonic form, which had been all but abandoned in the early years of the twentieth century by Debussy and Ravel, Stravinsky and Schoenberg. Diamond's Second Symphony is considered his first significant work, written, as Diamond himself pointed out, "during the days of tense world unrest, and I am quite sure that a certain amount of exterior emotional influence has affected the quality of the symphony. . . ." Diamond's musical language had been assimilated from many sources—his work with Rogers and Sessions, the exciting residence in Paris where he had the value of criticism from

Stravinsky and absorbed the neoromantic elements which he heard in the music of the younger composers.

A consistent winner of prizes and awards, it was in 1946 that Diamond received the New York Music Critics Circle citation for his *Rounds for String Orchestra* (1944), a piece which Olin Downes described as music with "vernal freshness and energy." His *Psalm for Orchestra* (1936), which he and Mlle. Boulanger had played for Stravinsky in a piano version and for which the Russian composer made certain suggestions, won Diamond the 1937 Juilliard Publication Award. Other orchestral works include *Elegy in Memory of Maurice Ravel* (1937), whom he greatly admired; two suites drawn from his incidental music for *Romeo and Juliet* (1947) and *The Tempest* (1947); a Symphonic Portrait, *Timon of Athens* (1949); two concertos for violin and orchestra (1936, 1947), a Cello Concerto (1938); a Concerto for chamber orchestra (1940), a Piano Concerto (1950), and a Sixth Symphony (1954).

Diamond's chamber-music works include three string quartets (1940-1947); a Concerto for string quartet (1936); Piano Quartet (1938); quintets for flute, strings, and piano (1937) and for clarinet, two violas, and two cellos (1950); Chaconne for violin and piano (1948); and a *Canticle and Perpetual Motion* for violin and piano (1946). There are also numerous piano and choral pieces, among the latter a *Sacred Service for the Sabbath Eve* (1951).

Later theatrical productions for which Diamond composed distinguished incidental music were *The Changeling* (1947); *The Rose Tattoo* (1950); and for the production of *Romeo and Juliet* which starred Olivia de Haviland (1950). He also wrote the background scores for the film *Anna Lucasta* (1949), and for the documentaries *A Place to Live* (1940) and *Strange Victory* (1948). His ballet scores are *Tom* (1936) and *The Dream of Audubon* (1941).

Paul Nordoff

The Philadelphian, Paul Nordoff (1909-   ), who taught at Michigan State College, was awarded Guggenheim Fellowships in 1933 and 1935, a Pulitzer Scholarship in 1940, while his *Prelude and Variations* for piano won the Bearns Prize from Columbia University in 1933. He studied composition at the Juilliard School of Music with Rubin Goldmark and piano with Olga Samaroff Stokowski. Before going to Michigan Nordoff was on the faculty of the

Philadelphia Conservatory of Music (1937-42), where Vincent Persichetti became his pupil.

Nordoff's orchestral works include a *Prelude and Three Fugues* (originally for two pianos, 1932), given its first full performance by the Pennsylvania WPA Orchestra in 1940; a Suite (1939), introduced by the St. Louis Symphony in 1940; and a *Little Concerto* for violin, viola, cello, double bass, and orchestra, played first by the New York Little Orchestra Society in 1950. In addition there are a *Secular Mass* (1934); two piano concertos (1934, 1936); two string quartets (1932, 1935); Piano Quintet (1936); Violin Sonata (1932); Cello Sonata (1941); a one-act operetta, *The Masterpiece* (1941); and incidental music for *Romeo and Juliet* (1935). For Martha Graham he has written three ballets: *Every Soul Is a Circus* (1938), *Salem Shore* (1942), and *Gospel of Eve* (1950).

Arthur V. Berger

Arthur V. Berger, born in New York City in 1912, was for many years a member of the music staff of the *New York Herald Tribune*. He was graduated from New York University and continued his studies at Harvard under Walter Piston. Receiving a Paine Fellowship from Harvard, Berger went to France where he studied with Nadia Boulanger. Later he worked with Darius Milhaud in California.

Berger's works are primarily in the field of chamber music and include a Quartet for woodwinds (1941); the *Serenade Concertante,* for solo violin and woodwind quartet, strings, and brass (1944, revised 1951); two Duos, No. 1 (1949) and No. 2 (1951), for violin and piano; a Duo for cello and piano (1952); a Duo for clarinet and oboe (1952). Francis Perkins wrote in the *Herald Tribune* of the Duo for cello and piano that its first movement, "with a distinctive profile, was inventively treated so that, without losing its characteristic outline, it varied from firm refractoriness to melodic flexibility, with a corresponding change of mood."

Berger has composed two orchestral works—*Three Pieces* for strings (1945) and *Ideas of Order* (1952), the latter on commission from Dimitri Mitropoulos, who conducted the first performance in April, 1953, with the New York Philharmonic-Symphony. The reviewer of *Musical America* wrote that "its form is quasi-variational, rather in the manner of some twelve-tone music, although its harmonic language is austerely diatonic. . . . It springs instantly into a kind of tense, athletic rhythmic play and refuses flatly, and successfully, to let down for an instant."

A group of very talented young composers began to have wide recognition about this time, all graduates of the Eastman School of Music, and passing on to their own students the academic traditions which they had used with such success.

Gardner Read

Gardner Read has won prizes with each of his two symphonies. In 1937 his First Symphony was awarded a $1000 prize by the New York Philharmonic-Symphony, and in 1943 his Second Symphony won the Paderewski Prize of equal amount. Born in Evanston, Illinois, in 1913, Read took his master's degree at the Eastman School, working with Rogers and Hanson, and later with Aaron Copland. At present he is the head of the music department at Boston University. Although he falls into the traditionalist group, Read has pronounced eclectic tendencies. His orchestral works include a symphonic poem, *The Lotus Eaters* (1932); two suites which reflect the American scene, *The Painted Desert* (1933) and *Sketches of the City* (1933); *Fantasy*, for viola and orchestra (1935); *Prelude and Toccata* (1937); *First Overture* (1943); *Night Flight* (1942); *Pennsylvania Suite* (1946); *Quiet Music*, for strings (1948); and the more recent dance-symphony, *The Temptation of St. Anthony* (after Flaubert) (1952). He has also written chamber and choral music, as well as songs and pieces for piano and organ.

Burrill Phillips

A native of Omaha, Nebraska, Burrill Phillips (1907-   ) arrived in Rochester in 1931 after studies in Denver. He made such an impression that he was appointed to the Eastman faculty in 1933, and remained there until 1949. He is now associate professor of composition at the University of Illinois. His style is technically adept and his better-known orchestral compositions include: *Selections from McGuffey's Reader* (1934); *Courthouse Square* (1936); *Tom Paine Overture* (1946); *American Dance*, for bassoon and orchestra;

Concerto for piano and orchestra (1937), first performed in 1949; and Symphony No. 1. Among his stage works is the comic opera for four singers and small orchestra, *Don't We All?* (1949). He has also written extensively for instrumental combinations as well as for piano.

Robert Palmer

Robert Palmer, now a member of the music department at Cornell University, was born in Syracuse, New York, in 1915, and had his first training at Eastman under Hanson and Rogers. Afterward he worked with Harris and Copland, who had a great influence on his style of writing. His major orchestral works include a Concerto for small orchestra (1943); Symphonic Variations, Chorale and Fugue (1947-54); and *Abraham Lincoln Walks at Midnight* (after Nicholas Vachel Lindsay) for chorus and orchestra (1948). There are also two string quartets (1939, 1947); a Quartet for piano and strings (1947); Three Preludes for piano (1941); and a *Toccata Ostinato* (1945) employing a typical boogie-woogie bass.

William Bergsma

William Bergsma, by the time he was thirty years old, already had a long list of works to his credit. Born in Oakland, California, in 1921, he was educated at the Eastman School, and in 1946 was awarded a Guggenheim Fellowship. He became a member of the faculty of the Juilliard School of Music, where he continued to compose an impressive list of works. He displayed his interest in American folk song in the Suite from his ballet *Paul Bunyan* (1937), played first by the Burlingame (California) High School Orchestra in 1938. Other orchestral pieces include *Siesta and Happy Dance* from the ballet *Gold and the Señor Commandante* (1941); *Trumpet Song and Jubilee* (1943); *Music on a Quiet Theme* (1943); *The Fortunate Islands* (1946), composed while he was in the West Indies on his Guggenheim Fellowship and played at the twenty-fifth anniversary concert of the League of Composers in 1949. There is also a Symphony for chamber orchestra (1942); and a Symphony No. 1, which had its première by the CBS Symphony in 1950. For the stage, besides the ballet *Gold and the Señor Commandante* (1941), Bergsma has written an opera, *The Wife of Martin Guerre* (1955).

His chamber music includes a Suite for Brass Quartet (1938); and three string quartets (1942, 1944, 1953).

Ulysses Kay

Ulysses Kay, a Negro born in Tucson, Arizona, in 1917, another Eastman alumnus, also studied with Paul Hindemith at the Berkshire Music Center and at Yale. As early as 1939 Kay's *Sinfonietta* was introduced by the Rochester Civic Orchestra, and his ballet *Danse Calinda* was performed in Rochester in 1941. Kay has won many prizes, including an American Academy Fellowship, Columbia University's Ditson Award, and the Gershwin Award. Other works include an orchestral piece, *The Quiet One*, performed by the New York Little Symphony (1948); a symphony (1956); *Brief Elegy*, for oboe and strings, played at the National Gallery in Washington in 1948; a Quintet for flute and strings (1942); Suite for oboe and piano (1942); and a Suite for strings, introduced at the Museum of Modern Art in New York in 1952.

ECLECTICS

William Schuman

Of the many young American composers who have had most of their music study in the United States and under the foremost American composers, none is a better example than William Schuman, who was born in New York City, August 4, 1910. Having organized a jazz band in high school, he started his career on Broadway as a song writer and arranger, but unlike George Gershwin he abandoned the popular field entirely. After taking his bachelor's and master's degrees in music at Columbia University, he went to Salzburg to study conducting in 1935. Upon his return he was appointed Professor of Music on the faculty of Sarah Lawrence College, where he remained until 1945, when he became president of the Juilliard School of Music. He was awarded a Guggenheim Fellowship in 1939 and again in 1940, and was given the first Pulitzer Prize for music in 1943 for his secular cantata no. 2, *A Free Song* (to a Whitman poem), introduced on March 26, 1943, by the Boston Symphony Orchestra.

Nathan Broder, in an article on Schuman in the *Musical Quarterly*

(January, 1945), wrote that the most prominent traits of his music are "boldness, originality, freshness, resourcefulness, and intensity of feeling." "There is little," Broder continued, "of what the average listener would be inclined to regard as grace or charm, but humor may be found, either of the burlesque sort . . . or of a subtler kind. But what strikes the listener most of all in this music is its complete honesty and integrity, its deep seriousness—even at its gayest—its unswerving fidelity to the highest aims. Schuman can be light and unpretentious but he is seldom trivial."

Schuman has returned to Broadway on occasion, for example, in his *Circus Overture,* a sketch for Billy Rose's Revue, *The Seven Lively Arts* (1944), which was undertaken as the work not of a Tin-Pan Alley composer but a serious musician. Jazz has its place in many of his major works, but there is also present the influence of Roy Harris, who was his adviser and critic for many years.

To date Schuman has composed six symphonies. The First was written in 1935, and is scored for eighteen instruments. The Second was composed in 1937; the Third, introduced in 1941 by the Boston Symphony, received the award of the New York Music Critics Circle in the spring of 1942. The Fourth was played first by the Cleveland Orchestra in 1942. The Fifth (1943) is a Symphony for Strings, and the Sixth was written in 1948. Schuman's interest in the American scene may be found in his *American Festival Overture* (1939), based on a three-note theme which the composer describes as a New York boys' street-call; his *William Billings Overture* (1943); his *Newsreel, in Five Shots* (1941), originally for band, but which has been arranged for orchestra. For band there is also *George Washington Bridge* (1950).

Schuman has composed three ballets—*Undertow* (1945); *Night Journey* (1947); and *Judith* (1949); music for a film, *Steeltown* (1944); and music for the play *Henry VIII* (1944). There is considerable chamber music, which is one of his best mediums, and among his major choral works are *Pioneers* (1937); *Holiday Song* (1942); and two secular cantatas, *This Is Our Time* (1940) and *A Free Song* (1942). His opera, *The Mighty Casey,* is discussed in chapter XV.

Paul Creston

Paul Creston, born in New York, is not an experimentalist, for although his harmonies are often advanced, the form and construction of his works are conservative. Born Joseph Guttoveggio (October 10, 1906), his childhood nickname Cress developed into Paul Creston. Creston studied various branches of music with Giuseppe Randegger, Gaston Déthier, and Pietro Yon, but he was self-taught in theory and composition. He had Guggenheim Fellowships in 1938 and 1939. His first success came with his two *Choric Dances* (1938), first played at Yaddo and by the Cleveland Federal Orchestra in that year. They are perhaps the most widely performed of his works. Creston's First Symphony (1940) was awarded the New York Music Critics Circle Award in 1942; and he has written two others—the Second, introduced by the New York Philharmonic, February 15, 1945, and the Third, composed in 1950.

Creston's interests are varied, ranging from acoustics and aesthetics to musicotherapy. He has a long list of works for solo instruments and orchestra: concertos for saxophones and orchestra (1941), piano and orchestra (1949), and two pianos and orchestra (1951); a Concertino for marimba and orchestra (1940); a Fantasy for piano and orchestra (1942); *Poem* for harp and orchestra (1945); and *Fantasy* for trombone and orchestra (1947). Other orchestral works include *Threnody* (1938), whose modal idiom stems from Gregorian chant; *Prelude and Dance* (1941); *Pastorale and Tarantella* (1941); *Chant of 1942; Frontiers* (1943); and *Dawn Mood* (1944). For band he has composed a *Legend* (1942) and *Zanoni* (1946); for chorus *Three Chorales from Tagore* (1936). He has also composed a long list of chamber works.

Norman Dello Joio

Norman Dello Joio, born in New York on January 24, 1913, was trained at the Institute of Musical Art and later at the Juilliard Graduate School. Prior to receiving a scholarship at Juilliard he had composed his Concertino for piano. The first work he wrote as a Juilliard student was his Concertino for flute and strings. He received a Guggenheim Fellowship in 1944, and in 1945 he succeeded William Schuman as head of the music department at Sarah Lawrence College. Recently he resigned to give all of his time to composition.

Louis Biancolli, in the *New York World-Telegram* (1946), called Dello Joio "one of the liveliest talents in today's symphonic arena." By the age of forty he already had an impressive list of orchestral works, which include Concertos for two pianos and orchestra (1941), for harp and orchestra (1942), for clarinet and orchestra (1943); and a *Ricercari* for piano and orchestra, introduced by the New York Philharmonic-Symphony in 1946. His dissonant neoclassic tendencies continued to manifest themselves in such works as his *Sinfonietta* for piano and orchestra (1941); *Serenade for Orchestra* (1948); *Magnificat* (1943); *Concert Music*, played by the Pittsburgh Symphony in 1946; and the *Variations, Chaconne and Finale* (1947), whose themes are derived from Gregorian chant. *Three Symphonic Dances* was first heard with the Pittsburgh Symphony in 1948 and *New York Profiles* with the New York Philharmonic-Symphony in 1951.

Dello Joio's opera *The Triumph of St. Joan* was first heard through excerpts in concert form at a League of Composers concert in February, 1950. The following spring it was given a full stage production at Sarah Lawrence College. Other stage works include the ballets *The Duke of Sacramento* (1942); *On Stage!* (1945); and *Diversion of Angels* (1948); a second opera, *The Ruby* (1954), given in May, 1955, at the University of Indiana; and the powerfully moving television opera, *The Trial at Rouen*, first telecast by NBC's Opera Theatre on April 8, 1956. His choral music has been an important contribution, including such works as *Western Star* (1944); *The Mystic Trumpeter* (1943); *A Jubilant Song* (1946); *A Psalm of David* (1950), which Virgil Thomson called a "distinguished work"; and *The Blue Bird* (1952). There are also four Piano Sonatas (1942, 1943, 1947, 1948), and considerable chamber music, including a Sextet for three recorders and three strings (1943).

Paul Bowles

Paul Bowles, also born in New York (1911), studied with Aaron Copland and Virgil Thomson, after which he spent much time in distant lands, urged on by his interest in exotic folk music and by what he himself terms his "itchy foot." His travels have taken him to Spain, Northern Africa, the Sahara, the Antilles, and Central and South America. It was natural then that he became an eclectic in every sense of the word. During the year that Bowles enjoyed a Guggenheim Fellowship (1941), he composed an opera to a play by García Lorca, *The Wind Remains*. For the stage he has written the ballets *Yankee Clipper* (1936), performed by Ballet Caravan in 1938 in New York; *Pastorela* (1941); *Sentimental Colloquy* (1944); and *Facsimile* (1946). Equally successful in writing incidental music for many plays, his list includes *Horse Eats Hat* and *Dr. Faustus* (1936), for Orson Welles' productions; *Watch on the Rhine* (1941); *Liberty Jones* (1941); *Jacobowsky and the Colonel* (1944); and *The Glass Menagerie* (1945) by Tennessee Williams. Now living in northern Africa, he has also written two books of fiction, *The Sheltering Sky* and *The Delicate Prey*.

Philip James

Philip James (1890-) became associated with the Music Department of New York University in 1923 and since 1933 has been its Chairman. In 1932 he was the winner of the first prize of $5000 in a contest sponsored by the National Broadcasting Company. His winning piece, *Station WGZBX*, was an orchestral satire on radio programs. Others of his orchestral works are an *Overture on French Noëls* (1926); a *Sea Symphony* (1928); *Judith* (1927), a ballet; an overture, *Bret Harte* (1936); besides much chamber music, short choral pieces, and anthems.

Bernard Wagenaar

Bernard Wagenaar, born in Holland in 1894, came to America in 1921, and since 1927 (the year he became an American citizen) he has been a teacher of composition at the Juilliard School of Music. His works include four symphonies, of which the Fourth was introduced by the Boston Symphony in 1950; a Triple Concerto for flute, harp, cello, and orchestra (1935); a Sinfonietta (1929); and a Divertimento for orchestra (1929). Besides chamber music his "operatic comedy," *Pieces of Eight* (1943), was presented by Columbia University in 1944.

Ray Green

Ray Green, born in Missouri in 1909, was for a number of years the head of the composition department of the San Francisco Conservatory. Since 1948 he has been executive secretary of the American Music Center in New York. His orchestral works include *The Birds* (1934); Concertino for piano and orchestra (1937); *Three Pieces for a Concert* (1948); and Concertante for viola and orchestra (1948). There are also the *Three Inventories of Casey Jones* for percussion

(1936), and *Jig for a Concert* for two pianos (1948). His best-known choral works are *Sea Calm,* for men's voices (1934); *Two Madrigals* (Whitman) (1933); *Westoon Wind* (1946); and in his *Sunday Sing Symphony* (1948), he has successfully delved into the past in his use of early American hymns and fuging tunes.

NATIONALISTS

Morton Gould

Superficially, it might seem that Morton Gould (born in New York, December 10, 1913) was a younger Gershwin, for he brings to his symphonic scores a strong flavor of the American popular-music idiom. His scores, a bit theatrical and in the Hollywood and Broadway manner, have achieved wide success. Gould, however, did not start on Broadway and then approach the concert hall, as did Gershwin. Instead, he had a thorough academic musical education. He studied at the Institute of Musical Art in New York, and completed a two-year course in theory and composition with Vincent Jones at New York University at the precocious age of fifteen. He became associated with the Radio City Music Hall and the National Broadcasting Company, and has since become well-known as a conductor in radio, for phonograph records, and in concerts.

One of Gould's earliest orchestral works to attract attention was his *Chorale and Fugue in Jazz* (1931), which Stokowski and the Philadelphia Orchestra played in 1936. This was followed in rapid succession by a string of major works. Of a series of four symphonies, the First (*American Symphonette*) (1936), has for one of its movements the popular *Pavane,* while the Fourth is the *Latin-American Symphonette* (1944). In *Foster Gallery* (1941) Gould paid tribute to Stephen Foster by developing several of his songs symphonically, in a manner the composer admits is more Gould than Foster. *An American Salute* (1942) uses as its theme *When Johnny Comes Marching Home. A Lincoln Legend* was introduced by the NBC Symphony in 1942, and *Spirituals in Five Movements,* for String Choir and Orchestra by the New York Philharmonic-Symphony in the same year. Gould's interest in the American scene is manifested in such scores as *Minstrel Show* (1946), *Philharmonic Waltzes* (1948), and *Big City Blues* (1950). There is also *Cowboy*

Rhapsody (1940), *Jericho* (1941), *Family Album* (1951), for band; as well as a symphonic work for orchestra entitled *Declaration,* based on the Declaration of Independence. This was first performed by the National Symphony Orchestra at its Inaugural Concert for President Eisenhower in 1957. In addition to an orchestra the score calls for a chorus of thirteen (representing the original states) and two soloists, one representing a Town Crier speaking for the revolutionists and the other a Tory.

Gould's other music includes scores for the motion pictures *Ring of Steel* (1941), *Delightfully Dangerous* (1945), and *San Francisco Conference* (1946); the ballets *Interplay* (1943) and *Fall River Legend* (1948); and the scores for two musical comedies, *Billion Dollar Baby* (1945) and *Arms and the Girl* (1950). One of his most novel scores is the *Concerto for Tap Dancer and Orchestra* (1952), which had its première in the Eastman Theatre, Rochester, New York, with the composer conducting the Rochester Civic Orchestra and Danny Daniels as the soloist, in November, 1952.

Don Gillis

Don Gillis has for a number of years been a radio production director for NBC, and as a composer he has been interested in all things American. Born in Missouri in 1912, Gillis injects a typical American humor in his scores, which sparkle with a brashness that reflects the popular tempo of the day. His many symphonies contain all types of American rhythms and often have curious titles, such as *Symphony 5½*, which, as he explained, was composed "for fun" between his Fifth and Sixth Symphonies. Some of his orchestral pieces have distinctive titles—*The Panhandle, Portrait of a Frontier Town, The Raven, Citizen Tom Paine, The Alamo, Scherzo-frenia,* and others.

Ernst Bacon

Ernst Bacon, born in Chicago, Illinois, May 26, 1898, was a pupil of Ernest Bloch, and in 1932 won a Pulitzer Scholarship. In 1939 and again in 1942 Bacon was awarded Guggenheim Fellowships. During the 1930s he was director of the Federal Music Project in San Francisco. His three Suites, *Country Roads, Unpaved* (1936), *Ford's Theatre* (1943), *From These States* (1943), show his preoccupation with Americana. So do his two folk operas, *A Tree on the*

Plains (1942), first performed at the Spartanburg Music Festival at Converse College in 1942, and *The Drumlin Legend* (1949), which had its première at the Columbia University Festival in 1949. His orchestral music includes two symphonies (1932, 1937) and a *Prelude and Fugue* (1926).

Elie Siegmeister

Elie Siegmeister, born in New York in 1909, has also identified himself with American folk music by compiling several collections of folk songs. His orchestral music includes a *Walt Whitman Overture* (1939), *Strange Funeral in Braddock* (1933), *Ozark Set* (1943), *Prairie Legend* (1944), *Western Suite* (1945), *Sunday in Brooklyn* (1946), *Summer Night,* and two symphonies (1946, 1948). For piano there is his *American Sonata* (1944).

Robert McBride

Robert McBride, born in Arizona in 1911, winner of a Guggenheim Fellowship in 1937, has specialized in short orchestral works which show where his youthful interests lay. *Strawberry Jam (Home Made)* (1941) is the title of a piece that was first introduced in New York in 1942. Others are entitled *Jingle Jangle* (1938), *Fugato on a Well-Known Theme* (1935), *Swing Stuff* (1938), *Wise-Apple Five* (1940), and the *Go Choruses* (1936), based on the adventures of a jazz band in which each player takes the chorus of the tune and "goes" with it.

Dai-Keong Lee

From Honolulu came Dai-Keong Lee (1915-   ) to study with Roger Sessions, Frederick Jacobi, and Aaron Copland, and to win Guggenheim Fellowships in 1945 and again in 1951. His music reflects the part of America he has known best and the titles speak for themselves. The orchestral pieces include *Prelude and Hula* (1939), *Hawaiian Festival Overture* (1940), *Introduction and Allegro* for strings (1941), *Golden Gate Overture* (1942), *Pacific Prayer* (1943), two symphonies (1946, 1950), and a Violin Concerto (1947). He has also composed three operas, *Open the Gates* (1948), *The River* (1950), and *Mary of Magdala* (1950); as well as a ballet, *Children's Caprice* (1948). Among his pieces for band are the *Hawaiian*

State March (1948) and *Tropical Overture* (1948). He has written for piano, organ, and various chamber combinations.

Ferde Grofé

Typical of many who moved from the realm of Broadway to the concert hall is Ferde Grofé, born in New York, 1892, the arranger who orchestrated Gershwin's *Rhapsody in Blue*. His many orchestral suites which brilliantly describe the American scene include: *Grand Canyon Suite* (1932), *Broadway at Night, Mississippi Suite* (1925), *Tabloid Suite* (1933), and *Hollywood Suite* (1935). These show the influence of arranging for Paul Whiteman, especially in the "harmony chorus" where a solo instrument, often a saxophone, croons the melody softly while the brass section gives it a subdued chord accompaniment. Then the more rhythmic sections would use the brass in a somewhat polite imitation of the hot jazz artists.

A MINORITY GROUP OF EXPERIMENTALISTS

John J. Becker

John J. Becker, a native of Henderson, Kentucky, where he was born in 1886, is a valiant champion of nonconformist music and a seeker of new and unusual orchestral sounds. His published works include three Symphonies, various Concertos with orchestra, several *Soundpieces* for string combinations; and stage works, including the ballets *Dance Figure* (1933) and *Obongo-Dance Primitive* (1933), the latter employing twenty-nine percussion instruments. In *A Marriage with Space* (1933) and *The Life of Man* (1937) (based on the play by Leonid Andreev), he has experimented with new combinations of music, dancing, and dramatic action. In the symposium *American Composers on American Music* he suggested that if we must learn by imitation, our study should be based on all of the musical systems, new and old, adding his own belief: "Laws are made for imitators. Creators make laws." Becker is at present at Barat College of the Sacred Heart, Lake Forest, Illinois, where he is composer-in-residence.

Henry Brant

Henry Brant, born in Montreal, Canada, in 1913, and now a resident of New York, studied at the Juilliard School of Music with

Goldmark and later worked with Copland, Antheil, and Riegger. He has experimented with what he calls "oblique harmony," and is concerned with the relationship of the sounds made by voices and/or instruments placed at various points about the concert hall. In commenting on his works and his idiom Brant has said: "No two of my works have any surface resemblance in technique and style." Repudiating such earlier works as his *Variations* (1930), he has rewritten his *Sonata Sacra* for hardware and piano as *Five and Ten Cent Store Music* for violin, piano, and kitchen utensils (1930-31) and his *Crying Jag* for Military Band as *Street Music* for Dance Band (1949).

Since 1950, Brant has written such pieces as *Millennium 1*, for eight trumpets, bells, and cymbals (1950); *Millennium 2*, for ten trumpets, ten trombones, eight French horns, four tubas, four percussion players and soprano (1954); and the series of *Galaxy* pieces for various wind and percussion instruments, which show his search for a new concept of polyphony, such as one finds in the exotic music of the Orient.

Alexei Haieff

Alexei Haieff studied with Nadia Boulanger after he had worked at the Juilliard School of Music. He was born in Siberia in 1914, and after living in China came to the United States at the age of seventeen. In 1946 he was awarded a Guggenheim Fellowship and in 1949 one at the American Academy in Rome. Experimenting with extreme dissonant sounds, his orchestral works include an early Symphony (1942); a Divertimento (1944) for chamber orchestra, introduced by the New York Little Symphony in 1946; a Violin Concerto (1948); and a Piano Concerto, played at the Columbia University Festival in 1952. In reviewing the Piano Concerto in the *Musical Quarterly* (July, 1952), Henry Cowell wrote that it seems conceived as a series of fanfares. "The effect of so many exclamations and explosions," he said, "kept up for so long that no possible resolution of the forces invoked could give proportionate relief, is exhausting; one leaves the concert hall feeling somewhat bruised and battered, if respectful."

Haieff has also composed two ballets: *The Princess Dondilda and Her Entourage* (1946) and *Beauty and the Beast* (1947). There is a

Sonata for two pianos (1945), as well as other instrumental pieces, and chamber works.

AMERICAN ORCHESTRAS DURING THE WAR YEARS

With the war in full swing, America's orchestral music went into its greatest period, as far as the growth of the smaller orchestras was concerned. The New York Philharmonic-Symphony was suffering because it had to play under an endless stream of guest conductors. Barbirolli was still conductor in name, but as the centenary approached in 1942, there was a noticeable lack of commissioned works and no American conductors. Alexander Smallens and Howard Barlow were good men and might have been asked to appear, if only to take part in the celebration of America's oldest orchestra. But what the orchestra needed most of all was the strict discipline that can only come with a permanent conductor. It found one later in Artur Rodzinski, but by 1947 he had left in a fit of temperament.

Koussevitzky, in his last years of tenure with the Boston Symphony, was still the dominant figure in American orchestral music. His talent was so many-sided, his work so consecrated, that his service to the composer and the public alike can never be forgotten. He seemed to draw strength from every phase of American musical life, and he played and commissioned more American music than any other one conductor.

The Philadelphia Orchestra continued under Ormandy to be one of the truly great orchestras. Ormandy could not emulate Stokowski's pioneering spirit in performing new music (others were already doing that), but he kept the marvelous tone of the group, if anything enhancing it, and the concerts have remained a delight.

The Chicago Symphony, preparing for its fiftieth anniversary, far outran the New York Philharmonic-Symphony in commissioning works. Frederick Stock conducted the opening of the Jubilee with his own *Festival Fanfare* on October 10, 1940. Darius Milhaud, who had recently arrived in America, conducted the world première of his First Symphony, seven days later. Other new works included John Alden Carpenter's *Symphony in C;* Roy Harris' *American Creed,* for chorus and orchestra; and Stravinsky conducting the world première of his newest work, *Symphony in C,* dedicating it in the words he had used ten years before for the Boston Symphony's celebration. When Stock died in 1942, he was only the second conductor the orchestra had had in over fifty years. Under his guidance it was a beautiful group, rich in tone, and maintaining the finest artistic principles. Stock, too, had been a great champion of American music and at a time when there were fewer composers of stature to draw from. Hans Lange took over for the 1942-43 season, and then Désiré Defauw, from Brussels, Belgium, became the conductor.

In Baltimore, the old municipal orchestra was completely reorganized in 1942, with Reginald Stewart as its conductor. With Otto Ortman's resignation as head of the Peabody Conservatory, Stewart had come from Canada in 1941 to head the school. From three or four concerts a season, Stewart and the board of directors put the orchestra on a professional level, with a nineteen-week season, and from the beginning its growth was incredible. In 1952, when Stewart resigned, Massimo Freccia was called from New Orleans, and under his superb musicianship, the orchestra continued to grow consistently, at last taking its place with the major orchestras of the nation.

Cleveland's orchestra under George Szell is excellent, and has attained new heights, becoming one of the half-dozen top orchestras in America. When Eugéne Goossens left Cincinnati for Australia at the close of the 1946-47 season, one of the most heartening signs of America's maturity was the appointment of the young American conductor, Thor Johnson, by Cincinnati's board.

The St. Louis orchestra, under Golschmann, continued to play elegantly and Pierre Monteux brought the greatest distinction to San Francisco's orchestra. Mitropoulos had immediate success in Minneapolis, when Ormandy left to go to Philadelphia, and the many outstanding recordings of the Minneapolis orchestra attest its vitality and style. Los Angeles heard many guest conductors after Otto Klemperer left in 1940, but in 1943-44 Alfred Wallenstein was appointed, and he quickly brought the orchestra into national prominence, not alone for its homogeneous tone, but as a leader in performing contemporary music. In the 1947-48 season, it led all the American orchestras in the performance of contemporary music.

The close of the war seemed to be a signal for many American cities to wake up and have their own orchestras. Massimo Freccia revitalized the New Orleans Symphony, which had been formed in 1936 after a successful free concert under Arthur Zack. In three years Saul Caston, Stokowski's assistant conductor as well as first trumpet of the Philadelphia Orchestra, brought Denver's orchestra into the "major league" class. Texas, not to be outdone, woke up to her cultural possibilities, and as the 1940s closed, it was the second state in the nation that could boast of three major orchestras. New York had the Philharmonic-Symphony, Rochester, and Buffalo orchestras; Texas had orchestras in Dallas, Houston, and San Antonio. The Dallas orchestra, serving the center of northeast Texas, became a vital force under Antal Dorati in 1948-49 (he later left to go to Minneapolis), particularly in the commissioning of new works. Dorati was followed by Walter Hendl, young American conductor. Houston, in southwest Texas, was fortunate in getting Efrem Kurtz from Kansas City (1948), for he built the orchestra into a virtuoso group, as fine as any in the North. In the Southwest, the San Antonio Symphony Orchestra, founded in 1940 by Max Reiter, was still alive and fresh, frequently gaining national prominence through its program policy. Like the other Texas orchestras, the San Antonio plays much American music and encourages Texas composers.

A vital and dedicated group was formed in New York in 1947, under Thomas K. Scherman. Called the Little Orchestra Society, it made a major point of presenting to New York each season neglected masterpieces and unfamiliar works of early orchestral and operatic music. It also championed the present-day composer. Many thought New York did not need another orchestra, and Scherman's imaginative powers were greatly underestimated at first. But with dogged persistence and despite frequent adverse critical reviews, he soon proved that he could accomplish his aims and his orchestra attained an enviable reputation for its unusual programs and clever children's concerts. Scherman's first concert is a good example of what he set out to do, and he has never changed his course. On October 20, 1947, he conducted the first performances anywhere of David Diamond's *Romeo and Juliet* music, a Concerto for harp and orchestra by Norman Dello Joio, and Douglas Moore's bright score, *A Farm Journal*.

At the close of the first half of the twentieth century, America was no longer provincial. Long since, her composers had faced the world confidently. In the growing recognition of the potentialities of her native conductors during and after the war, was yet another sign of the rightness of things. The Negro was also to take his place among his colleagues. When Dean Dixon, at twenty-six, led the New York Philharmonic-Symphony at a Stadium concert in August, 1941, he was the first of his race to have that honor. Since then he has been conducting in Europe where he has carried the message of American music with the greatest success.

RADIO GIVES WAY TO TELEVISION

Radio music had a fitful life during the war years, and little was done for the furthering of the serious repertory. Looking back it must be admitted in all fairness that in the 1940s nearly every important musical organization could be heard over the radio, and as most of the new works received their first performances from this source, perhaps there was not the need for radio's championship of the contemporary composer that there had been in the past. Certainly there were countless broadcasts, of every type of music, and it became as difficult to avoid hearing good music as it had been in past years to get the opportunity to hear it. Wallenstein did fine work from WOR until he left for the West Coast; Howard Barlow was in charge of CBS; and of course Stokowski continued to give first performances of new works when he conducted the NBC Orchestra while Toscanini was out of the country or appearing as a guest conductor with other orchestras. In 1941, the Columbia network broadcast a program of chamber music as the Eighteenth Festival of the International Society for Contemporary Music opened, the festival having been forced out of Europe because of the war. The broadcasts ran from May 17 through May 25. After that there were spasmodic performances and America could in no way approach the remarkable activity of the European radio stations after the war, nor has it to this day.

Television, meanwhile, was music's newest medium, and was already beginning to make the most of its great potentialities.

The first opera telecast in the United States (1940) was the first act of *Pagliacci*, sent out from studios in Radio City. Two years later the General Electric television station in Schenectady experimented with the complete *Hansel and Gretel*, sung in English by students from the Hartt School of Music in Hartford. In the 1944-45 season, NBC continued its project of telecasting operas, and with

Herbert Graf as the producer five operas in a condensed form and in English were heard. TV proved at once to be a better medium than radio for anything connected with the theater, be it opera or ballet. Scenery, costumes, expressive features, and movement are much better for telecasting than long orchestral programs in a studio or concert hall. However, 1948 brought two major orchestras to the television public on rival networks on March 20, when WCBS-TV featured Eugene Ormandy conducting the Philadelphia Orchestra in the Academy of Music, Philadelphia, and WNBT of the National Broadcasting Company transmitted Arturo Toscanini (who would be 81 in five days), in an all-Wagner program an hour later.

The Metropolitan Opera House had its opening night televised for the first time (November 29, 1948), through NBC—the opera being Verdi's *Otello*. It would also have Strauss's *Der Rosenkavalier* on the air the next season, and *Don Carlos* in 1950.

From 1948 on, as conditions improved and camera technique was developed, NBC-TV Opera Theatre came into being. With Peter Herman Adler at its head, excellent young singers were chosen, and in succeeding years a regular series was inaugurated which consisted of about eight operas a year, with a narrator cleverly piecing together the story. Those who have seen these productions know that the standards are on the highest artistic level. They have undoubtedly done much for the cause of American opera, as well as opera in English.

REBIRTH OF THE RECORDING INDUSTRY

When Dr. Peter Goldmark, Director of the CBS Engineering Research and Development Laboratories, demonstrated on June 18, 1948, the new LP (long-playing) Microgroove, nonbreakable twelve-inch, vinylite disc, he heralded a new era for the record industry. Capable of playing for fifty minutes, and sponsored jointly by Columbia Records (a CBS subsidiary) and Philco, the new record was to presage great things for both the makers and the consumers. With twenty-five minutes of playing time on each side (the old-style record played only about four and a half minutes), the new records were lighter, easier to store, wore better, and cost less to produce.

There followed a bitter war between Columbia and RCA Victor (who wished to produce only their own 45-rpm small records), but within two years the public made its decision, showing unquestionably that it preferred the less expensive and longer-playing 33⅓-rpm record. Columbia made its discoveries available to all companies, and in the next years nearly a hundred and fifty companies began issuing records in the United States alone. Most of the serious European repertory is now on LP records, while popular music may be had on the old 78-rpm or the newer 45 records. Consumers had the advantage of several different works on one record, as well as recordings of complete symphonies, while an uncut opera could be put on three records, as against about twenty of the older ones.

Public taste developed rapidly, and companies soon vied with each other in bringing out unusual or seldom-heard works. It would take several years before the serious American repertory would appear on records, but almost at once every other type of music was to be had. In reproduction and preservation, recording did for music what printing had done centuries before for language, and while the so-called "canned music" can never take the place of a live performance, records became more and more a power in the growth and training of intelligent listeners. The gramophone, motion pictures, and radio have revolutionized the life of all Americans, and with the advent of the half-century, only Hollywood has failed to make the best use of the many fine composers the studios have engaged. Once again the European industries have shown what can be done in the realm of the motion picture. They have proved that it can be an art form of the first rank, and they have consistently used their best composers. Hollywood, as an industry, has come close to it with Aaron Copland's superb score for *The Red Pony*. Certain documentary films have proved that it can be so, as in Virgil Thomson's music for *Louisiana Story* (for which he won the Pulitzer Prize in 1949), but Hollywood picture makers can never resist tampering with the lives of the people they attempt to portray, and so the pictures of the great musical figures—Chopin, Liszt, Melba, and Caruso—are distorted and unnatural. However, the miracle may yet happen, and only time may tell.

BERKSHIRE MUSIC CENTER

By 1949, the summer festival at Tanglewood was attracting large and enthusiastic audiences, but of far greater importance to America's musical scene had been the growth of the Berkshire Music Center, which had already attained an international standing. To be on its faculty or admitted to its student body was no small honor. Koussevitzky, in his mid-seventies, had proved to be an educator of whom Lowell Mason would have been justly proud. As a professional music school, the Center has attained far more prominence than the summer concerts of the Boston Symphony Orchestra alone could have engendered. The best men in the orchestra made up the faculty of the school, and of course the profits from the concerts were a substantial item in the school's maintenance. Aaron Copland was assistant to Koussevitzky, beginning in 1949. Richard Burgin, Leonard Bernstein, and Eleazar de Carvalho were the orchestral assistants, with Hugh Ross and Christopher Honass in the choral department. There was also a department of composition, headed by Copland and a different foreign visitor each summer—such as Darius Milhaud, Arthur Honegger, and Olivier Messiaen. Further, there was a department of opera, headed by Boris Goldovsky. Students appeared in orchestra and chamber concerts, there was a weekly concert of new works, and the opera group presented scenes or entire acts from the standard operas, as well as two unusual works—one old, one new—given in complete form. The student learned not only how to sing in opera, but received instruction in conducting, stage direction, and scenery and costume design. Stage lighting was not neglected, nor the difficult task of libretto writing. Thirty singers were chosen by auditions, and some forty auditors, not counting those who were interested in the purely technical side of opera. The choral department, originally directed by Robert Shaw, later by Ross and Honass, makes up the large Festival Chorus, a smaller Madrigal Chorus, and a Bach Choir. For their accompaniments there is a student orchestra.

The carefully selected student body, slightly less than five hundred, receive an unbelievably fine background. Even the layman is encouraged, both as auditor and participant in the choral singing classes, for the school quite wisely recognizes the importance of creating intelligent listeners. The stimulus of this remarkable school has been of incalculable worth to its students, instructors, and auditors, and could future generations of Americans have the advantage of similar schools, built around the many important symphonic groups throughout the nation, America's musical growth might know no limits.

RENAISSANCE OF CHORAL MUSIC

An interesting renaissance of choral music written by contemporary composers was to be noticed in the years after the war, as well as a new interest in oratorio. We have seen how Dudley Buck dominated the field of choral music before the turn of the century. Clarence Dickinson (1873-   ), as director of the School of Sacred Music at Union Theological Seminary, greatly enriched the church repertory, as did Mark Andrews (1875-1939) and Noble Cain (1896-   ). For the Catholic service, Pietro Yon (1886-1943) stands out, having come to America in 1907, and become organist at St. Patrick's Cathedral in New York in 1926. His *Gesu Bambino,* first composed as an organ piece, has become an American traditional Christmas song. His pupil, Paul Creston, as organist of St. Malachy's Church in New York, brought stature to the service with his *Missa Pro Defunctis* (1938) and a *Missa Solemnis.*

Two of the most eminent composers of Jewish liturgical music have been Ernest Bloch and Frederick Jacobi (1891-1952). Other important ones include Abraham W. Binder (1895-   ); Jacob Weinberg (1883-1956); and Lazare Saminsky (1882-   ), who has been director of music at Temple Emanu-El, New York, since 1924.

It might be said that renewed interest in choral music started with Bernard Rogers' oratorio *The Passion,* which had its première in Cincinnati, at the May Festival (1944) conducted by Eugène Goossens. Leonard Bernstein presented Marc Blitzstein's oratorio *Airborne,* on March 23, 1946, dramatic in its terseness and percussive style. Lukas Foss, no doubt deriving inspiration from Bach's solo cantatas, dedicated his new score, *The Song of Songs,* to Ellabelle Davis, who first performed the work with Koussevitzky and the Boston Symphony on March 7, 1947. Roy Harris "composed for the Catholic people of America" a *Mass for Men's Voices and Organ,* which was introduced at Columbia University's Festival of Music in New York on May 13, 1948, instead of in St. Patrick's, for which it had been intended.

In New York, Paul Boepple, conducting the Dessoff Choirs, brightened the musical scene with performances of Renaissance music, and Robert Shaw, of the original Collegiate Chorale, vied with John Finley Williamson (of Princeton's Westminster Choir School) and Hugh Ross of the Schola Cantorum in presenting major choral works. In later years, Shaw was to conduct many important premières, and to give series of concerts which featured established works, along with new ones.

This activity has been multiplied many times throughout America, as choirs and madrigal groups, as well as large choruses of amateurs or college students have given concerts in which programs included every type of choral music ever written.

Two groups of singers appeared in the late 1940s that might be said to recall the nineteenth century in America. Leonard De Paur and his Infantry Chorus, which came out of the war, were in every way superior to the earlier Negro singers, and have been of inestimable service to the Negro race. De Paur's magnificent group, beautifully disciplined and admirably trained, reminded America of its great heritage of Negro song. The other group was a singing family that came to America from abroad, as the earlier Rainer brothers had done—the Trapp Family Singers. They were a carry-over of many generations of family singers, and, led by their priest, they sang the finest music of their native Austria, drawn from both sacred and secular art song as well as folk song. The group's performances brought warmth and pleasure to many in America, and were an excellent illustration of the home-music of an age long since vanished.

THE CONTRIBUTION OF THE FOUNDATIONS

As national income taxes took their toll of the wealthy patron who had formerly subsidized the musician and given him freedom to compose, of sponsored chamber-music groups, or paid orchestral and operatic deficits, a further change took place in America's musical life. While occasionally the talented student or composer might still have the benefit of a generous patron of music, the vast majority of the individuals as well as the institutions became more and more dependent on the monies available through tax-free groups. With the resources of conservatories and even large universities dwindling after the war as living and running expenses mounted, the musician at mid-century was very much in need of the many foundations set up to help the deserving and talented individual. At a time when an artist needs the leisure to compose or create, such foundations as the Guggenheim are equipped to help him. The larger foundations such as the Rockefeller, the Mellon, and Ford, meet the needs of the many large projects, but even they cannot pay deficits, but must use their money (as with the Louisville Philharmonic and the New York City Center) for the commissioning of original works. Today it is possible to obtain a Pulitzer Traveling Scholarship from Columbia University for composition. From Yale University, a Charles H. Ditson Fellowship will help in graduate study abroad. Harvard University has the John Knowles Paine Traveling Scholarship in musicology or composition, while the Beebe Fund Fellowships are designed for persons who have passed the student age, and are granted for musical research as well as for composition.

For the performer, New York's Edgar M. Leventritt Foundation Award gives a solo appearance with the New York Philharmonic-Symphony, while Chicago's Michaels Memorial Award allows a thousand dollars for further study, in addition to an engagement with the Chicago Symphony at Ravinia Park. The Walter W. Naumburg Musical Foundation in New York gives a Town Hall debut recital for qualifying instrumentalists and vocalists between the ages of sixteen and thirty who have not already had a formal New York debut. With the National Federation of Music Clubs contests, and many others, there will always be hope for tomorrow's potential talent. As America reached the halfway mark in the twentieth century, life, as far as music was concerned, took on new meaning.

CHAPTER XV

Music at the Half-Century

MUSIC EDUCATION

Colleges and Universities

The colleges and the universities, as well as the conservatories and music schools that guide the destinies of the American student of music have in recent years begun to play a much more important and dramatic part in the life of their individual communities than ever before. Once students are trained, many of them are urged to return to their respective homes and to make every effort to raise the existing standards of music and revitalize the cultural life through cooperation with the related arts. Music cannot be a static thing, and even in such large cities as New York and Chicago conditions constantly change. There is always a place for new ideas and projects, if they are born of inspiration and genius.

There was a definite enriching of the musical life in the communities of the colleges and great universities as America went into the second half of the twentieth century, particularly as these centers became more and more self-sufficient and less dependent on music from the outside. Concerts were on the highest possible level, whether given by faculty members or students; opera workshops gave admirable performances, often in English, some of which might even be judged by professional standards; and there was a healthy revival of all types of music, both instrumental and vocal, with ancient and modern instruments.

With important composers in residence—such men as Piston and Thompson at Harvard, Bloch at the University of California, Sessions at Princeton, Hindemith at Yale—many of our universities have been completely independent of any center, such as New York, yet each in its way has dominated American music. Not all moved forward as much as they might have, yet many younger schools have forged to the front. Music in the Midwest is alive and vigorous, thanks to the vision of such universities as Northwestern and the University of Wisconsin. The latter has done a great service for chamber music by having the Pro-Arte Quartet in residence, and arranging for it to tour throughout the state.

The University of Southern California has a splendid opera workshop under Carl Ebert, who won an international reputation at the Mozart Festival in Glyndebourne, England. The University of Illinois, in planning its Annual Festival of Contemporary Music, does modern music a service through its symposium, where the music that is performed may be discussed. The quite young Brandeis University at Waltham, Massachusetts, held its first Annual Festival in 1952, with Leonard Bernstein in charge, and showed its catholic taste in planning programs that contained the finest music from all over the world. San Francisco has long been hospitable to chamber music, and Mills College in Oakland has for many years sponsored summer concerts by the London and the Budapest quartets—six at the College and six in San Francisco, matching similar concerts by the University of California at Berkeley.

As the European school of composition declined, native composers no longer had reason to go abroad for study, for the supremely gifted teachers of composition to be found in practically every major college and conservatory have been responsible for the creation of an American school of composition that has no peer.

Public Schools

If Lowell Mason could walk the earth again he would be amazed to see the state of music in the public schools. In hundreds of the larger schools excellent training is given in piano classes, in rhythm bands, and periods devoted to the singing of folk songs. Madrigals and larger choral works are performed in public concerts, and talented students may major in music and have their theory, sight-reading, and counterpoint in school time. Music, if only listening to records, is the order of the day, and not just confined to an isolated period as it was a few years ago.

The Music Educators National Conference (MENC) was responsible for the establishment of music education as a profession, and it has proceeded to promote music as a part of education. Now it is concerned with the functioning of music as a part of general education. It knows only too well that while there are many teachers who are inspired in the cause of the dissemination of good music, there are still many schools where the work is slack and slipshod. But the alert music educator knows that in many of the talented students there is the future of America's music, and that as they plan their careers they need the best guidance possible.

There are many teachers who can envision a future for music only as it is performed, while there are others who have proved the practical worth of exposing the supposedly unmusical child to periods of listening to music, without much attempt to guide. Both systems have their merits, for the former will feed the large army of practicing musicians, while the latter will supply the audiences of tomorrow. Today, save in isolated sections of the country, our children are exposed to music in a way that has made America unique among the nations of the world, save perhaps England. The greatest need is still for teachers who are themselves so well-trained and possessed of such a wide knowledge and experience that they will be able to keep their work on the highest artistic level.

Private Teachers

Another important factor in America's maturing has been the amazing development of the local teacher who maintains a private studio, and might be said to be the link between music in the public (or private) school and the later years spent in a college or conservatory. Having banded together as the Music Teacher's National Association (MTNA), this group of private teachers has grown into one of the most progressive groups in the nation. The winter conventions are made up of all kinds of forums, clinics, and seminars, in which all problems of teaching and methods of pedagogy are aired and discussed. Their standing has become so high, that conservatories and music-school administrators, and important college faculty members attend, and groups like the Music Library Association or the American Musicological Society (consisting of college and university scholars) now plan their meetings at the same time. All groups are stimulated and learn the problems that face the teacher, and the unusual concerts planned for each convention keep the members informed as to the newest trends in music. This is but another evidence of the healthy state of American music today.

The aspiring student soon learns that the profession of music includes many fields, and each year finds the profession nearer the earning capacities of comparable professions in other fields. Young America is at last realizing that there are countless opportunities in the field of music other than those of the concert artist—long the dream and ideal of the young musician. Teaching, performing in orchestras, singing and dancing in stage and television productions, directing choirs, writing or arranging for radio and television—all furnish ample opportunity for those students who have imagination and talent.

High Schools for the Arts

Already in New York a novel idea has borne fruit that may well spread over the country. Two public high schools—the High School of Music and Art, and High School of Performing Arts—have been established for the student who shows an aptitude in music or the other arts. Drawn from all classes throughout the city, regardless of race or color, these students receive a well-rounded academic education and an intensive training in music and art. They learn to write and perform, acquire a healthy respect for traditional music, and they do it with no more thought of its being unusual than students in other schools write and produce school plays or put out school magazines. When this begins to happen so naturally, America's future music is on a more solid foundation than ever before.

EXPERIMENTAL COMPOSERS

Charles Edward Ives

While America has seen many experiments come and go, and had witnessed the revolutionary tendencies of both European musicians and her own native sons, there had been in her midst since the turn of the century one of the most remarkable figures in all contemporary music—Charles Ives—who, unaided and without any knowledge of what was taking place in Europe, anticipated many of the radical changes which took place in the early years of the twentieth century, and for which composers like Stravinsky and Schoenberg got the credit. Not that they did not deserve them, for they ⌣⌣⌣, but it took America nearly fifty years to become aware of the work and significance of Ives.

Born in Danbury, Connecticut (1874), the son of a local musician who was a teacher of violin, piano, and theory, leader of the village choir, and member of the town band, Charles Ives had his earliest lessons from his father. To say that they were unorthodox would be an understatement, for George Ives, sensing the restless, seeking nature of his son, made him the companion for his experiments into the realm of unusual sound. The use of quarter-tones, attempts to recreate the echo of a horn sounded over Danbury Pond, the sounds of bands playing at the opposite ends of the village green and from the church tower during patriotic celebrations, the tinkle of glasses, and the sounding of bells—all such raw musical materials appealed to the father's free-ranging mind and figured in the early musical experiences of the boy Charles. In the old church hymns and revival songs, the exuberant dance tunes, even the shouting at baseball games, George Ives heard a natural expression of all things American, and he let none pass him by. But neither did he neglect the classics, for the chamber music of Handel, Bach, and Beethoven had an equal place in the Ives house. That his musical education might be a sound one, Charles was sent to Yale to continue his studies under Horatio Parker. He also had lessons with Harry R. Shelley, and studied organ with Dudley Buck. It was while he was at Yale that Ives wrote his First Symphony, which purported to be in D minor, but whose first subject was in some half-dozen keys. Parker neither liked it nor understood it, and insisted that Ives write conventionally. No doubt the practice was good for him, but in the seclusion of his own rooms Ives continued to write as he felt and he knew his father would approve.

When his college career was over and Ives had to choose his life work, he was in complete agreement with his father, who, he wrote: "felt that a man could keep his music interest stronger, cleaner, bigger and freer if he didn't try to make a living out of it." Thus he chose a business career so that he could support the music he loved. In the years which led to the first World War, Ives was as active in his business as he was in his music. In January, 1907, with Julian Myrick as a partner, he put into force millions of dollars' worth of new insurance. It seems ironical that the nation's insurance men had a healthy respect for Charles Ives, while the musical world, except for a very small group, knew him not at all, or if it did, viewed his music with condescending amusement. The Ives & Myrick training school for insurance agents was recognized as sound and was soon imitated throughout the nation. Another of Ives's ideas, that of proper "estate planning," was equally sound and today is one of the basic factors in the selling of life insurance.

Happily married (1908) to the former Harmony Twichell, Ives threw all of his creative energies into his business in the daytime and his musical composition at night and over the week ends. Overwork and artistic frustration, the derision of those who performed or heard his music for the first time, brought on a physical collapse just as World War I ended. The last part of his life was spent in retirement and partial invalidism.

The music world first heard of Ives in 1919, when he was enough recovered from his illness to plan a course of action. It was then that he published at his own expense and distributed without charge, a cloth-bound volume which contained his Second Pianoforte Sonata, "Concord, Mass., in the 1840's." This was accompanied by another cloth-bound volume entitled *Essays before a Sonata* (1920), with one essay for each of the Sonata's four movements: *Emerson, Hawthorne, The Alcotts,* and *Thoreau.* The composer wrote that his work was an attempt "to present one person's impression of the spirit of transcendentalism that is associated with the minds of Concord over a half century ago. This is undertaken in impressionistic pictures of Emerson and Thoreau, a sketch of the Alcotts, and a Scherzo supposed to reflect a lighter quality often found in the fantastic side of Hawthorne."

Musicians who examined the printed Sonata were puzzled, and many put it aside as too bizarre and unorganized to be worthy of further consideration. Equally abstruse was a volume of *114 Songs* which Ives himself published in 1922, saying "I have not written a book at all—I have merely cleaned house." Recognition, however, came in time. Part of the Sonata was played at the 1928 Salzburg Festival in Austria, but it was not until 1939 that America heard it. In that year the pianist John Kirkpatrick presented the entire work at a New York recital. Lawrence Gilman, then critic of the *New York Herald Tribune,* wrote that it was "exceptionally great music—it is, indeed, the greatest music composed by an American, and the most deeply and essentially American in impulse and implication." Kirkpatrick has recorded the work, and what once sounded like needless dissonance and inarticulate tonal crashes are today accepted as expressive and wholly sensitive representations of the thoughts of the mid-nineteenth-century transcendentalists.

Henry and Sidney Cowell finished their discerning biographical study of Charles Ives on May 15, 1954, just four days before the composer died in New York (May 19, 1954). In it is the fullest catalogue to date of Ives's works, with a discussion of Ives's use of musical materials by Mr. Cowell, as well as a detailed analysis of three of the most important works. It is an important and timely contribution about the man who is now called the "father of American music."

A few early performances of Ives's music included *Three Places in New England,* by Nicolas Slonimsky in Boston and New York (1931); *Decoration Day Music,* conducted by Slonimsky in San Francisco in 1932; and in 1937, when the young composer Lehman Engel directed his Madrigal Singers in the *67th Psalm.* It was not until the season of 1944-45, when Ives was seventy, that more of his chamber music was heard, in Los Angeles and at the Columbia University Music Festival. In 1947 Ives was awarded the Pulitzer Prize for his Third Symphony, conducted by Lou Harrison and the New York Little Symphony, which he had composed almost forty years before. Already recorded are the Second, Third, and Fourth symphonies; *Set of Pieces,* for chamber orchestra; Four Pieces for Orchestra; Sonatas for piano, Nos. 1 and 2 *(Concord);* Sonatas for violin and piano, Nos. 1 and 2; *67th Psalm;* and some of his songs.

The Cowells perfectly sum up the significance of Charles Ives when they point out that no one composed as he did because no one lived "in the same musical and philosophical world as he did." No one today "seems able to think up any kind of musical behavior that cannot be found, sometimes in embryo, sometimes fully worked out, in the music of Ives." Charles Ives takes his place as America's great creative figure in the early twentieth century, and beside him stand Schoenberg, Stravinsky, and Bartók.

John Cage

John Cage (1912) is another composer interested in percussive sound. When the Museum of Modern Art in New York presented his compositions written for a large group of players, many types of instruments and objects were used, producing a great variety of sound. Electric buzzers, flowerpots, brake-bands were heard, together with drums. To the informed auditor, the sounds seemed a combination of the gamelan orchestras of the East, the futuristic noisemakers of Marinetti, and the later experiments of Cowell, Antheil, and Varèse. Cage also attempted to create new sounds by writing compositions for what he calls a "prepared piano," in which he places small pieces of metal and leather at certain distances between the strings. In his writing Cage has derived many ideas from Schoenberg's twelve-tone harmonic system and his atonal music, by doing away with all sounds of a definite pitch and introducing a scale of unusual color. This is obtained by light thuds, delicate pluckings, etc., and is selected for its expressiveness. Freedom from conventional pitch has enabled the composer to concentrate on the rhythmic side of his music, and his technique is one of the most sophisticated of any present-day composer. His work is advanced, perhaps far ahead of his time, but his talent speaks through his original musical ideas, which are poetic expressions as well. Cage's *Concerto for Prepared Piano* was performed at Cooper Union in New York in 1952. There are also recordings for his Quartet (1950) and *Sonata Interludes,* for prepared piano.

ELECTRONIC MUSIC

A potential new art medium that in late years has been in a state of experimentation is the exploration of electronic means of capturing sounds. A pioneer of this idea is Edgar Varèse, whose experiments with new sounds by percussion instruments were the subject of heated controversies in the 1920s and 1930s. When he withdrew from active musical life, Varèse continued his experiments in electronics, new sounds, and unusual acoustical possibilities. In 1950, when the State Department asked him to conduct master classes in composition at Darmstadt, Germany, he quickly won to his cause many of the younger German composers. His ideas soon spread to France and Italy, and there has been not only an acceptance of his work, but Europe has made significant advances in tape recording. Varèse believes that the ear is the only true judge in music, and he prefers to use the term "organized sound" rather than "music," for in his opinion music's raw material is merely sound. In composing for tape, there need be no consideration for a performer, and as he works, the composer deals with tones and not notes.

At Columbia University Vladimir Ussachevsky and Otto Luening (as well as Henry Cowell) have been exponents of music for tape recording. In using tape, once the sound desired is recorded almost anything may be done with it. It may be made to play slower or faster, combine with itself, or play backwards. By splicing the tape, the composer may create unusual groupings of sounds, either natural sounds, or musical tones. If desired there may also be periods of dramatic silence. Ussachevsky and Luening have already performed in Los Angeles their *Poem in Cycles and Bells for Tape Recorder and Orchestra.* It was created from flute, piano, and percussion instruments, then developed from the tape. *Poem* was the combination of Luening's *Fantasy in Space* and Ussachevsky's *Sonic Contours,* played in synchronization. Pitches too high to be heard by the human ear may be used (like the dog whistle), and converted into audible sound electronically. Many composers feel that the medium has a great future, and Henry Cowell believes that it will be of the greatest value to the younger composer who can record all orchestral sounds and combine them as he wishes.

Otto Luening

Luening was born in Milwaukee, Wisconsin, in 1900. He won a Guggenheim Fellowship in 1930 and 1931, and has taught at the University of Arizona, the Eastman School, Bennington College, and more recently at Columbia University. He states that he has been designated by critics or audiences who are familiar with perhaps one or two of his works as "conservative, ultramodern, a stylist, vulgar, imposing, a melodist, folksy, insane." He believes that a composer should do a little experimenting, compose for any occasion for which he is called upon to supply music, expand all forms after having mastered them, create new forms, and generally interest himself and make himself useful wherever he can. Then, he feels, his immortality will be decided upon by audiences, critics, colleagues, and time.

Luening has composed for orchestra two Symphonic Poems (1921, 1924); a *Divertimento* (1936); *Two Symphonic Interludes* (1936); a *Serenade* (1927); a *Dirge* (1936); a Symphony (1937); a

Suite for strings (1937); and a *Pilgrim's Hymn*, introduced by the New York Philharmonic-Symphony in 1949. His opera, *Evangeline*, was produced at the Columbia University Music Festival in 1948. Among his recorded chamber music and piano pieces are *Short Sonata* (1939) for flute and harpsichord; Suite for soprano and flute (1939); Preludes Nos. 2, 5, 6, and 8, for piano; *Prelude to a Hymn Tune*, piano and eleven instruments; and *Three Inventions* for piano.

His tape music includes *Low Speed* (1952); *Incantation* (with Vladimir Ussachevsky); and *Rhapsodic Variation* for tape-recorder and orchestra (with Ussachevsky), a joint commission from the Louisville (Kentucky) Orchestra.

TWELVE-TONE MUSIC

In 1941, when Arnold Schoenberg became an American citizen, his system of writing twelve-tone music had not only interested many young American composers, but its very discipline had brought about a singular freedom in their writing. First developed by Schoenberg and two of his pupils, Alban Berg and Anton Webern, this system does away with all accepted scales, as the twelve tones which lie within the octave at once become the basis of the system, and may be used in any manner the composer desires. The series of tones, which the composer sets up, takes the place of key, scale, and tonality, and through the use of canons (the strictest musical imitation) the row may move forward or backward, be inverted or the inversion used backwards. Once the composer decides upon his row of tones, no tone may be repeated until all are used; at the same time these predetermined tones provide the melodies and harmonies of the composition. Rhythm is much freer than in traditional music and chords are not restricted to being built in the traditional manner, that is, in thirds, fourths, etc. Twelve-tone composing was soon to become one of the most progressive aspects of America's music.

Wallingford Riegger

Wallingford Riegger was entirely conventional in his early pieces but later became interested in atonality and composing in the twelve-tone system, Riegger left his romanticism behind him and made an about face when he composed his *Study in Sonority* for ten violins or "any multiple thereof," which was first performed at the Ithaca Conservatory on August 11, 1927, the composer conducting. Born in Albany, Georgia, in 1885, Riegger studied at the Institute of Musical Art, and later in Berlin. It was in the orchestral piece *Dichotomy* (1932) that he anticipated his later interest in twelve-tone writing, for by that time he had become convinced that the twentieth-century musician should learn to express his musical ideas fully, even if it meant violating tradition. To Riegger, violating tradition was quite different from overthrowing it, for he was fully aware of the way in which Bach, Wagner, and Debussy became innovators. Riegger is a serious and honest composer, one whose originality and expressive qualities were not fully recognized until the performance of his Symphony No. 3 at the 1948 Columbia University Festival. The symphony won the New York Music Critics Award. His works include *Canon for Woodwinds* (1931); a *Fantasy and Fugue* for orchestra and organ (1930-31); *Passacaglia and Fugue* for band (1942); three Symphonies (1944, 1945, 1947); *Funeral March* for band (1943); and *Music for Brass Choir* (1948-49). He has composed considerable music for the modern dance, written for Martha Graham, Charles Weidman, Doris Humphrey, Helen Tamiris, and others. The works include: *Bacchanale* (1930); *Frenetic Rhythms* (1933); (both for Graham); *Candide* (1937) (Weidman); *New Dance* (1935) and *Theatre Piece* (1935) (Humphrey-Weidman); and *Trojan Incident* (1938) (Tamiris). There are also chamber music works, choral music, and piano pieces.

Ben Weber

Ben Weber (born 1916) is another avowed atonalist, one of the younger composers to cultivate the twelve-tone technique. In an article in *Musical America* (February, 1951), Anthony Bruno wrote of him: "Weber simply prefers to do without tonality, and does not feel any great loss—perhaps because in his twelve-tone music he employs such devices and forms as recurrence of themes, recapitulation, sonata, and canon, which he admits borrowing from tonal operations."

Weber, a native of St. Louis, Missouri, is largely self-taught in composition. For a time he supported himself as a musical autographer. In 1950 he was given a Guggenheim Fellowship. His works include a *Symphony in Four Movements on Poems of William*

Blake, with baritone solo (1952 and recorded); *Sonata da Camera* (Fromm Award, 1954); *Concert Aria after Solomon* (1949); a Ballade for cello and piano; and a film score, *Image in the Snow*.

Other American composers who adopted the twelve-tone technique include Adolph Weiss (1891-   ); George Perle (1915-   ); Milton Babbitt (1916-   ); and Ross Lee Finney (1906-   ).

THE YOUNG TRADITIONALISTS

Vincent Persichetti

Vincent Persichetti (1915-   ) first studied at Combs College of Music, and in his home town of Philadelphia at the Curtis Institute and then at the Philadelphia Conservatory of Music, where he was a piano pupil of Olga Samaroff Stokowski and a composition student of Paul Nordoff. Later he studied with Roy Harris. Now a member of the Juilliard faculty, he has received many commissions and his works have been widely performed. Persichetti has chosen freely from all sources what has suited his musical requirements, whether it was from traditional classic forms and styles or his own adaptation of the twelve-tone technique. His works include four symphonies (1942, 1942, 1946, 1951); nine piano sonatas (1939 to 1952); a suite, *Fables* (1943); *The Hollow Men*, for trumpet and string orchestra (1944); *Dance Overture* (1942); Concertino, piano and orchestra (1941); a series of pieces called *Serenade*, for various combinations; and Concerto, for Piano Four Hands (1952). There are also two ballets for Martha Graham—*King Lear* (1947); and *The Eye of Anguish* (1950). His Quintet for piano and strings (1954), a commission from the Koussevitzky Foundation, was first performed in February, 1955, at the Library of Congress in Washington. Probably his most ambitious score is *Harmonium*, a cycle of twenty songs for soprano and piano (1951). There are a great number of works for chamber-music combinations, a Sonata for harpsichord (1951), and pieces for band, as well as for voices.

Peter Mennin

Peter Mennin, born in 1923 in Erie, Pennsylvania, is a graduate of the Eastman School and won a Guggenheim Fellowship in 1947. Before he was thirty he heard his Fifth Symphony performed by the Dallas Symphony, in 1950, and in the following year by the Boston Symphony. His Third Symphony (1946) was performed in 1949, by the New York Philharmonic-Symphony, and his Fourth Symphony, *The Cycle,* a commission from the Collegiate Chorale, was introduced by that group in the same year (1949). Other orchestral works include a *Folk Overture* (1945); *Fantasia* for strings (1947); *Concert Piece* (1949); *Sinfonia* for chamber orchestra (1946); and a *Concertino* for flute, strings, and percussion (1945). His *Canzona* for band was introduced by the Goldman Band in New York in 1951. The Cantata, *The Christmas Story,* (1949), was first sung by the Robert Shaw Chorale over the ABC network in 1949. In 1947 Mennin was appointed to the faculty of the Juilliard School of Music.

Robert Ward

Robert Ward (1917-   ) is another young member of the Juilliard faculty who trained at Eastman. Later he studied with Aaron Copland. Born in Cleveland, Ohio, Ward has written three Symphonies (1941, 1947, 1950) and the overture *Jubilation* (1946). Other works include Sonata No. 1, for violin and piano (1950); *Lamentation* (1948) and *Folk Dance* (1949), both for piano; *Hush'd Be the Camps Today* (1938); for chorus and orchestra; and commissioned by the League of Composers and Broadcast Music, Inc., *Concert Music* for orchestra (1948).

Harold Shapero

Harold Shapero (1920-   ) was trained at Harvard under Piston, and studied also with Ernst Křenek, Hindemith, and Copland. Harvard awarded him the Paine Fellowship, and he subsequently won the Rome Prize in 1951, the Bearns Prize, and Guggenheim and Naumburg Fellowships. For orchestra he has written a *Nine Minute Overture* (1940); *Symphony for Classical Orchestra* (1946); an Overture, *The Travellers;* and a Concerto for orchestra. There are also piano, violin, and trumpet sonatas, and a String Quartet (1940).

ECLECTICS

Howard Swanson

Howard Swanson, a Negro born in 1909 in Atlanta, Georgia, was a student of Herbert Elwell at the Cleveland Institute of Music, where he supplemented his income by working at the Cleveland post office. His unusual ability won him a Rosenwald Fellowship award and he went to Paris to study with Nadia Boulanger. With the approach of war in 1939 he left Europe and soon decided to devote all his time to music. His choice was a wise one, and when his songs were sung in recital by Marian Anderson and other distinguished singers, his talents began to be recognized both here and in Europe. In 1951 Swanson won the New York Music Critics' Award for his *Short Symphony,* composed in 1948, and given its first hearing in November 1950, by Mitropoulos and the New York Philharmonic-Symphony. Further honors came his way with a grant from the Academy of Arts and Letters and in 1952 a Guggenheim Fellowship. Other works include an earlier Symphony (1948); *Night Music* for orchestra (1950); *Music for Strings* (1952); *Soundpiece* for brass quintet; Sonata, for piano; Suite, for cello and piano; and numerous short instrumental pieces and songs.

Lukas Foss

Lukas Foss (1922-   ) was one of the most promising of the younger contemporary composers from the moment of his arrival in the United States. Born in Berlin, Germany, he went with his parents to Paris in 1933, and then came to America in 1937. Studying at the Curtis Institute and at the Berkshire Music Center, he attracted immediate attention in 1943 when his cantata *The Prairie* was broadcast by the Columbia Broadcasting System. In February, 1944, it was performed by the New York Philharmonic-Symphony, with the Westminster Choir and four soloists.

Foss's orchestral works include Two Symphonic Pieces (1939, 1940); two Piano Concertos (1942, 1951); Ode for Orchestra (1944); Symphony in G (1945); *Recordare* for orchestra (1948); Concerto for oboe and orchestra. Other choral works include *The Song of Songs* (1946), cantata for soprano and orchestra; *The Parable of Death,* for tenor, narrator, chorus, and orchestra (1952), one of his best scores; and *Behold I Build an House* (1951). He has also composed three ballets: *Within These Walls* (1944); *The Heart Remembers* (1944); and *Gift of the Magi* (1945); and an opera, *The Jumping Frog of Calaveras County,* written in 1949. There is also a *Suite for the Tempest* (1942), for chamber orchestra and a String Quartet in G (1947).

Harrison Kerr

Born in Cleveland, Ohio, in 1899, Harrison Kerr is now (1957) the Dean of the College of Fine Arts of the University of Oklahoma. A pupil of Nadia Boulanger in Paris, Kerr's earlier orchestral and chamber works are written in the conventional form. In recent years he has become interested in the twelve-tone technique, but he has leaned more toward Alban Berg's style than that of Schoenberg. His larger orchestral works include *Dance Suite* (1938); three symphonies (the First revised in 1938, No. 2 composed in 1943-45, and No. 3 (1945); and a Violin Concerto (1951). His chamber music includes a String Quartet (1937); suites; and trios. There are two sonatas for piano (1929, 1943), choral music, and songs.

Roger Goeb

Roger Goeb (1914-   ) has composed three symphonies. When the third was played at the Columbia University Festival in 1952, Henry Cowell wrote in the *Musical Quarterly* (July, 1952): "The work is a dynamo of activity; it is entirely free of sentimentality and pretentiousness. It has what is the most valuable expressive quality in any art: it betrays the personality of its maker directly and quite unintentionally. One hears in the music the speech of an honest, serious, and talented person whose only vital lack—surely a temporary one—is that of inner repose."

Goeb, a native of Cherokee, Iowa, studied with Otto Luening in New York, and, winning a Guggenheim Fellowship in 1950, went to Paris to study with Nadia Boulanger. His output has been large, already numbering over fifty works, including *Lyric Piece* for trumpet and orchestra (1947); *Three American Dances,* string orchestra (1952); and *Two American Dances* for orchestra (1952); besides many chamber pieces for all types of instrumental combinations.

Alan Hovhaness

Alan Hovhaness, of Armenian ancestry, has turned to the Near East for both the subject and source of much of his music. Born in Arlington, Massachusetts, in 1911, his early training was at the New England Conservatory. It was not until he was thirty that he turned in spirit to the land of his ancestors and concerned himself with modal melody, generally in a diatonic, Near Eastern mode. In reviewing Hovhaness' *Saint Vartan Symphony* in the *Musical Quarterly* (July, 1951), Henry Cowell wrote: "Hovhaness' music . . . sounds modern (but not ultra-modern) in a natural and uninhibited fashion, because he has found new ways to use the archaic materials with which he starts, by following their natural trend towards modal sequence and polymodalism. . . . His is moving, long-breathed music, splendidly written and unique in style. It is a contemporary development of the archaic and sounds like the music of nobody else at all."

The *Saint Vartan Symphony* was first performed in New York in March, 1952. It is not a symphony in the conventional form, but rather a suite of twenty-four short movements. Hovhaness' other works include a Concerto for piano, four trumpets, and percussion, entitled *Khaldis; Ancient God of the Universe; Pe-El-Amarna* (City of the Sun) for orchestra; Concerto No. 7, for orchestra (1954); Concerto No. 9, for piano and strings (1954); *Soci*, for violin, horn, timpani, gong, and strings; Quartet for flute, oboe, cello, and harpsichord (1952); and Prelude and Fugue for oboe and piano. He has composed also a quantity of choral music, and in many of the instrumental accompaniments he has sought to imitate the ancient Armenian instruments.

ORCHESTRAS IN THE 1950s

Of the hundreds of orchestras playing in the nation's concert halls, there might be said to be about thirty major organizations Nearly every city of over 400,000 persons maintains an orchestra that is considered in the music business a major group if its annual gross expenditure is over $100,000. The big three—New York, Philadelphia, and Boston—are million-dollar groups, while Chicago, Cleveland, and Cincinnati are far above half that amount. About seven cities provide public funds to help their orchestras—San Francisco, Philadelphia, Indianapolis, Baltimore, Detroit, Rochester, and Buffalo. There is a noticeable increase in American conductors —Alfred Wallenstein, Thor Johnson, Walter Hendl, and Howard Mitchell. San Antonio has Victor Alessandro, Oklahoma City, Guy Fraser Harrison. Leonard Bernstein has filled his schedule with guest appearences with all of the major orchestras, and in the 1957-

58 season became associate conductor of the New York Philharmonic Symphony.

COMMISSIONS AND PRIZES

A most interesting orchestra in recent years has been the Louisville (Kentucky) Orchestra, under Robert Whitney. Greatly helped by the city, Whitney had gained a fine reputation for the quality of his programs and for the commissioning of new scores. In April, 1953, the Rockefeller Foundation granted the orchestra $400,000, to be used in part over a period of four years for the commissioning of twenty-eight symphonic works and two one-hour operas. The project began in January, 1954, and each composer was to receive $1,000 for each work, plus $200 for scoring, while the opera composers receive $4,000. Each new work has received four performances, and has been recorded by Columbia Records and distributed through the orchestra to subscribers. In addition to professional commissions, the orchestra, through the grant, will choose twelve compositions written by students of composition in colleges and universities. Each student who wins is to receive $500 for each piece. These works will also have public hearings at the weekly concerts.

One of the outstanding works of the first season was the *Sinfonietta Flamenca* by Carlos Surinach, performed on January 9, 1954. Surinach came to America from Barcelona, Spain, and is becoming an American citizen. He is a first-class composer and a skillful technician, with the rare ability of combining the flavor of Spanish music with a contemporary idiom. American history is again repeating itself, as foreign musicians come to America and immediately become a part of its musical life.

Edgar Varèse is but one of many composers who are preparing works for Louisville. His new piece will be entitled *Trinum*, and is in three uninterrupted sections, which Varèse has based on three principal elements—tension, dynamics, and rhythm.

American composers continue to win international prizes. The International Festival, held in April, 1954, in Rome, gave five prizes for original works, one of which went to the American composer Lou Harrison, professor of composition at Black Mountain College, North Carolina. Mr. Harrison's prize-winning work was for soloist and chamber ensemble. It was sung by Leontyne Price (known from *Four Saints in Three Acts* and *Porgy and Bess*), the chamber ensemble led by Carlos Surinach.

OPERA COMPANIES IN THE 1950s

In New York

The half-century found the Metropolitan Opera with a new manager. In 1950, Rudolf Bing was called from London to succeed Edward Johnson, and a new era was inaugurated. Bing had become known through his outstanding work for the Edinburgh Festival of Music and Drama, and he let it be clearly known from the beginning that he wished to produce operas that were well-integrated and would appeal, through up-to-date staging, to a new and cosmopolitan audience. He gave the operatic stage directors added authority, and also sought help from the New York stage in putting on new productions. Margaret Webster, known for her Shakespearean productions, was the adviser for the new *Don Carlos;* Garson Kanin for the comedy *Die Fledermaus;* Alfred Lunt for *Così fan Tutte;* and Cyril Ritchard for *The Barber of Seville.* Herbert Graf's work was already well-known, and Roff Gerard came from Covent Garden and Glyndebourne to create new sets and costumes. The Metropolitan still kept its international reputation, but it now had the competition of the excellent productions at the more intimate City Center.

The Metropolitan showed its ability to perform large and difficult works, such as Moussorgsky's *Khovantichina,* while the City Center company revived Puccini's *Turandot* and won unanimous praise for restoring Prokofiev's *The Love for Three Oranges,* not heard since its Chicago première. The City Center company was about 100 per cent American, as against the Metropolitan's international personnel. After László Halász' dismissal, Joseph Rosenstock became the New York City Opera Company's artistic director. Rosenstock resigned at the end of the 1955-56 season, and Erich Leinsdorf, conductor of the Rochester Philharmonic, was named as general director.

In New York a group known as the American Opera Society has demonstrated its importance to the city's musical life by giving concert versions of operas never heard before in America (such as Cherubini's *Medea*, November 8, 1955), or less frequently heard works, such as those of Purcell *(Dido and Aeneas)* or Monteverdi *(Il Combattimento di Tancredi e di Clorinda)*, both given in December, 1955.

In Chicago

In the fall of 1954 Chicago again realized its desire to have its own opera company, rather than rely for its opera seasons on visiting companies from New York. The Lyric Theatre, organized largely through the efforts of Carol Fox, offered a brilliant array of singers and opera productions for a three-week season which included the debut of the New York-born soprano Maria Callas, and the première of a new opera, *Lord Byron's Love Letter,* composed by Rafael de Baufield to a libretto by Tennessee Williams.

Managerial disputes at the end of the 1955 season threatened to disrupt the entire organization. Miss Fox, general manager, and her managing and artistic directors were in such disagreement that the matter was taken to court with the result that the assets and liabilities of the Lyric Theatre were ordered transferred to a new organization formed by Miss Fox—the Opera Theatre Association. In spite of the fact that the liabilities totaled $120,000 and the assets consisted principally of contracts with artists, the resourceful Miss Fox obtained the necessary backing and opened the Lyric Theatre's 1956 season in October with a production of Puccini's *The Girl of the Golden West*. The novelties the company has presented include another American opera, Vittoria Giannini's *The Taming of the Shrew,* previously heard in Cincinnati.

In Other Cities

The San Francisco Opera Company continues its brilliant seasons every autumn both in its home city and in Los Angeles. In Philadelphia the City Council's Recreational Committee granted in 1954 $25,000 to the Philadelphia Grand Opera Company, which represented a merger of the Philadelphia La Scala Opera Company and the Civic Grand Opera Company.

In Hartford, Connecticut, the Connecticut Grand Opera serves not only its home city but surrounding communities as well. Other cities throughout the country enjoy short seasons of opera, using local symphony orchestras and choruses, and soloists imported from New York's Metropolitan and City Center. These cities include Kansas City, San Antonio, New Orleans, Miami, and Chattanooga. Summer opera seasons continue at Chautauqua (New York) Institution, Cincinnati, Central City, the Hollywood Bowl, and as part of the summer orchestral concerts in various cities.

One of the most idealistic opera companies that have come to prominence in the last five years is the Baltimore Civic Opera Company. Under the capable musical direction of Leigh Martinet (whose father, Eugene Martinet, founded the group) and giving three productions a year in Baltimore's Lyric Theatre, the company has enjoyed the invaluable assistance of the incomparable Rosa Ponselle as artistic adviser. The casts are all made up of local singers, and those who have the leading roles are personally coached by Miss Ponselle for months in advance. Two fine Violettas were developed during the spring of 1954, and both singers were auditioned by Rudolf Bing for the Metropolitan Opera. The winner was Shakeh Vartenissian, who made her debut the following fall. Another young Baltimore singer, Joshua Hecht, bass, went on to the New York City Opera, and Eva Bober and Kira Baklanova were chosen for operatic appearances in Germany and Italy. That smaller American opera companies have developed so far that young singers may gain valuable experience in secondary as well as leading roles before going on to the nation's larger houses, is one of the healthiest signs yet of America's operatic maturity.

Opera Workshops

Opera workshops have grown to amazing numbers, there being over a hundred in 1952. In New York, besides those at Columbia University and the Juilliard School of Music, the smaller Henry Street Settlement Music School and Greenwich House have excellent departments. The Peabody Conservatory in Baltimore had the benefit of Ernest Lert's wide experience until his death (1955); and there is Elemer Nagy at the Hartt School in Hartford and Carl Ebert at the University of Southern California, both of whom are known for their high standards of production. Indiana University, where the opera workshop gave the first performance of Weill's *Down in the Valley*, has also produced new operas by Lukas Foss,

Bernard Rogers, and Walter Kaufman. Its annual Palm Sunday production of Wagner's *Parsifal* is without parallel in the country.

The opera workshops may very likely prove one of the greatest factors in developing American opera, for they are very much in need of short operas, practical for production with limited resources. Through the large number of performances they have given to the shorter Menotti works, and others by such composers as Alec Wilder and Kurt Weill, they are offering a more gratifying and remunerative market to composers than can be provided by the few major opera companies of the nation.

AMERICAN OPERAS

The first opera given in Louisville, commissioned under the terms of the Rockefeller grant, was Peggy Glanville-Hicks' (1912-   ) two-act *The Transposed Heads,* based on Thomas Mann's story of the same name. This work, and other operas written on commission, emphasize the fact that since American composers appear to work more successfully under commission than on speculation, the musical theater in this country has every chance of a bright future if suitable commissions are forthcoming.

With Kurt Weill's death in April, 1950, America lost not only one of its finest opera composers, but one of the century's most significant writers in all forms of the musical theater. His passing left Gian-Carlo Menotti as the outstanding craftsman in American opera, a reputation that he more firmly established when his opera, *The Consul* opened in March, 1950. This work was mentioned in chapter XIV.

New operas continued to appear during the decade, some, like William Schuman's *The Mighty Casey,* a first operatic attempt by an established composer, others, like those of Vittorio Giannini and Menotti, the work of practical hands.

Vittorio Giannini

Vittorio Giannini (1903-   ), born in Philadelphia, and a product of the Juilliard School, had his most recent opera, *The Taming of the Shrew,* produced in 1953 in Cincinnati, Ohio, by the Music Drama Guild and the symphony orchestra of that city and later in Chicago by the Lyric Theatre. Virgil Thomson reviewed the performance for the *New York Herald Tribune* and called the work "a real opera, practical and effective. It is not very stylish or even original," he continued, "but it has power. That power comes from its composer's sweetness of mind, sincere skill and real gift for the theatre."

Giannini had been a Fellow at the Academy in Rome in the mid-1930s, and his first operas were produced in Europe—*Lucedia* in Munich, 1934, and *The Scarlet Letter* in Hamburg in 1938. The next two operas had radio performances by CBS—*Beauty and the Beast* in 1938, and *Blennerhassett* in 1939. Giannini has also written successfully in all other forms, including two concertos—Violin (1945) and Cello (1946)—and his Third Symphony (1948).

Schuman's "The Mighty Casey"

William Schuman, already an established composer, as well as the President of the Juilliard School of Music in New York, decided to try his hand at an opera, and chose a subject close to his heart— baseball. Based on Ernest Lawrence Thayer's *Casey at the Bat*, Schuman had Jeremy Gury write a libretto, and the outcome was Schuman's one-act opera, *The Mighty Casey*, which had its première on May 4, 1953, by the Julius Hartt Opera Guild, in Hartford, Connecticut. Many of the opera's songs were written in the style of Broadway's musical comedies, which style Schuman had learned through practical experience at the start of his career. Some of the song titles show how well Schuman drew a picture of America in the 1950s: *I'm fed to the teeth; Case on Casey*, for teen-age chorus; *Peanuts, Popcorn, Soda, Crackerjack; You're doing fine, kid.* It is too early to tell how significant Schuman's opera is, but it obviously inspired the 1955 Broadway musical, *Damn Yankees*, which apparently delighted a certain segment of the theatergoing public.

Weill's "The Threepenny Opera"

When Kurt Weill came to the United States in 1935, his adaptation of John Gay's *The Beggar's Opera* (which had been so popular in America before the Revolution) was already known. Entitled *The Threepenny Opera*, and composed in 1928, the work used the idioms of America's popular music. Marc Blitzstein adapted *The Threepenny Opera* in the summer of 1952, changing the locale to New York in the 1870s, and translating the lyrics into current slang.

In this form it had a concert performance at Brandeis University. It was subsequently revived in New York (1954 and 1955-56), with the locale once again returned to England.

Menotti's "The Saint of Bleecker Street" and a Ballet

When Gian-Carlo Menotti's latest opera, *The Saint of Bleecker Street*, reached New York on December 27, 1954, it raised a storm of controversy. Jay S. Harrison, writing in the Sunday edition of the *New York Herald Tribune* (January 9, 1955), pointed out that "whatever else one may think or say of Gian-Carlo Menotti and his talent and skills, his ability to split the musical world cleanly down the middle is nothing short of phenomenal." Set in the poor Italian quarter of New York's Bleecker Street, the plot concerns a simple Italian girl, Annina, who receives the bloody stigmata as she ponders on the Passion of Christ. Mr. Harrison, in reviewing *The Saint*, said: it "is without any question his finest work to date. In a sense it is a culmination of all his previous efforts and represents a complete synthesis of his lyrico-dramatic style." There were some who did not like the religious implications, or understand the simple life that is still to be found in a large city's ghetto-like district. Nevertheless, the opera won the coveted 1954 Music Critics Circle Award, and the 1955 Pulitzer Prize.

On October 21, 1956, Menotti's "madrigal-fable for chorus, dancers and orchestra" *The Unicorn, the Gorgon, and the Manticore*, commissioned by the Elizabeth Sprague Coolidge Foundation, was performed at the Library of Congress in Washington. The following January 15 (1957) it was presented at the City Center by the New York City Ballet. In reviewing the performance, Walter Terry, dance critic of the *New York Herald Tribune* called the work "sad, funny, wistful, simple, beautiful and altogether captivating," while Jay S. Harrison, writing of the music in the same journal, called it "a thumping fine work—deeply expressive, charged with humor, provocative, and wildly appealing in its bursts of sentiment."

Leonard Bernstein

Leonard Bernstein (1918-) composed a successful television opera, *Trouble in Tahiti*, a satire on married life in a typical American suburb. It was performed in New York in 1952. Bernstein already was well-known for his ballet, *Fancy Free* (1944), from which he drew some of the material for a Broadway musical comedy, *On the Town* (1944-45). Adding a number of gay, sparkling songs, for which Betty Comden and Adolph Green wrote the lyrics, *On the Town* enjoyed a long run, was taken on tour, and later made into a successful motion picture. In 1953 and again with the same lyric writers, Bernstein provided the music for *Wonderful Town*, a musical version of the popular play *My Sister Eileen*. Born in Lawrence, Massachusetts, Bernstein had an academic training at Harvard, and studied music with Hill and Piston. Extremely talented, he became a protégé of Koussevitzky while studying with the maestro at Tanglewood, and made the newspaper headlines in 1943 when he conducted the New York Philharmonic-Symphony for Bruno Walter, who was suddenly taken ill. Besides his two symphonies—*Jeremiah* (1944) and *The Age of Anxiety*, for piano and orchestra (1949)—both of which the critics felt were not completely convincing, he has written chamber music; two more ballets, *The Age of Anxiety* (drawn from the symphony) and *Facsimile* (1946); as well as incidental music for *Peter Pan*.

Hugo Weisgall

When Columbia recorded Hugo Weisgall's opera *The Stronger* in 1956, a new and highly promising operatic talent was able to reach a large audience. Born in Czechoslovakia in 1912, but long a resident of Baltimore, Maryland, and an American citizen, Weisgall has always had a deep love for the operatic stage. His earlier opera, *The Tenor*, had several performances, but the audiences were naturally limited, whereas *The Stronger* may be heard wherever there is a phonograph. But it is in his newest opera, *Six Characters in Search of an Author*, that Weisgall has achieved his finest work to date. Completed in the summer of 1956 in Italy, the composer and Denis Johnston based their libretto on the famous play of Luigi Pirandello. The setting is the stage of a small provincial opera house while a rehearsal is in progress, and the opera has a magnificent pace and variety of mood. Using a Mozartean orchestra of thirty-six players, Weisgall uses every conceivable operatic form and his music is richly varied and expressive and his rhythms are vital and dynamic. Add to this his fine gift of counterpoint and his ability to combine both the comic and tragic aspects of the story with consummate skill, and Weisgall's opera promises to be one of the most significant works of the decade.

RADIO AND TELEVISION

When NBC, in cooperation with ASCAP (American Society of Composers, Authors, and Publishers) and the Eastman School, broadcast in 1952-53 a weekly radio series known as "America's Composers," the lethargy of the previous decade seemed to end. The public had been greatly agitated when the Philharmonic-Symphony Sunday afternoon broadcasts were changed in the 1950-51 season (the time had been sold), and in answer to the many protests, the concerts were broadcast as usual in the next season. CBS's music coverage improved under the direction of James Fassett and Oliver Daniel, and WNYC's annual Festival of American Music became increasingly important. Yet it still seemed that most broadcasts were to deny the Federal Communication Commission's insistence that some serious music be broadcast as a public service, rather than any leadership being taken for the sake of playing a dominant role in America's musical life. Europe's radio transmission of music was still far ahead of anything in America. While many cities have good serious programs, there are still countless towns where, if there are no network programs of value, little worth-while music is to be heard.

Television, on the other hand, seems to give evidence of life. With the sensational success of Menotti's opera *Amahl and the Night Visitors,* the first opera written especially for television and commissioned by NBC and performed on December 24, 1951, new operas were announced to be forthcoming. The nation took *Amahl* to its heart, and the little crippled boy has already become as much a part of Christmas in America as Dicken's Tiny Tim.

RECORDS

While the advent of the LP record brought about the recording of a large part of the standard repertory, in 1950 there was very little serious American music to be found on discs. Columbia Records issued the first Walter W. Naumburg Foundation Recording Award, the *Second Symphony* of Roger Sessions, played by

Mitropoulos and the New York Philharmonic-Symphony. Columbia now has a long-range program, in which it will record all of the best American chamber music. Other foundations gave a helping hand—the Ditson; Eastman; and Koussevitzky. Mercury Records, under Howard Hanson's guidance, will issue the best orchestral works, while Capitol has recorded the complete Pittsburgh International Contemporary Music Festival, and while the records are not for sale, copies will be sent to colleges, universities, libraries, and other educational institutions. The American Recording Society has done the most for American classical music, in issuing some fifty-six compositions by fifty composers since 1951. Made in Vienna, with American conductors and soloists, these works were subsidized through a foundation, and over 100,000 LP records have been sold by mail subscription. Twenty-two works in all, they were mostly symphonic works. Remington will also do its share, all of which will greatly advance the appreciation of America's excellent concert repertory. Times have once more changed, and the record companies need the aid of the foundations. With what is soon to appear, and with what the smaller companies like Decca, Circle, Concert Hall, New Editions, and New Records have already done (not to count the invaluable folk music recordings of Folkways Records), American music will have its fulfillment as it becomes available and familiar to all people.

THE AMERICAN COMPOSER PROTECTS HIS INTERESTS

Early in the century it was impossible for anyone in this country to make a living merely by composing. Even MacDowell had to turn to concertizing and teaching. The composer not only received small return from his major compositions, he generally had to provide at his own effort and expense manuscript scores and parts to any orchestras willing to play them. Conditions are still far from the millennium in this regard, but there is a new conception of the composer's rights, and the value of his contribution to our culture that have improved his economic status.

Most of this improvement comes from the realization that the primary use of music is its performance. Publication is only a convenient means of making performance possible. Publication of books is an end in itself. Those who buy them read them, but the printing of music is only providing a script or scenario to those who will bring it to life by performing it in public. It is therefore logical that the composer should derive his livelihood directly from the primary use of his product—its performance.

The copyright laws of most countries give to the owner of a copyrighted musical work (either the composer himself or his assignee) the exclusive right to perform that work in public. In the United States this right is limited to public performance *for profit*. In France and the British Commonwealth and in most foreign countries anyone who performs copyrighted music in public, even in schools and churches, must have a license to do so. In America the composer cannot collect unless it can be established that the performer or the entrepreneur is profiting from the performance. Consequently the "for profit" limitation has caused much argument and even litigation to determine what performances are given for profit and which are exempt. When radio first came into being the broadcasters maintained that inasmuch as the audience itself did not pay for the programs they were not for profit. Court decisions were required to establish the principle that broadcasting was a profit-making enterprise.

Assertion of the performing right would be an impossible task for the individual composer, and securing a license to perform would be equally difficult, if the users had to seek out the copyright owner of each piece they wish to perform. For this reason there are in almost every country "performing rights" societies that administer these rights for composers and publishers by licensing the users of music and distributing the moneys received among their members (the composers and publishers) according to the number of performances each has received. Most of the societies are known by their initials: in England, P.R.S. (Performing Right Society, Limited); in France, SACEM (Société des Auteurs, Compositeurs et Editeurs de Musique); in Germany, GMA (Gesellschaft für Musikalische Aufführungs und Mechanische Vervielfältigungsrechte); and in the United States, ASCAP (American Society of Composers, Authors and Publishers), as well as BMI (Broadcast Music, Inc.), organized by the broadcasters themselves, and SESAC (Society of European Stage Authors and Composers), a privately owned corporation. The number of foreign societies with which ASCAP has reciprocal agreements is twenty-nine.

In America the justice of paying the composer for the right to use his music has not been easily gained. It is readily conceded that hall rent, lighting bills, printing of programs, janitors' salaries, piano tuning are necessary expenses, but payment to the man who has composed the raw material without which there would be no concert has required much persuasion and in some cases court action. The "for profit" limitation of the copyright act prevents composers whose works are used chiefly by choral societies, schools, and churches from collecting any payment from such organizations for the performance of their music.

Nevertheless, the licensing of those users of music who are ostensibly operating for profit has enabled many composers whose works are regularly played by such agencies to derive a substantial income from the performance of their works.

AMERICA: A WORLD MUSIC CENTER

In quickening tempo our century has witnessed fierce struggles, with two world wars and a serious economic crash. The manifestos, new styles and extravagant trends, many "isms" and conflicting theories of this period, have in themselves shown the vitality of the past fifty years. As America revived her belief in her native arts, music began to blossom. Europe was tired and ingrown, and the world turned to America, whose composers and music had a freshness and vitality that was most welcome. Many of the greatest musicians sought a refuge in America, never to return to their native countries. These eminent musicians shared the center of the stage with our own composers, and did not take it away from them as the foreign arrivals had done in former centuries. Meanwhile, the American composer made himself familiar with every style. He was an eclectic, drawing freely from all, and then writing as he wished. It was a healthy thing that no "American style" developed, for that would have hampered native originality. Nowhere in the world is the composer so free and informed as in America. Our Coplands, Barbers, Hansons, Thomsons, Menottis, Iveses, and the rest have now the international standing of the Milhauds, the Křeneks, the Hindemiths, and the others who have come to us from abroad. We no longer need protective tariffs to shield American composers from foreign competition. We have achieved reciprocity.

CHAPTER XVI

Toward the Bicentennial

As the bicentennial of the birth of the United States as a nation approaches, it will be of considerable interest to pause and evaluate objectively what the past decade produced musically. In the ten years which have passed since the first appearance of *A Short History of Music in America*, the United States has firmly held her place as a world center of music. There have been both surprises and disappointments, startling occurrences side by side with those potentials which were not fulfilled, the golden opportunities which were allowed to slip through our fingers.

But there is great promise for the future and the discernible trends have a solidity and a firmness that is rooted in deep ground. There are more young composers working actively in our midst than ever before, fine musicians expertly trained and equipped, with much better backgrounds than their counterparts in other countries of the world. These past years have seen revolutionary changes in our way of life, and the rising generation is quite sure of just what it expects from and wants of life.

There are several fields which have failed to expand and mature when compared with their accomplishments of a few years ago. Certainly commercial television seems to be more of a "barren wasteland" for creative music than the medium at first promised; American opera has had few productions that are likely to find their place in the permanent repertory; there has been a dearth of out-

standing film scores from Hollywood to match the stature of the
motion picture itself; and even though Broadway has had entertaining musicals that have been big financial successes, only one
in the past decade can be called great, for Leonard Bernstein's
West Side Story (1957) will ever remain in a class by itself.

The real worth, the lasting value, of much of the music that has
been composed can only be left to the judgment and test of time.
The increased interest in electronic music, now being used in nearly
every medium, must be reckoned with, even though it remains a
controversial subject among musicians and public alike. With more
chances for the performance and recording of his works; the great
number of available prizes, awards, and grants; the opportunity to
study in almost any country of his choosing; with conferences,
seminars, and panel discussions with the most distinguished composers and teachers, no young composer has had such ideal circumstances within his reach in the history of our Western music.

Yet the youth of this generation has had to live through a period
of shattered traditions, changing values, and difficult adjustments,
which may prove to have far deeper implications than the earlier
decade of transition known as the Roaring Twenties. There can be
no question that this young generation, in spite of the overly publicized minority groups, is better educated, more adventurous, and
has more character than many of its predecessors. With relentless
intent, it is making its own life with a sureness of purpose that is
astonishing, seeking the truth as it establishes its own rules and
revolts against the intolerance, selfishness, and bitter hatred which
it cannot fail to see on every side.

SOCIAL AND CULTURAL CHANGES

In the ten years which have passed since we discussed them, the
colleges and universities, the conservatories and music schools, have
continued to serve their individual communities, expanding their
programs, strengthening their faculties, and exploring new possibilities to further serve the student body. In some instances outstanding projects and festivals have been established, exchanges
with foreign groups and organizations made, all of which have been
fine examples of American foresight and imagination. But it has

been from the younger generation that most of the significant changes toward a new way of life have come, for this highly vocal group has rejected many inherited practices as impractical or outmoded and scorned the dictatorial, the dishonest, and the frequently immoral attitude of its elders. The younger generation is returning once more to the basic honesty and integrity that has been America's heritage, fulfilling the words of one of music's significant leaders when he said: "Violent reactions are in reality a continuation, an evolution."

ROCK 'N' ROLL MUSIC

The impact of rock 'n' roll music when it appeared had worldwide repercussions and it achieved a success that was unknown to any earlier type of popular music. At first a fad of the young teenagers (and detested by their elders), it soon answered a deep need for this restless group, with its steady, persistent, primitive beat, and has endured because it answered its purpose. With the increasing popularity of the guitar as an accompanying instrument and the song texts in rural dialects, this music, either for those participating or those merely listening, submerged everything with its relentless, ever-present beat as it mounted in intensity to the final moments of exaltation. Actually this mood is but a modern version of ancient ritual music, as old as man himself, once used to induce mystical ecstasy and long a part of both pagan ritual and religious ceremonies of worship.

By 1964 it was no surprise to find *The New York Times* using the word "frenzy" in an assessment of the important revival of folk songs. The guitar (one of the most ancient of all instruments) had superseded the piano as the popular instrument on which to learn music and in 1966 attained a sale of more than 1.5 million instruments in the United States alone, more than twenty-two times the number of all other stringed instruments bought.

Another factor important in contributing to this change was the popularity of Hootenanny shows, which soon gained millions of eager followers. It was not long before scheduled concerts, such as those in New York's Carnegie Hall, were sold out for weeks in advance. Eventually the demand to hear folk music had reached such overwhelming proportions that the Newport Folk Festival drew thousands more admissions than did the already famous Jazz Festival.

Throughout America, from one coast to the other, the young people flocked to the coffeehouses, concert halls, college gyms, and city parks to listen to groups of instrumentalists or singers accompanied by guitars (either acoustic or electric), banjos, and the more unusual folk instruments such as the mountain dulcimer or autoharp. To this was added, at the whim of those listening, all types of sound effects available, such as washboards, beer bottles, or wine jugs.

The programs included many types of songs: Irish rebel songs, old French ballads or love songs, early American Appalachian tunes and dances, the mournful blues songs, or any type of protest song that fitted the mood or topic of the day. The deeper meaning of this renaissance was not always apparent to many persons, but it foretold great changes in the outlook and viewpoint of today's younger generation. Other contributing factors in this new awareness had been the intense interest aroused around 1958 with such leaders as Huddie Ledbetter (better known as Leadbelly) and Woody Guthrie (whose many songs included *This Land Is Your Land,* now considered the anthem of the folk singer), as well as the two-million-dollar sale of the Kingston Trio's recording of *Tom Dooley,* which inflamed this young group that had cut its teeth on rock 'n' roll music and now included many college students.

As the campus became the popular place for all types of folk music, clubs and festivals of folk songs were planned in most of the leading colleges and universities. Magazine and newspaper articles soon pointed out the collegians' desire and actual need for the songs, which dealt with current problems or protests, just as earlier Americans used similar songs when the colonies were young and the clouds of war hung heavy over the land. The young people, turning to the simple songs of everyday life as known and experienced by themselves, passed through many confused and troubled hours in the search for a positive, ideal way of life. Out of it these future leaders of the destiny of our great nation rediscovered their basic American heritage of integrity and honesty. In the final eager desire to move forward at all costs, to see that all men have their chance regardless of race, color, creed, or religion, the younger generation ultimately relinquished its place as a spectator and became wholeheartedly involved as a participant.

THE PHENOMENON OF THE MUSIC FESTIVALS

Just as every spring fills the fields and wooded slopes with the simple beauty of countless wild flowers, so there blossomed throughout the land every type of music festival in similar profusion. This is a phenomenon such as America had never known quite to this extent. A few examples will give some idea of the size, scope, and variety of these festivals, which may be found in the largest cities or in the smallest communities.

New York City, after talking about having a summer music festival for far too long a time, in 1967 used the new Lincoln Center for the Performing Arts as a point of departure for the city's five boroughs. Each of the three largest units of this great complex contributed its share. The Metropolitan Opera House offered a season of opera which included ten performances by the Metropolitan Opera Company with its finest casts and the debut of The Hamburg State Opera from Germany giving productions from its brilliant repertoire. The New York Philharmonic, celebrating its 125th Anniversary in June, again offered the "Promenades" at popular prices and conducted by André Kostelanetz. These were followed by other concerts in Philharmonic Hall, conducted by Leonard Bernstein and guest conductors, with premières of some of the newly commissioned works. For its share, the New York State Theater offered its annual revival of one of Broadway's best musicals, *South Pacific,* with an all-star cast.

The entire Summer Festival 67 plan included everything from Pop at the Forest Hills Music Center to the Museum of Modern Art's "Jazz in the Garden" programs. In Central Park once again the magnificent productions of Shakespeare's plays were given in the outdoor Delacorte Theater and scores of free concerts were offered, as they were in other city parks. These included music in all its forms, from concerts by the New York Philharmonic and operas in concert form by the Metropolitan Opera Company to the Naumberg Orchestra and Goldman Band programs to personal appearances of jazz artists and folk singers to evenings of chamber music under the stars.

One of the newest festivals of the 1967 season, yet indicative of what the entire country was hearing in one way or another, was the Fair Lane Festival, named for the mansion on the Ford estate, which is now a part of the University of Michigan's Dearborn campus. Sponsored by the Musical Society of the University, with Gail W. Rector as the director, the ten concerts in the outdoor shell included four by the Chicago Symphony Baroque Orchestra under Jean Martinon; two small Britten operas from the Caramoor Festival at Katonah, New York; performances by the Bath (England) Festival Orchestra under Yehudi Menuhin, its founder-conductor; and two programs by the Stratford Festival Orchestra of Canada, conducted by Oscar Shumsky. Plans also called for sessions of electronic music in the section of Fair Lane where Thomas Edison worked.

Joining the many festivals along the Pacific Coast was the residence of the highly successful New York City Center Joffrey Ballet for four weeks on the campus of Pacific Lutheran University in Tacoma, Washington, before additional tours took the troupe to other cities and eventually to Alaska and Hawaii.

In 1957, Gian-Carlo Menotti felt the call of his native land with such urgency that he planned to return, thereby fulfilling a life's ambition. His "Festival of Two Worlds," a unique idea, was one of the most ambitious projects to be undertaken in many years. It was aimed "to bring young artists from the New World into contact with those of the Old," and so the small remote town of Spoleto, Italy, was given the miracle of returning to life. With the powerfully persuasive artistic personality of Menotti directing, young American singers, stage directors, conductors, and all those whose efforts are needed to create a lyric theater won the chance to make good, to learn both the Old and the New. Once again these young artists were able to demonstrate America's rare ability to draw from all sources, to use only what is best and practical, and to produce something beautiful that will endure. For 1967, plans called for a domed theater for the Spoleto Festival, designed by the American architect Buckminster Fuller, to be called the Spoleto-Sphere. Students of architecture from six countries would be in the labor force constructing the 350-seat theater under Mr. Fuller's supervision, with financial aid from Southern Illinois University and the National Endowment for the Arts.

WHAT OF AMERICAN OPERA?

Vast sums of money have been contributed to further the performance and creation of American operas. And there have appeared many scores of ability and unmistakable talent, of expert workmanship and deft characterizations, some with a marked melodic content and moments of dramatic grandeur. Yet too many have been dropped from the repertoire, a few revived from time to time or given amateur or semiprofessional performances, and the rest all but forgotten.

Some of the most flourishing operas, those which were sung more often than is the general average, belong to a particular period or are an expression of the times, an outgrowth of various phases of life under existing conditions, and consequently are not as topical (or as relevant) twenty-five years later. These would include such operas as Deems Taylor's *The King's Henchman* and *Peter Ibbetson*; Louis Gruenberg's *Emperor Jones*; Howard Hanson's *Merry Mount*; the delightful score of Virgil Thomson, *Four Saints in Three Acts*; and George Gershwin's beloved *Porgy and Bess*.

America has *no permanent opera repertory*. Only *Porgy and Bess*, which has been heard by more people throughout the world than any other American opera, has achieved the status of a masterwork. American opera has yet to match the peerless works of the European masters.

A NATIONAL OPERA COMPANY

When the present Opera Company of Boston was founded in 1958, the best available home for it was an ancient movie palace, a short walk from Symphony Hall. Its artistic director was the wise and dynamic Sarah Caldwell, who already knew just what she wanted for Boston audiences, especially the vast numbers of students in the city and nearby suburbs. There was no way of knowing then just how far-reaching the impact and influence of this vital group would be. Each season was carefully planned—five productions, which included masterworks from the standard operatic repertory and first performances of new or unheard controversial works to enrich the musical environment of both company and audience alike.

This young company soon became known in musical circles. Some of the world's greatest artists came to sing in certain operas that appealed to them. This, in turn, brought opera lovers to the city, which was already packing the "opera house" with its own audiences. The climax of the company's brief career came in 1966-67 with the American première of Arnold Schoenberg's opera *Moses and Aaron.*

Critical acclaim was immediate and praise came from all sides, not only for the company itself, but also for those who had planned so carefully and well. The insight and imagination, the belief in a dream, and the rare ability to make that dream become a reality made a deep impression on many of those who had obtained financial support for the company. Therefore, plans are now under way, with the Opera Company of Boston as a nucleus, for an opera company on the national level. To be known as the American National Opera Company, part of its support will come from the National Endowment for the Arts, headed by Roger L. Stevens. With the benefit of the trials and errors experienced in Boston, the original purpose of the founders can never be lost: They knew and believed that there was a public for beautiful music, theatrical excitement, and a variety of emotional experiences, and that is what they gave it.

BROADWAY AND OFF-BROADWAY

After the heights reached by the new type of Broadway musical in the 1940s, climaxed by *My Fair Lady* in 1956, there came a gap. Up to this time there had been a steady gain in brilliance and momentum, but then inspiration seemed to wane. This does not mean that there were no delightfully entertaining productions on Broadway, for many of them are still favorites of someone today. But to one who has had years of experience with this music, something was lacking; the musicals of the late fifties and early sixties did not fully measure up to those productions of the preceding decade.

Some worthy of mention include the last musical of Rodgers and Hammerstein before the latter's death in 1960, *The Sound of Music* (1959), whose superb film version broke many records. In 1962, working entirely alone, writing both the words and the music, Rodgers made a notable success with *No Strings*. *Gypsy* (1959) proved to be Jule Styne's best score of the decade, and Jerry Herman's two hits, *Hello, Dolly!* (1964) and *Mame* (1966), have bouncy, infectious tunes. In 1959 Jerry Bock and Sheldon Harnick won the Pulitzer Prize for *Fiorello*, their sketch of Mayor La-Guardia. And in 1964 they wrote one of the most memorable musical portraits of the decade, *Fiddler on the Roof*, the tender, pathetic story of the eternally persecuted Jewish peasants in a small Russian province. In this they captured the timeless, traditional dignity of any Jewish community, with its music and rituals and its solemn respect for family traditions, from which a warm sense of humor is never absent.

In more recent years Broadway has had artistic competition from off-Broadway productions. Originally located in Greenwich Village, off-Broadway today includes small theaters anywhere in the city. One off-Broadway hit, *Once Upon a Mattress* (1959), with music by Mary Rodgers (second generation), also lent itself to an excellent television performance. Another, now in its eighth year, was *The Fantasticks* (1960), by Harvey Schmidt and Tom Jones, who then proceeded to bring off a tour de force with their full-scale Broadway musical *I Do! I Do!* (1966), which had only two characters.

Twenty years ago the hope was expressed by some of our most thoughtful critics and aficionados that the United States might look to the final merger of Broadway and the opera house for a *real* American opera. Already Broadway and the concert hall have met successfully, for increasing numbers of our composers are thoroughly trained musicians, equally at home in either medium.

Leonard Bernstein's *West Side Story* (with its book by Arthur Laurents and lyrics by Stephen Sondheim), although slow in getting under way in 1957, soon became a financial success, and then was followed by the tremendously exciting film version. That Bernstein is a genius few will argue; supremely gifted in any medium in which he chooses to work, he has no peers among his contemporaries.

West Side Story is a unique theatrical experience, that rare combination of music, song, dance, and drama. Every part of the production—movements, gestures, words—move with an effortless grace and rhythm. The restlessness, the exploding energy, the unabashed sentiment, are as much a product of the *verismo* school as anything that came out of Italy near the beginning of the twentieth century. It pictures life as thousands have known and had to live it, yet its songs were heard on the jukeboxes throughout the land.

Who can say with any certainty that either *Porgy and Bess* or *West Side Story* (each of which pictured a phase of life that at the time was very real), or perhaps both, are not well on the way toward finding that opera so desperately being sought?

THE YOUNG AMERICAN COMPOSER TODAY

The young composer of 1967 is as thoroughly prepared as his older contemporaries and he has the good fortune to begin his life's work in a period of heightened activity, optimism, and an increased flourishing of music as an art. Standards of performance continue to improve and the composer has at last won respect as a creative talent. Trained and equipped for his craft, instinctively an eclectic, and knowledgeable and well informed, much more so than those in a comparable position in the other countries of the world, the young American composer of today has yet a new dilemma. Today he finds such a multiplicity of musical avenues that his position is both unprecedented and very difficult.

For the purpose of experimentation and research, electronic music undoubtedly offers the greatest challenge for many. Today, in the light of the great technological developments, the experience gained from years of experimentation in the three countries that led the way—France, the United States, and Germany—must be redirected. The new concentration must be on the sounds that are electronically produced—the "what" rather than the "how."

A Rockefeller grant was given to Columbia University in 1959 to further equip its laboratory for the expansion of experimental work. In 1960, under the joint jurisdiction of Otto Luening and Vladimir Ussachevsky, with Roger Sessions and Milton Babbitt of Princeton University, a recent development, the RCA Electronic Synthesizer, was installed at the Columbia-Princeton Center for Electronic Music. This highly expensive electronic system is able to generate any musical tone or combination of tones imaginable, in many varieties of pitch levels and timbres, as well as the most complex rhythmic patterns, far beyond the possibilities of the usual orchestral instruments.

Any attempt to name the promising young composers of the last ten years would be both impractical and all but impossible. Today the nation's leading newspapers and magazines keep the public informed about important new discoveries and individual artistic achievements, while the monthly record catalogues indicate which composers and what works are getting the chance of being heard.

BALLET AND DANCE GROUPS

One of the strongest mediums of our American music for more than twenty-five years has been the ballet, and it still has a large and devoted following. The nation can take great pride in its young dancers and choreographers, who not only have won their place in the world of the dance, but have maintained that position through the years. Still, these honors must also be shared with the composers, who have written some of the most significant ballets of our generation, scores undeniably American in flavor and in their use of folk themes and rhythms. The New York City Ballet still plays the leading role, at home in its new location in the New York State Theater in Lincoln Center or on extensive national and international tours.

The American Ballet Theater, the first to emerge in 1939 as Ballet Theater, has gone through some difficult years. With its reorganization in 1959 it has consistently grown in stature until the turning point—the 1966-67 season—when Clive Barnes wrote in *The New York Times*: ". . . the company looked like a genuinely creative artistic organization."

The presence of a new and exciting company in New York was not only a healthy sign, but one for rejoicing. Robert Joffrey had built his original ballet workshop in Greenwich Village into a company with a solid reputation. Its first tour in 1956 attracted much attention and justified the support of its patrons. The troupe was soon afterward offered a "trial" engagement at the old New York City Center. Success was immediate and with it came financial aid and a permanent home at City Center.

National recognition followed and the summer of 1967 was spent in appearances at festivals on the West Coast and short tours to nearby western cities and states, including Alaska and Hawaii. The tour was interrupted for four weeks of residence on the campus of Pacific Lutheran University in Tacoma, Washington. Of great significance to the Pacific Northwest, the university plans over the next three years to establish a permanent summer session of performances, classes, and lecture-demonstrations. Ballet in America has indeed come of age.

ORCHESTRAS AND COMMISSIONS

The orchestras of the United States are still internationally known for the reputation they made many years ago, especially in the 1920s. As their standards of performance, technical skill, the opulence of the strings and fiery spirit of the rhythmic sections were heard on the early electrical recordings and then in actual performances when various orchestral groups began to go abroad, their reputations were firmly established. Then, with the dramatic success of the Philadelphia Orchestra's visit to Japan in the spring of 1967, new friends were made in the Orient, still a large and untapped section of the world. With increasing frequency our conductors, constantly being invited to appear with various outstanding orchestras, are apt to turn up almost anywhere. This is a remarkable change from the old-fashioned notion many Americans had that a foreign name immediately signified superior musicianship.

Of the "big three" orchestras—New York, Boston, and Philadelphia—two have had, or are about to have, major changes in musical directors. In 1958 Leonard Bernstein, then associate conductor of the New York Philharmonic, was appointed its permanent musical director with the retirement of Dimitri Mitropoulos. Now Bernstein himself must soon be replaced since he plans to use more of his time for composing and other activities. In Boston Erich Leinsdorf took over the directorial post of the Boston Symphony Orchestra when Charles Munch retired to his native France in 1962. The distinguished conductor of the Philadelphia Orchestra since 1936, Eugene Ormandy, therefore, still holds the record of the longest tenure of the three.

New Yorkers found that they had a new orchestra in 1962 when the American Orchestra was founded by Leopold Stokowski. As its music director and conductor, Stokowski promised his public "concerts of great music within the means of everyone," to be played in beloved Carnegie Hall, so fortunately rescued from the wreckers. Still as vital and dynamic as ever at the age of eighty-five, Stokowski has no peer either as a conductor or as the champion of new music. Nor can the history of twentieth-century music in America show a similar span of more brilliant work or wizardry in getting any ensemble which he directs to play with the most magnificent tonal beauty.

Some of the country's major orchestras are revising their requirements in the selection of new, permanent conductors. The "name" conductor who contracts for a selected number of concerts each season, but spends little time in his temporary home, is a stimulus only for the immediate attention that the orchestra must have in order to survive. For a healthy, long-term gain, to build future audiences through popular and educational concerts, and to become the heart of a thoroughly integrated and actively functioning community musical life, the ultimate choice must be the rarest of individuals—a musician, a dynamic conductor respected by the orchestra, a diplomat, a businessman, and above all a man with a deep and consuming love of music.

Today our composers include some of the most active and alert conductors, directors who have already made a name in other mediums, such as choral groups or opera, and those gifted graduate student conductors, the winners of foundation grants, who already have had experience with major symphony orchestras.

An excellent example is Lukas Foss, one of the most talented and richly endowed of our contemporary American composers. As music director and conductor of the Buffalo Philharmonic and one of the guiding spirits in the city's new Center for Creative and Performing Arts, he is building a music center that has already attracted international attention. Besides the orchestra, Buffalo's Center has a chamber music ensemble performing the latest music with unlimited rehearsal time, nine months out of the year. At this point the performer is given considerable critical attention for his ability to master new and complex scores, as the European avant-garde has been doing for some time. Foss was correct when he wrote in an article in *The New York Times*: "Buffalo is interesting as a phenomenon symbolic of what is happening in the United States."

The history of the commissioning of new music in America is as old as the nation itself. Whether it consisted of songs to honor General George Washington, grand marches to celebrate a victorious battle, light entertainment to honor visiting celebrities in the eighteenth and nineteenth centuries, or the later Expositions and World's Fairs, such as those in St. Louis and Chicago, or Richard Wagner's empty, pompous *Centennial March* sent to the Philadelphia Centennial in 1876, there are few types which have not been heard. Today there are more commissions than ever, from the Coolidge Festival concert series' commissions, started over a half century ago and carried further by many famous galleries and the bequests of prominent persons, to Samuel Barber's *Antony and Cleopatra* opera composed to honor the gala opening of the new Metropolitan Opera House in Lincoln Center, New York, to the long series of commissions for the 125th Anniversary of the New York Philharmonic. Multiply these countless times and only then is it possible to get a picture of the average, hard-working American composer, now respected both as an artist and as a man.

POSTSCRIPT

Despite the fact that television has had the severest criticism, even abuse (much of which was justified), there is a positive side that in all fairness must be considered. Invariably any new medium raises controversies, and radio went through its own difficult times, yet today the combination of these two momentous discoveries is of the greatest importance in further discovering the vast wealth that is in our American music. With the gradual improvement of educational television, there is an opportunity for the serious student of music and the average music-lover to enrich his musical life and deepen his understanding.

The advent of stereo recordings for home use in 1958 was considerably hastened by the early experiments in and subsequent use of stereophonic sound in motion pictures by such pioneers as Walt Disney in his *Fantasia*, shown publicly in 1940. Just as perfection of electrical recording was the industry's answer to the threat of radio, in much the same way stereo recordings proved to be the impetus that revitalized the sale of records, which had been seriously affected by television.

Now with every type of music that can be heard ready to sound at the flick of a switch, day or night throughout the country, America can do full justice to her vast musical treasure. The celebration of her two hundred years of freedom is cause for great joy. And there is even greater promise for the years ahead, for at last American music, no longer a slave to foreign domination and influences, is free, too. Musically she has no peer, and like her new generation, America moves forward toward the future with high hopes and renewed faith.

Necrology

	DIED		DIED
ANTHEIL, George	1959	JACOBI, Frederick	1953
		JOSTEN, Werner	1963
BECKER, John J.	1961		
BLITZSTEIN, Marc	1964	KAHN, Erich Itor	1956
BLOCH, Ernest	1959	KURKA, Robert	1957
BOROWSKI, Felix	1956		
		McPHEE, Colin	1964
CHANLER, Theodore	1961	MITROPOULOS, Dimitri	1960
COWELL, Henry	1965		
		PORTER, Cole	1964
FARRAR, Geraldine	1967	PORTER, Quincy	1966
FINE, Irving	1962	POULENC, Francis	1963
		POWELL, John	1963
GARDEN, Mary	1967		
GIANNINI, Vittorio	1966	RIEGGER, Wallingford	1961
GRAINGER, Percy	1961		
GRUENBERG, Louis	1964		
		SALZEDO, Carlos	1961
		SAMINSKY, Lazare	1959
HAMMERSTEIN, Oscar II	1960	SCOTT, Tom	1961
HANDY, W. C.	1958	SHEPHERD, Arthur	1958
HART, Moss	1961		
HILL, Edward Burlingame	1960		
HINDEMITH, Paul	1963	TAYLOR, Deems	1966
HOFMANN, Josef	1957	TOCH, Ernst	1964
HOWARD, John Tasker	1964	TOSCANINI, Arturo	1957
HOWE, Mary	1964		
HUMPHREY, Doris	1958	VARESE, Edgar	1965

Supplementary Readings

CHAPTER I

Burton, Frederick R., *American Primitive Music* (New York, Moffat, Yard and Co., 1909).
Curtis, Natalie, *The Indians' Book* (New York, Harper and Brothers, 1907).
Howard, John Tasker, *Our American Music* (New York, Thomas Y. Crowell Company, revised ed., 1954), pp. 613-622.

For other books on Indian music see Bibliography of Howard, *Our American Music, op. cit.,* pp. 725-727.

CHAPTER II

The Spaniards in Mexico

Stevenson, Robert, *Music in Mexico* (New York, Thomas Y. Crowell Company, 1952).

The Pilgrims and Puritans

Foote, Henry Wilder, *Three Centuries of American Hymnody* (Cambridge, Harvard University Press, 1940), pp. 1-123.
Howard, John Tasker, *Our American Music, op. cit.,* pp. 3-20.
Pratt, Waldo Selden, *The Music of the Pilgrims* (Boston, Oliver Ditson Company, 1921).
Scholes, Percy A., *The Puritans and Music in England and New England* (New York, Oxford University Press, 1934), pp. 1-90.

Secular Music in the Colonies

Howard, John Tasker, *The Music of George Washington's Time* (Washington, D.C., United States George Washington Bicentennial Commission, 1931).

417

——, *Our American Music, op. cit.*, pp. 20-30.

Odell, George C. D., *Annals of the New York Stage* (New York, Columbia University Press, 1927), Vol. I, sections on concerts and opera.

Redway, Virginia Larkin, "A New York Concert in 1736," *Musical Quarterly*, April, 1936.

Sonneck, Oscar G., *Bibliography of Early Secular American Music*, rev. and enlarged by William Treat Upton (Washington, D.C., The Library of Congress, 1945).

——, *Early Concert Life in America* (New York, Musurgia Publishers, 1949).

——, *Early Opera in America* (New York, G. Schirmer, Inc., 1925).

The Minority Sects

David, Hans T., "Ephrata and Bethlehem in Pennsylvania: a Comparison." *American Musicological Society Papers*, 1941, pp. 97-104 (Oberlin, Ohio, 1946).

Foote, Henry Wilder, *Three Centuries of American Hymnody, op. cit.*, pp. 124-142.

Rau, Albert G., "John Frederick Peter," *Musical Quarterly*, July, 1937.

——, and Hans T. David, *A Catalogue of Music by American Moravians* (Bethlehem, Pa., The Moravian Seminary, 1938).

CHAPTER III

Daniel, Oliver, "America's First Troubadour" (William Billings), *Music Clubs Magazine*, January, 1953.

Foote, Henry Wilder, *Three Centuries of American Hymnody, op. cit.*, section on Billings, pp. 116-123.

Hastings, George E., *The Life and Works of Francis Hopkinson* (Chicago, University of Chicago Press, 1926).

Howard, John Tasker, *Our American Music, op. cit.*, pp. 37-57.

Lindstrom, Carl E., "William Billings and His Times," *Musical Quarterly*, October, 1939.

Sonneck, Oscar G., *Francis Hopkinson and James Lyon* (Washington, D.C., H. L. McQueen, 1905).

CHAPTER IV

Howard, John Tasker, *The Music of George Washington's Time, op. cit.*

——, *Our American Music, op. cit.*, pp. 58-110; 113-121.

Odell, George C. D., *Annals of the New York Stage, op. cit.*, vols. I and II, sections on concerts and opera.

Sonneck, Oscar G., *Bibliography of Early Secular American Music, op. cit.*

——, *Early Concert Life in America, op. cit.*

——, *Early Opera in America*, New York, *op. cit.*

CHAPTER V

General

Howard, John Tasker, *Our American Music, op. cit.*, pp. 121-128; 129-136.

Krohn, Ernst C., "Alexander Reinagle as Sonatist," *Musical Quarterly*, January, 1932.

Redway, Virginia Larkin, "The Carrs, American Music Publishers," *Musical Quarterly*, January, 1932.

Sonneck, Oscar G., *Report on the Star-Spangled Banner, Hail Columbia, America, Yankee Doodle* (Washington, D.C., Library of Congress, Government Printing Office, 1909).

Specific

Muller, Joseph, *The Star-Spangled Banner; Words and Music Issued between 1814-1864* (New York, G. A. Baker and Company, 1935).

Sonneck, Oscar G., *The Star-Spangled Banner* (Revised and enlarged from the Report of 1909) (Washington, D.C., Library of Congress, Government Printing Office, 1914).

Weybright, Victor, *Spangled Banner, The Life of Francis Scott Key* (New York, Farrar and Rinehart, 1935).

CHAPTER VI

General

Erskine, John, *The Philharmonic-Symphony Society of New York* (New York, The Macmillan Company, 1943).

Foote, Henry Wilder, *Three Centuries of American Hymnody, op. cit.*, pp. 143-258.

Howard, John Tasker, *Our American Music, op. cit.*, pp. 129-252.

Johnson, Harold Earle, "The Germania Musical Society," *Musical Quarterly*, January, 1953.

——, *Musical Interludes in Boston*, 1795-1830 (New York, Columbia University Press, 1943).

Krehbiel, Henry E., *Chapters of Opera* (New York, Henry Holt and Company, 1909).

Mattfeld, Julius, *A Hundred Years of Grand Opera in New York* (New York, New York Public Library, 1927), pp. 10-119.

——, comp., *Variety Music Cavalcade, 1620-1950* (Englewood Cliffs, N.J., Prentice-Hall, Inc., 1952).

Metcalf, Frank J., *American Writers and Compilers of Sacred Music* (New York, The Abingdon Press, 1925).

Odell, George C. D., *Annals of the New York Stage, op. cit.,* Vols. II, III, IV, V, sections on concerts and opera.

Ryan, Thomas, *Recollections of an Old Musician* (New York, E. P. Dutton and Company, 1899).

Specific

Benét, Laura, *Enchanting Jenny Lind* (New York, Dodd, Mead and Company, 1939).

Brink, Carol, *Harps in the Wind, The Story of the Singing Hutchinsons* (New York, The Macmillan Company, 1947).

Gottschalk, Louis Moreau, *Notes of a Pianist,* ed. by Clara Gottschalk, translated by Robert E. Peterson (Philadelphia, J. B. Lippincott Company, 1881).

Howard, John Tasker, "Louis Moreau Gottschalk, as Portrayed by Himself," *Musical Quarterly,* January, 1932.

——, *Stephen Foster, America's Troubadour* (New York, Thomas Y. Crowell Company, rev. ed., 1953).

Jordan, Philip O., *Singin' Yankees* (Minneapolis, The University of Minnesota Press, 1946).

Maginty, Edward A., "'America': The Origin of Its Melody," *Musical Quarterly,* July, 1934.

Smith, Mortimer B., *The Life of Ole Bull* (Princeton, Princeton University Press, 1943).

Upton, William Treat, *Anthony Philip Heinrich, A Nineteenth-Century Composer in America* (New York, Columbia University Press, 1939).

Wagenknecht, Charles Edward, *Jenny Lind* (Boston, Houghton Mifflin Company, 1931).

CHAPTER VII

General

Browne, C. A., *The Story of Our National Ballads* (New York, Thomas Y. Crowell Company, rev. ed., 1931).

Dolph, Edward A., *Sound Off! Soldier Songs from the Revolution to World War II* (New York, Farrar and Rinehart, 1942).

Howard, John Tasker, *Our American Music, op. cit.,* songs of the Civil War, pp. 255-268; after the Civil War, 269-306.

Niles, John J., Douglas Moore and A. A. Wallgreen, *Songs My Mother Never Taught Me* (New York, The Macaulay Company, 1929).

Swan, Howard, *Music in the Southwest, 1825-1950* (San Marino, California, The Huntington Library, 1952).

Upton, George P., *Musical Memories* (Chicago, A. C. McClurg and Company, 1908).

Specific

Harwell, Richard B., *Confederate Music* (Chapel Hill, N.C., The University of North Carolina Press, 1950).

Howe, M. A. De Wolfe, "John Knowles Paine," *Musical Quarterly,* July, 1939.

Russell, Charles Edward, *The American Orchestra and Theodore Thomas* (Garden City, Doubleday, Doran and Company, 1927).

CHAPTER VIII

General

Howard, John Tasker, *Our American Music, op. cit.,* "The Parents of Our Contemporaries," pp. 294-306; "The Boston Group," pp. 306-323; "Edward MacDowell," pp. 323-344.

Specific

Currier, T. P., "MacDowell as I Knew Him," *Musical Quarterly,* January, 1915.

Engel, Carl, "Charles Martin Loeffler," *Musical Quarterly,* July, 1925.

——, "George W. Chadwick," *Musical Quarterly,* July, 1924.

Erskine, John, "MacDowell at Columbia: Some Recollections," *Musical Quarterly,* October, 1942.

Gilman, Lawrence, *Edward MacDowell, A Study* (New York, John Lane Company, 1908).

Langley, Allen Lincoln, "George Chadwick and the New England Conservatory of Music," *Musical Quarterly,* January, 1935.

MacDowell, Marian, "MacDowell's 'Peterboro Idea,'" *Musical Quarterly,* January, 1932.

Semler, Isabel Parker, *Horatio Parker* (New York, G. P. Putnam's Sons, 1942).

Smith, David Stanley, "A Study of Horatio Parker," *Musical Quarterly*, April, 1930.

Tuthill, Burnet C., "Daniel Gregory Mason," *Musical Quarterly*, January, 1948.

——, "Mrs. H. H. A. Beach," *Musical Quarterly*, July, 1940.

Waters, Edward N., "John Sullivan Dwight, First American Critic of Music," *Musical Quarterly*, January, 1935.

CHAPTER IX

Boardman, H. R., *Henry Hadley, Ambassador of Harmony* (Atlanta, Ga., Barnes Press, Emory University, 1932).

Carter, Elliott, "American Figure, with Landscape," (Henry F. Gilbert) *Modern Music*, May-June, 1943.

Downes, Olin, "An American Composer," (Henry F. Gilbert) *Musical Quarterly*, January, 1918.

CHAPTER X

Borowski, Felix, "John Alden Carpenter," *Musical Quarterly*, October, 1930.

Downes, Olin, "John Alden Carpenter," *Musical Quarterly*, October, 1930.

Gatti, G. M., "Ernest Bloch," *Musical Quarterly*, January, 1921.

Goss, Madeleine, *Modern Music Makers* (New York, E. P. Dutton and Company, 1952). "John Alden Carpenter," pp. 34-56.

Hughes, Charles W., "Percy Grainger, Cosmopolitan Composer," *Musical Quarterly*, April, 1937.

Maisel, Edward M., *Charles T. Griffes, The Life of an American Composer* (New York, Alfred A. Knopf, Inc., 1943).

Newlin, Dika, "The Later Works of Ernest Bloch," *Musical Quarterly*, October, 1947.

Panassié, Hugues, *The Real Jazz*, tr. by Anne Sorelle Williams (New York, Smith and Durrell, 1942).

Sargeant, Winthrop, *Jazz: Hot and Hybrid* (New York, E. P. Dutton and Company, 1946).

Sessions, Roger, "Ernest Bloch," *Modern Music*, November, 1927.

Tuthill, Burnet C., "David Stanley Smith," *Musical Quarterly*, January, 1942.

Ulanov, Barry, *A History of Jazz in America* (New York, The Viking Press, Inc., 1952)

For general references for chapters X to XV inclusive, see the following:

Chase, Gilbert, *America's Music* (New York, McGraw-Hill Book Company, Inc., 1955), see index.

Cowell, Henry, ed., *American Composers on American Music* (Stanford University, Cal., Stanford University Press, 1933), see index.

Howard, John Tasker, *Our American Music*, see index.

Howard, John Tasker, *Our Contemporary Composers* (New York, Thomas Y. Crowell Company, 1941), see index.

McNamara, Daniel, ed., *The ASCAP Biographical Dictionary* (New York, Thomas Y. Crowell Company, rev. 1952).

Reis, Claire R., *Composers in America*, revised ed. (New York, The Macmillan Company, 1947).

CHAPTER XI

General

Howard, John Tasker, *Our American Music*, pp. 446-452.

Specific

Antheil, George, *Bad Boy of Music* (Garden City, N.Y., Doubleday, Doran and Company, 1945).

Armitage, Merle, ed., *George Gershwin* (New York, Longmans, Green and Company, 1938).

Cowell, Henry, "The Music of Edgar Varèse," *Modern Music*, January, 1928.

Duke, Vernon, "Gershwin, Schillinger, and Dukelsky: Some Reminiscences," *Musical Quarterly*, January, 1947.

Ewen, David, *The Story of George Gershwin* (New York, Henry Holt and Company, 1943).

Gerschefski, Edwin, "Henry Cowell," *Modern Music*, Fall, 1946.

Goss, Madeleine, *Modern Music Makers* (New York, E. P. Dutton and Company, 1952), "George Antheil," pp. 334-345; "Henry Cowell," pp. 267-281; "Howard Hanson," pp. 223-236.

Hirsch, Stefan, "Portrait of Varèse," *Modern Music*, January, 1928.

Levant, Oscar, *A Smattering of Ignorance* (Garden City, N.Y., Doubleday, Doran and Co., 1940), chapters on Gershwin.

Smith, Julia, *Aaron Copland* (New York, E. P. Dutton and Company, 1955).

Thompson, Randall, "George Antheil," *Modern Music*, May-June, 1931.

Tuthill, Burnet C., "Howard Hanson," *Musical Quarterly*, April, 1936.

CHAPTER XII

General

Goss, Madeleine, *Modern Music Makers* (New York, E. P. Dutton and Company, 1952), see index for composers.

Specific

Arvey, Verna, *William Grant Still* (New York, J. Fischer and Bro., 1939).

Barlow, S. L. M., "Virgil Thomson," *Modern Music*, May-June, 1941.

Blitzstein, Marc, "Towards a New Form," *Musical Quarterly*, April, 1934.

Broder, Nathan, "The Music of Samuel Barber," *Musical Quarterly*, July, 1948.

Brunswick, Mark, "Roger Huntington Sessions," *Modern Music*, May-June, 1933.

Carter, Elliott, "Walter Piston," *Musical Quarterly*, July, 1946.

Citkowitz, Israel, "Walter Piston, Classicist," *Modern Music*, January-February, 1936.

Damrosch, Walter, *My Musical Life* (New York, Charles Scribner's Sons, 1923).

Diamond, David, "Bernard Rogers," *Musical Quarterly*, April, 1947.

Farwell, Arthur, "Roy Harris," *Musical Quarterly*, January, 1932.

Forbes, Elliott, "The Music of Randall Thompson," *Musical Quarterly*, January, 1949.

Glanville-Hicks, P., "Virgil Thomson," *Musical Quarterly*, April, 1949.

Hanson, Howard, "Bernard Rogers," *Modern Music*, March-April, 1945.

Henderson, William, J., "Walter Damrosch," *Musical Quarterly*, January, 1932.

Horan, Robert, "Samuel Barber," *Modern Music*, March-April, 1943.

Howard, John Tasker, *Deems Taylor* (New York, J. Fischer and Bro., 1927).

Kramer, A. Walter, "Louis Gruenberg," *Modern Music*, November-December, 1930.

Luening, Otto, "Douglas Moore," *Modern Music*, March-April, 1953.

Porter, Quincy, "Randall Thompson," *Modern Music*, May-June, 1942.

Schubart, Mark, "Roger Sessions, Portrait of an American Composer," *Musical Quarterly*, April, 1946.

Slonimsky, Nicolas, "Roy Harris," *Musical Quarterly*, January, 1947.

Sternfeld, Frederick W., "Copland as a Film Composer," *Musical Quarterly*, April, 1951.

Thomson, Virgil, "Aaron Copland," *Modern Music*, January-February, 1932.

Tuthill, Burnet C., "Leo Sowerby," *Musical Quarterly*, July, 1938.

CHAPTER XIII

General

Downes, Olin, and Elie Siegmeister, *A Treasury of American Song* (New York, Alfred A. Knopf, Inc., 1943).

Haywood, Charles, *A Bibliography of North American Folklore and Folksong* (New York, Greenberg: Publisher, Inc., 1951).

Howard, John Tasker, *Our American Music, op. cit.*, pp. 592-612, 613-642.

Lomax, John A., and Alan Lomax, *American Ballads and Folk Songs* (New York, The Macmillan Company, 1934).

——, *Folk Song U.S.A.* (New York, Duell, Sloan and Pearce, Inc., 1947).

Negro Music

Handy, W. C., and Abbe Niles, *A Treasury of the Blues* (New York, Simon and Schuster, Inc., 1949).

Odum, H. W., and G. B. Johnson, *The Negro and His Songs* (Chapel Hill, N.C., University of North Carolina Press, 1925).

Scarborough, Dorothy, *On the Trail of Negro Folk-Songs* (Cambridge, Harvard University Press, 1925).

Work, John W., *American Negro Songs* (New York, Howell, Soskin and Company, 1940).

Anglo-American Folk Songs

Sharp, Cecil J., and Olive D. Campbell, *English Folksongs from the Southern Appalachians* (2nd ed., London, Oxford University Press, 1932), 2 vols.

Scarborough, Dorothy, *A Song Catcher in the Southern Mountains* (New York, Columbia University Press, 1937).

Cowboy Songs

Lomax, John, A., and Alan Lomax, *Cowboy Songs and Other Frontier Ballads* (New York, The Macmillan Company, rev., 1938).

Folk Hymns and Gospel Songs

Foote, Henry Wilder, *Three Centuries of American Hymnody, op. cit.*, pp. 263-386.

Jackson, George Pullen, *The Story of the Sacred Harp, 1844-1944* (Nashville, Tenn., Vanderbilt University Press, 1944).

——, *White Spirituals in the Southern Uplands* (Chapel Hill, N.C., University of North Carolina Press, 1933).

Metcalf, Frank J., *American Writers and Compilers of Sacred Music* (Nashville, Tenn., Abingdon Press, 1925).

For books on regional folk songs see Bibliography of Howard, *Our American Music, op. cit.*, pp. 731-735.

CHAPTER XIV

General

Goss, Madeleine, *Modern Music Makers* (New York, E. P. Dutton and Company, 1952), see index for composers.

Howard, John Tasker, *Our American Music, op. cit.*, see index for composers.

Palmer, Edgar A., *G.I. Songs* (New York, Sheridan House, 1944).

Posselt, Erick, *Give Out! Songs of, by, and for the Men in the Service* (New York, Arrowhead Press, 1943).

Specific

Burton, Jack, *The Blue Book of Tin Pan Alley* (Watkins Glen, New York, Century House, 1950).

Cowell, Henry, "Paul Creston," *Musical Quarterly*, October, 1948.

Ewen, David, *Men of Popular Music* (Chicago-New York, Ziff-Davis Publishing Co., 1944).

——, *The Story of Irving Berlin* (New York, Henry Holt and Company, 1950).

——, *The Story of Jerome Kern* (New York, Henry Holt and Company, 1953).

Green, Abel, and Joe Laurie, Jr., *Show Biz from Vaude to Video* (New York, Henry Holt and Company, 1951).

Haywood, Charles, comp., *The James A. Bland Album of Outstanding Songs* (New York, E. B. Marks Corp., 1946).

McNamara, Daniel, ed., *The ASCAP Biographical Dictionary* (New York, Thomas Y. Crowell Company, rev. ed., 1952).

Mattfield, Julius, comp., *Variety Music Cavalcade, 1620-1950* (Englewood Cliffs, N.J., Prentice-Hall, Inc., 1952).

Spaeth, Sigmund, *A History of Popular Music in America* (New York, Random House, Inc., 1948).

Smith, Cecil, *Musical Comedy in America* (New York, Theatre Arts Books, 1950).

Taylor, Deems, *Some Enchanted Evenings, The Story of Rodgers and Hammerstein* (New York, Harper and Brothers, 1953).

Waters, Edward N., *Victor Herbert, His Life and Work* (New York, The Macmillan Company, 1955).

CHAPTER XV

Bellamann, Henry, "Charles Ives, The Man and His Music," *Musical Quarterly*, January, 1933.

Carpenter, Paul S., *Music as Art and a Business* (Norman, Okla., University of Oklahoma Press, 1950).

Carter, Elliott, "Ives Today: His Vision and Challenge," *Modern Music*, May-June, 1944.

Cowell, Henry and Sidney, *Charles Ives* (New York, Oxford University Press, 1955).

Goldman, Richard F., "The Music of Wallingford Riegger," *Musical Quarterly*, January, 1950.

Goss, Madeleine, *Modern Music Makers* (New York, E. P. Dutton and Company, 1952), "Charles Ives," pp. 13-32; "Wallingford Riegger," pp. 117-127.

Heinsheimer, H. W., *Fanfare for 2 Pigeons* (New York, Doubleday and Company, Inc., 1952).

——, *Menagerie in F sharp* (New York, Doubleday and Company, Inc., 1947).

Smith, Cecil, *Worlds of Music* (Philadelphia, J. B. Lippincott Company, 1952).

Recordings of American Music

As the American composer and his works are the main object of interest in this *Short History,* and because of lack of space, no attempt has been made to name the artists or instrumental groups recording these works. Nor has there been any listing of the album numbers; those that are readily available are constantly being changed. However, all detailed information will be found in the excellent, carefully edited Schwann *Long Playing Record Catalog* (published by W. Schwann, Inc., 137 Newbury Street, Boston, Mass. 02116). The *Catalog* is issued monthly as a guide to mono and stereo records in more than thirty-eight hundred record shops throughout the United States and in thirty-eight foreign countries.

The continued and rapid growth of American music and its recording in the last ten years is well ahead of any earlier listing and is difficult to compile at any time. This list may be used as a point of departure, for it includes the music (often with original casts) of many of the important Broadway musical productions, as well as the music of numerous original film scores. Generous lists of folk music and albums devoted to the highlights of American jazz may also be found.

Previously the recordings of the Louisville (Kentucky) Symphony Orchestra and the American Recording Society have been available only through subscriptions, but gradually many works of these organizations will be found among the new monthly releases.

In the spring of 1956, the first complete catalogue of prerecorded tapes appeared. Either reel or cartridge tapes are sold, in the fields of classical and folk music, as well as jazz.

ABRAMSON, Robert
  Dance Variations for Piano and Orchestra (1965)
AMRAM, David
  Dirge and Variations
  Piano Sonata
  Shakespearean Concerto
  Sonata for Violin and Piano
ANDERSON, Leroy
  Irish Suite
  Music of Leroy Anderson
ANTHEIL, George
  Ballet Mécanique (1924)
  Capital of the World (1953)
  Serenade No. 1, for Strings (1948)
  Sonata No. 2, for Violin and Piano (1947)
  Symphony No. 4 (1942)
  The Wish (1955)
BABBITT, Milton
  All Set (1957)
  Composition for Four Instruments (1948)
  Composition for Synthesizer (1964)
  Composition for Twelve Instruments (1948)
  Composition for Viola and Piano (1950)
  "Du" (song cycle) (1951)
BACON, Ernst
  Enchanted Island (1954)
  Five Hymns
  Five Poems by Emily Dickinson
  Ford's Theatre (1943)
  From Emily's Diary (1944)
  Sonata for Cello (1948)
BARBER, Samuel
  Adagio for Strings (from Quartet, Op. 11) (1936)
  Andromache's Farewell, Op. 39 (1963)
  Capricorn Concerto (1944)
  Commando March (1943)
  Concerto for Cello (1946)
  Concerto for Piano and Orchestra, Op. 38 (1962)
  Concerto for Violin and Orchestra, Op. 14 (1941)
  Essay No. 1, for Orchestra

Essay No. 2, for Orchestra
Hand of Bridge (1959)
Hermit Songs (1953)
Knoxville: Summer of 1915 (1948)
Medea, Op. 23 (ballet suite) (1946)
Medea's Meditation and Dance of Vengeance, Op. 23-A
Music for a Scene from Shelley (1935)
Nocturne (Homage to John Field)
Nuvoletta, Op. 25 (1947)
Overture to the School for Scandal (1933)
Quartet No. 1, Op. 11 (1936)
Serenade for String Quartet (arr. orch.) (1929)
Sonata for Cello and Piano, Op. 6 (1932)
Sonata for Piano, Op. 26 (1949)
Stopwatch and Ordnance Map, Op. 15 (1940)
Summer Music for Woodwind Quintet, Op. 31 (1956)
Symphony No. 1 in One Movement, Op. 9 (1936)
Three Reincarnations, Op. 16 (1936; 1940)
Toccata Festiva, Op. 36 (1961)
Vanessa (1958)
BARLOW, Samuel
Ballo Sardo: Cortege (1928)
Circus Overture
Mon ami Pierrot: Overture (1935)
BAUER, Marion
Prelude and Fugue (1948)
Suite for Strings (1940)
BEACH, Mrs. H. H. A.
Improvisations (5) for Piano
Trio for Violin, Cello, Piano, Op. 150 (1939)
BECKER, John J.
Concerto Arabesque, for Piano and Orchestra (1930)
BEESON, Jack
Hello Out There
Lizzie Borden
Symphony No. 1 in A (1959)
BENNETT, Richard Rodney
Calendar, for Chamber Orchestra (1962)
Tom O'Bedlam's Song
Trio for Flute, Oboe and Clarinet

BENNETT, Robert Russell
  Commemoration Symphony, "Stephen Foster" (1959)
  Hexapoda (Five Studies in Jitteroptera) (1940)
  Song Sonata for Violin and Piano (1927)
  Suite of Old American Dances
  Symphonic Songs for Band (1958)
  Symphonic Story of Jerome Kern
BEREZOWSKY, Nicolai
  Brass Suite, Op. 24 (1939)
  Christmas Festival Overture (1943)
BERGER, Arthur
  Bagatelle (1946)
  Cello and Piano Duo (1951)
  Intermezzo (1947)
  Polyphony for Orchestra (1956)
  Quartet (1958)
  Serenade Concertante (1944; rev. 1951)
  Wind Quartet (1941)
BERGSMA, William
  Carol on Twelfth Night (1954)
  Chameleon Variations (1960)
  The Fortunate Islands, for String Orchestra (1947; rev. 1956)
  March with Trumpets (1957)
  Music on a Quiet Theme (1943)
  Quartet No. 2 (1944)
  Quartet No. 3
  The Wife of Martin Guerre (selections) (1956)
BERNSTEIN, Leonard
  Age of Anxiety (Symphony No. 2)
  Candide: Overture
  Chichester Psalms for Chorus and Orchestra (1965)
  Facsimile (ballet) (1947)
  Fancy Free (1944)
  Jeremiah Symphony (1943)
  Music of Leonard Bernstein
  On the Town (ballet music)
  On the Waterfront: Symphonic Suite (1955)
  Prelude, Fugue and Riffs (1950)
  Symphony No. 3—Kaddish (1963)
  Trouble in Tahiti (1952)
  West Side Story (ballet music)

BINKERD, Gordon
  Ad te levavi (1959)
  Sonata for Piano (1955)
  Symphony No. 2 (1960)
BLACKWOOD, Easley
  Chamber Symphony for Fourteen Winds, Op. 2 (1955)
BLITZSTEIN, Marc
  The Cradle Will Rock (1937)
  Regina (1949)
BLOCH, Ernest
  Abodah, for Violin and Piano (1929)
  Baal Shem for Violin and Piano (1923)
  Concerto for Violin and Orchestra (1938)
  Concerto Grosso No. 1 for Strings and Piano (1924-25)
  Concerto Grosso No. 2
  Fantasie for Violin and Piano (1899)
  Five Sketches in Sepia
  Israel Symphony (1912-16)
  Nigun from "Baal Shem" Suite
  Poems of the Sea
  Prelude and Two Psalms (Nos. 114 and 137) (1912-14)
  Proclamation for Trumpet and Orchestra (1955)
  Quartet No. 5 (1956)
  Quintet for Piano and Strings (1923)
  Sacred Service, "Avodath Hakodesh" (1930-33)
  Schelomo, Rhapsody for Cello and Orchestra (1915)
  Scherzo Fantasque, for Piano and Orchestra (1950)
  Sonata for Piano (1935)
  Sonata No. 1 for Violin and Piano (1920)
  Suite for Violin (1958)
  Three Nocturnes for Piano Trio (1924)
  Trois Poèmes Juifs (1913)
BOROWSKI, Felix
  The Mirror (1954)
BOWLES, Paul
  Blue Mountain Ballads
  Music for a Farce (1938)
  Preludes for Piano (1934-45)
  Scènes d'Anabase (1932)
BRANT, Henry
  Angels and Devils—Concerto for Flute (1932)

CHADWICK, George Whitefield
Tam O'Shanter (symphonic ballad) (1915)
CHANLER, Theodore
Epitaphs (1937; 1940)
Pot of Fat (1955)
CLAFIN, Avery
Concerto for Piano ("Concerto Giocoso")
Design for the Atomic Age
Fishhouse Punch (1947-48)
La Grande Bretèche (1945-47)
Lament for April 15
The Quangle Wangle's Hat
Teen Scenes (1954-55)
CONVERSE, Frederick Shepherd
Mystic Trumpeter (1905)
COPLAND, Aaron
Appalachian Spring (complete ballet, 1944)
Appalachian Spring: Suite
Billy the Kid: Suite (1938)
Concerto for Clarinet and Orchestra (1948)
Concerto for Piano and Orchestra (1927)
Connotations for Orchestra (1962)
Dance Symphony (1922; 1925)
Danzón Cubano (1942)
El Salón México (1936)
Fanfare for the Common Man (1944)
In the Beginning (1947)
Lark (1939)
Las Agachadas (1942)
Lincoln Portrait
Music for a Great City (symphonic suite) (1964)
Music for the Theatre (1925)
Old American Songs (1950; 1954)
Orchestral Variations (1957)
Our Town (suite) (1940)
Outdoor Overture (1938)
Passacaglia for Piano (1922)
Piano Fantasy (1957)
Piano Variations (1930)
Quiet City, for Trumpet, English Horn, Orchestra (1940)

COPLAND, Aaron—*Continued*
  Red Pony (1948)
  Rodeo (1942)
  Second Hurricane (1937)
  Sonata for Piano (1941)
  Sonata for Violin and Piano (1943)
  Statements for Orchestra (1933-35)
  Symphony No. 3 (1946)
  The Tender Land (abridged)
  The Tender Land (orchestral suite) (1954)
  Twelve Poems of Emily Dickinson (1950)
  Vitebsk, Study on a Jewish Theme (1929)
COWELL, Henry
  Ancient Desert Drone (1940)
  Homage to Iran (1959)
  ". . . if He please" (1954)
  Music 1957 (1957)
  Ongaku for Orchestra (1957)
  Ostinato Pianissimo for Percussion Orchestra (1934)
  Persian Set (1957)
  Prelude for Violin and Harpsichord
  Quartets No. 2 "Movement" (1934)
          No. 3 "Mosaic" (1935)
          No. 4 "United" (1936)
  Sonata No. 1 for Violin and Piano (1945)
  Symphony No. 5 (1949)
  Symphony No. 7 (1952)
  Symphony No. 11 ("Seven Rites of Music") (1954)
  Symphony No. 15 ("Thesis") (1961)
  Symphony No. 16 ("Icelandic") (1962)
  Toccanta for Soprano, Flute, Cello and Piano (1938)
  Trio for Violin, Cello and Piano (1965)
CRESTON, Paul
  Celebration Overture, Op. 61 (1955)
  Choric Dances (1938)
  Corinthians XIII
  Dance Overture (1954)
  Dedication (1965)
  Invocation and Dance, Op. 68 (1953)
  Partita for Flute, Violin and Strings (1937)

Prelude and Dance, Op. 76
Sonata for Saxophone and Piano, Op. 19 (1939)
Symphonies Nos. 2 (1945) and 3 (1950)
CUMMING, Richard
  Knight's Page
  Sonata for Piano (1951)
DAHL, Ingolf
  Allegro and Arioso (1942)
  Music for Brass Instruments (1944)
  Tower of St. Barbara—Symphonic Legend (1955)
DELLO JOIO, Norman
  Epigraph (1951)
  Fantasy and Variations for Piano and Orchestra
  Meditations on Ecclesiastes (1956)
  New York Profiles (1949)
  Serenade (1948)
  Sonata No. 3 for Piano (1947)
  Suite for Piano (1941)
  Variations and Capriccio for Violin (1948)
DENNY, William Dene
  Partita for Organ
DIAMOND, David Leo
  Quartet No. 4 (1951)
  Rounds for String Orchestra (1944)
  Timon of Athens: Portrait after Shakespeare (1949)
  World of Paul Klee (1957)
DONOVAN, Richard
  Epos (1963)
  Passacaglia on Vermont Folk Tunes (1949)
DUKE, Vernon
  Etude for Violin and Bassoon
  Oboe Variations on Old Russian Chant
  Parisian Suite
  Quartet in C
  Sonata in D for Violin and Piano (1949)
  Souvenir de Venise (Piano Sonata No. 2) (1948)
  Surrealist Suite (1939)
  Three Caprices
DVORKIN, Judith
  Maurice (1955)

ELWELL, Herbert
   Concert Suite for Violin and Orchestra (1957)
FINE, Irving
   Diversions (1960)
   Fantasia for String Trio
   Music for Piano (1947)
   Mutability (1952)
   Partita for Wind Quintet (1948)
   Quartet (1952)
   Romanza (1963)
   Serious Song: Lament for String Orchestra (1955)
   Symphony (1962)
   Toccata Concertante (1948)
FINE, Vivian
   Alcestis (ballet music) (1960)
   Concertante for Piano and Orchestra (1944)
   Sinfonia and Fugato for Piano (1963)
FINNEY, Ross Lee
   Piano Quintet
   Quartet No. 6 in F (1950)
   Symphony No. 1 (Communiqué 1943) (1943)
   Symphony No. 2
   Symphony No. 3 (1964)
FLANAGAN, William
   Chapters from Ecclesiastes (1962)
   Concert Ode (1951)
   Lady of Tearful Regret (1959)
FLOYD, Carlisle
   Mystery (Five Songs of Motherhood)
FOOTE, William Arthur
   Night Piece, for Flute and Strings (1917)
   Suite in E for Strings, Op. 63
FOSS, Lukas
   Behold! I Build an House (1950)
   Capriccio for Cello
   Echoi, for Four Soloists (1963)
   Jumping Frog of Calaveras County (1950)
   Parable of Death
   Psalms (1957)
   Quartet No. 1 (1947)

Time Cycle (1960)
Time Cycle (chamber version) (1963)
FOSTER, Stephen
Music of Stephen Foster
GERSCHEFSKI, Edwin
Saugatuck Suite (1938)
GERSHWIN, George
American in Paris (1928)
Concerto in F for Piano and Orchestra (1925)
Cuban Overture (1932)
"I Got Rhythm" Variations for Piano and Orchestra
Music of George Gershwin
Porgy and Bess (1935)
Porgy and Bess (selections)
Porgy and Bess (original suite)
Porgy and Bess (symphonic picture)
Preludes (3) for Piano (1926)
Rhapsody in Blue (1924)
Second Rhapsody for Piano and Orchestra (1931)
GIANNINI, Vittorio
Divertimento No. 2 (1961)
Symphony No. 3
GIDEON, Miriam
Lyric Piece for Strings (1941)
Suite No. 3 for Piano (1963)
Symphonia Brevis (1953)
GILBERT, Henry F. B.
Dance in Place Congo (1906)
GLANVILLE-HICKS, Peggy
Nausicaa (selections) (1961)
Sonata for Harp (1953)
Transposed Heads (1953)
GOEB, Roger
Concertino II for Orchestra (1956)
Concertino for Trombone and Strings (1950)
Prairie Song, for Woodwind Quintet (1947)
Quintet for Woodwinds No. 2 (1956)
Symphony No. 3 (1951)
Symphony No. 4 (1955)
GOEHR, Alexander
Choruses (2), Op. 14

GOTTSCHALK, Louis Moreau
  Gran Tarantella for Piano and Orchestra
  Nuit des Tropiques (symphonic poem)
  Piano Music
GOULD, Morton
  Ballad for Band
  Derivations for Clarinet and Band
  Fall River Legend (ballet suite) (1948)
  Interplay for Piano and Orchestra
  Jericho
  Latin American Symphonette (1941)
  St. Lawrence Suite
  Spirituals for Orchestra (1941)
  Symphony No. 4 for Band, "West Point" (1952)
GRAINGER, Percy
  Children's March (1918)
  Hill-Song No. 2 (1929)
  Lincolnshire Posy
  Music of Percy Grainger
  Walking Tune, for Woodwind Quintet
GREEN, Ray
  Sunday Sing Symphony (1946)
GRIFFES, Charles Tomlinson
  Bacchanale
  Clouds (1917)
  Pleasure Dome (1919)
  Poem for Flute and Orchestra (1918)
  Poems (3) for Voice, Op. 11
  Roman Sketches, Op. 7
  Sonata for Piano (1919)
  Songs
  White Peacock (from Roman Sketches, Op. 7) (1917)
GROFE, Ferde
  Atlantic Crossing
  Concerto in d for Piano and Orchestra
  Death Valley Suite
  Grand Canyon Suite (1931)
  Mississippi Suite
GRUENBERG, Louis
  Concerto for Violin and Orchestra (1944)

HAIEFF, Alexei
  Ballet in E (1955)
  Concerto for Piano (1952)
  Divertimento (1944)
  Quartet, No. 1 (1953)
  Three Bagatelles for Harpsichord
HANSON, Howard
  Chorale and Alleluia (1953)
  Concerto for Piano (1948)
  For the First Time (1962)
  Lament for Beowulf, Op. 25 (1925)
  Merry Mount Suite (1937)
  Mosaics
  Psalms (4)
  Serenade for Flute, Harp and Strings (1946)
  Songs from "Drum Taps" (1935)
  Symphony No. 2, "Romantic" (1930)
  Symphony No. 3
  Symphony No. 4 (1943)
HARMAN, Carter
  A Hymn to the Virgin (1956)
HARRIS, Roy
  Elegy and Dance (1958)
  Epilogue to Profiles in Courage: J. F. K. (1964)
  Kentucky Spring (1949)
  Quintet for Piano and Strings (1936)
  Sonata for Violin and Piano (1942)
  Symphony No. 3 (1938)
  Symphony No. 4, "Folksong" (1940)
  Symphony No. 5 (1943)
  Trio (piano) (1934)
HARRISON, Lou
  Canticle No. 1 for Percussion (1940)
  Canticle No. 3 for Percussion (1941)
  Four Strict Songs for Eight Baritones and Orchestra (1956)
  Song of Queztecoatl (1941)
  Suite for Symphonic Strings (1960-63)
  Suite for Violin, Piano and Small Orchestra (1957)
HELM, Everett
  Concerto No. 2 for Piano (1956)

HERBERT, Victor
  Concerto No. 2 for Cello, Op. 30
  Irish Rhapsody (1910)
  Music of Victor Herbert
HERDER, Ronald
  Movements for Orchestra (1963)
HEWITT, James
  Battle of Trenton
HILL, Edward Burlingame
  Sextet for Piano and Winds (1934)
HIVELY, Wells
  Summer Holiday (Rive Gauche) (1944)
HOIBY, Lee
  Beatrice (1959)
HOLLINGSWORTH, Stanley
  Stabat Mater (1957)
HOVHANESS, Alan Scott
  Concerto No. 2 for Violin
  Concerto No. 7 for Orchestra (1953)
  Duet for Violin and Harpsichord (1954)
  Fantasy on Japanese Woodprints (1965)
  In the Beginning Was the Word (oratorio)
  "Khaldis," Concerto for Piano, Four Trumpets and Percussion
  Koke no niwa ("Moss Garden")
  Lousadzak for Piano and Strings
  Magnificat, Op. 157 (1959)
  Meditation on Orpheus (1958)
  Mysterious Mountain, Op. 132
  October Mountain
  Prelude and Quadruple Fugue
  Sharagan and Fugue for Brass Choir, Op. 58
  Silver Pilgrimage (Symphony No. 15)
  Sonata for Solo Flute
  Suite for Violin, Piano and Percussion
  Symphony No. 4, Op. 165
  Upon Enchanted Ground (1951)
HOWE, Mary
  Castellana for Two Pianos and Orchestra (1935)
  Sand (1928)
  Spring Pastorale (1936)
  Stars (1937)

IMBRIE, Andrew W.
  Concerto for Violin and Orchestra (1958)
  Legend for Orchestra (1959)
  Quartet in B flat Major (1944)
  Quartet No. 2 (1953)
  Quartet No. 3 (1957)
  Sonata for Piano (1947)
IVES, Charles
  Anti-Abolitionist Riots (1908)
  Browning Overture (1911)
  Central Park in the Dark (1898-1907)
  Circus Band
  December
  "Decoration Day" (from Symphony: Holidays) (1912)
  "Fourth of July" (from Symphony: Holidays) (1913)
  General William Booth Enters Into Heaven (1914)
  Hallowe'en (1911)
  Harvest Home Chorale No. 3 (c. 1912)
  Harvest Home Chorales (1898-1912)
  Hymn (1903-14)
  Indians (1912)
  Largo for Violin, Clarinet and Piano (1902)
  New River
  Over the Pavements (1913)
  The Pond (1906)
  Psalms 24, 67, 90, 100, 150
  Quartet No. 1 (1896)
  Quartet No. 2 (1913)
  Rainbow (1914)
  Serenity
  Some Southpaw Pitching (1908)
  Sonata No. 1 for Piano (1909)
  Sonata No. 2, "Concord, Mass., 1840, 1860" (1909-15)
  Sonatas (4) for Violin and Piano (1908-14)
  Songs
  Symphony: Holidays (complete) (1904-13)
  Symphony No. 1 in d (1896-98)
  Symphony No. 2 (1897-1902)
  Symphony No. 3 (1901-04)
  Symphony No. 4 (1910-16)

IVES, Charles—*Continued*
  "Thanksgiving and/or Forefathers' Day" (from Symphony: Holidays) (1904)
  Theatre Set: In the Inn (1904-11)
  Three-Page Sonata for Piano (1905)
  Three Places in New England (1903-14)
  Three Protests (1914)
  Tone Roads Nos. 1 (1911) and 3 (1915)
  Trio for Violin, Cello and Piano (1911)
  Twenty-two (1912)
  The Unanswered Question (1908)
  Variations on "America," for Organ (1891)
  Variations on "America" (orchestrated by William Schuman)
  "Washington's Birthday" (from Symphony: Holidays) (1913)
JACOBI, Frederick
  Ballade for Violin (1942)
  Concerto for Cello and Orchestra (1932)
  Fantasy for Viola (1941)
  Hagiographa, Three Biblical Narratives for String Quartet and Piano (1938)
  Quartet No. 3 (1945)
JOHNSON, Hunter
  Trio for Flute, Oboe and Piano (1954)
JOSTEN, Werner
  Concerto Sacro I-II (1925)
KAHN, Erich Itor
  Ciaconna dei tempi di guerra (1943)
  Eight Inventions (1937)
  Five Short Piano Pieces (1951)
KAY, Hershy
  Cakewalk (ballet), (after Gottschalk) (selections)
KAY, Ulysses
  Brass Quartet (1952)
  Choral Triptych (1962)
  Fantasy Variations (1963)
  How Stands the Glass Around (1954)
  Round Dance and Polka (1954)
  Serenade for Orchestra (1954)
  Sinfonia in E (1950)
  Umbrian Scene (1964)
  What's in a Name? (1954)

KELLER, Homer
  Symphony No. 3 (1956)
KERR, Harrison
  Concerto for Violin and Orchestra (1950-51)
  Trio for Violin, Cello and Piano (1938)
KIRCHNER, Leon
  Duo for Violin and Piano (1947)
  Quartet No. 1 (1949)
KOHS, Ellis B.
  Chamber Concerto for Viola and Strings (1949)
  Psalm 23 (1957-58)
  Short Concert for String Quartet (1948)
  Symphony No. 1 (1950)
KRAFT, William
  Concerto Grosso (1961-62)
KUBIK, Gail
  Celebrations and Epilogue
  Divertimenti 1 and 2 for Thirteen and Eight Players
  Sonata for Piano
  Sonatina for Clarinet and Piano
  Sonatina for Piano (1941)
  Symphony No. 2 in F (1956)
KUPFERMAN, Meyer
  Chamber Symphony (1950)
  Divertimento for Orchestra (1948)
  Line Fantasies from Infinities I
  Little Sonata (1948)
  Lyric Symphony (1956)
  Ostinato Burlesco (orch. 1954)
  Quartet No. 4 (1958)
  Sonata on Jazz Elements (1958)
  Symphony No. 4 (1956)
  Variations for Orchestra (1959)
  Variations for Piano (1948)
KURKA, Robert
  Good Soldier Schweik: Suite
  Serenade for Small Orchestra, Op. 25 (1954)
  Symphony No. 2, Op. 24 (1953)
LADERMAN, Ezra
  Quartet (1959)
  Theme, Variations and Finale (1957)

LaMONTAINE, John
  Birds of Paradise
  Concerto for Piano and Orchestra, Op. 9 (1958)
LAYTON, Billy Jim
  Quartet in Two Movements (1955-56)
LEE, Dai-Keong
  Polynesian Suite (1959)
  Symphony No. 1 (1947)
LEES, Benjamin
  Concerto for Orchestra (1962)
  Prologue, Capriccio and Epilogue (1959)
  Symphony No. 2 (1957-58)
LESSARD, John
  Concerto for Winds and Strings (1952)
  Octet for Winds (1954)
  Partita for Wind Quintet
  Sonata for Cello (1953-54)
  Toccata (1955)
LIST, Kurt
  Remember (1956)
LOCKWOOD, Normand
  Inscriptions from the Catacombs (1935)
  Sing unto the Lord a New Song (1952)
LOEFFLER, Charles Martin
  Memories of Childhood (1925)
  Poem (1923)
LOPATNIKOFF, Nikolai
  Music for Orchestra, Op. 39 (1958)
  Variazioni Concertanti
LO PRESTI, Ronald
  Sketch for Percussion
LUENING, Otto
  Gargoyles (1962)
  Kentucky Rondo (1951)
  Symphonic Fantasy (1924)
LUENING, Otto and Vladimir USSACHEVSKY
  King Lear Suite (1955)
  Poem in Cycles and Bells, Tape Recorder and Orchestra (1954)
  Rhapsodie Variations for Tape Recorder and Orchestra (1954)
McBRIDE, Robert
  Concerto for Violin (1954)
  Pumpkin Eater's Little Fugue (1952)

Punch and Judy (1941)
Workout for Small Orchestra (1936)
MacDOWELL, Edward
  Concerto No. 1 in a, Op. 15, for Piano and Orchestra (1885)
  Concerto No. 2 in d, Op. 23, for Piano and Orchestra (1890)
  Sonata No. 1, "Tragica," Op. 45, for Piano
  Sonata No. 4, "Keltic," Op. 59, for Piano (1901)
  Songs
  Suite No. 1 for Orchestra, Op. 42
  Suite No. 2 (Indian Suite), Op. 48
  Woodland Sketches, Op. 51 (1896)
McPHEE, Colin
  Concerto for Piano and Winds (1928)
  Symphony No. 2, "Pastoral" (1957)
MAMLOK, Ursula
  Variations for Solo Flute
MASON, Daniel Gregory
  Chanticleer (A Festival Overture) (1928)
MENNIN, Peter
  Canto and Toccata (from Five Pieces for Piano) (1950)
  Canzona for Band
  Concertato for Orchestra
  Quartet No. 2
  Symphony No. 5 (1951)
  Symphony No. 6 (1953)
MENOTTI, Gian-Carlo
  Amahl and the Night Visitors (1951)
  Concerto in F, for Piano and Orchestra (1945)
  The Consul (1950)
  The Medium (1946)
  The Telephone (1947)
  The Unicorn, the Gorgon, and the Manticore (1956)
MILLS, Charles
  Centaur and the Phoenix (1960)
  Prelude and Dithyramb (1951; rev. 1954)
  Summer Song (1960)
  The True Beauty (1950)
MOORE, Douglas
  The Ballad of Baby Doe (1956)
  Cotillion Suite (1952)
  The Devil and Daniel Webster (1939)

MOORE, Douglas—*Continued*
 Farm Journal (1947)
 In Memoriam (1943)
 People's Choice
 Quintet for Clarinet, 2 Violins, Viola and Cello (1946)
 Symphony No. 2 in A (1946)
MOROSS, Jerome
 Frankie and Johnnie (ballet) (1938)
MOURANT, Walter
 Air and Scherzo (1955)
 Aria for Orchestra ("Harper's Ferry, W. Va.") (1960)
 Sleepy Hollow (1955)
 Valley of the Moon (1955)
MULLER, Paul
 Concerto for Cello and Orchestra, Op. 55 (1954)
MURRAY, Bain
 Safe in their Alabaster Chambers (1962)
NIXON, Roger
 Quartet No. 1
 Six Moods of Love (Song Cycle)
 Wine of Astonishment (Cantata from the Psalms)
NORDOFF, Paul
 Winter Symphony (No. 1) (1954)
PALMER, Robert
 Memorial Music (1957)
 Nabuchodonosor (1964)
 Quartet for Piano and Strings (1948)
PARKER, Horatio
 Hora Novissima (Oratorio)
PARTCH, Harry
 Bewitched: Scene 10 and Epilogue (1957)
 Cloud Chamber Music (1950)
 Plectra and Percussion Dances: Castor and Pollux (1953)
 Wayward: Letter (1943)
 Windsong (film track) (1958)
PERLE, George
 Monody No. I
 Monody No. II for Unaccompanied Double Bass (1962)
 Quintet for Strings, Op. 35 (1958)
 Rhapsody for Orchestra (1954)
 Six Preludes, Op. 20B (1946)

PERSICHETTI, Vincent
  Concerto for Piano, Four Hands, Op. 56
  Divertimento for Band (1950)
  Pageant for Band (1953)
  Pastoral, for Woodwind Quintet (1945)
  Psalm for Band
  Serenade No. 5, for Orchestra (1950)
  Serenade No. 12, for Solo Tuba, Op. 88 (1961)
  Symphony No. 5, for Strings, Op. 61 (1953)
PHILLIPS, Burrill
  Selections from McGuffey's Reader (1934)
  Tunes
PINKHAM, Daniel
  Cantilena and Capriccio for Violin and Harpsichord (1956)
  Concertante No. 1 (1954)
  Concerto for Celeste and Harpsichord Soli (1955)
  Folk Song: Elegy (1947)
  Glory Be to God (1957)
  Madrigal (1955)
  Partita for Harpsichord
  Symphony No. 2 (1963)
PISTON, Walter
  Carnival Song (1940)
  Chromatic Study on B.A.C.H. (organ) (1940)
  Concertino for Piano and Chamber Orchestra (1937)
  Concerto for Viola and Orchestra (1958)
  Divertimento for Nine Instruments (1946)
  Incredible Flutist (ballet suite) (1938)
  Quintet for Piano and String Quartet (1949)
  Serenata (1956)
  Sonata for Flute and Piano (1930)
  Symphony No. 2 (1944)
  Symphony No. 4 (1949)
  Symphony No. 5 (1956)
  Three Pieces for Flute, Clarinet and Bassoon (1925)
  Tunbridge Fair
PORTER, Quincy
  Concerto Concertante for Two Pianos (1953)
  Concerto for Viola and Orchestra (1948)
  Dance (arr. Wilson)
  Dance in Three Time (1937)

PORTER, Quincy—*Continued*
  Quartet No. 8 (1950)
  Symphony No. 1 (1934)
  Symphony No. 2 (1961-62)
POWELL, John
  Rhapsodie Nègre, for Piano and Orchestra (1918)
POWELL, Mel
  Divertimento for Five Winds (1956)
  Divertimento for Violin and Harp (1955)
  Electronic Setting (1961)
  Filigree Setting for String Quartet (1959)
  Haiku Settings (1960)
  Trio for Violin, Cello and Piano (1956)
RATNER, Leonard
  Piano Sonata
  Serenade for Oboe, Horn, Quartet
READ, Gardner
  Night Flight, Op. 44 (1944)
  Toccata Giocosa, Op. 94 (1953)
REED, H. Owen
  Concerto for Cello (1949)
  La Fiesta Mexicana (1956)
RIEGGER, Wallingford
  Canon and Fugue in d for Strings (1939)
  Concerto for Piano and Woodwinds, Op. 53 (1952)
  Dance Rhythm, Op. 58 (1955)
  Music for Orchestra, Op. 50
  Romanza, Op. 56a
  Suite for Solo Flute (1929)
  Symphony No. 4 (1957)
  Variations for Piano and Orchestra, Op. 54 (1952-53)
  Variations for Violin and Orchestra, Op. 71 (1959)
RIETI, Vittorio
  Concertino for Five Instruments
  Concerto for Cello
  Concerto for Harpsichord (1930)
  Introduzione e Gioco delle Ore (1954)
  Liriche Italiane (4)
  Medieval Variations
  Partita for Flute, Oboe, String Quartet and Harpsichord
  Sei pezzi brevi

Sonata all Antica (1946)

ROCHBERG, George
Bagatelles (12) (1952)
Night Music (1949)
Quartet No. 2 with Soprano (1961)
Symphony No. 1 (1949-55)
Symphony No. 2 (1958)

ROGERS, Bernard
Dance Scenes (1953)
Leaves from the Tale of Pinocchio (1950)
Three Japanese Dances (1933)
Variations on a Song by Moussorgsky (1960)

ROREM, Ned
Design for Orchestra (1955)
Eleven Studies for Eleven Players (1963)
Lovers, for Harpsichord, Oboe, Cello and Percussion (1964)
Poems of Love and Rain (1963)
Sonata (1959)
Two Psalms and a Proverb (1962)

RUGGLES, Carl
Evocations (1945)
Lilacs (1924)
Organum for Orchestra (1945-46)
Portals (1925)
Sun-Treader (1932)

SALZEDO, Carlos
Chanson dans la nuit
Concert Variations on O Tannenbaum

SANDERS, Robert
Little Symphony No. 1 in G (1939)
Little Symphony No. 2 in B flat (1953)
Quintet in B flat (1942)
Symphony in A (1954-55)

SCHIFRIN, Seymour
Serenade for Five Instruments (1954)

SCHULLER, Gunther
Abstraction
Concertino for Jazz Quartet and Orchestra (1959)
Conversations (1959)
Densities I (1962)
Dramatic Overture (1951)

SCHULLER, Gunther—*Continued*
  Fantasy—Quartet for Four Celli (1958)
  Music for Brass Quintet (1961)
  Night Music (1962)
  Seven Studies on Themes of Paul Klee (1959)
  Transformation (1957)
  Woodwind Quintet (1958)
SCHUMAN, William
  American Festival Overture (1939)
  Canonic Choruses (1932; 1933)
  Carols of Death
  Chester (Overture for Band) (1956)
  George Washington Bridge (1950)
  Judith (choreographic poem) (1950)
  New England Triptych, Three Pieces for Orchestra (1956)
  Prelude for Voices (1939)
  Song of Orpheus (Fantasy for Cello and Orchestra) (1963)
  Symphony No. 3 (1941)
  Symphony No. 6 (1948)
  Symphony No. 8 (1962)
  Undertow (ballet) (1945)
  Voyage for Piano (1953)
SCHWARTZ, Paul
  Concertino for Chamber Orchestra (1937; 1947)
SCOTT, Tom
  Binorie Variations (1953)
  Creation
  Go Down Death (1954)
  Hornpipe and Chantey (1944)
SESSIONS, Roger
  The Black Maskers: Suite
  Chorale Preludes for Organ (4) (1938)
  From My Diary (1940)
  Idyl of Theocritus for Soprano and Orchestra (1954)
  Quartet No. 2 (1950)
  Sonata No. 2 (1946)
  Sonata No. 1 for Piano (1930)
  Sonata No. 2 for Piano (1946)
  Sonata for Violin Solo (1953)
  Symphony No. 1 (1927)

SHAPERO, Harold
  Credo for Orchestra (1955)
  On Green Mountain (1958)
  Quartet No. 1 (1940)
  Sonata for Piano—Four Hands (1941)
  Three Sonatas for Piano (1944)
SIEGMEISTER, Elie
  Quartet No. 2 (1960)
  Symphony No. 3 (1957)
SMITH, Russell
  Tetrameron (1959)
SOWERBY, Leo
  All On a Summer's Day (1954)
  Classic Concerto for Organ and Orchestra (1944)
  Pop Goes the Weasel (1927)
  Prairie (symphonic poem) (1929)
STARER, Robert
  Five Miniatures for Brass
  Sonata for Piano (1950)
STEIN, Leon
  Quintet for Saxophone and String Quartet
  Sonata for Solo Violin
  Sonata for Violin and Piano
STEVENS, Halsey
  Like as the Culver (1954)
  Psalm 98 (1955)
  Sinfonia Breve (1957)
  Sonata for Solo Cello (1958)
  Symphonic Dances (1958)
  Symphony No. 1 (1945; rev. 1950)
  Triskelion (1953)
STOUT, Alan
  Great Day of the Lord (1956)
SURINACH, Carlos
  Overture, Feria Magica (1956)
  Sinfonietta Flamenca (1953)
  Symphonic Variations
SWANSON, Howard
  Night Music (1950)
  Songs (7)

TALMA, Louise
  Corona (Holy Sonnets of John Donne)
  Toccata for Orchestra (1944)
TAYLOR, Deems
  Portrait of a Lady (1918)
  Through the Looking-Glass (1917-19; rev. 1921-22)
THOMPSON, Randall
  Alleluia (1940)
  Last Words of David
  Peaceable Kingdom (1936)
  Symphony No. 2 (1932)
  Testament of Freedom (1943)
THOMSON, Virgil
  Cantabile: Portrait of Nicolas de Châtelain (1940)
  Concerto for Flute, Strings and Percussion (1954)
  Feast of Love
  Four Saints in Three Acts (1934)
  Louisiana Story: Acadian Songs and Dances (1948)
  Mass for Two-Part Chorus and Percussion (1934)
  Plow That Broke the Plains (1936)
  Praises and Prayers (1963)
  Psalms Nos. 123 and 126
  Quartet No. 2 (1932)
  The River: Suite (1942)
  Scenes from Holy Infancy: Joseph and Angels (1937)
  A Solemn Music (1919)
  Sonata (1926)
  Sonata for Violin (1930)
  Sonata No. 14 "Guggenheim Jeune" (1940)
  Symphony on a Hymn Tune (1928)
  Variations on Sunday School Tunes (1927-30)
TOCH, Ernst
  Geographical Fugue (from Spoken Music Suite) (1930)
  Jephta, Rhapsodic Poem (Symphony No. 5) (1964)
  Notturno (1953)
  Peter Pan, "Fairy Tale," Op. 76 (1955-56)
  Poems to Martha, for Voice and Strings (1946)
  Quartet in D flat, Op. 18 (1909)
  Serenade in G, Op. 25 (1917)
  Trio, Op. 63 (1937)

Quartet No. 7, Op. 70
Quartet No. 10, Op. 28 (1921)
Quartet No. 13, Op. 74 (1954)
Quintet for Piano and Strings, Op. 64 (1938)
TRIMBLE, Lester
  Closing Piece (1957)
  Five Episodes
  Four Fragments from Canterbury Tales (1958)
  Symphony in Two Movements
TURNER, Charles
  Serenade for Icarus, for Violin and Piano (1960)
USSACHEVSKY, Vladimir
  Composition
  Creation—Prologue (1962)
  Improvisation 4711
  Linear Contrasts (1958)
  Metamorphosis (1957)
  Piece for Tape Recorder (1955)
  Sonic Contours
  Underwater Waltz
VARESE, Edgar
  Amèriques (1926)
  Arcana
  Arcana (1927)
  Deserts (1954)
  Density 21.5 (1935)
  Hyperprism (1923)
  Intégrales (1925)
  Ionisation (1931)
  Octandre (1924)
  Offrandes (1922)
  Poème Électronique (1958)
VERRALL, John W.
  Quartet No. 4 (1949)
VINCENT, John
  Consort for Piano and Strings (1960)
  Quartet in G
  Symphony in D (1955)
WAGENAAR, Bernard
  Concert Overture (1953)

WAGENAAR, Bernard—*Continued*
  Symphony No. 4 (1949)
WARD, Robert
  Crucible (1961)
  Divertimento for Orchestra
  Euphony for Orchestra (1954)
  "Hush'd be the Camps Today" (1941)
  Jubilation Overture (1946)
  Songs for Pantheists (1951)
  Symphony No. 1 (1941)
  Symphony No. 2 (1947)
  Symphony No. 3 (1950)
WEBER, Ben
  Concert-Aria after Solomon, Op. 29
  Prelude and Passacaglia, Op. 42 (1954)
  Serenade, Flute, Oboe, Cello and Harpsichord, Op. 39 (1953)
  Symphony on Poems of William Blake (1952)
WEISGALL, Hugo
  The Stronger (1952)
  The Tenor (1952)
WIGGLESWORTH, Frank
  Lake Music
  Symphony No. 1 (1957)
WOLPE, Stefan
  Passacaglia
  Percussion Quartet
  Sonata for Violin
  Ten Songs from the Hebrew
WYNER, Yehudi
  Concert Duo for Violin and Piano (1956)
  Serenade for Seven Instruments (1958)
YARDUMIAN, Richard
  Chorale-Prelude (1959)
  Symphony No. 1 (1950)
  Symphony No. 2 (Psalms for Medium Voice and Orchestra) (1965)

Index

457